God Is

Ending Hell with *A Course In Miracles*

Also by brother hermit:

The Ladder of Prayer: What *A Course In Miracles* Teaches About Prayer, Forgiveness and Healing (2019)

Available in hardcover edition from:
   RiverSanctuaryPublishing.com
   Amazon.com

God Is

Ending Hell with *A Course In Miracles*

brother hermit

River Sanctuary
PUBLISHING

God Is—Ending Hell with *A Course In Miracles*

Cover photograph by George Provost

Back cover photograph by brother hermit

ISBN 978-1-935914-75-4

Revision 3

Printed in the United States of America

To order additional copies please visit:

www.riversanctuarypublishing.com

RIVER SANCTUARY PUBLISHING
P.O Box 1561
Felton, CA 95018
www.riversanctuarypublishing.com
Dedicated to the awakening of the New Earth

ACKNOWLEDGMENTS

I am grateful for the help of many people in the making of this book. Ginny provided a peaceful place of silence and solitude where I could park my bus. My brothers and mother provided financial assistance. Several friends and family read the manuscript and provided helpful suggestions.

This book is a true story. Certain names and details were changed to protect privacy.

All quotes from *A Course In Miracles*© are from the 2nd Edition, published in 1992. They are used with written permission from the copyright holder and publisher, the Foundation for Inner Peace, P.O. Box 598, Mill Valley, CA 94942-0598, www.acim.org and info@acim.org.

Brief excerpts from pp. 94, 95, 97, 98, 102 from *The Art of Spiritual Healing* by Joel S. Goldsmith. Copyright © 1959 by Joel S. Goldsmith. Reprinted by permission of HarperCollins Publishers

Brief excerpts from pp. 145, 149, 161, 162, 163, 168, 172, 173, 175 from *The Infinite Way* by Joel S. Goldsmith ISBN 9780875163093 © 1947 reprinted by permission of DeVorss Publications www.devorss.com

CONTENTS

Preface 1

Prologue 3

Introduction 9

Part I: Preparation

Chapter 1. A Course In Miracles 17

Chapter 2. Words about Words 24

Chapter 3. Resolving Dilemmas 34

Chapter 4. Open Mind 53

Part II: Main Ideas

Chapter 5. The Nature of Depression: Cause and Effect 87

Chapter 6. Who Am I: Identity 114

Chapter 7. When Egos Collide: Relationships 143

Chapter 8. As The World Turns It Burns, You Learn 172

Chapter 9. Time is Temporary 198

Part III: Ending Hell

Chapter 10. True Forgiveness and the End of Guilt 237

Chapter 11. Mind Your Mind 262

Chapter 12. Joining: The Unitive Teaching of Non-Duality ... 288

Chapter 13. Responsibility 322

Chapter 14. How To Perform Miracles 352

Chapter 15. I Need Do Nothing 371

Epilogue 397

References 415

Bibliography 421

Dedicated to all who suffer depression.

PREFACE

Imagine you are lost in a desert dying of thirst. The temperature is 120 degrees Fahrenheit and there is no shade. Your skin is burned and blistered by the brutal sun and your throat is so parched that it scrapes like sandpaper when you try to swallow. All your desperate efforts to find water have failed. You are suffering deadly dehydration and losing all hope except to find relief through death.

You remember your holy book: *All About Water.* You pull it out and read again what you already memorized from repeated readings. "Water is wonderful, life-giving and lifesaving. Cool, pure, water. Water tastes so good and is so good. Living wet water is all you need." But you can't find any. Duped by many mirages, despair displaces hope. The pretty pictures of water in your book are of no help. You were fooled to search for water where there was none. The memory of water is no help. Your mind tortures you with constant craving thoughts about water that are as hellish as, or worse than, the physical thirst itself. Now you are terribly tired and too thirsty to go any further. You have lost all hope. You pray for a quick death. Suicide makes sense.

A stranger seems to appear, looking thirsty too. You can't tell the difference between a dream and reality. Your mind is playing tricks on you. Am I awake or asleep? Maybe this apparition is part of dying.

Your weak voice whispers in desperation, "Water?"

"No," declares the stranger softly.

"I need water," you plead.

"So do I," says the stranger.

"This is grim. I can't go on," you cry.

"Don't give up. I hold a map that shows where water is," the stranger says.

"A map? How do you know it's true?" you ask.

"I trust the sister who gave it to me," the stranger replies.

1

The stranger takes your hand in his and smiles, "Come, join with me and we will find water together."

This book is a map for those dying of thirst in the desert of depression. This book shares a spiritual path out of hell.

**There is a secret medicine given only to those
who hurt so hard they can't hope.**[1]

~Rumi

PROLOGUE

In the summer of 1976, I was a member of a monastic community in New Mexico, and something spiritual happened one evening. I hesitate sharing this "holy happening" because the experience is indescribable and even the word "experience" is misleading. Usually, when I report an experience, I describe something perceivable. I share something seen, heard, smelled, tasted, or touched. Mental sensing is similar to a physical sense, like when dreaming I "see" certain places or people while my eyes are closed. If I remember the dream, I can tell what I "perceived." So one challenge in describing what I experienced is that I did not perceive anything with physical or mental senses. How to describe that?

Besides this difficulty, my attempt to describe the phenomenon falls short and the danger that people might get the wrong idea made me wary of talking about it. Even though it seemed somehow important to share the experience, I preferred to keep silent about it rather than mislead people, or somehow defile something sacred.

Also, as I will explain, the experience produced three main dilemmas within me that continued unresolved for many years. Until I resolved these dilemmas, sharing seemed premature. In fact, I needed to digest and integrate the experience before trying to share something I did not understand. Another danger is "spiritual pride." Monks tended not to talk about their spiritual experiences. More humble that way, or not. (If I am proud of my humility, am I humble?) I will try to describe what happened forty years ago without much context. By context I mean my own spiritual journey. I will share the larger context later in this book. At the time this happened, I felt fine, not sad at all. Depression came later.

On that evening, after final communal prayers in the chapel, I went back into the chapel to pray and be alone. A handful of people sat scattered throughout the small, dimly-lit chapel in private, silent

3

prayer. In an uncharacteristic move, I invited everyone present to join in a circle, sitting on the floor, to pray together.

Those present joined and took turns in spontaneous prayer, as is common in charismatic circles. A young woman on my immediate left spoke to Jesus, saying something like she wished she had a direct phone line to Him so she could talk to Him and hear Him talking back to her. When she finished her prayer, I spoke up and asked her to imagine she is sitting on soft grass, scented with wild flowers, in a beautiful landscape, watching a river flow by. The weather is perfect and the atmosphere peaceful. I asked her to imagine Jesus sitting relaxed right next to her and she could be with him for as long as she wanted. Jesus was in no hurry to go anywhere. Then a spinning sensation started.

My eyes were closed and I felt a spinning within. I started to feel dizzy. The feeling was unpleasant; I felt I might get sick if the spinning continued, much like nausea from motion sickness. Then the spinning stopped and I felt no discomfort. I was no longer conscious of the chapel, or the people I invited to prayer, or even of my own body, but I was aware. This awareness is not of the senses or mind, but prior to those ways of perception. I became aware of an invisible, most holy presence, a holiness I had not experienced before. I perceived nothing, no light, no sound; not even a mental image; nothing but a basic awareness of this holy presence. The presence seemed somehow personal, and I was aware of three, invisible, silent beings. One in the middle seemed primary, or of a higher order. Two other beings accompanied, one on each side of the central one. The presence did not identify itself and I speculated for years as to its identity. Neither did I speak and my attention was riveted to this invisible, holy presence. There wasn't any fear. As far as I remember, there wasn't any thinking going on; just awareness and awe.

I was aware also of invisible "rays" (for lack of a better word) coming from this presence and passing through me like an x-ray might. I did not know what these rays were but I sensed "healing" and "purification," not so much in words or thoughts, but as an intuitive, non-verbal impression. The rays passing through me seemed like an immersion or a baptism. Could this be the baptism in the Holy Spirit I sought?

Then I noticed something different, also like an invisible ray. I can best describe it as the greatest love I ever experienced. It seemed like the most powerful, most stable thing in the universe. To call it a thing is not right, words fail here. It was not a thing as in an object. It was more like an activity or a power, and attitude. I had not experienced this kind of love before, not from any person, even though I did feel the rare person loved me. The difference in nature and magnitude between this higher love and human love seemed immense and categorical.

This experience of love included an awareness of the attitude of this indescribable, numinous presence towards me. I describe this attitude as unconditional acceptance. This acceptance is not like, "I accept you warts and all," but somehow It saw me as perfect and even delightful. Without using words, it communicated "I take delight in you."

I do not know how long this experience lasted; there was no sense of time. But when I was back sitting in the circle, little, if any, time had passed.

As the small group ended its prayer and people started to stand up, an excited buzz burned through the group. Everyone received a spiritual experience, but everyone's was different. People started talking and sharing, but I wanted to be alone and just sit with what had happened. I felt that if I talked about it, I might somehow contaminate it, or dilute it. Still in a bit of a pleasant daze, I didn't know how to speak about it or attempt to describe what exactly happened. It seemed too sacred to speak of. A blissful, almost drug-like high gradually dispersed over a couple hours. Joy remained within me for many months though not as intense as the night of the experience. My secret was this: God's love is way better than advertised. It is unconditional and contingent on nothing. I couldn't lose it if I tried. Yet I could, and did, lose the experience of it. All experience is temporary and changes into a memory, and then memory of memories. And thus began a long, long, dark night where the love-light seemed lost.

When I tried to share this experience, I would say something like, "I felt a great love," and the words seemed stupid, inaccurate, corny, romantic, probably because the word love is used in so many ways. I could not describe it. Language is not capable of it.

The morning following my mystical experience, the Abbot called me to his office. He heard that something spiritual had happened in the chapel the night before. I told him as best I could what I experienced. He asked me to pray for him and I did. Then he gave me a prophetic message. He said I was in for a long journey. I did not know what he meant. Now, after forty years lost and wandering in the dry desert of this world, I have some idea what the Abbot meant. I was out of Egypt, thank God, yet the desert and its gold cows loomed.

As I tried to understand what had happened, three dilemmas arose. First, this unconditional love/acceptance seemed to run counter to all my religious conditioning. Love, or acceptance, is conditional, according to the authorities. I knew of no priest or preacher who taught that God's love is unconditional, and I was familiar with Catholic, Orthodox, and Protestant theologies. Raised on fear of eternal damnation in hell, I learned there are conditions to determine placement after death. Can you imagine a university with no conditions for admission? There is no easy resolution to this dilemma; many years passed before I began to find an answer. Later in this book, I go into more detail about my own spiritual conditioning. Conditioning forms core beliefs, and pours the false-foundation of identity. These beliefs are often unconscious, stubborn, and persistent, like a concrete cornerstone hidden stories below the visible structure. Fear reinforces these hardened beliefs despite experiential evidence that contradicts what I believe.

The second dilemma is closely related to the first. If this Love is unconditional, it means I do not earn it. No one earns it. Unconditional, by definition, means it is inclusive of everyone. For anyone to be excluded there must be conditions for exclusion, such as sin and guilt. I experienced an all-inclusive love, yet my conditioning trained me to believe God's love is exclusive and conditional. How could it include everyone without exception? Why go to church if it had nothing to do with salvation? I was confused. The pieces of the puzzle were not fitting together.

The third dilemma is that this presence saw me as perfect. How could this be? I knew for certain I was not perfect. I was a sinner, plain as could be. Should I argue with this numinous presence and disagree with it? No, I could not argue with Holiness. Yet I recognized two opposing and irreconcilable views. Who am I to challenge 2,000 years of Christian theology based on a single experience I did not understand, and could not even begin to describe? I trusted this unconditional love absolutely. Nothing is stronger or more stable. Despite these unresolved dilemmas, I was confident, almost recklessly so, of God's love and sure that His love is not contingent on anything I did or didn't do. And because this love is unconditional, it is extended to everyone without exception.

I had had the most significant experience of my life, dwarfing anything else I knew. I was left with a knowing that nothing in this world compares to that love and holy presence, and a confidence I could trust this higher love. Before this happened, I had lived for five years in a Catholic seminary and almost two years in contemplative monasteries. I read certain saints' writings on mystical, contemplative experience but I did not find a description that matched my experience, even though most spoke of a great love. After that experience, nothing else really interested me; nothing in the world came close. I wondered about the spinning sensation and dizziness. Is it related to the whirling dance of Sufi dervishes?

> **Most scholars agree that the whirling dance was taught to Rumi by Shams. It is said that this dance is symbolic of the circular motion of the soul...**[1]

Is it related to the "revolving" St. Simeon the New Theologian described?

I was twenty-one years old when I experienced Holy Love. Fast forward thirty-seven years to the Fall of 2013. I woke up in the emergency room of a hospital in Reno with no memory of what happened, although I had a hunch. Nothing was wrong physically but I was a mental wreck. I was involuntarily hospitalized for suicide ideation. I didn't remember arguing with the paramedics; I had a full drunken blackout. I told the ER staff, "I'm not suicidal." Someone replied, "That's not what you said in your emails." My memory of the emails was vague. Yes, perhaps I did send emails saying goodbye, but I wasn't sure. I did not try to kill myself, but I was severely depressed, the third major depressive episode of my life. Wearied with life, I had wished and prayed to be done with the whole mess. I still believed in the love I experienced at age twenty-one, but so much time passed, and so much went wrong. So what the hell happened between age twenty-one and fifty-seven? Hell happened.

I do not want to write a book about myself. My separate-self-story is part of the past, unimportant, and soon to be gratefully forgotten. I share aspects of my spiritual journey on the chance it might help others. The past is gone, thank God. Memory of experience is a poor substitute for the reality.

Specifically, this book is about how the spiritual teaching, *A Course In Miracles* (ACIM) helped me understand the spiritual experience heretofore described, address the dilemmas mentioned, and heal from depression. I hope this book helps others connect the dots in ACIM. When one is in the deepest pit of depression, it seems that there is no solution and death is a reasonable and merciful option. I include in this writing some of my story to demonstrate how my life experience confirmed ACIM. ACIM is a map of the spiritual journey that found me when I was lost and dying in the hell-desert. Maybe it will help you too.

INTRODUCTION

Are you sad? Have you ever been sad? Do you know anyone, or love anyone, who suffers severe sadness? I have been all of these. Because depression is so common, most of us can answer yes to one of those questions. Depression is something many experience journeying back to Paradise lost. Henry Thoreau noted in *Walden*:

The mass of men lead lives of quiet desperation.[1]

This book shares a spiritual approach to suffering: what it is, what causes it, what heals it.

A Course In Miracles is not for everyone and makes no claim to being the only way. That's one of the refreshing things about it. It is for those who are ready to hear it. Perhaps those dealing with depression, who tried many treatments without lasting relief, will benefit from this specific spiritual approach. After all, what have you to lose? It might also benefit spiritual seekers who still haven't found what they are looking for. Have you met God or is god a concept? If you want to meet God, you can, according to ACIM. When you meet God, you do not see anything, yet you "know" God.

A Course In Miracles teaches that even though there are many forms of sickness, suffering and pain, there is only one cause and one solution. Depression is a particularly nasty form of suffering because it is the opposite of joy. I could be dying of cancer and still be happy. I cannot be depressed and happy at the same time. Blues management might prevent suicide, or not, but why settle for a sad life?

For some of us, just the perception of so much suffering is depressing. Even if I seem personally free of suffering, there is still the collective suffering, the collective mental illness, the collective depression. Suicide statistics don't lie. Self-murder is more common than murder. The get-out-of-hell-free card costs a lot, it seems. But it costs even more to stay in hell. Seeing suffering is what drove Gautama on his mission for the liberation of all beings. I feel close to the Awake One because I am tired of suffering.

Even though this book addresses the specific form of suffering called depression, the teaching applies to any and all forms of suffering. Understanding true cause and effect is fundamental. The teaching is basically simple, but not necessarily quick to grasp, because, even though simple, it represents a completely different thought system. ACIM seems complicated, but it is not. I could read the whole thing and scratch my head wondering what it means. It seems complicated because it challenges everything I think I know. Sticking with it, one learns ACIM is simple.

ACIM repeats the same basic ideas in a holographic way. The whole course is summed up over and over again in various passages throughout the book. It boils down to a simple choice between two views. It seems complex because those two views have many forms and the course's thought system includes understandings of identity, Source (or how we came to exist), the meaning of existence, the nature of the time/space continuum, cause and effect, conditioning, mind and unconscious mind, relationships, evolution, psychology, spirituality, suffering, suicide, death, hell, Heaven, Truth, and God. A little something for anyone interested.

This book is designed in three parts and each part forms the foundation for what follows. I behoove the reader to read this book in the order presented.

The first part, *Preparation*, introduces ACIM, explains how the course helped me understand the experience of 1976, and resolve the dilemmas described. Part one also includes chapters on open-mindedness, and the challenges and limits of using language in a spiritual context.

The second part, *Main Ideas*, presents the core concepts of ACIM and the relationship between these ideas and depression. These ideas include the true cause of suffering, identity, relationships, the world, and time.

Part three, *Ending Hell*, is about practicing the teaching. Here one learns how to heal depression and perform miracles. An intellectual foundation is necessary, but not sufficient to end suffering. Healing happens in the application. Here I get my get-out-of-hell-free card, if I want it. As the course teaches, I do not need to believe any of this to reap the benefits, but I do need to apply the ideas.

The various concepts are all related and interwoven to form a simple, whole, and useful spiritual cartography. The ideas all reinforce one another and gradually integrate into a simple system of thought. Although approaching truth from different angles, we are looking at one truth; we are like blind persons, each describing the elephant in different ways, depending on what part they touch: tusk, trunk, tail or toe. Yet there is just one elephant.

Because the ideas presented in ACIM are so spiritually radical, the reader is urged to withhold judgment about the ideas until they are considered and comprehended. This open-mindedness is more of a challenge than it might seem. Just getting to the point where I understand the teaching is a major challenge. I can't accept it or reject it if I don't understand it, right?

Although the various ideas of ACIM are consistent and basically simple, if radical, it takes a while for these ideas to sink in. In the course itself there is much necessary repetition because the ideas tend to go against what I think I know. After studying the course for twenty-three years, I still can read a passage and it seems like I never read it before. There is a certain "slipperiness" to the ideas. ACIM replaces an ancient, entrenched thought system with a new thought system. It is like learning a new language, and that doesn't happen overnight; so, blessed are the patiently persistent. Constructing this map is a bit like putting together a puzzle. Random pieces don't make much sense, but as they come together they form the big picture. "God is" is saying the Truth in two words. The rest is unpacking what that means.

Today, we are more sensitive to the politically correct use of language. Some sixty years ago a shift began to change from male-biased language to gender inclusive language. ACIM uses the traditional male bias in language referring to everyone as a "brother" and God, Christ (the Sonship), and the Holy Spirit, as "He." Understandably, in the age of the rise of feminism, many of us find this masculine bias in language exclusive, objectionable, and even offensive. I ask that you relax judgment about sexist language until understanding core course ideas about identity. For now, it might help to know that the course teaches, with much repetition, that I am not a body. Female and male has to do with bodies, not spirit. From the perspective of ACIM, it does not matter if I use *sister* in place of *brother*, or refer to God as *She*. God is not male or female. The course teaches of a radical, unconditional, and inclusive equality that is non-dual.

In writing this book, I grappled over what approach to take regarding gender-biased language. The solution is not simple and the options awkward. I could use both genders and use "sister and brother" instead of "brother." Or "his and her" instead of "his," and so forth. This adds more words to read in order to express the same idea. Should I place the female pronoun first, the male pronoun first, or alternate priority? Or, do I use one gender term and alternate, using "sister" sometimes, and "brother" sometimes. Do I use "She" for God sometimes and "He" at other times? How do I respect everyone? In a certain sense, attempting to use gender-inclusive language supports the idea that we are bodies. ACIM teaches letting go of body-identification. Because I quote ACIM frequently, I opted to follow the way used in the course for the sake of consistency. Please forgive my poor attempt to speak of the unspeakable. Feel free to substitute feminine pronouns and words whenever you like. Our language is not only dualistic; it is sexist.

Throughout the book, various true autobiographical stories, called *sidetracks*, describe my personal spiritual journey.

In this book are many of my favorite spiritual quotations, mostly from ACIM, but also many quotes from the Bible and other sources. I present a variety of other sources congruent with ACIM. Quotes from ACIM are perhaps the most important part of this book. They are organized by topic, so several course quotes from different chapters are presented together about a specific topic. Organizing the quotes this way demonstrates how consistent ACIM is, and how the basic ideas are repeated and reinforced. Reading ACIM from start to finish, one does not get the same effect because the quotes are spread out over 1,249 pages. One of the challenges for students of the course is that it is not written in a linear fashion. It does not go from beginning to middle to end. It is written in a holographic fashion. Various ideas are presented and then later the ideas are presented again. Many readers find this non-linear style challenging.

Unless indicated otherwise, the quotes are from ACIM. Italics for emphasis in the quotes are original and not added by the writer. In some quotes, I have added for clarification, in brackets, the meaning of a pronoun or a word served by a larger context than that provided in the quote. Page location for the quotes is listed in the *References* in the back of the book.

PART I

PREPARATION

Hell exists even in this life for people who
endure unbearable mental suffering.[1]

~Thomas Keating

Chapter One

A COURSE IN MIRACLES

*J*n 1992, I was 37 and experiencing my second bout of severe depression. My marriage of almost ten years was on the rocks. I had no idea what was next, and the future looked grim. I still hadn't resolved the dilemmas of the 1976 experience. Although on the verge of some sort of breakdown I tried to hold it together for the sake of my two young children, a girl, age four, and a boy, age two. At this time I came across a personally poignant quote about sharing:

Nothing real can be increased except by sharing.[1]

The quote is from a book called *A Course In Miracles* (ACIM), and until then I hadn't heard of it. I shared this experience with only a few persons and I wondered if my hesitancy to share it explained why my spiritual life seemed to be such a failure. Why hadn't I experience that love again? I began to think that perhaps I should somehow share this experience. My Jonah-like reluctance to do so might be one possible reason for my whale-sized unhappiness.

I became quite curious about the course and bought the second edition combined volume in 1992. My worn and blue-covered book contains three parts, a 669-page *Text*, a 488-page *Workbook For Students*, with 365 lessons, and a 92-page *Manual For Teachers*. Current volumes include two short supplements: *Psychotherapy: Purpose, Process and Practice*, and *Song Of Prayer: Prayer, Forgiveness, Healing*. It is 1296 pages of dense, Shakespearean free verse and iambic pentameter style of writing. I hadn't read any Shakespeare since the required plays in High School. Not exactly my cup of tea, but I understood the respect for Shakespeare. The point is, ACIM is not a quick or easy read.

For such a long and dense book, the Introduction to the *Text* is only twelve sentences, two of which struck me at first reading as personally significant:

> **The course does not aim at teaching the meaning of love, for that is beyond what can be taught. It does aim, however, at removing the blocks to the awareness of love's presence, which is your natural inheritance.[2]**

Since the experience of 1976, whenever I came across any spiritual writing about love, my attention perked up and I checked to see if it described something similar to my experience of unspeakable presence and love. Now, here is ACIM saying the meaning of love is unteachable. The course aims, however, to remove blocks to the awareness of love's presence. That sounded good to me. My awareness of love was painfully blocked. Could this book explain what happened in 1976? Could it help solve my dilemmas and heal depression? Early in the course, answers came.

In the second section of the first chapter, the course describes a spiritual experience it calls *revelation*.

> **Revelation induces a state in which fear has already been abolished.[3]**

I noticed no fear during the experience. Apparently, the abolishing of fear, even temporarily, is a prerequisite for this experience of revelation, because fear blocks the awareness of love.

> **When you return to your original form of communication with God by direct revelation, the need for miracles is over.[4]**

Could my experience be communication with God? The presence did not identify itself. How could I know if it was God or not? What is this "revelation" the course speaks about? Perhaps God does not identify

Himself with words, "Hello hermit, I am God." Anyone can say the words. Perhaps God identifies Himself by His Love, which no man imitates. I wanted to know more and kept reading.

> Revelation is intensely personal and cannot be
> meaningfully translated. That is why any attempt to
> describe it in words is impossible. Revelation induces only
> experience. Revelation is literally unspeakable because it
> is an experience of unspeakable love.[5]

My interest grew. *To describe it in words is impossible*: my experience *exactly*. It is truly unspeakable love. That is one of the reasons I hesitated to share it. Although many mystics know words fail to describe their experience, they still want to share anyway. It is the nature of true love that it is shared. If my experience was the *original form of communication with God*, then that form of communication is an expression of unconditional love, unconditional acceptance and unconditional delight. Before the experience, I believed God loved me; after the experience, and still now, I know it, even if my awareness of it is painfully blocked. Is this what it means to live by faith? Knowing something is true, despite not experiencing it now? Could this blockage be related to my depression? How do I know this divine love is real, when I don't experience it? The single experience of it, forty years ago, demonstrated that this love is so stable, so strong, so holy, so magnificent, that my confidence in it remains unshakable. Why don't I experience it on a regular or continual basis? There are blocks to my awareness of it.

God is Love now made more sense. Love is not simply an activity of God, but in some mysterious way, what God *Is*. Love wants to share itself by extending itself, giving itself, with no conditions. Our nature is love (divine) because love (God) creates us like Itself and one with Itself, as an extension of Itself. Divine love is spiritual, invisible; it is not made out of atoms; it has no form, no shape, no color, no weight, no mass, no length, no image of any kind, no sound, no smell, no taste; it can't be measured, perceived, or described, yet we can know it through a nonsensual spiritual experience.

> Awe should be reserved for revelation, to which it is perfectly and correctly applicable…a state of awe is worshipful, implying that one of a lessor order stands before his Creator. You are a perfect creation, and should experience awe only in the presence of the Creator of perfection.[6]

Worshipful awe describes my response to the presence exactly. Also, I seemed to be *one of a lessor order* before this presence, whatever it was. Although the presence did not identify itself as my Creator, it seemed to be of a higher, more holy, and more loving order. At the time, God seemed to be something I could not experience in this world. I wondered if the presence I experienced in the summer of 1976 was an angel or other spiritual agent of God? Why is the direct experience of God so seemingly rare?

Regarding spiritual experiences, some involve a spiritual perception, like a vision, or visible light, like when the apostles experienced the transfiguration of Jesus into the Christ. Another type of spiritual experience does not involve any perception, as happened to me. Heaven is the realm of knowledge or awareness, not perception. Perception is in the domain of duality, requiring the perceiver and the perceived.

> A "vision of God" would be a miracle rather than a revelation. The fact that perception is involved at all removes the experience from the realm of knowledge. That is why visions, however holy, do not last.[7]

Experiences come and go, *however holy*. Holy happenings do, however, reveal knowledge that is permanent. Or *timeless*.

> Knowledge is the result of revelation and induces only thought. Even in its most spiritualized form perception involves the body. Knowledge comes from the altar within and is timeless because it is certain. To perceive the truth is not the same as to know it.[8]

Zen Buddhists share a strange saying: "If you meet the Buddha, kill him." The meaning of the saying is that any "vision," or anything I perceive, is not the reality. A vision of God is a vision of an image, not God Itself, Who is not visible. Any image of God is graven. It is easy to get stuck on visions, which come and go in time. So kill it. Don't be fooled. This makes more sense after having a spiritual experience that does not involve any perception, mental or physical. The danger of spiritual experience is ego may hijack visions into vainglory. Then I can consider myself as spiritually special, holier than you, chosen by God, etc.

In the same way as a vision, a concept of God is not God. It is easy to confuse the two. A concept is a mental perception. Using the term "spiritual" is a little sloppy. Spiritual can mean many things and there are different levels within the spiritual. Four broad levels within the spiritual are psychic, subtle, causal, and non-dual. Each of those levels are further differentiated in the transpersonal literature. There is much written about the various levels of spirituality, yet that discussion is beyond the scope of this book. ACIM is simpler.

ACIM impressed me after reading only the introduction and first chapter, sixteen pages out of 1296. In describing the experience of revelation, the course offered a precise description of what I experienced in the summer of 1976. Finally, after sixteen years, had I found an oasis in the desert? What more did it hold?

I wondered when ACIM was written. I turned to the title page and read: *A Course In Miracles was first published in three volumes in June 1976.* The synchronicity of date startled me. I believe there are no accidents, no coincidences. Although I felt I should share my experience, it made more sense after I read this:

> Revelation is not enough, because it is only
> communication from God. God does not need revelation
> returned to Him, which would clearly be impossible,
> but He does want it brought to others. This cannot be
> done with the actual revelation; its content cannot be
> expressed, because it is intensely personal to the mind that
> receives it. It can, however, be returned by that mind to
> other minds, through the attitudes the knowledge from
> the revelation brings.[9]

So it is true that the experience brought knowledge of holiness and unconditional love, and this knowledge resulted in certain attitudes that remain present still, and that much I can share. The experience itself is temporary and passing, only a memory. I could not control it, duplicate it, or repeat it. I could not give the experience to someone else. Yet the experience left a knowledge not temporary. The Truth is not temporary. The blocks to the awareness of love's presence are temporary. God's love is not temporary. ACIM confirmed my experience. I had finally found a precise description of what I experienced. I share this so you may know that the experience of revelation described in ACIM does, in fact, literally, happen. The course states it does not happen to everyone, and, like all experience, it is temporary. Apparently, I cannot live in the body in this state for long:

> Sometimes a teacher of God may have a brief experience
> of direct union with God. In this world, it is almost
> impossible that this endure. It can, perhaps, be won after
> much devotion and dedication, and then be maintained
> for much of the time on earth. But this is so rare that it
> cannot be considered a realistic goal. If it happens, so
> be it. If it does not happen, so be it as well. All worldly

states must be illusionary. If God were reached directly in sustained awareness, the body would not be long maintained. Those who have laid the body down merely to extend their helpfulness to those remaining behind are few indeed.[10]

The course quote above is from the *Manual For Teachers*, which is presented in a question and answer format. In this case, the quote is a partial answer to the question, *Can God Be Reached Directly?* Rather than choosing ACIM, it seemed to be choosing me.

Chapter Two

WORDS ABOUT WORDS

*T*he development of language, speaking, alphabets, and writing seems to be an amazing mystery. How many different languages and dialects developed over human history? Language developed to facilitate communication because the original form of perfect communication, or communion, became blocked. Therefore, language is a substitute for communion because I perceive and think that you are separate from me. Besides oral and written words, there is body language and other, non-verbal forms of communication.

Thought appears dependent on language. Thought appears as cognitive commentary or conversation. How did people think before language? Did I think in images or feelings before words emerged? Words are so common and familiar that I easily, and automatically, take them for granted. There is a danger in words, written more than spoken. Words cannot be truth. At best, words provide an orientation pointing in the right direction. If I invest too heavily in words, I become a fundamentalist. Then the letter of the law is valued more than the spirit of the law. This is the challenge of language, and I best remember the limits of language, most especially when communicating about spirituality. Why spirituality? Because spirituality, God, truth, are unspeakable. Words are too limited to express it. To confuse language and words with the Word results in rigid, closed-minded, fear-based fundamentalism, and its fruits.

Spiritual communication, through language, is successful along a continuum corresponding to how inspired the communication is. Are the words helpful or not? Or, perhaps, somewhere in between? Is the map accurate or not? All words are temporary tools towards meaning. Certain words might trigger reactions. Recovering religious junkies might have hangovers associated with certain words like God,

24

Christ, or the Holy Spirit due to lame conditioning or due to proselytizing by judgmental fear-mongers. Forget about the traditional
meaning of these "gray" words. A concept of God is not God. ACIM
uses these words frequently but with different meanings. Words are
like clothes a child wears. When I grow up, children's clothes no
longer fit. Why would I try to wear them? They still might be useful
for children though. Masters liked Jesus and Buddha did not write
words, as far as we know. Written words are more dangerous because
they can become carved in stone, rigid, hard, a graven block to truth.
I hesitated to write a book for this reason. Hence I preface this book
with words about words. Words are symbols. The word God is not
God. This may seem obvious, but it easy to forget it and get lost in
symbols. It's easy to confuse the intellectual and the spiritual. If it
involves words, it is intellectual.

> I [Jesus] have made every effort to use words that are
> almost impossible to distort, but it is always possible to
> twist symbols around if you wish.[1]

Words help or hurt. I can distort and twist words, misinterpret the
meaning of words, and use them to confirm what I already consider
true. I can unconsciously, or automatically, assume the meaning of
words. I can hear with the ear, yet not listen with the heart.

> All terms are potentially controversial, and those
> who seek controversy will find it. Yet those who seek
> clarification will find it as well.[2]

Words can confuse or clarify. There are words and then there is my
interpretation of the words.

Within many spiritual paths there is the concept of non-duality.
ACIM is a non-dual spiritual teaching. Non-duality is a tricky concept to communicate because language is fundamentally dualistic.
A sentence includes subject and object. The best that words can do is
point towards non-dual Spirit. In naming anything, I objectify what

is named. The word "spirit" is a name/symbol for a reality changed into an object by naming it. Now I can talk about Spirit as if it is a thing, an object. Language is too limited to express Spirit, yet spiritual experience happens. One who does experience Spirit feels an enthusiastic urge to share it. Thus inspired, the mystic attempts to articulate the truth, even though handicapped by a lame, limping language of duality. Sometimes poetry is the best approach. ACIM tells me not to expect an intellectually satisfying answer, because there cannot be one. Even with these challenges, I make these "raids on the unspeakable" to share with others, to serve, to help facilitate the ending of suffering.

It is easy to confuse the spiritual and the intellectual. Most religious beliefs are intellectual, based on thinking, based on words, based on concepts, based on the past. Human reason is of the personal realm, not the transpersonal realm. The spectrum of consciousness ranges from the pre-personal (pre-rational), to the personal (rational), and to the transpersonal (transrational). When we use words to speak about spirituality, we are in the personal (rational) realm and we should not confuse intellectual understanding with spiritual experience that is beyond the intellectual.

> **We are not concerned with intellectual feats nor logical toys. We are dealing only in the very obvious, which has been overlooked in the clouds of complexity in which you think you think.**[3]

Luke's Gospel:

> **In that same hour he rejoiced in the Holy Spirit and said, "I thank thee, Father, Lord of Heaven and earth, that thou has hidden these things from the wise and and revealed them to babes; yea, Father, for such was thy gracious will."**[4]

The more I think I know, the less I understand. Rational thought cannot comprehend Spirit.

> This is not a course in philosophical speculation, nor is it concerned with precise terminology.[5]

Philosophers play with ideas. Many spiritual teachers, including Buddha, Ramana Maharshi, and Krishnamurti, show no interest in intellectual theories or spiritual speculation. The professor of philosophy, Raymond Martin, taped several conversations with Krishnamurti. About Krishnamurti and his own academic practice, Martin wrote:

> ...Krishnamurti's thought is quite removed from academic philosophy, particularly in the analytical tradition. There is a simple reason why this should be so: Krishnamurti wasn't interested in presenting theories; and theories are what academic philosophy is all about.[6]

Likewise, ACIM is not interested in speculation about the truth. Words are symbols, temporary means to *what lies beyond symbols*. They are not important in themselves. When used skillfully, they are means of communication. Speculative thinking is for philosophers; silence and stillness is for mystics.

> The ego will demand many answers that this course does not give. It does not recognize as questions the mere form of a question to which an answer is impossible. The ego may ask, "How did the impossible occur?", "To what did the impossible happen?", and may ask this in many forms. Yet there is no answer; only an experience. Seek only this, and do not let theology delay you.[7]

Can God make a rock so big he cannot pick it up? Intellectual games and speculative theology slow progress. Truth is not told in wordy tales. Truth is trans-verbal and trans-ideological, but words and the intellect serve as a temporary transitional tools. Until I return to wordless communion, I use words. Some even give up using words while still in this world.

Finally, beyond all thought is an experience that answers all intellectual questions, not with an intellectual answer, but by dissolving the questions, like the warm sun dissolves fog. In the bliss of union, questions are gone like wind-blown gnats. Concepts, for better or worse, provide a context for interpreting and sharing the non-verbal experience.

Realizing the limits of language, mystics still strive to share ideas using language, and try to refine communication to be as precise as possible in the hope that meaning and eventually experience is shared by minds. The course's use of language makes subtle distinctions to increase clarity and decrease confusion, within the limits of language. For example, as we already saw in the *Introduction* to the *Text*, ACIM teaches that its goal is the removal of blocks to the awareness of love. The precision of this language is astonishing because in two sentences it overcomes a basic flaw in many spiritual teachings that promise salvation or awakening *in the future*. The love of God is fully present right now. It does not come and go, begin here or end there. It is the eternal reality beyond the space/time continuum. "Was" and "will be" are terms of time. Divine love is not temporary. I cannot attain it in the future. I did not lose it in the past. It simply is, now, with no past or future. However, there are blocks to my awareness of this beneficence, and so I seem to suffer. When the blocks to awareness of love are removed, depression is shined away. Removal of these blocks does not require time, only willingness. God does not need time. My release does not happen in the future. My acceptance of the truth seems to take time.

It is possible to be stuck in a conceptual world, a wordy world, an intellectual world, without realizing it. So I need reminding frequently: the description is not the described; the map is not the territory. Words are symbols, symbolic, conceptual. The words and pictures of water in the thirsty desert person's book do not quench his thirst. This might seem obvious, but it is easy to forget and intellectualize spirituality.

Ideally, words direct one from the conceptual to the real; from intellectual understanding to realization. ACIM takes this radically further. The "reality" words point to is also not real. Thus words are considered symbols *twice removed*.

> God does not understand words, for they were made by separated minds to keep them in the illusion of separation. Words can be helpful, particularly for the beginner, in helping concentration and facilitating the exclusion, or at least the control, of extraneous thoughts. Let us not forget, however, that words are but symbols of symbols. They are thus twice removed from reality.[8]

There is this dichotomy I attempt to balance. Words are limited; words fail; and yet I use words to communicate with other souls who think they are separate and have forgotten about mind-in-mind direct and wordless communion. Then, if I am going to attempt to speak of the unspeakable, I must be careful how I use words. Sloppy use can confuse. ACIM achieves this balance beautifully. It uses a lot of words. The more I study it, the more I see how consistent and careful ACIM is in its use of words.

There is a tendency in certain spiritual circles to see all concepts as illusionary and develop an anti-intellectual stance. It is true that ultimately all concepts are illusionary, but ACIM teaches that correct concepts are necessary to realize liberation from concepts. I use concepts like I use a map when lost. Once I arrive at the destination the map is no longer needed. It is useful while lost, but not the end in itself. The conceptual map is a temporary aid to be gratefully given away when no longer needed.

> Salvation does not seek to use a means as yet too alien to your thinking to be helpful, nor to make the kinds of change you could not recognize. Concepts are needed while perception lasts, and changing concepts is salvation's task.[9]

In Buddhism one of the core teachings is the Four Noble Truths. The fourth of these describes the "Eight-fold Noble Path," the first of which is "Right View." This right view is the intellectual, conceptual map that guides my way, a world view, a frame of reference. Each of us uses such a map, for better or worse. The better the map, the sooner I get home, ideally. Though ACIM is a unique spiritual teaching, it mirrors many of the teachings of Buddhism, Vedanta, and Christianity. Maybe my map is pretty good, but is there a better map? Has the terrain changed? If I am using a map to find water in the desert and someone comes along and says, "Your map is out-dated, that stream is dry; there is a quicker route to water," what am I going to do? Instead of rejecting all concepts (which might be a way of avoiding what I do not want to see, or the baby-boomer resistance to all authority and hierarchy), consider that *concepts are needed*, for a while. Whenever I use words, I am in conceptual territory.

Many common words are problematic because the meaning of the word is not clear. Often there are many meanings for one word. Words like love, truth, God, mind, spirit, reality, are "gray" words that have as many different meanings as there are people who use them. ACIM uses many words with a different meaning than the usual. Often the meaning is so different I wish I could coin a new word for the new meaning.

For example, ACIM uses the word "forgiveness" in a different way than normally understood. Sometimes the word might be qualified with an adjective like "true forgiveness," implying there is a false forgiveness. There is a pseudo-forgiveness the course calls *forgiveness to kill*, and *forgiveness-to-destroy*. So what does the word *mean*? If I read a sentence defining the word *forgiveness* as ACIM means it, I might immediately disagree with it because it is so different from the common use. Also, many statements need a qualifier such as "seems" for the correct understanding. Ideas we might think of as true might be better expressed as "seems to be true." ACIM uses many words familiar in Christian theology, such as "Atonement," but with a different meaning or interpretation. The new meanings will be unpacked as we go along. Beware of understanding words according to traditional understandings.

The interpretation of words is also context dependent. Does a sign on the side of a road saying "Shoulder Work" refer to a chiropractor's office? Thus right interpretation requires context, a preparation, a certain unpacking, before one learns how ACIM uses the word. As you read *God Is*, patience with temporary ambiguity will help and pay off with clarity. As you read, questions might arise. If you keep reading you might find your questions answered. Each chapter assumes you gained the context of the previous chapter.

ACIM is not meant to be read. It is meant to be studied. Slowly. Carefully. It is mind training that completely reverses and replaces conditioned thinking, what the course calls "wrong-mindedness." It is more like learning a new language than simply reading. I do not learn a new language by reading about it. It takes serious study, or immersion. Its 1296 pages is not an easy read and a quick read will not do. It is not written in a traditional linear fashion. It takes careful, slow, focused study and attention to detail. I might feel like I don't have time for immersive study. That's okay; I go at my own pace. How fast I proceed is up to me. In my case, I "dropped out" of society for a few years. My retreat into solitude permitted an immersive study of ACIM. Life more or less forced me into hermit life. In terms of functioning in the world, I was disabled. There is a stigma associated with dropping out. I learned to detach from the opinions of others. I quit my job and lived as frugally as possible. I lived in a bus I converted into my house on wheels. No rent, no utilities, no TV, no Internet, few distractions. This gave me plenty of time to read and study the course and other spiritual teachers. I began this retreat from the world more than twenty years after I started studying the course. It's like I went from being an undergraduate student to being a graduate student. This reclusion is not a course requirement; not every student needs to drop out to study the course. In this book, I share what I learned during my immersive study. Perhaps the reader can benefit from my extended retreat. Ideally, this book accelerates comprehension of ACIM.

Here is another paradox about the course. ACIM makes a bold claim: it leads to liberation faster than any other way. ACIM came to accelerate spiritual transformation. Faster than other ways means it saves time. This does not mean it is easy, or quick. The course language is designed to force one to slow down. Today, many prefer sound bytes of a few seconds and tweets of a few words. ACIM is the antidote for the contemporary collective attention deficit disorder. Who has time to read books when there is Netflix? I am free to binge eat, binge watch TV, and binge drink as long as I want to, but am I not interested in ending hell?

Besides the challenges of language and words, another impediment to understanding is conditioning. I am conditioned. If I learned any language at all, linguistic conditioning of the past acts as a filter, affecting my interpretation and thus understanding, or misunderstanding. Usually I am unaware of this filtering process. It is like driving a car with an automatic transmission vs. a stick shift. The driver does not think about changing gears; it happens automatically. It helps to stay aware of this potential and usually automatic challenge to understanding. When immediately disagreeing with an idea, pause, and inquire, "Why do I disagree?" Is it past conditioning being threatened? Is it fear? Conditioning is discussed in more detail in Chapter Four.

> Beneath your words is written the Word of God. The truth upsets you now, but when your words have been erased, you will see His.[10]

Why does the truth upset me? Because truth challenges what I already "know."

> Is it loss to find all things you really want, and know they have no ending and they will remain exactly as you want

them throughout time? Yet even they will be exchanged at last for what we cannot speak of, for you go from there to where words fail entirely, into a silence where the language is unspoken and yet surely understood.

Communication, unambiguous and plain as day, remains unlimited for all eternity. And God Himself speaks to His Son, as His Son speaks to Him. Their language has no words, for what They say cannot be symbolized. Their knowledge is direct and wholly shared and wholly one.[11]

Words are temporary tools, like the life jacket I take off when the boat arrives at its destination.

The mystic healer and teacher Joel S. Goldsmith died in 1964, the year before the scribing of ACIM began. Mr. Goldsmith said about words:

Truth is infinite; therefore, truth cannot be known in finite terms.[12]

Words are finite terms.

Chapter Three

RESOLVING DILEMMAS

How can God know me as perfect when evidence demonstrates otherwise? One of my dilemmas was that God viewed me as perfect and yet in my own view I was far from perfect. God is perfect and the Creator of perfection. All that God creates is perfect. Why would God create anything less than perfect? All of us are the one Son of God. The course is unambiguous about our God-given perfection. This is God's Will. Take it or leave it.

My Son is pure and holy as Myself.[1]

Be you perfect as Myself, for you can never be apart from Me.[2]

God's Son is perfect, or he cannot be God's Son. I thank you Father for Your perfect Son, and in His glory will I see my own.[3]

God's perfect Son remembers His creation. But in guilt he has forgotten what he really is.[4]

You have not only been fully created, but have also been created perfect.[5]

If God created you perfect, you are perfect.[6]

You had already taught yourself wrongly, having believed what was not true. You did not believe in your own perfection.[7]

As these teachings accumulated, I started to see how God knows me as perfect, even though I seem to have evidence to the contrary. ACIM even uses the same word – "perfect" I used to describe how that invisible presence knew me. The course was washing my mind of previous brain-washing.

In 1976 I knew little about spiritual teachings concerning the false separated self, the ego, and my true identity. Like most people, I assumed my identity was simply "me," without close examination. In fact, I identified with my separate self, the ego/body, and so I could not reconcile being both a sinner and perfect. I still identified as the thinker of my thoughts, instead of as the witness to the thinking process. I did not yet understand how God could see me as perfect. It is a relatively slow process to replace a thought system. In time, I remembered a past full of evidence demonstrating my lack of perfection.

Another dilemma concerned God's love being unconditional when the deist religions taught that God's love is conditional. For the Jews it is conditioned on a blood sacrifice of an animal and obeying the Hebrew laws. For the Christian it is conditioned on the blood sacrifice of Jesus in the crucifixion, and on the Christian's faith, and perhaps Baptism, and maybe living according to a specific moral code. There are a whole lot of conditions to achieve salvation. Salvation is of God, not self. Grace trumps all effort.

In everyday life between humans, love is conditional. Children learn from an early age how easy it is to receive disapproval and punishment. Regardless of all the disagreements among the religions and within religions concerning what conditions God demands for salvation, there are always ample conditions. *Unconditional* is the scariest word in the world to organized religions. It collapses their whole conditional theology. It might collapse their bottom line. Tithers might not want to continue tithing to a church preaching fear of hell and judgmental wrath of an angry God. Some fear also that if God's love is unconditional, then people will go crazy with licentious hedonism, and worse. Without fear of extreme punishment, we humans go wilder than topless coeds on spring break in Florida. I would probably speed a sports car if a speeding ticket did not concern me. Fear driven morality is selfish. Seriously though, if I found out that God's mercy is truly unconditional, what would I do? Would I then desire to kill, steal, and lie? If my motivation for loving my brother is fear of punishment, then I am not yet ready for Heaven.

A universal theology is not possible. Truth is true, not my version of the truth. Dogma is not necessarily true. Words fail. Truth is unspeakable, but knowable. The unspeakable experience is what matters, not words. Then, perhaps, an attempt is made to translate experience into words. Truth is lost in translation.

> **A universal theology is impossible but a universal experience is not only possible, but necessary.**[8]

God's is the only reality that's real. In the *Introduction* to the *Text*, the course teaches that love is all-encompassing. Fear *seems* to be the opposite of love, but fear is an illusion. If God has *all* power, then there is no other power that exists. To believe in a power that opposes God is believing in two powers, or duality.

> *Only perfect love exists.*
>
> *If there is fear,*
>
> *It produces a state that does not exist.*[9]

Yet I do experience fear, right? How do I experience something that does not exist? I experience illusions as well as truth. I believe that illusions are true. Dreams seem real when they are happening. I see train rails that converge in the distance, yet they don't.

The course is uncompromising in its teaching that God's love is perfect and unconditional. This teaching resolved my related dilemma. Unconditional love is all-inclusive. Absolutely no one is excluded. To exclude anyone means a condition exists for exclusion. Exclusion means there is a second power opposing God. Inclusiveness contradicts deist dogma that divides people into those going to Heaven, and those going to hell, and also those going to purgatory, or limbo, or somewhere else in the Bardo. The course teaches over and over again that the fullness and the completeness of the Son of God requires the holy rejoining of every mind in perfect wholeness. The truth of unconditional inclusiveness is not contingent on anything, because that's how God created it to be. Holy wholeness is God's Will. How is God whole if part of Him is missing?

> But exempt no one from your love, or you will be hiding a dark place in your mind where the Holy Spirit is not welcome. And thus you will exempt yourself from His healing power, for by not offering total love you will not be healed completely.[10]

The implications are significant. If I exclude anyone, I exclude myself.

I *delay* the completion of God's joy, and my own, by procrastination. Delay, for millions of years, or not, is my choice, but the good end for everyone is inevitable. ACIM came about specifically to shorten the delay.

> What God knows is that His communication channels are not open to Him, so that he cannot impart His joy and know that His children are wholly joyous. Giving His joy is an ongoing process, not in time but in eternity. God's extending outward, not His completeness, is blocked when the Sonship does not communicate with Him as one. So He thought, "My children sleep and must be awakened."[11]

Notice: *God's extending outward* is blocked, but *His completeness* is not blocked. The course often makes these fine distinctions. God's extension is the extension of divine Love. The *Introduction* makes a related distinction. The course aims to remove the blocks to the awareness of

Love's presence. The extension of God's Love is blocked only in my awareness, not in fact. God's Love extends eternally. It is here right now, but fear blocks my awareness of it. Yet fear is not real. Fear does not exist, yet belief in fear does make it seem real. At night the sun is still shining but it might seem dark because the sun rays are blocked. The moon's reflection of the sun's light serves to remind lunatics like me that the sun is shining, even when my senses demonstrate darkness. The sun does not set or rise and the earth blocks only a tiny bit of the sun's light, and that blockage is temporary.

> **But unless you take your part in the creation, His [God's] joy is not complete because yours is incomplete. And this He does know. He knows it in His Own Being and its experience of His Son's experience. The constant going out of His Love is blocked when His channels are closed, and He is lonely when the minds He created do not communicate fully with Him.**[12]

Love is offered, not forced, and God is lonely if I am closed to communion with Him. It is God who removes the blocks I maintain. God accomplishes the perfect reunion of every mind into His one Son through the Holy Spirit.

The fullness of joy requires everyone. At twenty years of age I thought that Heaven could not be complete if it excluded someone I loved. Could I be happy in Heaven while someone I loved suffered in hell? Heaven is inclusive, not exclusive.

> **God loves every brother as He loves you; neither less nor more. He needs them all equally, and so do you.**[13]

As I studied ACIM I gradually came to understand what happened that summer evening in 1976, and my dilemmas dissolved. If the course teaches that God's creation is perfect as God is perfect, then how does it explain our world of blatant imperfection and our lives that seem nowhere near perfect? If God has all power then why is there suffering? More dilemmas. Patience. We will learn how the course dissects these dilemmas.

Since this book is based on the teachings in ACIM, it is reasonable for the reader to ask, "Why ACIM?" Besides its explanation of my spiritual experience, and the resolution of the dilemmas resulting from that experience, here are ten more reasons why brother hermit embraces ACIM:

(1) ACIM is different from most religious teachings in that it states that it is not for everyone. Most religions teach their way is the only way. They claim an exclusive on the truth. It is their way or the highway to hell. This insistence is so strong that it involves killing non-believers. Freedom from insisting that ACIM is the only way is way refreshing. There is only one truth but many, even thousands, of ways of expressing it. There are so many roads home.

> **The form of the course varies greatly. So do the particular teaching aids involved. But the content of the course never changes…This is a manual for a special curriculum, intended for teachers of a special form of the universal course. There are many thousands of other forms, all with the same outcome.**[14]

I am free to take it or leave it. There is no condemnation, nor punishment, if one chooses to say, "Thanks, but no thanks." People who study and teach the course are from any and all religions or no religion at all.

> **They come from all over the world. They come from all religions and from no religion.**[15]

(2) Even though the course states it is not for everyone, it makes the daring claim to be the most efficient or the fastest way to awakening and liberation. ACIM aims to save me time in the return to Heaven. ACIM might have particular appeal to those with less time.

> Many have spent a lifetime in preparation, and have indeed achieved their instants of success. This course does not attempt to teach more than they learned in time, but it does aim at saving time.[16]

The course saves time and is different from other spiritual methodologies that require a *lifetime in preparation*. ACIM is calling for miracle workers, or teachers of God, to save time.

> It calls for teachers to speak for It and redeem the world. Many hear It, but few will answer. Yet it is all a matter of time. Everyone will answer in the end, but the end can be a long, long way off. It is because of this that the plan of the teachers was established. Their function is to save time…And each one saves a thousand years of time as the world judges it. To the Call Itself time has no meaning.[17]

If I enjoy this world, I probably want more time; but if I am depressed, I want my pain to end, sooner rather than later. Death is preferable to depression.

> They [God's teachers] merely save time. Yet it is time alone that winds on wearily, and the world is very tired now. It is old and worn and without hope. There was never a question of outcome, for what can change the Will of God? But time, with its illusions of change and death, wears out the world and all things in it. Yet time has an ending, and it is this that the teachers of God are appointed to bring about. For time is in their hands. Such was their choice, and it is given them.[18]

Is not depression associated with being weary and tired? Would I rather end suffering sooner or later?

(3) There is no ACIM church, religion, or teaching authority. There is no pope, priests, Dali Lama, or any hierarchy. There are various independent teachers and students. It is primarily a spiritual and psychological self-study course in mind training and mind healing. There are many various independent and optional ACIM study groups. There is no hierarchical, ecclesiastical organization. All my life I rebelled against authority, irrational authority, authoritarians with a need to control others. What do I do with church authorities who proclaim war is just? ACIM is a refreshing break from external authorities. True authority is within. The *Epilogue* of the *Workbook for Students* states:

> No more specific lessons are assigned, for there is no more need of them. Henceforth, hear but the Voice for God and for your Self when you retire from the world, to seek reality instead. He will direct your efforts, telling you exactly what to do, how to direct your mind, and when to come to Him in silence, asking for His sure direction and his certain Word.[19]

The true authority, the *Voice for God*, is in me, not outside of myself.

(4) The *Voice for God* refers to the Holy Spirit. Notice the subtle distinction: it is not the voice of God; it is the voice *for* God. In ACIM the Holy Spirit is indistinguishable from the Holy Spirit in the New Testament. The Holy Spirit is the divine Spirit of Love, that is God, dwelling in everyone. The Holy Spirit is what unites us.

> The Holy Spirit is referred to as the Healer, the Comforter and the Guide.[20]

The Holy Spirit guides me out of my imaginary hell. If hell is an illusion should the word and concept of hell be dropped? The course uses the term 128 times. Depression is a hellish state. Here, the illusion of hell is experienced as if real.

> Do not, then, think that following the Holy Spirit's
> guidance is necessary merely because of your own
> inadequacies. It is the way out of hell for you.[21]

The Holy Spirit brings joy, not depression. Comedians are healers.
Laughter and depression can't coexist.

> The Holy Spirit's curriculum is never depressing because
> it is a curriculum of joy. Whenever the reaction to
> learning is depression, it is because the true goal of the
> curriculum has been lost sight of.[22]

At the time of the spiritual experience described in the *Prologue*,
I identified as a Roman Catholic Christian, and I focused first on the
Holy Spirit. In my fifth, and last year in the seminary, I embraced the
Catholic Pentecostal movement, which placed emphasis on the Holy
Spirit. As I studied the New Testament, and in particular the sayings
of Jesus, I noticed His emphasis on the Holy Spirit, saying the Father
sends the Holy Spirit in Jesus' name, and how the Holy Spirit reveals
all truth to us. Jesus is no longer on earth as an individual man. He
transformed into the Christ. Now He offers the Holy Spirit to help us
join Him as the Christ. Jesus in John's Gospel:

> These things I have spoken to you, while I am still with
> you. But the Counselor, the Holy Spirit, whom the Father
> will send in my name, he will teach you all things, and
> bring to your remembrance all that I have said to you.[23]

In ACIM Jesus refers to his own promise in the New Testament regarding the Holy Spirit:

> I myself said, "If I go I will send you another Comforter
> and He will abide with you."[24]

ACIM:

> The Holy Spirit is in your right mind, as he was in mine
> [Jesus']. The Bible says, "May the mind be in you that
> was also in Christ Jesus," and uses this as a blessing. It is
> a blessing of miracle-mindedness. It asks that you may
> think as I thought, joining with me in Christ thinking.[25]

New Testament:

> And I will pray the Father, and he will give you another
> Counselor, to be with you forever, even the Spirit of truth,
> whom the world cannot receive, because it neither sees
> him nor knows him; you know him, for he dwells with
> you, and will be in you.[26]

ACIM:

> The Holy Spirit is the Christ Mind which is aware of the
> knowledge that lies beyond perception.[27]

The term *Holy Spirit* occurs 564 times in ACIM.

(5) ACIM is contemporary. There are serious challenges with the old scriptures. Jesus and Buddha did not write their teachings. An oral tradition guided the believers until disciples started writing things down, sometimes years, sometimes hundreds of years, after the transition of the Teacher. How accurate is the oral transmission? Research in psychology suggests that when a story is told from one person to the next via memory, changes are introduced to the story. Over many re-tellings and selective memory, the story may change dramatically.

Until the invention of the printing press by Johannes Gutenberg in 1439, writers and copiers hand-wrote (or carved) and hand-copied books, and few people could read and write. Have you ever made a mistake copying something in writing? To make matters worse, for most ancient scriptures we do not hold the originals; we use copies and fragments to construct our best guess at the original. And, we do not know what other complimentary or contemporaneous writings existed that did not survive the passage of time, nor the censorship of the authorities. Besides this, many different authors, human authors, with their own conditioning and politics filtering what they believed and how they interpreted the teaching, wrote the Bible. The discovery of the Dead Sea Scrolls in the 20th century introduced new writings contemporary with the New Testament. Further complicating matters is the issue of translation, and translations of translations. It is hard to know how true the writings are to the original message of the teacher. The original message was translated, interpreted, re-translated, re-interpreted, over and over for thousands of years through the individual and cultural filters of the writers, readers, and translators. The point of all this is that ACIM was first published in 1976, in English, and "scribed" by one author. The actual scribing began October 21, 1965, exactly fifty years ago as I write this.

> **Of all the messages you have received and failed
> to understand, this course alone is open to your
> understanding and can be understood. This is *your*
> language.**[28]

English readers are fortunate to be free of translations, copies, or fragments. We enjoy the luxury of the complete original in our own language. Even so, there is still interpretation. ACIM is public now for less than forty years and already there are many interpretations.

(6) I discovered confirmation of ACIM teachings in the work of several other spiritual teachers and writers, some of whom died before the course was published. These include Meister Eckhart, Ramana Maharshi, Wei Wu Wei, Joel S. Goldsmith, Eckhart Tolle and Byron Katie. I also found Biblical quotes in agreement with the course, though the course is not congruent with traditional Jewish or Christian theology. One of my favorite writers on spirituality is Wei Wu Wei. He is known for his writing on non-duality, Buddhism and Taoism. His

second book is titled, *Why Lazarus Laughed: The Essential Doctrine Zen-Advaita-Tantra*. Regarding the subtitle of this book, he wrote,

> Under the title of this book only three religions are cited, those that are formally non-dualist. But this apparent limitation does not imply that such is not also the essential "doctrine" of the three Semitic faiths, Judaism, Christianity, and Islam, which are formally dualist, and whose esoteric aspects are Kabala, Gnosis, and Sufism.

> …Therefore the Christian evidence chiefly resides in Gnostic records that are little known, in the early Fathers, and in sages and saints such as Meister Eckhart and St. John of the Cross, who were obliged by the dogmas of the Church to cloak the nondualism which is implicit in their realization of the truth. For this reason it is unpractical to use Christian evidence in such a collection as this.

> However, in view of the tidal-wave of interest in metaphysics which reveals a considerable percentage of modern man as being driven to seek the truth concerning himself and the universe, it seems inevitable that the day will arrive when the doctrines of Iesous Christos will once more be revealed to mankind.[29]

I wondered if ACIM is the realization of this prediction by Wei Wu Wei. ACIM is often compared with Gnostic writings. ACIM does share some Gnostic ideas, but it is not Gnosticism.

(7) In my spiritual journey I studied other spiritual teachings besides the Christian ones I learned growing up, including Jiddu Krishnamurti, Buddhism, and Sufism, my favorites. When I started reading the course, I thought of it as a synthesis of eastern and western spiritual teachings. This integration of east and west appealed tremendously because I respected these other teachings and I did not share

the belief in Christian exclusiveness. I hoped to integrate and include east and west. Bill Thetford, the psychologist who worked with Helen Schucman to produce ACIM, called the course Christian Vedanta. He meant an integration of Christianity and mystical Hinduism. Ramana Maharshi's teaching is harmonious with ACIM.

Some commentators on the course see it as more a Buddhist teaching than Christian. This appears so because in contemporary Christianity, the sheep have strayed so far from the Shepherd so as to be unrecognizable as related to Christ. Buddhism in a non-theist religion. ACIM uses the word "God" 2207 times, the term "Holy Spirit" 564 times, the word "Christ" 273 times, the word "Creator" 195 times, and the term "Holy Trinity" seven times. It uses the word "crucifixion", or its variants, 79 times. It uses the word "resurrection" 35 times, and the word "Atonement," or its variants 189 times. There are hundreds of references to the Bible. ACIM is neither Christian nor Buddhist, but embraces truth, regardless of flavor. The truth is true, regardless of the teacher, and ACIM warns about delaying our liberation because of theological and philosophical speculation. Christianity developed and derailed after Jesus. ACIM seems to be Jesus applying correction.

(8) Related to it being contemporary, ACIM is a spiritual teaching making use of modern psychology. The insights of modern psychology were not available until the 20th century. Freud first published *The Interpretation of Dreams* in 1900. Older spiritual technologies do not hold this advantage, despite deep insights into the workings of the mind. ACIM came through clinical psychologists. The three primary people associated with the publication of ACIM were Helen Schucman, William Thetford, and Kenneth Wapnick, all PhD clinical psychologists. Helen and Bill worked primarily as academic research psychologists at Columbia University in New York City. Hence the academic flavor of the course. It is called a "course," and a "required course." It contains a *Text* (theory), *Workbook For Students* (lab), and a *Manual For Teachers,* including a *Clarification Of Terms.* It speaks of lessons, students, teachers and a curriculum. Modern psychological

ideas of the unconscious mind and defense mechanisms are fundamental to the course.

Bill Thetford studied as a graduate student and assistant to Carl Rogers, my favorite clinical psychologist, in Chicago. Kenneth Wapnick, a Jew and psychologist, converted to Catholicism after reading Thomas Merton and being attracted to the monastic life Merton described. Wapnick made a retreat at the Trappist Monastery Gethsemane in Kentucky, famous for being the monastery of Thomas Merton, who died in 1968. I wonder what might be Merton's opinion of ACIM, since he was one of the first Catholics to try to build bridges of deep ecumenism between west and east. Merton especially liked Zen and Sufism. Wapnick also spent time in Christian Monasteries in Israel, and planned on a monastic vocation there, before he met Helen and Bill and learned of the course. Kenneth became devoted to the course, and to Helen, and helped with the chapter titles and organization of the book. He died in 2013, and is known as one of the greatest teachers of the course.

(9) Also related to it being contemporary is the benefit of quantum physics and modern technology. Teachings in the course are so advanced that students are challenged understanding and remembering the ideas. If I don't understand an idea, then I'm not likely to remember it. Familiarity with modern physics theory is helpful and even supportive of radical course ideas about reality, time, and space. Post-modern quantum physicists babble like mystics about "reality." Modern ideas and technology such as "virtual realities," motion pictures, holography, and flight simulation serve as metaphors for radical course ideas.

(10) The course makes frequent references to the Bible. Often it offers a different interpretation than the traditional. At age sixteen I developed a desire for studying the New Testament. I found much agreement between the words of Jesus in the course and in the Gospels, in particular John's Gospel, considered more Gnostic than the three synoptic Gospels.

Where did ACIM come from; whose teaching is it? It uses many Christian terms, but the theology is not Christian. It shares a lot of ideas with Buddhism, Taoism, Vedanta Hinduism, Gnostic thought, and depth psychology. Although a psychologist scribed the course, it is not her teaching. It came through her. Helen Schucman heard a voice in her head and wrote down what it said over a seven year period, 1965-1972. The voice spoke rapidly and she used her own method of shorthand to write it down. Day by day, she read what she took as a type of mental dictation to her colleague, Bill Thetford, who typed what she read. She said she could stop at any time, even mid-sentence, and later pick it up right where she left off. She describes herself as:

> **Psychologist, educator, conservative in theory and
> atheistic in belief, I was working in a prestigious and
> highly academic setting.**[30]

The size of the course, writing style, and the fact that Helen, Bill, and Kenneth wrote, typed, and edited it without computers or word-processing programs is impressive. The voice she heard claimed to be Jesus, the same Jesus of Christianity. The course teaches that it is not necessary to believe the source is Jesus. The teaching stands as truth, regardless of who I believe the source is. Anyone, however, who is interested in Jesus, and is concerned with the variety of Christian theologies, might approach the course with an open mind.
Jesus in the New Testament:

> **I have yet many things to say to you, but you cannot bear
> them now. When the Spirit of truth comes, he will guide
> you into all the truth.**[31]

The course addresses the above quote:

> **As you read the teachings of the Apostles, remember
> that I told them myself that there was much they would
> understand later, because they were not wholly ready to
> follow me at the time.**[32]

The course addresses traditional Christian theology frequently:

> A further point must be perfectly clear before any
> residual fear still associated with miracles can disappear.
> The crucifixion did not establish the Atonement;
> the resurrection did. Many sincere Christians have
> misunderstood this...Yet the real Christian should
> pause and ask, "How could this be?" Is it likely that God
> Himself would be capable of the kind of thinking which
> His Own words have clearly stated is unworthy of His
> Son?[33]

Essentially, people were unable to hear and understand his complete teaching two thousand years ago. The majority of people he spoke to were Jews, and conditioned by generations of Judaism. Jesus' teaching remains too radical even today. What is it about "Love your enemies," that Christians don't get? Jesus was Jewish, but transcended Judaism, and his followers misunderstood his teaching because they filtered it through their Hebrew conditioning. In particular, Jewish ideas of blood sacrifice to atone for sin are continued in Christianity. Christian theology developed long after Jesus' death. Jesus did not write any of the New Testament. Paul wrote most of it. The earliest Gospels presented sayings of Jesus, like the *Gospel of Thomas*.

What exactly then does ACIM say about Jesus?

> He has become the risen Son of God. He has overcome
> death because he has accepted life. He
> has recognized himself as God created him, and
> in so doing he has recognized all living things as part of
> him. There is now no limit on his power, because it is the
> power of God. So has his name become the Name of God,
> for he no longer sees himself as separate from Him.

> What does this mean for you? It means that in
> remembering Jesus you are remembering God...

Is he still available for help? What did he say about this? Remember his promises, and ask yourself honestly whether it is likely that he will fail to keep them. Can God fail His Son? And can one who is one with God be unlike Him?

Remembering the name of Jesus Christ is to give thanks for all the gifts that God has given you. And gratitude to God becomes the way in which He is remembered, for love cannot be far behind a grateful heart and thankful mind. God enters easily, for these are the true conditions for your homecoming.

Jesus has led the way.

This course has come from him because his words have reached you in a language you can love and understand.[34]

It is easy to forget something important here. I remember God via gratitude. The *true conditions* of my return to Heaven are a *grateful heart and thankful mind*.

The name of *Jesus* is the name of one who was a man but saw the face of Christ in all his brothers and remembered God. So he became identified with Christ, a man no longer, but at one with God.

Jesus remains a Savior because he saw the false without accepting it as true. And Christ needed his form that He might appear to men and save them from their own illusions.

In his complete identification with the Christ –the perfect Son of God, His one creation and His happiness, forever like Himself and One with Him – Jesus became what all of you must be. He led the way for you to follow him. He leads you back to God because he saw the road before him, and he followed it. He made a clear distinction, still obscure to you, between the false and true. He offered you a final demonstration that it is impossible to kill God's Son; nor can his life in any way be changed by sin and evil, malice, fear or death.

And therefore all your sins have been forgiven because they carried no effects at all.[35]

ACIM teaches that Jesus is the first to graduate from this world.

The Holy Spirit is described throughout the course as giving us the answer to the separation and bringing the plan of the Atonement to us, establishing our particular part in it and showing us exactly what it is. He has established Jesus as the leader in carrying out His plan since he was the first to complete his own part perfectly. All power in Heaven and earth is therefore given him and he will share it with you when you have completed yours.[36]

I see ACIM as the corrected teaching of Jesus. The Jesus of the course frequently refers to himself as the Jesus of the New Testament. The theologies of the course and Christianity are certainly different. In particular, the entrenched Jewish-Christian notion of blood sacrifice for sins is diametrically opposed to the course teaching. Yet even the Bible frequently agrees with the course: *I desire mercy and not sacrifice.* Many course teachings are closer to Buddhism, Taoism, and Hinduism than Christianity, but as far I as I can tell, the Jesus of the course is the same Jesus of the Gospels, though not the Jesus of Christian theology. The truth of Jesus is available in the Gospels, including the *Gospel of Thomas*, but the truth continues to be confused and compromised by thousands of years of theological misinterpretation. That's why Jesus said he had many more things to tell us, but we could not understand him, *at that time.*

All spiritual teachers are limited by the culture they lived in. Two thousand years ago Jesus presented the truth to people limited in what they could understand. The limit was not in Jesus but in the people of his time. Even the apostles closest to Jesus misunderstood Jesus' teaching about his return. They believed it was to happen soon. Even after living in direct contact with Jesus for three years, the Apostles misunderstood. They simply were not capable yet of understanding. So, if even the Apostles, who spent time directly with Jesus, did not get it, why should I assume that Christians today get it? Fundamentalists base their faith on a book written by others who misunderstood Jesus. Christians still can't agree among themselves about Jesus and his teaching and thus divide into thousands of denominations. Is the rapture pre-tribulation, mid-tribulation, or post-tribulation? Not long ago American Christians used the Bible to justify slavery. Beliefs change, fortunately. It seems that few other than the rare mystic shift from the intellectual, theological map to experiencing the true spiritual territory. Now, more people are ready to hear and apply the radical truth.

ACIM is likely to appeal particularly to those who experience much suffering and fail to find sustained relief or a solution to existential issues of identity, meaning of life, suffering, and death. The course clearly explains the cause of, and solution for, depression.

ACIM is also likely to appeal to the spiritual seeker who still has not found what he is looking for. Those who embrace a Christian faith but are challenged with various church divisions and politics might find the course to be just what is needed.

For further information about how the course came about, events preceding the scribing of the course, and the life of Helen Schucman, Kenneth Wapnick's biography of Helen, *Absence of Felicity*, is excellent. An important distinction for me in this book is Kenneth's teaching that the *form* of the course came from Helen and the *content* of the course came from Jesus.

Chapter Four

OPEN MIND

*a*m I open-minded? Most of us like to think so. We tend to see close-mindedness as a negative and open-mindedness as desirable. What does it mean to be open-minded?

> Heaven itself is reached with empty hands and open
> minds, which come with nothing to find everything and
> claim it as their own.[1]

It is one thing to assume I am open-minded and another to *come with nothing* but *empty hands*. How does emptying happen? From an early age most of us are in the process of filling our mental hands and accumulating more and more, not less and less.

When asked if one is open, the open-minded answer is "I don't know." I prefer to believe I am open-minded, even if it is not true. Sometimes it is hard to see. Sometimes it is in retrospect that I see my closed-mindedness. It is harder to see the more dangerous resistance currently present, right now. Closed-mindedness is there automatically, and unconsciously, because our minds are already filled with so much learning obtained from the authorities of family, church, state, school, media, and experience. We all get brainwashed. To be open-minded is more of a challenge than one might think.

> Yet the essential thing is learning that you do not know.
> Knowledge is power, and all power is of God. Yet all that
> stands between you and the power of God in you is but
> your learning of the false, and of your attempts to undo
> the true.
>
> Be willing, then, for all of it to be undone, and be glad
> that you are not bound to it forever.[2]

My *learning of the false* blinds me to the truth and this learning is undone if I want the freedom of the truth. It is perfectly okay to say "I don't know." Knowing I do not know frees me from slavery to the past. Regardless of what I think and believe, truth does not change. The truth of what I am does not change yet my understanding of my identity does change.

> *I will not use my own past learning as the light to guide me now.*[3]

I might not like being called ignorant, but thank God it is true. I am ignorant to believe and do the things I do. When men nailed Jesus to the tree, he asked his Father to forgive his executioners because they were ignorant. They did not know his identity and they did not know their own identities.

> **To learn this course requires willingness to question every value that you hold.**[4]

Values are beliefs and ideas important to me. Am I willing to question everything I value? Where do my values come from? Are children born with values? No, values are learned. When certain values challenge different values, the result is often war, like the American Civil War. Humans kill each other over ideologies and yet we consider ourselves intelligent.

> **Resign now as your own teacher.**[5]

This means shifting authority from self to God, the true Author. Why should I assume my values are valid and different values are not? All of them are learned.

The ideas presented in ACIM are radically different from what I already learned. Even to consider these ideas requires the mental door to be opened at least a crack. What shuts and locks the door of mind? In a word, fear. What I already "know" is a result of past conditioning, based on fear. I fear losing what I already learned, what I believe to be true or useful. I fear the loss of pseudo-control my knowledge seems to provide. I fear loss of the pseudo-security my beliefs seem to provide. I fear the loss of pseudo-salvation, as if salvation depended on ideas and God is waiting to condemn His beloved child for an error in thinking. If my mental hands are full I cannot receive new knowledge.

To be a learner is to be able to say, "I don't know." If I don't know, learning is possible. Can I drink wine poured into a glass full of dirt? I employ a "frame of reference" limiting open-mindedness. Am I willing let my frame of reference retire? It is not easy to do. Using memory, I teach myself, accumulating the past and constructing illusory images of God, self, other, and the world.

> **Remember nothing that you taught yourself, for you were badly taught. And who would keep a senseless lesson?**[6]

It is not easy to question my core beliefs, but unless I willingly inquire, I am stuck in the past.

> **If you are willing to renounce the role of guardian of your thought system and open it to me, I [Jesus] will correct it very gently and lead you back to God.**[7]

How well is past learning serving me? Has it ended depression?

The course teaches, simply, that there are only two thought systems, the thought system of the Holy Spirit and the thought system of my own, also called the ego's thought system. One is right-minded and the other is wrong-minded. Guess which one doesn't count? Even though there are only two thought systems, the ego's wrong-mindedness takes many forms. A closed-minded person is likely to resist seeing that his thinking is wrong. Most of us want to be the *guardian* of our own thought system. Each of us is close-minded, or limited, by our frame of reference that was constructed by conditioning. Do I want to see how I am wrong? No. I want to be right, even if it hurts me.

> Seek not outside yourself. For all your pain comes simply
> from a futile search for what you want, insisting where it
> must be found. What if it is not there? Do you prefer that
> you be right or happy?[8]

When I insist on what I want and where to find it I am not open
to hearing a different opinion. Unhappiness might be the blessed key
that unlocks the door of my mind. Can I even consider that I might
be wrong in my opinion? At least I know that my worldview does not
lead to happiness. Is there a better way? Is happiness possible at all?
Do I want to find out?

When someone presents a new idea, I naturally evaluate it according to my pre-existing database of learnings. Just because an idea is
new does not mean it is true or useful. The new idea either fits in
accord with what I already know, or it does not, or it might be somewhere in between. Usually, I base my acceptance or rejection of the
idea accordingly. Sometimes an idea is planted like a seed and remains
dormant until my mind is right for the seed to sprout life and grow.

It is difficult to consider a new idea that challenges my pre-existing
bias. My judgment is already made, before I even hear the new idea.
Krishnamurti called open mind, *Freedom from the known*. How free
am I from what I already know? Usually, if I accept an idea, I merely
accept what supports or agrees with what I already believe or "know"
to be "true." The more I know – the more I am the expert – the harder
it is to be open and receive new ideas that replace older, incompatible
ideas. Conditioning trains me into the rut of reinforcing my ideas
with repetitious ruminations, playing the same mental tape over and
over, fortifying and guarding a structure of thought until it is mas-
sively defended. When I believe what I was taught about God, I am
like Pavlov's dog, salivating at the gong of God, not God, as God is.

> Many stand guard over their ideas because they want to
> protect their thought systems as they are, and learning
> means change.[9]

When we are able to keep a curious mind, beginners mind, empty mind, open mind, previous conditioning is undone, or at least loosened. I might try to remove my muddy boots without loosening the laces, yet that doesn't work, does it? I allow undoing when I willingly consider the new without insisting on the old. Is there even one chance in a million I might have misunderstood or misinterpreted truth? Nothing is forced on anyone. Readiness varies.

Perhaps even more radical than questioning my thoughts and beliefs, ACIM asks me to question perception – what the five senses report as true.

> **Do not make the mistake of believing that you**
> **understand what you perceive, for its meaning is lost to**
> **you.**[10]

One way the course describes its goal is as perception correction.

> **It** [the course] **is concerned only with Atonement, or the**
> **correction of perception.**[11]

I trust my senses, most of the time. If I see something, it is real, yes?

> **You do not know the meaning of anything you perceive.**
> **Not one thought you hold is wholly true. The recognition**
> **of this is your firm beginning…instruction in perception**
> **is your great need; for you understand nothing.**[12]

So much for eye witnesses. So, the *firm beginning* is my recognition that I do not know. I understand neither my thoughts nor my sense perceptions. Am I willing to question my thoughts, beliefs, perceptions and what the authorities claim is good, true, and beautiful? Illusionists use slight of hand and distraction to convince me that what I see is true, even if it isn't. Perception is magic.

True authority is the Voice for God, the Holy Spirit, that is within everyone. External authority is illusionary. Perception presents an exterior world, with various authorities. Don't believe it.

> Seek not outside yourself. For it will fail, and you will
> weep each time an idol falls. Heaven cannot be found
> where it is not, and there can be no peace excepting
> there.[13]

External authorities condition as they were conditioned. It's a hard loop to break. Like a person abused as a child becoming an abuser himself. How often do people continue in the same religion or political party as their parents? People who challenge the status quo generally are not treated well. What do Jesus, Gandhi, and Martin Luther King share in common? They promoted non-violence and they were assassinated. Their ideas challenged status quo thinking that remained closed to hearing the truth. Ideas cannot be killed.

Do social fears feed the need to conform, to be accepted, to be part of a group? I might fear losing my job if I stray too far from what is "expected." Fear of rejection might keep the door of my mind closed, locked, and barricaded. Fear of the devil or hell might prevent an open mind. Fear in general is a warning. Inquire. What is this fear about? What is its cause? Resistance to the different is common across the board. Try getting insurance to pay for alternative treatments when covered and toxic treatments don't work. The Catholic Church discovered the solution for heretics: excommunication. Ever received or given someone the silent treatment? Is refusing to talk to someone ex-communication?

At about age nineteen I realized that my own strongly held beliefs and opinions were subject to change. So if my previous thinking evolved, why should I be so certain of my current ideas? Maybe my current, cherishly held concepts will end up in the recycling bin, or the dump. The truth is, beliefs develop and evolve and so perhaps *expecting* ideas to change frees me from the usual resistance to change that blocks awareness of the truth. If I am growing, will my ideas change? Without flexibility, giant steel skyscrapers break with a shake. Tall trees bend wisely in the wind, joyfully, and sing, "Thanks!" Could interpretation of ideas change? Do adults still eat baby food? Some do. Have you ever thought, "I used to think that was true; now I see it differently?" Often, ideas that challenge core beliefs are threatening and need to be harshly opposed, even with violence. Hence, wars are fought over beliefs, ideologies. How did *Thou shall not kill* becoming killing for God?

Academia is seriously conservative, continuing the past into the future. That's its job. Liberals are as rigid and resistant to a different idea as are conservatives. Ideas become institutionalized, protected by the professional experts – the rigorous academic authorities – despite evidence that knowledge evolves and changes. The professional peers who review and control what is published in the literature are all conditioned in the same way. Minds once fluid, questioning and open are cured like cement and become "experts."

The past is continued so that the future is identical to the past, while most miss out on the new that is *now*. I seem to prefer the stable slavery of continuity to freedom from the known. World peace is always in the future, not now. But why would I want to continue past pain? Is there a better way? Why fear to find out?

Since happiness hides in the future, I settle for pride in being right. If I am depressed, despite my current thought system (or maybe even because of my current thought system), then perhaps I can consider if there might be a better way. Depression, and all kinds suffering, might be the fire compelling me to consider alternatives, despite the usual need to be right. A depressed person might be able to say: "This is not working. Is there a way out of feeling this bad that actually works?" If I did not feel depressed, I might not be even curious about alternatives. If my house is burning down, I get out, or I get burned.

Integral theorist and writer Ken Wilber shares a view about suffering and the purpose of suffering:

> The movement of descent and discovery begins at the moment you consciously become dissatisfied with life.

> Contrary to most professional opinion, this gnawing
> dissatisfaction with life is not a sign of mental illness, nor
> an indication of poor social adjustment, nor a character
> disorder. For concealed within this basic unhappiness
> with life and existence is the embryo of a growing
> intelligence, a special intelligence usually buried under
> the immense weight of social shams. A person who is
> beginning to sense the suffering of life is, at the same
> time, beginning to awaken to deeper realities, truer
> realities. For suffering smashes to pieces the complacency
> of normal fictions about reality...[14]

Wilber goes on to say the problem is getting stuck in suffering, which
is a pretty good description of chronic depression. The usefulness of
suffering decreases when I get stuck in it. I get breakdown rather than
breakthrough. Instead of pain pushing me forward it blocks forward
progress. Why delay the ending of depression?

> The curriculum you set yourself is depressing indeed.
> Resign now as your own teacher. This resignation will
> not lead to depression.[15]

This book attempts to show why and how I delay liberation so I can
cooperate in clearing what blocks liberation. It's roto-rooter for the
constipated mind.

Fear prevents inquiry. I value core beliefs I won't question, let alone
relinquish. The most reinforced, cemented, and defended ideas are
usually related to religion and identity. Am I willing to risk the collapse of the foundation of my identity, my entire world? It may sound
scary, but staying stuck in sadness is worse.

Why have 3,000 years of Judaism, 2,500 years of Buddhism, and
2,000 years of Christianity failed to end killing?

The world has not yet experienced any comprehensive reawakening or rebirth.[16]

ACIM offers a rare spiritual and psychological approach that includes healing and purification of unconscious material. This is not psychological shadow work; it is spiritual shadow work, probing deeper to the core, hidden source of problems psychology does not even know about. The unconscious mind is a relatively new concept. Some people intuited *something* unknown affecting them. When St. Paul described the conflict between what he wanted to do and what he did, he gave a good description of the effect of the unconscious mind.

> I do not understand my own actions. For I do not do what I want, but I do the very thing I hate…I can will what is right, but I cannot do it. For I do not do the good I want, but the evil I do not want is what I do.[17]

Start simply by withholding judgment, neither agreeing nor disagreeing with the ideas, if possible. First see what the ideas are and once understanding that much, say yes or no. Or maybe. Or whatever. Meister Eckhart:

The more we know, the less we understand.[18]

ACIM promises peace when I remember that I know nothing. The ego is a know-it-all.

> Those who remember always that they know nothing and have become willing to learn everything, will learn it. But whenever they trust themselves, they will not learn. They have destroyed their motivation for learning by thinking they already know. Whenever you fully realize that you know not, peace will return for you have abandoned the ego.[19]

Krishnamurti is clear in explaining the challenge of freedom from conditioning:

> Our difficulty lies in that we have built around ourselves conclusions which we call "understanding." These conclusions are hindrances to understanding. If you go into this more deeply, you will see that there must be complete abandonment of all that has been accumulated for the being of understanding and wisdom. To be simple is not a conclusion, an intellectual concept for which you strive. There can be simplicity only when the self with its accumulation ceases.
>
> It is comparatively easy to renounce family, property, fame, things of the world; that is only the beginning; but it is extremely difficult to put away all knowledge, all conditioned memory.[20]

Is this not a radical teaching? *To put away all knowledge, all conditioned memory?* Who does it? ACIM teaches about believing or accepting the course itself:

> Some of the ideas the workbook presents you will find hard to believe, and others may seem quite startling. This does not matter. You are merely asked to apply the ideas as you are directed to do. You are not asked to judge them at all. You are asked only to use them. It is their use that will show you that they are true.
>
> Remember only this: you need not believe the ideas, you need not accept them, and you need not even welcome them. Some of them you may actively resist. None of this will matter, or decrease their efficacy.[21]

Application of the ideas is important, not believing them. So I do not need to agree with the ideas. The proof is in the practice.

> Therefore ask not of yourself what you need, for you do not know, and your advice to yourself will hurt you. For what you think you need will merely serve to tighten up your world against the light, and render you unwilling to question the value that this world can really hold for you.[22]

A mystic is longing for God. What do I know about God? Have I met God? If not, then all I know about God is what others, who, like me, have not met God, told me, or what I read in a book. The conditioned condition as they were conditioned. Even if I do not know anything about God, I might believe many things *about* God. Belief is not knowing. To become open-minded is to be emptied of all I "know." I am curious why many religions associate the direct experience of God with the devil. The last thing the devil wants is for anyone to experience God.

Even the correct conditioning the course provides to replace illusions is temporary and released when it is no longer needed. It is not needed in Heaven. And even before that, I might get confused or misinterpret what the course teaches and need to relinquish a previous understanding of the course. A powerful lesson from the *Workbook* asks me to empty myself of all conditioning, including the course itself:

> Simply do this: Be still, and lay aside all thoughts of what you are and what God is; all concepts you have learned about the world; all images you hold about yourself. Empty your mind of everything it thinks is either true or false, or good or bad, of every thought it judges worthy, and all the ideas of which it is ashamed. Hold onto nothing. Do not bring with you one thought the past has taught, nor one belief you ever learned before from anything. Forget this world, forget this course, and come with wholly empty hands unto your God.[23]

SIDETRACK: 1954-1974

Religious conditioning might be the most rigid and effective block to an open mind regarding spirituality. Because ACIM and this book are about spirituality, spiritual conditioning can prevent even a curious read. It is easy to scare the shit out of a small child with religious teachings that describe burning in hell for eternity. At a young age, pre-rational kids believe what they are told regardless of the logic. A baby's unconditioned mind is ripe for conditioning because there is not yet a pre-existing database to offer resistance to conditioning. Bruce Lipton:

> **Between birth and two years of age, the human brain predominantly operates at the lowest EEG frequency, 0.5 to 4 cycles per second (Hz), known as delta waves…A child begins to spend more time at a higher level of EEG activity characterized as theta (4-8 Hz) between two and six years of age. Hypnotherapists drop their patient's brain activity into delta and theta because these low frequency brain waves put them into a more suggestible, programmable state.[24]**

Later in life, when rational logic kicks in, a lame belief might be reinforced, kicked out, or hidden in the unconscious vault. Because belief in eternal, burning pain is so frightening, it grips the mind, compelling cautious consideration. I better be careful, just in case, even remotely, the hell teaching is true. And since so many millions of men believed in hell for thousands of years, it could be true, right? Who am I to argue with millenniums of infallible popes? And it is not just Christians who believe in eternal hell.

My story is an example of extensive religious conditioning. My dilemmas described in the *Prologue* were a result of my religious conditioning being challenged by a spiritual experience. It took decades to tie the knots, and decades to untie them.

My Mother and Father were born and raised Roman Catholics in Providence, Rhode Island. In my case, Baptism happened eight days after my birth. Mom was Irish Catholic and Dad was French-Canadian Catholic. They married in Modesto, California, where my Dad's parents were then living, in November 1953. Mom was eighteen and Dad was twenty-two. Three months later, Mom was with child and I came forth in November 1954 in Monterey County, California, where the army stationed my Dad. I was the first-born of five boys. No sisters. From the farming town where I first breathed air, King City, it is thirty miles due west, over the coastal range to the Big Sur coast and New Camoldoli, the Catholic Hermitage where holy hermits introduced me to the contemplative aspect of Catholicism, twenty years after my birth. The hermitage started in the 50's too. But that is getting a little ahead of the story.

Regarding being born, I came across the writings of Dr. Stan Grof. Grof is a psychiatrist who did research with LSD before it became illegal. He then developed holotropic breathwork to replace LSD. He regressed many people to the point of re-experiencing their human birth. It turns out that being born can be severely traumatic. We already know it is hard on the mother, but most of us retain no conscious memory of birth and it is not considered an issue. Grof's research suggests that birth trauma can have serious consequences. Just because the trauma is unconscious does not mean it is not there. Grof describes four stages of being born, or "basic perinatal matrices" (BPM). BPM I is the entire time of pregnancy. BPM II to IV are stages of the actual birth process. He discovered a relationship between problems at various BPM stages and specific mental disorders later in life.

In the case of my birth, I got stuck in BPM II. My Mother was nineteen and a novice at giving birth. The labor lasted twenty-four hours. Grof describes BPM II:

> **Reliving the fully developed first stage of biological birth – when the uterus is contracting, but the cervix is**

> not yet open (BPM II) – is one of the worst experiences
> a human being can have. We feel caught in a monstrous
> claustrophobic nightmare, suffer agonizing emotional
> and physical pain, and experience utter helplessness and
> hopelessness. Our feelings of loneliness, guilt, absurdity
> of life, and existential despair can reach metaphysical
> proportions. We lose connection with linear time and
> become convinced that this situation will never end and
> that there is absolutely no way out. There is no doubt
> in our mind that what is happening to us is what the
> religions refer to as hell – unbearable emotional and
> physical torment without any hope of redemption.[25]

One of the worst tortures I dread is confinement so tight that movement is impossible. I wonder if birth trauma is related to my rebellion against all authority and resistance to any kind of control. Grof goes on to discuss a kind of depression related to BPM II trauma:

> Inhibited depression can typically be traced to the second
> perinatal matrix. Subjects reliving BPM II in holotropic
> or psychedelic sessions show all the essential features
> of deep depression. Under the influence of BPM II, an
> individual experiences agonizing mental pain, despair,
> overwhelming feelings of guilt and inadequacy, deep
> anxiety, lack of initiative, loss of interest in anything and
> an inability to enjoy existence.[26]

Grof's research confirms what ACIM says about the birth process:

> For this world is the symbol of punishment, and all the
> laws that seem to govern it are the laws of death. Children
> are born into it through pain and in pain.[27]

In *Genesis* "God" says:

> **I will multiply your pains in childbearing, you
> shall give birth to your children in pain.**[28]

Usually birth is celebrated as a great blessing while death is feared and avoided, yet birth is accompanied by pain, even severe pain, for mother and child. Birth is the prerequisite for death. Birth is a separation event.

My Father was strict and serious about his religion. His mother, Grandma Rose, was a devout Catholic. My maternal Grandmother, Dorothy Maguire, worked at a Catholic retreat house the last ten years of her life. My Dad wanted to be a priest, but, for reasons unknown to me, authorities at the seminary deemed him unsuitable for priesthood. A common tradition in Catholic families then meant presenting the first-born son to the Church to become a priest. This practice comes from the Old Testament. And so it happened Dad conditioned me from an early age to prepare for priesthood. My biggest fear wasn't death, but worse: going to hell after I died. In kid-logic I figured if I became a priest, my chances of going to hell decreased significantly.

After discharge from the military my father worked a variety of jobs and we moved often but stayed in the state of California. We moved from King City to South San Francisco where my next two brothers, first Robert and then Mickey were born, and that's where my first memories are from. Then we moved to Southern California. I remember going to three different kindergarten schools in one year because we moved so often. I wonder if the frequent moves affected my social skills. I did not experience a lasting friendship until third grade. Also, because my birth month is November, I tended to be the youngest person in my classes. The book *Tipping Point* describes the effects of birth month. The difference between starting school at five or at six is significant because one year of development is huge at that age.

Here are a few facts about Catholicism: Catholics are required to go to Mass once a week, on Sunday or Saturday evening. If one missed this obligation, one committed a serious offense, a mortal sin. A mortal sin means that if I die before confessing the sin to a priest, I go straight to hell. That's how easy it is to achieve permanent damnation.

Mass is offered daily. Usually weekday Mass is early in the morning so people can attend before work. My Dad attended Mass daily and started taking me with him at age five. This attention from Dad contributed to my feeling special because my two younger brothers were too young. I felt a little superior to them with this privilege. Before Vatican II the Mass was in Latin, adding to the mysteriousness of the candle-lit, frankincensed ceremony. I remained a daily communicant pretty much until I married in 1982, two weeks before my twenty-eighth birthday.

Practicing Catholicism, I established some sort of relationship with a "God" I did not know. This relationship was between a hellish concept of God, and me. This relationship was based on fear and it reflected my relationship with my Dad. He criticized, found fault, and punished me by spanking my bare ass with a belt. Meanwhile my Mother spoiled me in certain ways. I think some of my brothers were belted worse than me. So God, like Dad, policed me, catching every sin or mistake I made because God is all-knowing. And God is also just, so punishment is in order. I hoped to make it to purgatory after this life and so avoid hell. Nothing like getting a kid started off on guilt and fear early. It is called "having a good conscience." The more guilt I feel, the more sensitive is my conscience. All the saints had sensitive consciences. "Father," whether as God or Dad, meant someone who saw my sin, judged me guilty, and provided punishment. I did not have a good relationship with either. Later, when I was in elementary school, my father ran his own appliance repair business. As I approached our house walking home from school, I could tell whether he was home or not by the presence or absence of his truck. I hoped he would not be home because I feared him. If I fear God, then I don't want to be with Him. Who wants to be with someone they fear? Fear repels. Love attracts. Fear blocks union.

Like many Catholics, my parents wanted their children to go to Catholic school. For grades one and two I attended St. Bridget of Sweden Catholic School and made my First Communion and Confession in the second grade. Imagine a seven-year-old coming up with a list of sins to confess to the priest. I was not old enough yet to have "impure thoughts." Why are sin and sex synonymous? Based on the mass media of film and television, sex and nudity are far more forbidden than violence, torture, and murder.

Two early events in first and second grades bear mentioning. In first or second grade my parents bought me a bike. My Dad, being frugal, bought an over-sized bike that I could grow into. He attached thick wood blocks to the pedals to make them reachable with my seven-year-old legs. I loved that bike and used it for many years. The bicycle became important in various ways. I consider it one of the greatest inventions ever. I developed a life-long love of bicycles and cycling. A bicycle symbolized freedom and independence. I eventually traveled long distances by bike. Now, at sixty, I have not owned a car for ten years; I use a nice full-suspension mountain bike.

In second grade, roughhousing in the back yard with my brothers and neighborhood boys, I broke my right wrist. Immobilized in a cast for a while, I could not write. In school, when the rest of the second graders were practicing writing, the Sister had me read instead of write. I became a good reader at an early age.

From third grade on we settled in the San Francisco Bay Area, first in Monte Vista near Cupertino and then for a long time in Los Altos. Now the Bay Area is the most expensive place to live in the United States, largely because of Silicon Valley and all that. But when my Dad bought the house in Los Altos in 1963, it cost $19,000.

Reaching a certain vantage point, maybe age fifty or so, I reflected on my life and recognized certain stable passions or patterns. These aspects of my life emerged early on and stayed throughout my life. I identified four primary life-long patterns: spirituality, wilderness, art, and relationship issues.

Identifying myself as a seriously devoted Catholic started early and persisted into my thirties. I wanted to go to Heaven after I died. Salvation required the practice of Catholicism. I prayed and considered theological things. My religiousness gradually shifted to spirituality and this remains my primary interest now. My spiritual journey is the subject of most of the *sidetrack* sections in this book.

As far as wilderness goes, I enjoyed the camping trips my father took my brothers and I on. I had fun fishing and catching critters like crayfish, snakes, lizards, salamanders, and frogs. Later I joined the Boy Scouts and looked forward to the monthly camping trips with Troop 35. I recall a two-week Boy Scout summer camp that was especially fun and I discovered backpacking (vs. family car camping). During this camp I swam a lot in the lake and increased the distance I swam each day so as to be able to complete the "mile swim" at the end of camp. I swam across Lake Arrowhead. We started before dawn to avoid boat traffic. First the swimmers boated across the lake, and then swam back solo, each boy going at his own pace. The goal was to make it across the lake, not win a competitive race. My Father rowed along as I swam across the cold mountain lake. I made it and received my badge proudly.

Though not good at competitive sports, I enjoyed fishing, swimming, cycling and hiking. These activities were fun and non-competitive with no need to qualify or "make" the team as with the usual school sports. I did not like aggressive sports and my brothers performed much better than me in competitive sports like basketball and soccer. In eighth grade I tried out for the school baseball team, and surprisingly enough made the team, barely. I sat on the bench the entire season. In the last inning of the last game, the coach, named Osario, allowed me one at-bat and I struck out. In High School I ran on the cross-country team. I identified as a naturalist and a fisherman. I wanted to be either a park ranger or an oceanographer when I grew up (if I did not become a priest). I completed many backpacking trips, mostly in the Sierra Nevada mountain wilderness where I also fished for trout. I especially like the thin-aired, clean, open, high country, above the tree line, with big, endless granite views. I spent a lot of time in the wilderness. I eventually spent twenty-five years living in Alaska (1987-2013), a great, gigantic wilderness area with few people and that suited me fine. There is a spiritual connection with this as well. The Apostles were fisherman. John the Baptist was a voice in the wilderness. Jesus went into the wilderness to fast and be tempted by the devil before starting his ministry. I felt most sane when in wilderness solitude. In the world was insanity. And people.

I identified also as an artist. In elementary school I started drawing, then using watercolors, then acrylic paints, and finally oil paints. My paintings were amateurish, but I enjoyed making things and felt more expressive via painting than with words. A Catholic friend of my father's, a sort of pre-hippy, beat, bohemian artist, provided free lessons. I opted into all the art projects in the seminary and took painting classes in college. The emphasis on visual arts shifted to music at about age 18. Several seminary friends played guitar. The folk-Mass was popular then and most Masses at the seminary featured guitars accompanying the singing. Sometimes guitars, bass, and drums rocked "Bossa Nova" Masses. I bought my first guitar at age nineteen when living in San Francisco. Over the years I continued with the guitar, preferring to compose and record my own music.

In 1986, two college art classes influenced me strongly: photography and film-making. Later in Alaska, I worked as a fine art photographer and this medium I loved and excelled in. Black and white photography complemented my love of wilderness, in particular the Sierras. I saw in Ansel Adams' photographs of the High Sierras the same appreciation as my own for that beautiful granite wilderness and dramatic cloudy skies, naturally shades of gray. No surprise the landscape genre grabbed me. Self-taught except for a beginning photography class and workshops, I settled on the 8x10 view camera like Adams and my favorite photographers – Edward Weston, Paul Strand, Michael A. Smith and Paula Chamlee – used. I passionately studied Adams' technical books, *The Camera, The Negative*, and *The Print* like I studied the Bible. Creative work is spiritual work because creating is what God does. I tried to practice photography with pure "seeing," without distractions that fragment seeing. Later I learned how to make and edit videos.

A negative social pattern developed early and lasted. Relationships, both with family and friends, challenged me. My interpersonal skills didn't develop normally, whatever "normal" is. After many failures in friendship, I made the conscious decision, at age eighteen, to be a loner. I concluded that I could not count on people, and I would not set myself up for painful disappointment by depending on anyone. In the seminary, my spiritual director asked, "What is your biggest problem?" I answered, "Relationships." He disagreed. He said relationships change, come and go. My attitude caused problems. I did not understand what he meant by attitude, and I didn't know what attitude I owned that caused problems. Later, I learned that my unconscious attitude did, perhaps partly, stress my relationships, and my mother's favoring me over my brothers was partly responsible for this attitude. Being the oldest, I was bigger than my brothers for a long time. We played a game where I stood while my two younger brothers would try to wrestle me to the ground. They each grabbed a leg and I tossed them off like toys. I was bigger, older, stronger, etc. These relationship problems exposed a serious moral conflict. Where is the love? I suffered this conflict all my life, first with my Father, then with my brothers, and then with many others. ACIM presents a particularly helpful view on the subject of relationships.

From grades three to eight I attended St. Nicholas School in Los Altos. I walked to and from school, about a mile away from home. The parish church was even closer, just down the street from our house. I became an altar boy in fourth or fifth grade. Once an altar boy, I received assignments as to when I "served" Mass. Besides the six daily Masses each week, there are four or five Masses on Sundays, the day all the Catholics are obligated to attend. Altar boys frequently did not show up for the early morning daily Masses. Since I was a regular at daily Mass, the sacristan snagged me to serve the weekday Masses frequently. Thus, from an early age I felt familiar and comfortable with the ceremonies and rituals of the Catholic Church. Serving at Mass I had the best and closest seats to watch the priest carefully. He actually changed bread and wine into the body and blood of Jesus. We knelt for that part of the Mass, the Consecration, and I rang a little bell right after the hocus pocus. I stayed focused because everyone in the church, including the priest, expected to hear the bell after the words, "This is my body," and "This is my blood," (but in Latin). When I started as an altar boy the Mass was still in Latin, but soon changed to the vernacular. The nice thing about the Latin Mass is one could attend Mass anywhere in the world and it would feel familiar. I remember the old Irish priest, Fr. Meade. His index fingers and thumbs were permanently bent from being pressed tightly together at Mass, as was required then.

Being an introvert, a strange dichotomy developed between my inner life and my exterior life. Within, I seemed to be OK, even happy. All my problems seemed to come from without, from other people. I loved thinking and thinking about thinking. What was thought, I wondered? In Junior High School, Friday nights were my thinking nights, which I enjoyed. No school on Saturday so I stayed awake Fridays and thought about things. I made a mental list of several things to think about. I started with the first thing on my list and enjoyed as much time as I wanted thinking about it. Then I thought about the second thing on the list, and so forth until I finished the list or fell asleep. What was on the list? Enjoyable things like a planned fishing trip, or what I wanted to do in Boy Scouts, or God, or the girl who sat in front of me at school. We used to pass notes back and forth. Usually I thought about something I looked forward to. Glad anticipation. Sometimes I might worry about something, but usually I enjoyed this interior time. One optimistic idea persisted for quite a while. I believed I could easily solve almost any problem that bothered anyone. Some of my thinking involved guilt-producing remembering and worrying about events from the past. One rather strange thinking process involved imagining the smallest thing I could imagine and the thing took on the form of a strange, unpleasant, interior sound, something like the "ping" of a drop of liquid, with reverb. The sound seemed almost sickening so I didn't stay with it long. Sometimes thinking about my relations with others led to tearful feelings of rejection.

My Dad joined a church organization called the Knights of Columbus. I didn't understand this group but once a month, they held an "all-night adoration." This is where member Knights took turns being in the church, all night, in adoration of Jesus, who is physically present in the tabernacle or the monstrance (because bread changed into the Body of Christ is stored in the tabernacle or displayed in the monstrance). Because of Jesus' physical presence there, Catholics genuflect towards the tabernacle before and after entering the pew. There are cloistered Catholic communities of nuns who engage in "perpetual adoration" 24/7. The sisters take turns being present in the chapel. Later in life I frequented such a monastery in Anchorage, Alaska. So at whatever time they scheduled my Dad's hour, two AM or three AM, I went with him and this strange, middle of the night experience seemed somehow exciting. It proved my seriousness about God. I didn't see any other kids there in the middle of the night. There were lots of other services as well, such as novenas, rosaries, stations of the cross. We recited the rosary as a family, kneeling on the hardwood floor. My Dad became a member of the Third Order of St. Francis and he took me to their meetings. We often visited a Poor Clare monastery in the anything but poor Los Altos Hills.

I remember the November day in fourth grade when the school intercom system announced that someone shot President Kennedy. Catholics loved Kennedy, the first Catholic president. Most Catholic homes hung a picture of the Irish-Catholic president. Sister Mary Fatima had the whole class on our knees praying the rosary for JFK.

I tend to notice dates and numbers. I found it interesting that Aldous Huxley died in a blaze of LSD glory the same day as John F. Kennedy died. Likewise, Thomas Merton died the same day as the famous Protestant theologian, Karl Barth.

My parents birthed their children in two batches, 1954-1957, and 1963-1966. In 1963 my third brother, Gerry, was born. In 1966 my fourth brother, Philip, was born. In 1968 I moved out of the house into the seminary, so I had less to do with Gerry and Philip then with Robert and Mickey. Problems plagued my parents' marriage from the beginning and gradually grew worse. The family dynamics were screwed up, with my parents fighting and my Mother favoring me and my Father favoring Robert. I disliked my Father from an early age. I felt my mother loved me, yet as time plowed on, distance accumulated. She is eighty-one now and we talk each week. My Father died in 2008. As a father myself I experienced the change in my relationship with my children as they grew. The infant is beginning the gradual process of building emotional walls and developing a private self. It doesn't take long. By the time of the terrible twos, ego is established.

At an early age I started to dwell on death. I feared dying because of the hell factor. I held two particular death fears – dying in a car accident and dying in my sleep. Thus I feared riding in a car and feared going to sleep at night. I became car sick on any drive longer than thirty minutes. Being in a boat was worse. I believed I would die before reaching age thirty. But here I am, still going at sixty. My interest in death and life after death continues. I started reading all I found about death, starting with Elizabeth Kubler Ross, and I once heard her speak. I became a direct care volunteer with Hospice in Alaska. During graduate school I worked for a year as a personal assistant to one of the psychologist professors as he died of brain cancer. I enjoyed hanging out casually with many of the psychologists teaching at the university. I became relatively comfortable with death and in my depression periods, I prayed for it. Many spiritual teachings place an emphasis on death and remembering the temporariness of life on earth. ACIM teaches a much different understanding of death, however.

At my eighth grade graduation in 1968 I read the Epistle at the graduation Mass, probably because I was the only one in my class headed for the seminary.

Seminary

At age thirteen I began five years in the Catholic seminary – four years in St. Joseph's High School and one year at St. Patrick's College (same campus in Mt. View). My teachers went from nuns to priests. In both the parochial school and the seminary, religious education is part of the curriculum. The seminary, a Catholic boarding school for boys, about five miles from my family's house, became my residence for the next five years. This seminary supplied priests to the Archdiocese of San Francisco. Lots of Catholic Churches in the Bay Area needed a priest or two. Many towns are named after a Catholic saint: San Francisco, San Jose, Santa Clara, San Rafael, Santa Cruz, San Juan Baptista, San Bruno, Santa Rosa, and so forth. Overall I liked the seminary because I did not like my life in the family home. My relationship with my father grew gradually worse and sibling rivalry ruined my relationships with my brothers. I wanted to get away from my family and move out. Homesickness didn't bother me. My worst memories from the seminary are being bullied by classmates. The seminary boarded gay priests and gay seminarians but they didn't molest me, though once a priest tried. My parents separated and divorced during my seminary years.

The summer of 1970, following my sophomore year, my friend since third grade, Chris, and I experienced our first solo backpacking trip. We loved it and savored our freedom from parental authority for two weeks in Desolation Wilderness near Lake Tahoe. We climbed Pyramid Peak and repeat trips to Desolation Wilderness to climb Pyramid Peak became an annual pilgrimage, sometimes alone and sometimes with friends and family.

In a previous summer Chris and I had run away from our homes together for a few days. We ran away in rebellion against parental authority. We planned our escape for months, gradually buying what we needed – sleeping bags, backpacks, etc. We hid our equipment behind a false fireplace in my house accessed through the attic. We left a note for our parents in the mailbox, telling them of our departure. We hitchhiked over the mountains to Santa Cruz. On our return a few days later, Chris' family caught us as we were fishing from the dam at Stevens Creek Reservoir. My Dad grounded me for the rest of the summer.

As soon as I turned sixteen I obtained my driver's license. I borrowed my parents Rambler for my first date, a double date, where I drove. I picked up my date and her friend, and on the way to pick up her friend's date, my date looked through pictures in my wallet. I looked over to see what pictures she viewed so I could name those pictured. When I looked back to the road, I saw a car stopped in front of us waiting to make a left turn across the four lane expressway against oncoming traffic. I knew immediately I could not stop in time, said, "Oh no," and jumped on the brakes just before the awful sound of crunching steel. My date's head cracked the windshield. I broke the steering wheel with my chest. Both cars were totaled. People in the car I hit were injured. It was a bad day for a teenager. I did not want to drive for six months. Even though I felt depressed about the whole situation, it put other irritating issues into perspective. My parents noticed a positive shift in my attitude. My constant anger with them lessened. Now anger at myself for causing this horrendous car accident replaced anger towards my parents.

In the summer of 1971, between my junior and senior years of High School, age sixteen, my father sent me to a week-long Christian convention for young people called "Campus Crusade for Christ," a fundamentalist, evangelical, Protestant event. I remember natural steam pools and bikini-clad teenage girls. I experienced a conversion.

I underwent a typical Protestant experience of accepting Jesus as my personal Lord and Savior. I felt like singing. As I heard the Gospel preached, something inside me said, "Yes, this is the truth. I want this." Evangelical Protestantism is theologically different from Catholicism, yet each breeds fundamentalists. Brand new baby Christians, like myself, went door to to door proselytizing, using a little pamphlet called *The Four Spiritual Laws.* We also did this "witnessing" on a beach. We emphasized sin and personal salvation. Catholics didn't talk about Jesus, even in the seminary. Jesus is less personal for Catholics, whose faith is more about a sort of abstract Christ. I became a "Jesus freak." I stayed in the seminary and tried to balance both the Catholic and the Protestant sides of my faith. I attended a non-denominational, evangelical church on weekends. I started reading the New Testament with great interest. I grappled with contradictions between the Catholic and Protestant theologies without resolving the dilemmas.

The summer of 1972, following graduation from High School, I completed my first long distance backpacking trip. My younger brother Mickey, and Fred, a seminary friend, and I, hiked the Tahoe-Yosemite trail from Meeks Bay, Lake Tahoe, to Tuolumne Meadows in Yosemite National Park. This is a 200-mile section of the Pacific Crest Trail. I suffered severe blisters most of the way thanks to my new, unbroken in, hiking boots. Chris and I had covered the Desolation Wilderness section of the trail in the summer of '70. This backpacking trip ended when a bear dragged my pack away (that was laying next to my head) and bear-clawed it into shreds to get the food. The bear shredded Fred's borrowed pack too. Despite the challenges, I loved backpacking in the High Sierra and already looked forward to the next trip. That same summer of 1972 I attended my first Grateful Dead concert in Berkeley, California. Eventually they became my favorite band.

Next on my spiritual journey I embraced the Catholic charismatic movement. This followed naturally my Protestant conversion experience. The Catholic charismatics were like the Protestant Pentecostals, except Catholic. There is emphasis on the Holy Spirit, the baptism of the Holy Spirit, healing, laying on of hands, and praying in tongues. Charismatics held weekly prayer meetings at the seminary. My focus shifted a little from Jesus to the Holy Spirit. Whatever spiritual experience I was seeking, however, still eluded me.

At the non-denominational church, Peninsula Bible Church (PBC), I met a beautiful blonde girl my age with a Scandinavian last name and she became my first serious girlfriend, though I had had crushes on several other girls, starting in the seventh grade. She rode a nice bike and I wanted one too. I saved my earnings from gardening jobs and eventually bought a shiny new Motobecane 10-speed! The day after I bought it I rode it up Moody Road and Page Mill Road, up to Skyline Boulevard, a long climb for a bicycle. On that ride I crashed, the first of three serious bike crashes. Near the top, after miles of continual climbing, I sped down a short downhill section on my fancy new bike and did not make the turn at the bottom of the hill, crashing face first into a wall of dirt and rocks. I don't remember the impact. The next thing I remember is sitting on the ground and looking at the bike. The impact destroyed the front wheel. I couldn't remember where the bike came from. I wondered if I could fix it and keep riding (impossible). A car drove slowly by and the elderly driver looked over with an expression of horror, but did not stop. I looked down, embarrassed. Pretty soon a VW van with a couple hippies in it stopped and picked me up. They took me to their commune nearby and called my home. There must be a parable here. My Dad came and picked me up and took me to the hospital where they tried to clean the dirt and pebbles out of my face. My entire face became scabbed and healed, with minor scars. God only knows what brain damage I did besides short term memory loss.

At age eighteen I registered for the draft as the Vietnam war still raged. I registered as a conscientious objector. But the draft soon ended. After the first year of college seminary I was weary of school and wanted a break from it. I developed a cynical attitude towards education. For thirteen years I attended Catholic school. Catholicism conditioned my mind almost completely, yet rebelliousness raged at the same time. I wanted a vacation. So I planned a long, inexpensive bicycle tour. I already owned a pretty good bike (now repaired from the crash). I started out the summer working as an orderly at an alcoholic detox ward in San Jose to save up funds for the bike trip. Leaving in August 1973, I rode solo from the Bay Area up to Vancouver, Canada, and then across Canada to northern Ontario where a car collided with me. The local newspaper ran a short blurb about it. The impact badly bruised my left thigh but otherwise I appeared to be okay. I spent five days in the hospital and about all I remember is the beautiful young nurse who talked to me every day. Bike crash number two. I rode about 4,000 miles in two months and it cost me about $300.00. I visited Canada several more times in the future. It is a country I came to like better than my own, with great, beautiful wilderness and not too many people. Maybe my French-Canadian ancestry influenced me.

After the bike tour, I visited family on the east coast, and then went back to the same job as an orderly. One day at work something strange happened. I thought it might be a LSD flash back but I don't know what it was. I was in the bathroom looking at my face in the mirror when I suddenly saw a third eye on my forehead, between my eyes and above them. Then a Catholic charismatic friend of mine, Jon, told me about a similar job at a hospital in San Francisco where he worked. They hired me and I moved to San Francisco in February of 1974, age nineteen now. I found a nice apartment in the Mission district, 18th and Valencia, for $50.00 per month and bought my first guitar, an acoustic. Without going into all the details, within about seven months I ended up feeling confused and unhappy about my life and in particular about my spiritual life. I engaged in the usual adolescent exploration and experimentation. I smoked marijuana and took LSD regularly. I didn't like it that most males working at the hospital were gay. I went to rock concerts weekly at Winterland.

I saw Traffic, The Grateful Dead, Neil Young, Jethro Tull, Pink Floyd, The Who, to name a few. I started going to rock concerts in 1970 and developed a passion for live rock music. Now I lived in *the* city and concerts with classic bands happened frequently. I grew my hair long. I quit my job and joined a weird survivalist cult.

I did a short bicycle tour with my seminary and backpacking friend Fred through Marin County, north of San Francisco. On the third day we were going down a long downhill stretch and I didn't make it down the hill. Major bike accident number three. Speeding down this hill I ran into gravel on the shoulder of the road, lost control, and crashed. Again, I don't remember hitting the ground. Drivers stopped and someone called an ambulance. One driver, traveling the opposite direction, said the front wheel had come off the bike. At the ER, a doc asked me where it hurt and I said, "Everywhere." A few stitches and a big shot of Demerol and I was off to recover. Despite my third serious bike crash, I didn't lose my love of bikes and riding. A lot happened in seven months in San Francisco.

A roommate from the seminary, Shan, told me about the Hermitage in Big Sur where he made a retreat. He said men stayed there as auxiliary workers without becoming monks. It sounded good, but I did not know how to contact them or how to apply to become an "auxiliary." In those pre-internet days one called "information" to get a non-local phone number, but I did not know what the Hermitage was called. Strange enough, right then, in my Bible, I found a sheet of stationery from the Hermitage, with its address! Synchronicity strikes. I don't know how the piece of paper appeared in my Bible. Perhaps my seminary friend borrowed my Bible for his Hermitage retreat.

Near the end of my SF adventure, Jon, my Catholic charismatic friend, gave me a book called *The Way of a Pilgrim*. This book influenced me significantly and served as a great preparation for life in the Hermitage. The book introduced the *Jesus Prayer*, a mantra type prayer used by monks and pilgrims of the Russian and Greek

Orthodox churches. The first split in Christianity, the "great schism," divided Roman Catholic and Eastern Orthodox churches centuries before Martin Luther started the Protestant Reformation. This book introduced me to contemplative prayer and mystical experience. I hadn't heard about mystical experience in the seminary. I suppose St. John of the Cross and St. Theresa of Avila were not teenage fare. In the Jesus Prayer, a person repeats the prayer, "Lord Jesus Christ, have mercy on me." A longer version is "Lord Jesus Christ, Son of the living God, have mercy on me, a sinner." Sophisticated practitioners coordinated the prayer with the breath and/or heartbeat. The goal is the movement of prayer from the head to the heart. It is also called "Prayer of the Heart." It is based on a similar New Testament verse, "Jesus, Son of God, have mercy on me," and St. Paul's admonition to "pray ceaselessly."

My story can be easily summarized: raised on religion and fed on fear. It is no wonder dilemmas arose when Holy experience challenged religious conditioning. It is no wonder I languished in these dilemmas for many years. My Catholic conditioning started at an early age, the pre-rational stage of development, before the "age of reason." Then family, church, school, seminary, etc. reinforced my religious conditioning. By the age of twenty-one, when the revelation experience happened, I had attended Mass about 5,000 times, spent thirteen years in Catholic school – five of those years in seminary – plus a year and a half in monasteries. It is hard to imagine a person more conditioned than I was. The course repeatedly asks us to let go of past conditioning in order to receive the truth.

I share the story of my own conditioning as an encouragement to the reader. If even I, conditioned as can be escaped that pain-washed prison, then anyone can, not to say that it's easy or quick, though. My past history, the story of "me," is unimportant to me now. I share it in the hope of helping. I read other helpful biographies and so am sharing parts of mine as simply and honestly as I can. I am nurtured by learning about what other spiritual seekers have seen on the deep sea dive. Perhaps the reader deserves some account of the writer's life as Thoreau suggested:

> **Moreover, I, on my side, require of every writer, first or last, a simple and sincere account of his own life, and not merely what he has heard of other men's lives…[29]**

PART II

MAIN IDEAS

...the end of hell is near.[1]

~A Course In Miracles

Chapter Five

THE NATURE OF DEPRESSION: CAUSE AND EFFECT

*D*o you want to feel good? Is there anything you might lose by being happy? Who wants a killer headache? Who wants a terrible toothache? Who wants a horrible heartache? Who wants depression? Not me. But it is interesting how long it takes us to tire of suffering. ACIM describes a temptation:

> ...to make yourself a thing that you are not.[1]

This mistaken identity is described:

> **It is a thing of madness, pain and death; a thing of treachery and black despair, of failing dreams and no remaining hope except to die, and end the dream of fear.[2]**

Does this sound like a depressed person? The course articulates the experience of depression quite well.

ACIM places emphasis on not confusing cause and effect. I want the cause of depression healed, not effects. The symptoms of depression are effects, and painfully felt. Treating symptoms of depression might bring symptom relief, but it is like treating cancer with pain killers. In the mental health system, the causes of depression are complex and often unknown. ACIM teaches there is simply one cause. The many causes proposed by psychological and medical research are actually layers of symptoms, not cause.

The psychiatrist considers depression to be a brain disorder; the cause is physical and in the brain. ACIM says the cause is in the mind, including the unconscious mind. ACIM also teaches that the mind is not the brain. So, brain chemistry, such as a neurotransmitter imbalance, is another layer of symptom and not cause. Chemical imbalance might be alleviated by certain medications, which also produce certain unpleasant side effects, requiring further pharmaceutical interventions, yet cause remains. One side-effect of these medications is increased suicide ideation. Another side-effect is avolition, where a person loses will or motivation for change or healing. Rather than a brain chemical imbalance causing depression, depression causes the chemical imbalance. It is the classic confusion of the horse and the cart, which ACIM calls confusing cause and effect, or "level confusion." The mind and the body/brain system are two different levels. Even so, ACIM states directly that if people find the truth fearful (which is true for most of us), medications and other magic methods, such as psychotherapy, can be used. I would not undergo heart surgery without the magic of anesthesia.

Why is the mental health system so inadequate in relieving mental suffering? Psychology means "study of the psyche." Psyche is dictionary defined as: 1) that which is responsible for one's thoughts and feelings; the seat of the faculty of reason, and 2) the immaterial part of a person; the actuating cause of an individual life. Around 1900, psychology emerged as a new science. Scientists did not respect the new science of psyche as even deserving of the name science. They considered psychology to be a soft science vs. hard, "real" science like biology, chemistry, and physics. Scientists are uncomfortable with terms like "the immaterial part of a person." Solid science is all about measurement. If I can measure it, it must be real. Mind stuff is hard to measure. But I can measure brain chemicals. I can measure behavior, things I can observe and count. So study of the psyche became analysis of behavior and study of the brain, a subcategory of biology. Psychology wanted to be respected as a real science and hence it conformed to science's requirement of measurement. Behaviorism is not study of the psyche. Behavioral health or illness is an effect, a symptom. Behavioral modification is meaningless. It is teaching the circus dog to jump through the burning hoop. How much does a thought weigh? How heavy is guilt? How big is my mind? Where are the edges, the boundaries, of my mind? How can I measure it without a border designating where mind starts and where it ends? I can count the neurons in a brain but I can't observe awareness. Awareness does the observing.

Without healing the cause of depression, the illness returns, one way or another. Some people get symptom relief with various treatments, and some people have "treatment-resistant" depression. Getting stuck in chronic depression is hell. A person may become "depressionalized." This is similar to a person being institutionalized. He is like a prisoner in a prison not locked. He knows he is depressed and complains about it. He keeps trying different treatments, but none of them work for long because they treat symptoms that grow right back like shaved whiskers. He stopped believing in any solution for himself and prefers the prison because it is all he knows. It is familiar. In a strange way it feels safer than the unpredictable unknown outside the prison, and there are certain prison benefits he might lose if he walked out. His friends and family treat him with kid gloves and walk on eggshells around him because of fear he will kill himself and/or fear of the harsh anger and irritation expressed by him inappropriately.

> The crucified give pain because they are in pain.[3]

He is dependent on the prison. At best he might try to improve the prison, but not leave it. On the few short trips outside the prison he gets uncomfortable (anxious) and wants to return to the security of his prison home.

> Prisoners bound with heavy chains for years, starved
> and emaciated, weak, and with eyes so long cast down in
> darkness they remember not the light, do not leap up in
> joy the instant they are made free.[4]

A person with treatment-resistant depression might hold an advantage, however. He can't settle for symptom relief. Symptoms of suffering motivate him to find the cause. So, what is the one cause of depression? The answer comes after peeling away the layers of effects confused as causal.

Deprivation

Depression is closely related to feeling lack, a sense of deprivation. I might contend that deprivation causes depression and the argument is logical enough, just not deep enough.

> **Lack implies that you would be better off in a state somehow different from the one you are in.**[5]

If I seek to be better off, it means I find the present lacking. If only I had this; if only I had that: the wish for misery. If only I wasn't depressed; if only I wasn't deprived. Anyone or anything I treasure, I will lose, or have already lost. Meister Eckhart:

> **And further, I maintain that all sorrow comes from love of those things of which loss deprives me. If I mind the loss of outward things it is a certain sign that I am fond of outward things and really love sorrow and discomfort... no wonder I am gloomy and wretched!**[6]

Meister Eckhart says that when I want outward things, I opt for misery and pain, because those things can be lost, and will be lost, sooner or later. And while I wait I worry about the worst case scenario. He goes on to describe three levels of deprivation: things, friends, and self.

> **Three kinds of trouble may fall upon a man and plunge him into distress: first, harm to his external possessions; next to his dearest friends; lastly, shame, hardship, physical pain, and distress of mind to himself.**[7]

Do I feel deprived? Is not a depressed person deprived of joy? Is it not true that anything I might cherish in this world can be taken away at any time? Relationships, health, wealth, possessions, position, career, whatever it is, I can, and eventually will, lose. Some sooner, some later. Deprived of love. Deprived of respect. Deprived of fairness. Deprived of peace. Finally, the depressing end you and I have coming, deprived of life by death. Depressing, isn't it?

> **Anything in this world that you believe is good and valuable and worth striving for can hurt you, and will do so because you have denied it is but an illusion, and made it real.**[8]

When I want something I do not have, I suffer craving. Withdrawal from a substance is an example of the hell of craving. It is the paradox of addiction. Whatever I use to escape pain plunges me into more pain. This is the devil's methodology. My restless mind is constantly looking for distraction from its restlessness.

> **When you are sad, know this need not be. Depression comes from a sense of being deprived of something you want and do not have.**[9]

Is deprivation true or is it a belief? Is it possible to live without believing in lack? Tao Te Ching:

> **Be content with what you have; rejoice in the way things are. When you realize there is nothing lacking, the whole world belongs to you.**[10]

A sense of deprivation leads to neediness and wanting. Feeling deprived, I need to get.

> **Everything the ego tells you that you need will hurt you. The ego urges you again and again to get.**[11]

A sense of deprivation seems to cause depression, but what causes the sense of deprivation?

The Collective Mental Illness

ACIM calls this world a *slaughterhouse*, a *battleground*, a *world of sorrow*, a *detour into fear*, and a *world of pain*. Sound like a happy place filled with happy people? Can you imagine a worse place to live than a slaughterhouse or battlefield? What happens in those places? The question is not why am I depressed but how could I not be depressed? The spiritual teacher Eckhart Tolle says our whole society is collectively mentally ill. Krishnamurti said that it is no sign of health to be well-adjusted to a sick society. According to professional psychiatry, if I am well adjusted then I'm not sick. In fact, we all suffer an adjustment disorder I call separation anxiety, or separation sadness, or both, whether we admit it or not. Adjustment to separation from God is ego's mission impossible.

Who is more sick, the sane or the insane? The Trappist monk Thomas Merton wrote about the collective insanity of this slaughterhouse world in his essay *A Devout Meditation in Memory of Adolf Eichmann*, from his book *Raids on the Unspeakable*:

> It is the sane ones, the well-adapted ones, who can without qualms and without nausea aim the missiles and press the buttons that will initiate the great festival of destruction that they, the sane ones, have prepared. What makes us so sure, after all, that the danger comes from a psychotic getting into a position to fire the first shot in a nuclear war? Psychotics will be suspect. The sane ones will keep them far from the button. No one suspects the sane, and the sane ones will have perfectly good reasons, logical, well adjusted reasons, for firing the shot. They will be obeying sane orders that have come sanely down the chain of command. And because of their sanity they will have no qualms at all...We can no longer assume that because a man is "sane" he is therefore in his "right mind."

> The whole concept of sanity in a society where spiritual values have lost their meaning is itself meaningless…God knows, perhaps such people can be perfectly adjusted even in hell itself.[12]

Besides my personal suffering, there is the suffering of others, of the animals, of all living beings. Even if I'm not suffering, can I ignore the collective pain? The collective suffering drove the Buddha to seek liberation. This course quote could have come from Buddha himself:

> This world is the symbol of punishment and laws of death. Children are born into it through pain and in pain. Their growth is attended by suffering and they learn of sorrow and separation and death. Their minds seem to be trapped in their brain and its powers decline if their bodies are hurt. They seem to love, yet they desert and are deserted. They appear to lose what they love, perhaps the most insane belief of all. And their bodies wither and gasp and are laid in the ground and are no more. None of them but has the thought that God is cruel.[13]

ACIM is like Buddhism in that it understands the suffering of separation: illusions of identity, others, world, and time. ACIM is original and new because it incorporates modern psychology discoveries of the unconscious mind, collective unconscious, and defense mechanisms. These new ideas were not understood at the time of Buddha and Jesus, or even little more than a hundred years ago. The First Noble Truth of the Buddha is his observation that there is suffering. From Jack Kerouac's *Wake Up*:

> The birth of anything means the death of the thing: and this is decay, this is horror, change, this is pain.[14]

To be born into this world is to be born into suffering. To be born means I die, sooner or later. Along the way to death I get to experience deprivation, disparity, sickness, pain, aging, etc. And maybe I get teased by brief, passing moments of pleasure. Some people appear happier than others. The happy train, however, arrives at the same destination as the sad train: derailment and death. All aboard die. There is no way to avoid this fact, but I can, and do, attempt to avoid it.

> He [you and I] goes uncertainly about in endless search, seeking in darkness what he cannot find; not recognizing what it is he seeks. A thousand homes he makes, yet none contents his restless mind. He does not understand he builds in vain. The home he seeks can not be made by him. There is no substitute for Heaven. All he ever made was hell.[15]

Depressing, isn't it?

Let's say I become a Buddhist and desire to end suffering, be harmless, and hurt no living thing. Giving up killing, lying, and stealing is pretty straight forward. So I become a vegetarian so as not to kill or hurt animals. Then I discover that in digging in the dirt to plant my celery seeds I cut a worm in two. The vegan farmer plows the field killing reptiles and rodents. Then as the plants grow the grower fights off insects, birds, and animals competing for the crop. It is an eat and be eaten world. In the end, worms eat my buried body. And until death, parasites suck my blood and consume my flesh. Sleeping with spiders and ticks is not fun, is it? Unfortunately, there is no way to be in this world without causing harm to creatures. Today, in huge factory farms, hundreds of millions of animals, sentient beings, spend their entire lives in a cage so small the creature cannot take a single step and never experiences the natural, outdoor world. The truth about the suffering caused to animals so I can eat them is depressing indeed. How long is this supposed to go on? How many lifetimes?

> Until you accept the journey to the cross as your own
> last useless journey, your life is indeed wasted. It merely

> re-enacts the separation, and finally the crucifixion,
> or death. Such repetitions are endless until they are
> voluntarily given up. Until then you are free to crucify
> yourself as often as you choose.[16]

The phrase *you are free to crucify yourself as often as you choose* refers to reincarnation, or the continuation of suffering, the continuation of birth and death. ACIM teaches that technically there is no reincarnation and I don't actually "incarnate" into a body. I appear to reincarnate in what are more like serial dreams, in which my life *re-enacts the separation, and finally the crucifixion, or death.* It is like confusing a TV series with reality. Do I want to keep coming back for more episodes, or graduate? Wanting to get to the bottom of it, I ask, what causes suffering, a sense of deprivation, depression, a mind in hell? In seeking the answer, do I do so with an open mind or a mind blocked and locked into past, traditional explanations? How well are traditional answers working?

The Separation

Depression, deprivation, and all irritation are results (symptoms) of "the separation." The separation is similar to the term "the fall" in Christian theology.

> Until the "separation," which is the meaning of the "fall,"
> nothing was lacking. There were no needs at all.[17]

What is meant by "the separation"? I wished to separate from God. The "fall" is the fall from the Grace of union with God. Like a teenager, I wanted "freedom" from authority; I wanted independence. To experience this unnatural state of autonomy, I needed to make a whole other world, and a way of being a separate individual in that world, because nothing existed but the union of God and His Creation, or Heaven, before the fall, or separation from Heaven. I made up a new identity as a separate being with a private mind and autonomous will, and a place, the world, for this individual to dwell. The 3-D space called the universe also required time. Space implies distance, which requires time to travel distance. It takes time to travel. In order to perceive the three-dimensional world, I view it from a fourth dimension, time. This is the basic setup of how I came to be here in this "world of pain." I now seem to be in the period of the separation. Before the separation, needs and deprivation did not exist. Separation from God is deprivation, if such a state was possible.

The separation is the prime cause of all suffering including depression. This first cause leads to a chain of "causes" (that are actually effects), like sin, guilt for sin, fear of punishment, sickness, and a sense of needy lack, deprivation. Separation is the opposite of union. The perceived loss of union with God is painfully depressing.

All sickness comes from separation.[18]

Pre-separation, I existed as one person, one Son of God, one Christ, one with God, an extension of God, the dwelling place of God, in Heaven, before the time/space continuum began. That is my true home, identity, and destiny, expressed metaphorically, because language cannot describe it literally. The post-separation condition is like the pre-separation, except for one thing. Before the separation I did not know the effect of separation, the price of independence. Post-separation I do. Pre-separation, I wanted pseudo-freedom; I did not appreciate Heaven because I did not know anything else. And I didn't yet know the fruits of false freedom. Adam and Eve did not appreciate Eden because they knew nothing else.

Although there is not a satisfying intellectual answer as to why the separation, or the fall, "happened," one of the best metaphors for the separation is in the Biblical story of the prodigal son, told by Jesus. A father had two sons. The family had wealth and needed nothing. The younger son asks his father to give him his inheritance so he can leave his father's house and go explore the world. I know the feeling as a teenager to want my own autonomy, independence, freedom. I begin to separate from my parents. I rebel against the ruling authorities and go my own way: "You're not the boss of me!" How many of us wish we didn't have a big boss man?

The Master's prodigal parable continues: the son travels to a far land, and eventually, after a certain amount of pleasure and pain in the world, hungry and homeless, he realizes that his declaration of independence was a mistake and he might be better off going back to his Father's house, even as a slave. Dad always has a full fridge. Despite his guilty feelings for hurting his father and wasting his inheritance, he journeys back, hoping his father will accept him back as a servant, for even the servants lived better than he, and besides that, because of his sins, he does not deserve the status of "son" anymore. I give up Sonship because of shame.

And as the story goes, the father is waiting, watching, and longing for his son to return. When the son is returning, the father sees him in the distance and rushes to meet him. The father rejoices and welcomes the son home with a huge celebration. I look forward to that party, which is not in the future.

The story also tells of an older son, who did not depart from his father. This represents my pre-separation state. When the prodigal son returns, he represents the post-separation state. Perhaps I do not appreciate Grace until I seem to lose it. The older son hadn't lost paradise and cannot appreciate it like the younger son. The older son is jealous of the younger son, thinking that his brother experienced the freedom and fleshy pleasures of the world, yet older bro doesn't understand that the world is hell. Younger bro does – by painful experience, not by reading about it. The father seems to love the younger son more than the older son because the younger son vanished for a while. Imagine a mother with two children whom she loves equally. One of her children falls into a coma that seems permanent. When the child wakes from the coma, the mother rejoices. Her other child might feel neglected, like his sister received all the attention because of her illness.

One of the biggest obstacles to the son's return, if not the biggest, is guilt. A primary consequence of the idea to separate from oneness is a profound sense of guilt. To want separation is *the* big sin, even an attack against God. This guilt is so painful that it cannot be maintained in consciousness and so becomes hidden, forbidden, and forgotten in the unconscious mind, and then projected as the dualistic world of pain and punishment I perceive. The unconscious mind is for this purpose, to hide what I can't bear to feel. It is a rational defense.

> **The real vision** [spiritual vision, not eyesight] **is obscured, because you cannot endure to see your own defiled altar. But since the altar has been defiled, your state becomes doubly dangerous unless it is perceived.**[19]

It is a *doubly dangerous* defilement because it is unconscious and delays progress without my even being aware it. Like a killer who tries to hide the victim's body by burying it, I repress, deny, displace, and dissociate the unbearable trauma. These mental methods are called, in psychology, defense mechanisms. I defend my defiled mind in pain with denial and other defense mechanisms. ACIM teaches specifically how to alleviate this unconscious guilt. This hidden guilt is first revealed in order to be healed. Religions deal with conscious guilt, being unaware of deepest unconscious guilt. Here ACIM offers something new and original among the various spiritual maps available. And this is why ACIM saves time over other spiritual paths. Some forms of "depth" psychology use a similar method, but do not go deep enough.

The Atonement

ACIM goes on to teach, however, that the separation did not actually happen. The impossibility of the separation is what the course calls *the Atonement*. The Atonement is God's answer to the separation. The separation only seemed to happen. My apparent reality (this world, including all bodies) is similar to a virtual reality, or a dream, or even a movie. My so-called reality is projected on the movie screen of my mind from the collective unconscious mind, just as I "perceive" a populated dream world while sleeping.

When I requested autonomy, God responded, "Request denied."

> **You were at peace until you asked for special favor. And God did not give it for the request was alien to Him, and you could not ask this of a Father Who truly loved His Son.**[20]

God creates by His Love to share His Love. Separation, simply, is not, and cannot be. And then, apparently, I insisted on the special favor of autonomy.

> **Therefore you made of Him an unloving father, demanding of Him what only such a father could give.**[21]

In my demand for separation I made God into what He is not: unloving. Only an unloving Father could agree to separation. The Atonement is the solution for this dilemma.

> **God did not allow this to happen. Yet you demanded that it happen, and therefore believed that it was so.**[22]

Like a spoiled brat, I received whatever I wanted. Therefore I believed God granted my request.

> **And the peace of God's Son was shattered, for he no longer understood His Father. He feared what he had made, but still more did he fear his real Father, having attacked his own glorious equality with Him.**[23]

Fear is fear of punishment that is deserved because of the shame of sin: guilt. The greatest shame comes from the belief I committed the greatest sin: rejecting God, and in so doing, I divided oneness and denied God and His Heaven complete joy. The Atonement says the separation did not happen because God did not allow it, would not allow it; it is not His Will.

> He [God] denied you only your request for pain, for
> suffering is not of His creation.[24]

In requesting autonomy, I unknowingly demanded pain and suffering, which is impossible for a loving Father to give to His Son.

What is the warning about eating the forbidden fruit of duality? I will die. If I don't heed the warning I detour into duality, the world of good and evil, pleasure and pain, birth and death. Before this, Adam and Eve were naked without shame. After eating the fruit of separation, they experienced shame, and the chain reaction consequences of duality: the pain of childbirth multiplied; inequality between man and woman, with men dominating women; short-lived survival through suffering and hard labor, until the opposite of painful birth: a painful death. Welcome to duality. It did not take long for the tree of duality to ripen its first fruit. Cain killed his brother Abel over their differences. Yet the Biblical story implies Adam and Eve are set up for this fall with reverse psychology, and tempted by the serpent, the "most subtle" of all the wild beasts, also created by Yahweh. "Don't do that" practically guarantees the doing.

So if the separation did not happen, why do I experience suffering? I experience suffering in the sleep of separation, in the desire to be different. The course describes the fall as a *mad idea* possible of *accomplishment and real effects*:

> Into eternity, where all is one, there crept a tiny, mad idea,
> at which the Son of God remembered not to laugh. In
> his forgetting did the thought become a serious idea, and
> possible of both accomplishment and real effects.[25]

The Course teaches how this seeming contradiction works by comparing it to my dreaming while I sleep. The accomplishment and real effects of the separation I imagine to be true and experience *as if* true.

> Dreams show you that you have the power to make a
> world as you would have it be. While you see it you do not

doubt that it is real. Yet here is a world, clearly within your mind, that seems to be outside.[26]

When I dream at night, where is the dream taking place? Is it outside or inside me? It *appears* to be outside me, because I view it from a subjective perspective, and yet my eyes are closed, I'm asleep, and I don't see anything outside myself.

> You have chosen a sleep in which you have had bad dreams, but the sleep is not real and God calls you to awake.[27]

While I dream, the dream seems real. Is depression a bad dream? Would it be better if my depressing life is a nightmare or true? Sleep and nightmares are my choice because I asked God for separation.

ACIM frequently refers to Bible passages and in referring to the Biblical creation stories, an interesting point is made.

> What is seen in dreams seems to be very real. Yet the Bible says that a deep sleep fell upon Adam, and nowhere is there reference to his waking up.[28]

Is Adam (mankind) still sleeping? Is Adam dreaming nightmares? What interior world is Adam projecting as an exterior world?

> Only after the deep sleep fell upon Adam could he experience nightmares.[29]

The first thing to happen after Adam fell into his deep sleep is the separation of Adam into Adam and Eve. This preceded the duality concepts of good and evil brought about by partaking in the forbidden fruit.

Although the separation did not happen, I believe it did happen, and this belief, together with the wanting for it, makes it seem real. The perceptive trick is quite impressive, as intended.

> What you believe is true for you. In this sense the
> separation has occurred, and to deny it is merely to use
> denial inappropriately.[30]

Therefore, from the human level, I experience the separation as real. The course often refers to level confusion and this is a good example. On the level of truth, the separation did not happen. On the level of the dream, the separation is occurring. So both statements are true: The separation did not happen; the separation did happen. There is no contradiction. The statements refer to two different levels.

Again, the first cause of all forms of suffering, including depression, is the separation and the chain reaction of consequences that are the seemingly real effects of separation. These effects, that include sin, shame, guilt, fear, sickness, and depression, are beliefs in erroneous ideas, an *illusion of despair*.

The solution to any form of suffering, including depression, is to wake up from the dream of separation. This re-awakening means I no longer believe the lies of the serpent. This transformation means I *give faith to truth* instead of giving faith to illusions, and until I make this shift in faith, I experience painful strain and conflict. To think I can remain in the dream of separation and find happiness is a sad and illogical illusion. Instead, I learn how to deal with the true cause of depression. Remove the cause and all the effects tumble.

> Grace is the natural state of every Son of God. When he is
> not in a state of grace, he is out of his natural environment
> and does not function well. Everything he does becomes
> a strain, because he was not created for the environment
> he has made. He therefore cannot adapt to it, nor can he
> adapt it to him. There is no point in trying. A Son of God
> is happy only when he knows he is with God. That is the
> only environment in which he will not experience strain,
> because that is where he belongs.[31]

There is no point in trying to adjust to the world because it will not work, and the frustration of futility produces intolerable strain. Substitutes for Heaven fail, every time. To be well-adjusted to hell is still hell.

Suffering on the Spiritual Journey

Besides the separation as the source of suffering, I experience challenges, including significant suffering, as part of the spiritual return to Heaven. Most of us learn the hard way, via experience. The prodigal son did not enjoy fasting while feeding the swine. The course makes it clear that the process of transformation is difficult and painful. It does not need to be this way, but usually is so experienced. I might endure a depression, a dark night, as I go through the desert, "dying" to the thirsty false self, releasing needy false relationships, and denying false perceptions. Meister Eckhart:

> The kingdom of God is for none but the thoroughly dead.[32]

Getting to the point where I willingly let go of my old ways is difficult. I experience hell to know I don't want it. I learn what does not work, what leads to pain, by trying it. I learn fire burns by touching it, not by reading about it.

> Who can make a choice between the wish for Heaven and the wish for hell unless he recognizes they are not the same? This is the learning goal this course has set.[33]

How do I learn that Heaven and hell are not the same? How do I know what happens when I choose independence? How do I know what ice cream tastes like?

> Who would be willing to be turned away from all the roadways of the world, unless he understood their real futility.[34]

How do I get to the point of understanding that *all* the roadways of the world are futile, and thus be willing to renounce them? I try them and find out hell is not fun. Without experiencing hell, hell is a concept, an idea, something read about in a book. Seeing my misery and failure may lead to despair. Especially when I see that my failure is forever. No exit. No solution. This despair is not necessarily useless. It can be the fire that makes me ready to renounce the idea of separate self and all its plans. I detour into despair until I am ready to surrender self.

> How could this readiness be reached save through the
> sight of all your misery, and the awareness that your plan
> has failed, and will forever fail to bring you peace and joy
> of any kind? Through this despair you travel now, yet it is
> but illusion of despair. [35]

The *readiness* referred to here is the readiness to accept God's plan for salvation, called the Atonement, in place of my own plans, which feature the world and the ways of the world. Preceding readiness is hard schooling, by excruciating experience of the difference between Heaven and hell. Joel S. Goldsmith on surrender of self in *The Infinite Way*:

> Withdraw from personal consciousness as rapidly as
> possible. Let "I" die. [36]

"I" is the separated self, me as different from you. Goldsmith:

> To those on the way, harmony in human affairs often is
> a lack of spiritual awakening, and, therefore, when the
> battle leading to the overcoming of "this world" is on,
> the initiate will remain as quiet as possible under adverse
> circumstances, endeavoring to refrain from fighting
> erroneous conditions and insofar as possible "letting" the
> warfare go on until the moment of transition arrives. [37]

I refrain from *fighting erroneous conditions* because opposing illusions makes them seem real. Otherwise, why would I oppose them? I oppose them because I believe they are real. My resistance gives energy to what is resisted. Why did Jesus say, "Resist not evil?" Goldsmith:

> When your spiritual study is sincere, the breaking-up of your material world – the desertion of friends, students, or family, a change of health or other outer activity – often ushers in the spiritual transition, or rebirth. This is the attainment of that which you have sought.[38]

Some spiritual teachings are sugar-coated. ACIM is not one of those. Neither is Goldsmith:

> To those unfolding on the spiritual path, come the discordant experiences of human life, until the transition from "this world" has been completely accomplished. The desire is to avoid or escape these inharmonies of mind, body, or economic affairs – but this cannot be done, since the discords result solely from the battle with spirit and "the flesh," that is, with spiritual consciousness and material sense.[39]

If I am serious about the spiritual journey, I can expect things to fall apart, with no escape. Truly trusting God makes this collapse acceptable. Goldsmith:

> When the spiritual student's house of cards crumbles, he is near to "a house not made with hands, eternal in the heavens."[40]

If I resist this collapse I prolong my suffering. If I accept whatever happens, I end my suffering. Maybe, when everything falls apart, a wise response is, "Thank you." Goldsmith:

> **Spiritual student! Rejoice as the outer building tumbles down, for the inner temple is to be revealed.**[41]

Joel S. Goldsmith describes a stage of the spiritual journey where one feels a sense of spiritual failure and abandonment.

> **On the spiritual way, many come to barren places – the desert, the wilderness – and believe that God has forsaken them. Often it appears as if Christ had forsaken them.**[42]

Can we know what Jesus experienced in the crucifixion? *Why have You forsaken me?* Some say the story of Abraham sacrificing his son prefigured God's sacrificing of His only Son. Except in the Old Testament story, angels intervene at the last second, as poor Abe is about to plunge the knife into his son. Did Jesus expect a similar intervention? After six hours of hanging nailed and naked, had his Father abandoned him? When God stopped the sacrifice of Isaac, He called for the end of human sacrifice. He promotes mercy, not blood.

Other spiritual travelers journeyed before me. They left maps, teachings, to help others on the way. They do this because it is the nature of love to give. Joy is not complete until it is shared by all. Hence we help one another. In this chapter a map of the true cause of depression, and two kinds of depression, is presented. The first is the depression caused by the separation. This includes experiencing hell so I learn, for sure, that I do not want hell. The serpent paints separation as a pleasure palace. I learn the hard way that it is actually a hell-hole. The second kind of depression is the suffering I experience as I prepare to be "reborn" back into union with everyone, and God, in Heaven. Surrender of self is dying before I die. The transitions of birth and rebirth are full of pain. If I open my eyes from a deep sleep into direct sunlight, the contrast is blinding and painful. I might say, "Close the curtains. That light hurts my eyes."

SIDETRACK: 1974-1976

From February to October, 1974, I lived in the city named after St. Francis. Now I wanted to leave the city. I wrote to the Hermitage on their own stationary and asked if I could become an auxiliary worker, and informed them a little of my Catholic background and five years in the seminary. They wrote back and invited me to come for a retreat and then we would discuss whether or not I stayed longer. We scheduled a retreat for mid-October, 1974. I tied up loose ends so if they let me stay, I could. I did not own a car and so boarded a bus to Monterey with a backpack and guitar. The hermit-monks from Big Sur made the fifty-mile trip north to Carmel and Monterey once a week, Saturdays, to pick up food donated by grocery stores. The food consisted mostly of vegetables destined to be thrown out, eggs, and expired dairy products. So on a Saturday the monks picked me up at the bus station in Monterey and we rode to the Hermitage in their van. The hermit-monks impressed me with their peaceful friendliness. Excited about my guitar, they asked me to play some and they sang along. The charismatic movement even made it to the monastery. And so we jammed our way south on Highway One (the non-dual highway!). When we arrived, the beautiful location overlooking the Pacific, not far from Esalen, impressed me deeply. Wilderness mountains, oak and redwood trees, a certain appealing atmosphere. And few people. My kind of camp. What is the energy in the air? Is it prayer or a saturation of silence? The silence is what I remember most. The quiet reminded me of the wilderness silence in the High Sierra, an absence of noisy vibrations. I checked into a room in the retreat house and began my retreat.

After a short retreat the monks allowed a two-week trial. I moved from the retreat house outside the cloister to a small room inside the auxiliary's quarters. After the trial period I became an auxiliary. Auxiliaries worked five or six hours a day in exchange for room and board. No pay, and no need for money because the community provided whatever I needed, including medical and dental services. Most of the auxiliaries also joined the monks in community prayer. Although this is a community of hermits, everyone except the recluse come together three times a day for prayer and Mass. About twenty hermit-monks, one recluse (whom I hadn't met yet), and about five other auxiliaries lived in the community. At nineteen, I was the youngest. The hermitage was not like the seminary. I fell in love with the place and the community immediately. It seemed like the real deal spiritually, whereas the seminary seemed a secular and intellectual environment. The monks were amazing. The monks figured out a way to live outside the rat race materialism and consumerism of the world. I began considering a monastic vocation and gave up the idea of becoming a parish priest.

The first service, called Vigils, is held at 3:30 AM half the year and 12:30 AM half the year. This schedule is for the novices, postulants, and novice master, but auxiliaries could attend. The regular, professed monks chose either to break their sleep into two periods (rising to say Vigils at 12:30 AM), or take their rest in one session and say Vigils at 3:30 AM, but they did it privately, in little cement block cabins called "cells." The ceremonies are beautiful and sacred. The monks were serious about their spirituality. All the services except Mass focused on chanting the Psalms. It takes them a week to chant each of the 150 Psalms of the Old Testament. They were supposedly written by David, a musician; Psalms are best chanted. Many of the monks memorized the Psalms and rose in the dark to sing the Psalms without turning on the lights. It is easier to remember words when combined with melody and rhythm.

One of my earliest memories there demonstrates the difference between monastic life and secular church life in the world. At Catholic services, like Mass, the priest says something and the congregation responds collectively. Example: the priest says, "The Lord be with you," and the congregation responds, "And with your spirit." The response comes immediately after the priest's "call." In the monastery however, when the priest said, "The Lord be with you," I responded alone. Then, after a slight delay, the monks responded. For the monks, the response is not an automatic, instant reaction. It is deliberate and considered, a conscious response. The short pause before responding made all the difference in the world.

A process called "Healing of the Memories" highlighted my hermitage year. In this process I recalled painful memories. As each memory is shared, the priest prays for the release and healing of that memory. At the same time, the priest offers the Sacrament of Penance, or Confession, for the forgiveness of sins. I read of the Healing of Memories process and wished to do it and I requested to do it with the recluse, Fr. Joseph. He stayed in his cell/garden and did not join the community for services, except perhaps once a year at Easter. I requested Fr. Joseph because I would not otherwise see him on a day to day basis within the community.

Fr. Prior granted my request and I began the process with the recluse. Fr. Joseph amazed me. He had a long white beard, was thin, bright-eyed, and joyful. He practically hopped when he walked around. I felt blessed to have this holy man help clear and release bad memories. I knelt in his little chapel where he said Mass and confessed a disturbing memory. Then he laid his hands on my head and prayed for the Holy Spirit to heal the memory. At the end of the session he pronounced the absolution of the Sacrament of Penance. I held plenty of bad memories. After several sessions I worked my way through all the conscious memories disturbing my peace of mind. Afterward I felt grateful and much lighter, as if a heavy load lifted from my shoulders. I gained insight into the unconscious mind because forgotten memories rose to the surface as conscious memories were healed.

As I considered the possibility of a monastic vocation, I wanted to visit other monasteries to see my options. The novice master, Father Adam, agreed, and they sent me for a one week retreat with the Trappists at New Clairvaux Abbey, in Vina, northern California, traveling by bus. I did not warm up to this monastery. The location is flat and weather hot, not sharing the wilderness isolation and beauty of Big Sur. The Trappists seemed a different breed from the Camaldolese.

After a year at the Hermitage I left on a trip to visit three other monastic possibilities. The day before I left a person making a retreat offered me peyote. I accepted the gift and planned to consume the cacti buttons when I camped alone in the Arizona or New Mexico wilderness desert. The monks gave me $300.00 cash, quite a sum for 1975, that I did not expect. I traveled alone by hitchhiking. I went from the Hermitage to Highway One and stuck out my thumb heading south in October 1975, exactly forty years ago as I write this.

My plan was to travel first to the Trappist Abbey in Snowmass, Colorado, where I intended to spend my twenty-first birthday. Then I would visit Christ in the Desert Monastery near Abiquiu, New Mexico, a hybrid Trappist/Benedictine monastic experiment. After that I would hitchhike to the Benedictine Abbey in Pecos, New Mexico, a new kind of co-ed and charismatic community. I hoped to determine whether or not God was calling me to a monastic life.

Along the way I visited a few friends. I visited Howard, another auxiliary from the Hermitage, who was now living in Costa Mesa, near Los Angeles, where he joined a large nondenominational, fundamentalist church. He and I both kept seeking, not fully convinced one way or the other about the Catholic Church. I attended a couple services at Howard's church and decided to be baptized (full immersion). Since I did not remember my infant baptism, nor choose it, I wanted to choose baptism. Baptism in the Holy Spirit interested me most. So I did it, but nothing mystical happened. Disappointed that I did not meet the Holy Spirit, I hitchhiked east. I remember getting picked up by two young women, one a singer/songwriter, in bad weather. They picked me up because they saw my guitar. They were broke and needed money, and so, being flush with cash, I helped them out. We ended up in Boulder, Colorado, jamming and drinking beer. I liked the young singer, but I intended to get to Snowmass by my birthday and thumbed my way southwest the next day.

St. Benedict's Cistercian Monastery is in a beautiful valley in the Colorado Rockies. The monastery structure itself is beautiful architecture. I liked the place. I anticipated joining up there but the Hermitage held the edge, perhaps because I spent more time there. Next I went to the visually stunning Christ in the Desert Monastery. This contemplative community is in a desert wilderness, more isolated than any of the other monasteries. Also a small community, less than ten people. Father Tarcisius asked if I read much Thomas Merton. "A little," I replied. Thomas Merton's writings about a reformed monastic community for contemporary contemplatives influenced this monastic experiment deeply. The last place on my pilgrimage-tour was Pecos and since I had a couple weeks before my scheduled retreat I decided to go backpacking in the desert for a week of wilderness solitude. I thought I might take the peyote then and did so. After the standard nausea and vomit-purge I enjoyed a blissful mescaline journey.

Pecos was much different. This Benedictine institution supported a much larger community of both men and women. It seemed more "active," and less contemplative. Large retreats happened frequently. The setting is beautiful high desert, near Santa Fe, and bordering the Sangre de Cristo Mountains. This was my least favorite monastery mainly because of all the commotion and people, both community members and those there for retreat. The Abbot took an interest in me and tried to "recruit" me more than the other monasteries. He wanted me to start playing guitar at services right away, even though three community members, including the Abbot, played guitar. Catholic charismatic services featured folk style singing with acoustic guitars. Playing guitar for the community appealed to me. Also, I noticed attractive young females in the community and decided to try out this place for a longer stay. Strange in a way because from a spiritual perspective, Big Sur, Snowmass, and Christ in the Desert, all appealed to me more than Pecos. Guitars and girls led this twenty-one year old to try out Pecos.

I hitchhiked back to the Bay Area and made plans to move to New Mexico in January 1976. I joined the community and although I liked playing guitar at services, I found living in the community quite difficult. I found so much personal interaction difficult. Life at the Hermitage in Big Sur encouraged solitude and silence. My discomfort at Pecos increased. I started to see the Abbot as a typical authority figure, like my Father, that I rebelled against, a pattern in my life. I was quite angry with him once, and told him so.

As I struggled with my situation, the big impasse seem to be vocation. In the Catholic church, there are basically two choices regarding vocation, religious life or married life. A celibate single life as a lay person is also an option but rare. In the religious life there are a variety of options. I could join an order, become a parish priest, become a brother, teacher, missionary, or engage in social services (this was the age of liberation theology), or withdraw from the world in a cloistered contemplative life, the life of a monk or hermit. At twenty-one years of age I struggled with what to do, what vocation to pursue. I thought I wanted to do God's Will, but I did not know God's Will, nor my motivation for doing God's Will. Vocation is not so much a choice as it is a calling.

As I prayed and sought discernment about what to do, or what God willed, I received a poignant insight, perhaps my first major realization. It hit hard and still shines. I realized my struggle was selfish. Seeking the Will of God was actually all about me. *My* salvation, *my* spiritual success, avoiding the pain of *my* damnation. Something in me collapsed. How horrible: all my lifelong pursuit of God and Heaven, or avoiding hell, was egocentric. Spiritual ambition, spiritual pride, spiritual materialism defiled my devotion. Spiritual practice was about getting something, gaining something, and avoiding something, in a selfish way. This self-centric spirituality is disguised and unconscious, until it isn't. Now it seemed no matter what I chose to do, my motivation was selfish. Damned if I did; damned if I didn't. I was less sure than ever about what to do.

Soon, unhappy living there, I asked for and received permission from the Abbott to spend time alone in the nearby wilderness, backpacking. I went into wilderness solitude to find peace. Perhaps I used retreat into solitude to avoid unpleasant personal interaction. My first attempt to find peace in wilderness solitude happened in May or June, and after three days in the wilderness a late spring blizzard dropped snow in the high desert and the Abbot, concerned for my safety, sent a brother to find me and bring me back. The brother, an outdoorsman, knew the area well but did not know my location other than a general idea based on the trailhead location where I started hiking. Amazingly enough, the guy found me in the snow storm. The smell of my campfire smoke guided him. He appeared like an apparition. Staying warm in my sleeping bag, near the fire, I saw his face emerge from the falling snow. He said the Abbot sent him to collect me and so I went back. Later in the summer I tried it again. This time the weather cooperated and I spent four weeks alone hiking the Sangre de Cristo Wilderness, the southern most sub-range of the Rocky Mountains, with mountain peaks over 14,000 feet high. After two weeks the only food left was oatmeal. For the next two weeks I lived on fresh caught trout, oatmeal, and dandelion leaves. I planned to leave Pecos after the wilderness time, return to California, and attend the wedding of a seminary friend, Tom.

After this completely sober wilderness trip I returned to the monastery for a few days before the return trip to California. On the third evening after returning from the wilderness, the holy happening described in the *Prologue* happened. This brings the story of my spiritual journey up to date of that experience. To be continued.

Chapter Six

WHO AM I: IDENTITY

*I*dentity is primary. From my sense of identity proceeds everything else. I mis-identify as image of self. I confuse self and self-concept. If I don't know who I am, then who is depressed? Who is saved? Who is in relationship with who?

> **Where concepts of the self have been laid by is truth revealed exactly as it is…There is no statement that the world is more afraid to hear than this:** *I do not know the thing I am, and therefore do not know what I am doing, where I am, or how to look upon the world or on myself.*[1]

How to look upon the world or on myself is my worldview, which is based on my identity. Thus ignorance of identity is corrected before anything else in my worldview makes sense.

> **The reason for the course is that you do not know what you are.**[2]

The reason for the course is identity-confusion. If I know my true identity, then I cannot be depressed, because who I truly am cannot be depressed.

> **If you will accept yourself as God created you, you will be incapable of suffering.**[3]

Incapable of suffering? Really? It might sound impossible but what if the course is right about this? Has anything else worked? In the dream of separation I sleep and identify with a character in a dream. It is an elaborate slight of mind. The dream actor tricks me about who I am. Lowercase "self" means separate self, individual self, private self,

114

special self, unique self, the me, myself, and I, as different than you, other than you. Uppercase "Self" is the true unitive Self, also called the Sonship, the Son of God, and the Christ. In the New Testament, the metaphor "the Body of Christ" is used to describe the collective Self.

There is good news and bad news about the self. The bad news: the me does not exist. The good news: the me does not exist. Naturally, I might resist the idea that I do not exist. It seems quite obvious I do exist, and my mind-movie dream drama proves it. Who else is reading this book? I want the continuity of the "me," even if I don't know who me is. The truth is, I do not exist as I think I exist: Identity-confusion. I identify with an image of self. I identify with a concept of self. I don't know what I am. I don't know *that* I am.

ACIM is not unique or original in teaching that I am not aware of my true identity, and that the identity I have adopted, with a name, history, and face, is a fiction. My horribly hysterical history is only his-story. Jesus in John's Gospel:

> **Truly, truly, I say to you, unless a grain of wheat falls into the earth and dies, it remains alone; but if it dies, it bears much fruit.**[4]

To remain alone is to remain separate. When the grain of wheat falls into the earth and dies, it gives birth to something much greater than a single seed. My separate self-sense ends when I want liberation, and want nothing else. This is not a criticism of solitude or the hermit life. Monks (same root as the word "mono") know that for certain people, periods of being alone and in retreat from the world of others is necessary and beneficial, not that it is for everyone. I find freedom in solitude. As soon as another person appears, self-consciousness arises. Now I need to act in certain way. Now I worry about what the other thinks of me.

Lao-tzu:

> **Ordinary men hate solitude. But the Master makes use of
> it, embracing his aloneness, realizing he is one with the
> whole universe.**[5]

The hermit is seeking the unitive state, which is not union with other
egos. The hermit prefers solitude to the insane drama of human conflict. The hermit is alone, not lonely. Some hermits are hermits because
life in the world is too difficult for them. The hermit's aloneness is all-
one, not separate. Bodies remain separate whether in solitude or not.

In the spiritual journey I discover my true Self, and lay down my
false self. Jesus in John's Gospel:

> **For this reason the Father loves me, because I lay down
> my life, that I may take it again. No one takes it from me,
> but I lay it down of my own accord.**[6]

Jesus lays down his life as a separate individual in order to realize his
true Self as the Christ. Then He gives himself to everyone, and unites
himself with everyone, through the shared Holy Spirit. He does this
himself, and does it willingly, in order to end the dream of separation
and unite all in Him and in God. Willingly means his will is united
with the Will of the Father; their wills are not separate, which is where
I, also, am heading. One Will.

The true nature of life, and my true identity, is eternal, and does
not die. To die is a lie. That's why it is difficult to imagine one's own
death. But the false self fades away, not by force, but by seeing it for
what it is. I see that it is an illusionary, and exclusionary, identity,
and stop identifying with it. I stop believing a lie about who I am.
In this way I do not destroy my false identity, but relinquish it. My
part in this transformation is desire and willingness. I want to know
the truth about what I am and I welcome the truth when I see it. I
fear and resist this willingness to let go of my false identity, because
it is the only identity I seem to know. I fear and resist losing my

little treasure, the *idea* of "me" that I seem to be. In that fear-driven resistance I delay release and prolong suffering because I continue the wish for separation.

The great Christian mystic, Meister Eckhart, knew about the difference between self and Self:

> **There is no greater valor and no sterner fight than that of self-effacement, self oblivion.**[7]

In the next quote, Eckhart describes three levels of renunciation.

> **Whoever has three things is beloved of God: the first is removal of goods, the second is removal of friends, and the third is removal of self.**[8]

Notice the progression of removals. Each removal is a release towards freedom. First is the removal of goods: material things, physical things, property, etc. I identify with what I own by placing the word "my" before an object. My house, my car, my money, etc. The second level is the removal of friends. This may sound counter-intuitive because friends seems like a good thing to keep. Yet I identify with "my" friends. But if I do not know who I am, then who is in relationship with friends? If I don't know who I am, then I don't know who my friends are either. The third and final level is the removal of self. This is the ending of my false identity as a separate self. I am free when I have nothing left to lose, especially my precious self. How many of us see the loss of goods, loss of friends, and even loss of self, as a good thing? Albert Einstein:

> **The value of a human being is determined primarily by the measure and sense in which he has attained liberation from the self.**[9]

What is this so-called "self?" If it is God-created, true, good, and beautiful, why would I relinquish it? Why do I need liberation from it? What is the relationship between identity and depression?

The separation event happened (seemed to happen) because of a *mad idea*. This mad idea is the wish for autonomy. To be independent, individual and unique. To be separate. To be my own boss (control my own will). To be *special*. A primary effect of the separation wish is to identify as being a separate body/brain, an individual mind with private thoughts, and with my own will. This is to identify with an illusionary self-made self that is different from others. Yet this pseudo-identity is only a concept, wishful thinking, willful thinking. What's so bad about being someone? I confuse self with Self and this is the identity confusion leading to depression and all forms of conflict and suffering.

Christian writers from St. Paul on describe various dichotomies of self including true self vs. false self, the new man vs. the old man, the inner man vs. the exterior man, spiritual man vs. carnal man, etc. The contemporary contemplative writer Bernadette Roberts described her spiritual journey to "no self" as moving beyond the concepts of both true and false selves. The Trappist monk Thomas Keating wrote:

> The sense of a separate self is the ultimate cause of all our problems in the first place, even more fundamental than the false self.[10]

At issue is the fact that even the so-called "true" self is still considered a separate self. I have my true self and you have yours, in the dream. Buddha clarifies different aspects of the separate self sense:

> Cease to follow the way of the world, cease to follow the way of the flesh, cease to follow the way of tradition, get rid of this false identification and know the true Atman. Cease to identify yourself with race, clan, name, form, and walk of life. These belong to the body, the garment of decay. Abandon, also, the idea that you are the doer of actions or the thinker of thoughts. These belong to the ego, the subtle covering. Realize that you are that

being which is eternal happiness. Man's life of bondage to the world of birth and death has many causes. The root of them all is the ego [the separate self sense], the first begotten child of ignorance. As long as man identifies himself with his wicked ego, there can be no possibility of liberation, for liberation is its very opposite.[11]

The body is the gross *garment of decay*. The ego is the *subtle covering*, the mind that thinks it is separate, with private, secret thoughts, and directs its own autonomous will, *doer of actions and thinker of thoughts*. Identity-confusion is presented here from four perspectives: body-identification, ego-identification, autonomous will, and the unconscious mind.

Body-identification

Clearly, bodies *are* separate. One exception might be twins co-joined at birth. When this happens, what is the first thing surgeons try to do, if possible? Is it not to separate them? In rare cases co-joined twins are not separated and grow up as a "two-headed" body that most of us would not choose. I prefer to be me, separate and autonomous. My identity is based on how I am different from you. Do you have the same name as me?

In this world, to be born, to be a body, means to die. Life of the body is temporary. No matter how much I may love my life as a separate individual, that life will end and is already in the process of ending right now. Birth and death are two sides of the same bad-luck coin. It is well known that many of the most "successful" people: wealthy, famous, talented, respected, beautiful, etc., end up killing themselves. And of those who do not commit suicide, most are not happy. Either way, no-body gets out alive.

As long as you perceive the body as your reality, so long will you perceive yourself as lonely and deprived.[12]

If I identify as a physical body, I will feel lonely and needy. The body *is* alone and needy.

> **It is impossible to seek for pleasure through the body and not find pain.**[13]

Pleasure and pain both come with the same nervous system. Pleasure and pain serve the same deceptive purpose: to convince me the body is real and that I am a body. And it is a pretty convincing argument evidenced by the sensual experiences of pain and pleasure.

> **Pain demonstrates that the body must be real. It is a loud, obscuring voice whose shrieks would silence what the Holy Spirit says. Pain compels attention – focusing on itself. Its purpose is the same as pleasure, for they are both means to make the body real. Pleasure and pain are equally unreal.**[14]

I use the body for comfort and pleasure, but pleasure can become pain in an instant. I know the body is temporary. It could die at any time and suffer pain at any time. Yet I avoid these unpleasant facts.

> **Equating yourself with the body is the invitation to pain.**[15]

The Indian sage Ramana Maharshi's whole teaching is simple: discover the Self. Find out my true identity and the rest falls into place. Ramana, who died in 1950, said in his humorous way:

> **To identify with the body is like attempting to cross a river on the back of an alligator.**[16]

The body is going to die and likely suffer before it dies. How far across the river will I get before the alligator wants a snack? Identifying with the body leads to depression.

> **When you equate yourself with a body, you will always experience depression.**[17]

If I think about torture, rape, and death enough, I might get depressed. In the face of death, what is the point of suffering? Do I suffer for the hell of it?

One of the primary aspects of body-identification is identification as male or female. Bodies and brains are male or female. Perception demonstrates differences. Minds are not male or female, yet minds are conditioned to identify as male or female. Sexes are separate, and opposite. Psychologists who study sex say the first thing we notice about anybody is their sex. Is it a boy or girl? Is she hot, or not? Jesus, in the *Gospel of Thomas*, refers to this gender-identity issue:

> **When you make the two into one, and when you make the inner like the outer and the outer like the inner, and the upper like the lower, and when you make male and female into a single one, so the male will not be male and the female will not be female, then you will enter the Kingdom.**[18]

I also body-identify as being of a certain race that includes different skin colors, and other, different, physical characteristics. Races are separate and frequently opposed. Some are masters, some slaves. How much suffering and persecution is based on race? Racism is one form of body-identification. I also body-identify by nationality. People identify as a Russian, or an American, or any other country, usually based on where birth of the body happened, where the body matures, or where the body is now residing. Nations are separate and war against each other. Sexism, nationalism, and patriotism divide humanity, setting us up for destructive conflict. Boundaries are defended. War is the way of the world.

> **The body is the central figure in the dreaming of the world...it acts as if it were a person to be seen and believed. It takes the central place in every dream, which tells the story of how it was made by other bodies, born**

> into the world outside the body, lives a little while and
> dies, to be united in the dust with other bodies as its
> friends and enemies. It's safety is its main concern. Its
> comfort is its guiding rule. It tries to look for pleasure,
> and avoid the things that would be hurtful. Above all, it
> tries to teach itself its pains and joys are different and can
> be told apart.[19]

Does the quote ring true? Do I tend to seek for physical comfort and
safety, look for pleasure and avoid pain?

> The dreaming of the world takes many forms, because the
> body seeks in many ways to prove it is autonomous and
> real. It puts things on itself that it has bought with little
> metal discs or paper strips the world proclaims as valuable
> and real. It works to get them, doing senseless things, and
> tosses them away for senseless things it does not need and
> does not even want.[20]

Jesus in Luke's Gospel:

> Therefore I tell you, do not be anxious about your life,
> what you shall eat, nor about your body, what you shall
> put on...consider the ravens: they neither sow nor reap,
> they have neither storehouse nor barn.[21]

Is a worried person happy? What does the body put on itself?
Clothes, jewelry, tattoos, makeup, etc. all of which cost money I earn
via a job: *doing senseless things*. The term *little metal discs or paper
strips* is curious. It refers to cash and coins as what they actually are...
little metal discs and paper strips. They are of no value in themselves.
Their only value is the value the world places on them that I make
"real" by sharing the belief in said value.

Imagine you love a great dog. One evening you cook t-bone steaks
for dinner. After dinner you offer your dog a choice of either the

delicious t-bone, or tasteless hundred dollars cash. Which does the dog take? Sniffing shows that the money doesn't smell so good. How about a thousand dollars, or a million? How about diamonds, or gold? The dog chooses the bone, but only every time. The money, jewelry, and precious metals are not so precious to the dog.

The quote goes on further to describe how I spend my life: doing *senseless* jobs to earn more money and spend it on *senseless things it does not need and does not even want*. So I work a stupid job I hate, watching the clock for quitting time and cocktail hour, living for the weekend or summer vacation. I do this for money, to buy more things, be a good consumer, and get ahead of my neighbor, even though most of the things I buy are unnecessary and not really wanted. I willingly do my patriotic part to promote the military-industrial complex by paying taxes. In the strange ways of the world I am not satisfied with *What Is* and want more, more, and still more. Finally, I live a little while, get sick, pay the doctors and lawyers, and die. Eat, drink, and be sorry, for tomorrow I die. Is this meaningful? Consumerism, materialism, hedonism, racism, sexism, patriotism. The American dream: getting ahead. To acquire more money than the next guy. Is it any wonder I'm depressed?

I refer to my body as "mine." Our bodies, ourselves. *My* body, as if it were a possession like a car or house. Well who is it that seems to own and occupy this bloody bag of skin and bones? Me? Let's say I think that I do not identify primarily with my body and rather identify more with my mind. The intellectual, cerebral type. Thinking that does not make it true.

How do I live my days? How much time and energy is invested in the body? Consider all the things I do for the body: bathing, brushing, grooming, flossing; putting on make up, shaving, plucking, urinating and defecating; dressing, eating, drinking, preparing food; having sex, thinking about sex, worrying about sex, shopping for sex; shopping for food, clothes, etc.; sleeping, exercising, going to the chiropractor, doctor or dentist; plastic surgery, Botox, breast implants, liposuction;

and working my way to the top to make more money to pay for all these things. How much time is left for anything else? Are these things done for the body or the mind? Perhaps I might say I gain more peace of mind when I do these things for the body, implying that I carry a lot of fear and worry about the body. How many hours a day are devoted to the care, grooming, feeding, pleasure, and protection of the body?

How much do I suffer because of body-identification? Our society places huge emphasis on the body beautiful, and young. What is worse than being fat? Maybe getting old and fat? The pursuit of youth and beauty, being "hot" and sexy, attractive, etc. demonstrates my conditioned worries, fears, vanity, and identity centering around the body. Most of us do not want to be poor, or worse, homeless. Where would I sleep? On the ground? What about weather, rain, snow, bugs, rodents, and reptiles? How did the Buddha do that for forty-five years in India where tigers roamed? These fears revolve around the body, seeking bodily comfort and pleasure and avoiding pain. If I run into a tiger on the trail, it isn't my mind I'm worried about. Wasn't Jesus homeless too? He and his gang of unemployed fishermen couch surfed or camped out, apparently. How did abundance avoid these masters of mercy? Humans are homeless outside of Heaven.

> Jesus said to him, "Foxes have their holes, and birds of the air have nests; but the Son of Man has nowhere to lay his head."[22]

Since bodies are separate I vainly compare bodies, making judgments, adding to my misery and fear. I worry about my "appearance." I worry about what other people think about my body. Are my teeth white enough? Am I pretty enough? Am I tall enough? Am I having a bad hair day? How do I compare to you?

Christian theology and interpretation of the Bible place special emphasis on the body. Crucifixion and resurrection are of the body. The death of Jesus meant the death of a body. How many billions of bodies already died? How many more billions of bodies will die? All of them. How many billions of bodies are due to die in the next 100 years? Do the math. The resurrection demonstrates that he did not die. The crucifixion did not, and could not, kill him. It killed a body. The crucifixion is one of millions of murders. Why should salvation depend on the torture and execution of an innocent man? And if the Father did demand the torture and slow death by crucifixion of His only Son, then why isn't that enough? Why do I need to suffer and die as well? Is there any end to blood sacrifice?

There is emphasis in the Gospels of Matthew and Luke to lay out the genealogy of Jesus, tracing his ancestors back to King David, or Adam. Just the male ancestors. However, the story goes on to tell of the virgin birth and thus Joseph, engaged to Mary, is not the physical father. So why the genealogy? The genealogy is further emphasis on the body: physical genes, connection to other bodies, bloodlines.

When Jesus gave his teaching about being the Bread of Life and how believers must eat his flesh and drink his blood, those who did not accept vampire cannibalism fell away from the fold. But notice the response of Jesus:

> **It is the spirit that gives life, the flesh is of no avail; the words I have spoken to you are spirit and life.**[23]

ACIM does not see the body as something evil or bad. To see it as evil or be against it is to make it real. To identify with it is a painful mistake. That identification process is a function of the mind, not the body. ACIM teaches that the proper use of the body is as a means of communication with other parts of the creation who are still confused about their identity. The Holy Spirit uses the body for communication. If my job is to raise the consciousness of ants, how could I do that? How could I communicate with ants? I become an ant first to be able to speak their ant language. It takes one to know one. The problem is not the body but my identification with the body.

Ego-identification

Closely related to body-identification is ego-identification. Both are symbols of separation. ACIM uses the term ego frequently, 475 times.

> The ego's fundamental wish is to replace God. In fact,
> the ego is the physical embodiment of that wish. For it
> is that wish that seems to surround the mind with a body,
> keeping it separate and alone, and unable to reach other
> minds except through the body that was made to
> imprison it.[24]

Being nothing, the ego is hard to define. I tend to think of it, as my discursive mind, the thinker of thoughts. The ego represents a thought system of separation. This is the thinking of the world: I'm not you and you aren't me; our minds, thoughts, feelings, beliefs, and desires are separate and different. If I said, "I am you," I might end up in the hospital. In *I am the Walrus* the Beatles sing, *I am he as you are he as you are me and we are all together.*

> The ego's goal is quite explicitly ego autonomy. From the
> beginning then its purpose is to be separate, sufficient
> unto itself and independent of any power except its own.
> That is why it is the symbol of separation.[25]

The body/ego feels deprived, and it is deprived, of the joy, love, and peace of union, and seeks to get through appetites. Appetites are getting mechanisms.

> That is why the concept of "getting" arose in the ego's
> thought system. Appetites are "getting" mechanisms,
> representing the ego's need to confirm itself.[26]

I want more and nothing satisfies. Who eats a single french fry? Refrigerator doors have durable hinges.

The ego's wish for separate independence is virtually opposite to the Kingdom of God, where the reality is unitive. The way of the world is clearly aligned with the ego's thought system. The wish to be independent required the making of a whole other way of being...a disguised identity, independent, autonomous, starring in the heroic role of "me." I traded non-duality for duality. Not really, but I think I did, believe I did, dream I did, and experience "real" consequences. Being a dream figure, the separate "me" who experiences suffering is not real.

> The one error can be described as a substitution: illusion for truth, fragmentation for wholeness. It has become so splintered and subdivided and divided again, over and over, that now it is almost impossible to perceive that it once was one. You do not realize the magnitude of that one error. It was so vast and completely incredible that from it a whole world of total unreality had to emerge.[27]

There is no separate self, even though there is a belief in a separate self and a perception of a separate self. Because I wanted to be independent, a world for separation *had* to be made because there was no other way to be separate.

Splitting the Son produced far greater dream consequences than did splitting the atom. God created His Son to share the same creative ability as Himself. Using the metaphor of Father and Son means that both are of the same nature. In the human world, a father and son are both equal human beings, sharing the same human nature. We share the same creative ability as God. The creative ability to make a whole other world where I seem to experience autonomy is God-given. This ability cannot, however, create against the Will of God. So what to do? How did the impossible happen? Because I wished for independence, God allows learning the consequences of separateness, in a dream only, like a pilot learns to fly in a flight simulator. My creative abilities are spent dreaming of separation, without violating the Will of God, which is impossible to do anyway.

The fruit of separation in this world is clear: conflict and competition, disparity, wars, killing, greed, me vs. you, us vs. them, and so forth and so on. I learn the hard way that separation does not work, tempting as it was, and is, to try out. After thousands of years of religions promoting peace, love, and so-called spiritual values, the earth is still a place of war, violence and killing.

How did the false, separate sense of identity come about?

God did not create your ego.[28]

Who did make the ego then? I did. You did. We did. God created His Son with the ability to create. John's Gospel tells us all things were made through the logos, and without the logos was not anything made that was made.

> **Everyone makes an ego or a self for himself, which is subject to enormous variation because of its instability. He also makes an ego for everyone else he perceives, which is equally variable.**[29]

The ego is unstable. It changes over time. What we made is pretty impressive, especially the body/brain symbol of separate identity. But upon close inquiry the illusion is seen. It does not work, unless I prefer pain. Sure, I get just enough seeming pleasure to keep me coming back for more, until I start to see through the veil of tears. After getting beat up by the world of separated egos, the prodigal son chooses to return to his Father's house. That choice is mine as well. That choice is the power of decision, the part of will still free and accessible.

The best end is inevitable. This is the real good news. I will choose to remember what I am, return to the Kingdom of Heaven, and help complete the reunion of God's Son. Yet it is not forced; I cooperate with willingness, or not. I can correct a wrong-minded choice and choose again. This is how depression and all suffering ends.

> The ego arose from the separation, and its continued
> existence depends on your continuing belief in
> separation.[30]

The ego's continuity depends on the belief that I am separate, as my senses say.

> The ego is the part of the mind that believes your
> existence is defined by separation.[31]

The ego is identity-confusion – only a concept of self – a thought, a desire, an image of self, not Self, as It is. I get what I want. Who wants to move back in with their parents? I want independence.

> The ego is but a dream of what you really are. A thought
> that you are apart from your creator. A wish to be what he
> created not. The ego is a thing of madness and unreal.[32]

I wished for the false freedom of independence, and fell into a deep dream of duality, madness.

> The ego is a wrong-minded attempt to perceive yourself as
> you wish to be, rather than as you are.[33]

Ego is only a wish, yet wishes are powerful and manifest. Perception is distorted by wrong-minded, egocentric desire. The ego is self-centered, not God-centered. It is interested in itself. Ego activity is exploitation. "Praise me, praise me."

> The ego tries to exploit all situations into forms of praise
> for itself.[34]

However, the ego is not real and does not exist. Yet, since I believe it exists, it seems real. My faith in it gives it appearance. Science tested the power of belief. Placebo pills prevent pain. The hypnotist convinces the hypnotized that a cold pin is a hot pin and a blister forms when the pin touches the skin.

The ego is nothing more than a part of your belief about yourself.[35]

To imagine I find happiness in a false identity and living in an illusionary world is a mistake with a high price: endless disappointment and frustration leading to depression, despair, and death.

I am teaching you to associate misery with the ego and joy with the spirit.[36]

Mis-identifying with ego as a separate self makes me miserable. Identifying with spirit produces the opposite of depression: joy. Why are spirit and joy synonymous? Spirit means no death, eternal life, wholeness, perfect love, and perfect peace.

The course offers a simple measure to determine whether or not a teacher is coming from ego or spirit:

Egos clash is any situation...the ego-oriented teacher's goal is concerned with the effect of his ego on other egos, and therefore interprets their interaction as a means of ego preservation.[37]

The ego uses the body for different purposes than what the Holy Spirit uses the body for. When I see myself as influencing you, the ego uses this as proof of its reality, importance, and superiority.

The ego uses the body for attack, for pleasure, and for pride.[38]

And what pleasure truly satisfies? How long is it before I want more? Or want something else, someone else? What distraction satisfies my restless mind for long? When I seek pleasure for the body, ego is operating. When I see myself attack another (even a passing mental criticism) I can know that this is ego operating. When I want pride, or when I feel the sting of a put down, I can know that this is ego operating.

You must have noticed an outstanding characteristic of every end that the ego has accepted as its own. When you have achieved it, *it has not satisfied you.* This is why the ego is forced to shift ceaselessly from one goal to another, so that you will continue to hope it can yet offer you something.[39]

This ceaseless goal shifting is the ego's trick to keep me in the crying game. Billions of years are the ego's imitation of eternity. If I continue to chase the ego's carrots, I continue the ego's dream of existence, because I *want* it.

The ego believes it is an autonomous mind with private thoughts. I might find it frightening to believe my thoughts are not private. But the truth is my mind is not separate from other minds, though I pretend they are separate and private. The belief that my mind is separate is ego-identification and ego-sustaining. If minds are connected, direct communication is possible, mind in mind communion, without words, talking, writing, or telephones. Privacy requires separation. There are no walls in Heaven. Nothing hidden, nothing secret, nothing unconscious.

ACIM teaches a core idea called *the holy instant,* that is presented in more detail in the chapter on time. For now though it bears a radical teaching about private thoughts and true, transparent and complete communication:

> The holy instant is a time in which you receive and give
> perfect communication. This means, however, that it
> is a time in which your mind is open, both to receive
> and give. It is the recognition that all minds are in
> communication...How can you do this when you would
> prefer to have private thoughts and keep them? The
> only way you could do that would be to deny the perfect
> communication that makes the holy instant what it is.[40]

Even though private thoughts of a separate mind is an ego illusion, I believe in, and demand, privacy. Related to a loss of privacy is fear, fear of embarrassment, fear of the blow to my pride when the truth is known, and the façade is failing.

Some spiritual paths advocate destroying the ego. Some paths advocate befriending the ego: "Welcome back old buddy, you're not so bad. Sorry I was so judgmental." Some paths suggest a compromise: keep your cake and take it too, or, transcend and include. As much as I might want to include the ego in God's Kingdom, it can't be done. ACIM does not advocate trying to kill the ego, nor making friends with it, nor putting it in its place and integrating it in a holistic way. Illusions are not destroyed any more than I destroy my shadow on a sunny day. Illusions are seen for what they are: nothing. I can neither destroy, nor integrate, nothing.

> **The ego is not destroyed but relinquished. To attack it would be to believe it is real.**[41]

Does it make any sense to attack my shadow by shooting it or stabbing it? Can I kill a shadow? Can a shadow feel anything? Same goes for the ego. Jesus said "Resist not evil," because if I resist evil I make it stronger and seemingly real. Why would I resist evil unless I thought it was real? This resistance, however, feeds the ego, gives energy to the ego, as if it was real. Two arms wrestling resist each other, and in the process both arms strengthen. If I resist evil, then it means I believe evil is real. Stop making evil seem real; stop giving energy to it. Why would I want to integrate the ego if the ego is not real?

Autonomous Will

My belief in a separate, autonomous will is closely related to the ego. When I think or talk about what I want to do, my plans, my desires, I refer to my own will, independent and separate. Conflict between wills is life on earth. Don't interfere with what I want to do.

My resistance to giving up my own will is probably stronger than the resistance to dis-identifying with the body and ego. The only free will is God's Will. Seven billion free wills doesn't work, unless I want war.

A painful consequence of the separation is that my will is imprisoned, or limited, for my protection, because my mind is split. Mind split into separateness means that Will is also split and diminished for individuals. In my unified, pre-separation state, my will is united with God's as one loving Will, free and unlimited.

> In the creation, God extended Himself to His creations and imbued them with the same loving Will to create... Because of your likeness to your Creator you are creative.[42]

Pre-separation or post-separation, collective Will is creative and free. Fragmented in the dream of separation we do not share one Will. Many wills means conflict and opposition. There are not many wills in Heaven, nor opposition and conflict.

> ...you cannot depart entirely from your creator, who set limits on your ability to miscreate.[43]

These "limits" refer to limits on my will, as a protection. Imagine the horror if the ego enjoyed full, unlimited, creative, Will. On the other hand, a limited will is quite painful. Like the restriction of heavy chains, or confinement of a straight jacket.

> An imprisoned will engenders a situation which, in the extreme, becomes altogether intolerable. Tolerance for pain may be high, but it is not without limit. Eventually everyone begins to recognize, however dimly, that there must be a better way.[44]

The limit on my will is also described as a disabling or reduction of the power of my mind. When this will-power is renewed I find the situation even *more* painful:

> Spiritual vision looks within and recognizes immediately
> that the altar has been defiled and needs to be repaired
> and protected…because of the strength of its vision, it
> brings the mind into its service. This re-establishes the
> power of the mind and makes it increasingly unable to
> tolerate delay, realizing that it only adds unnecessary pain.
> As a result, the mind becomes increasingly sensitive to
> what it once would have regarded as very minor intrusions
> of discomfort.[45]

This suffering of limited will pushes me to seek a solution, a different direction. When I look within and realize what is happening, my mind is energized to find a better way and seek liberation of will back to its unrestricted freedom to love and create. Once the mind, in service to Spirit, realizes there is a way out of pain, mind becomes increasingly sensitive, and delay in ending pain becomes increasingly intolerable. Prior to the mind choosing to serve Spirit instead of ego, it is less sensitive to suffering, particularly the suffering of others.

The Unconscious Mind

Part of my identity is unconscious. The shared unconscious is the collective unconscious. The unconscious mind is the ultimate private mind. It is designed to separate and keep secret what is most disturbing. Jesus in Luke's Gospel:

> Nothing is covered up that will not be revealed, or
> hidden that will not be known. Whatever you have said
> in the dark shall be heard in the light, and what you have
> whispered in private rooms shall be proclaimed upon the
> housetops.[46]

So much for secrets. ACIM places significant emphasis on healing what is hidden in my unconscious mind. I seem to keep apart my own private thoughts, and also my own private, traumatic, unconscious, forgotten, repressed, denied, and dissociated thoughts and memories. This sense of privacy denies oneness. Keep out: private property.

> **When you have become willing to hide nothing, you will not only be willing to enter into communion but will also understand peace and joy.**[47]

How often do I hide something? Why do I fear honest transparency? Fear interferes with willingness for truly transparent communication. Realizing that my unconscious darkness is publicly proclaimed makes the egotistical form of fear called embarrassment. Looked at the right way, it is hilarious, as many movies demonstrate. I want nothing to do with this rude invasion of privacy. I keep the unconscious private from the conscious for a reason. Secrets for the separated.

Perceiving what is unconscious means it is no longer unconscious. Freedom from the wish to hide my shadow in the unconscious (where it is hidden from myself) comes when I see the futility of hiding anything. I am like a child playing hide and seek. I hide, thinking my playmates can't see me, but they can. Eventually I come to the realization...

> **...the recognition that there is nothing you want to hide even if you could.**[48]

Am I ready for true transparency? It is not forced, because that might cause fear and fear blocks transparency, defeating the whole purpose. The Holy Spirit works to decrease fear, not to increase it. I am ready for the holy instant – communion – when there is nothing I want to hide.

When I cannot endure to experience something, I use various defense mechanisms to protect myself and they deploy automatically, like airbags in a car crash. In some situations I simply forget what I don't want to see or remember, and it becomes unconscious. In dissociation I dissociate from a painful experience and appear to watch it happening from a safer place...as if it were happening to someone else. Then the memory of the traumatic event is stored away in the locked vault of the unconscious where I neither see it nor remember it. But I'm not rid of it. It is hidden in the dark and light is forbidden in the psychological game of hide and go seek, but do not find. If I lose my contact lens in a dark cave, it's going to be hard to find without a light. The unconscious is associated with darkness, where the unwanted hide like enemies under the cover of darkness. The healing process involves bringing the unconscious to the conscious, the hidden to revealing, the darkness to the light. Using defense mechanisms is like trying to clean up the mess in my room by throwing everything into the closet. As long as the closet door stays closed, the room looks livable. The real cleanup is, however, ahead.

> **No one can escape from illusions unless he looks at them, for not looking is the way they are protected.**[49]

I make a pretense of law and order by keeping a locked lid on the unconscious. My house looks clean enough for company as long as no one sees the basement and so I lock, block, and defend that door.

> **You must look upon your illusions and not keep them hidden...**[50]

Avoiding what is painful to see prolongs pain by preventing the revealing of what needs healing.

ACIM teaches why unconscious illusions of sin, guilt, and fear are revealed in order to be healed. It is because these illusions are hiding something else, underneath these illusions, even deeper in the unconscious: a mind in pain. This mind in pain, cloaked beneath illusions of shame, remains hidden until the layers of illusions are made conscious and peeled away.

> **For beneath them, [unconscious illusions of sin and guilt] and concealed as long as they are hidden, is the loving mind that thought it made them [illusions] in anger. And the pain in this mind is so apparent, when it is uncovered,**

> that its need of healing cannot be denied. Not all the
> tricks and games you offer it can heal it, for here is the real
> crucifixion of God's Son.[51]

The mind in pain, buried deep in the unconscious, is actually a loving mind, as God created it, but it is overwhelmed with guilt about the wish to separate from God. My loving mind is hidden, deep in the unconscious mind. This holy mind is revealed when the unconscious material hiding it is made conscious. The revealing is healing. To resist this uncovering is to hide, stay unconscious, and continue pain. Yet I tend to resist this uncovering that leaves me naked and vulnerable, with no makeup mask to hide behind.

> **Do not hide suffering from His** [the Holy Spirit's] **sight,
> but bring it gladly to Him. Lay before his eternal sanity
> all your hurt, and let Him heal you. Do not leave any spot
> of pain hidden from His Light, and search your mind
> carefully for any thoughts you may fear to uncover.**[52]

The Holy Spirit heals the mind in pain to the extent I allow it. I allow it by surrendering my attempts to hide this pain in the unconscious. I drop my guard. Revealed, it can be healed.

> **Discomfort is aroused only to bring the need for
> correction into awareness.**[53]

Although this process is often painful, the discomfort is necessary, otherwise I might not know what is wrong or perhaps would not even suspect that anything is wrong. If I'm on a cold camping trip and trying to warm up my freezing feet by the fire, and I did not feel it when my feet started to burn, that is a problem. The ego's job, directly opposed to the Holy Spirit's job, is to keep the lid on the unconscious locked. As long as the problem stays hidden, the ego's world continues. The ego is not my friend, and if I start to choose for the Holy Spirit instead of the ego, the ego fights for its survival.

> As long as the ego is reasonably satisfied with you, as its
> reasoning goes, it offers you oblivion. When it becomes
> overtly savage, it offers you hell.[54]

I experience the Holy Spirit's healing work as painful because it threatens the ego's continuity. If I identify with the ego, it threatens my continuity.

> Undermining the ego's thought system must be perceived
> as painful, even though this is anything but true. Babies
> scream in rage if you take away a knife or scissors,
> although they may well harm themselves if you do not.
> In this sense you are still a baby.[55]

I'm like a toddler who does not know what is helpful from what is harmful. As I crawl along the world's carpet I'm willing to put anything I find into my mouth, a marble or a meatball.

The psychological concepts of the unconscious mind, defense mechanisms, and projection were not available until recently. The approach ACIM provides needs these new notions. Helen, the scribe, trained in Freudian psychology from 1952-1957.

Specialness

ACIM uses the word "special" in association with the separated self. To be special is to be different, unique, unequal, superior, inferior. To identify as special is to identify as separate. How often do parents tell their children that they are special?

> The "better" self the ego seeks is always one that is more
> special.[56]

How important is it to feel I am special, more special, most special?

> But the pursuit of specialness must bring you pain. Here
> is a goal that would defeat salvation, and thus run counter

> to the Will of God. To value specialness is to esteem an
> alien will to which illusions of yourself are dearer than the
> truth.[57]

The alien will is my own, separate and special will, based on the illusion
of a separate self. It is a desire for a different identity that is special.

> Specialness is the function that you gave yourself. It
> stands for you alone, as self-created, self-maintained, in
> need of nothing, and unjoined with anything beyond the
> body.[58]

All this attention on the separate self is necessary so that I learn what
I'm not. Uncovering the ego for what it is helps to free me of the illusionary identity. Do I want to be duped by deception? The ego keeps
plenty of tricks and treats up its sleeves. I learn to unmask it. The kid
in a wolf-man costume is not a wolf-man.

Studying about the special, separate, self sense is a lot of unpleasant news. Necessary to know, but still bad news. There is, however,
good news about my true identity:

> Forgive yourself your madness, and forget all senseless
> journeys and all goal-less aims. They have no meaning.
> You cannot escape from what you are. For God is
> merciful, and did not let His Son abandon Him. For what
> He is be thankful, for in that is your escape from madness
> and from death.[59]

I cannot escape from my true identity, only forget about it temporarily,
because God is merciful and loves unconditionally. My true identity
is as God created it: holy, perfect, innocent, unlimited, safe, healthy,
whole, free to love, free to create: I am Spirit. My false identity is a
temporary dream detour that deceives. Gratefully, the restoration of
my true identity is the promise of my merciful Father. I do not do it.

It is done. It is not done in fact, because the separation did not happen. It is done in my mind, where the belief in separation persists.

So if feeling depressed, ask, "Who is depressed? What is depressed?" According to the course, who I am cannot be depressed. From this view, depression is an identity-confusion disorder. This identity-confusion is a result, a requirement, of the separation. If I insist on continued identity with body, ego, and autonomous will, depression will continue. If I refuse the revealing of unconscious material I handicap healing. Who am I?

> **The death of specialness is not your death, but your awakening into life eternal. You but emerge from an illusion of what you are to the acceptance of yourself as God created you.**[60]

Four Fingers

Once upon a time, four fingers were born together. They were little but content and lived together closely, even though they did not know they were called fingers, or even know what they were at all. They were young and soft and slept right next to each other.

Now each finger appeared as unique and different. So they identified themselves as individuals, and, lo and behold, there were four individual fingers.

Someone named the fingers to tell them apart because they had the same last name: Finger. So, there was named Index Finger (nicknamed Indy), The Finger (nicknamed Theo), Ring Finger (nicknamed Ringo), and Pink Finger (nicknamed Pinky).

Gradually they grew and became stronger and smarter. They now did all kinds of things they could not do before skills developed. They found that by working together they achieved amazing things.

They play piano! They type poems! They bend guitar strings! They braided and beaded! In cooperation they created.

Then one day Indy said to the other brothers, "Well you know bros, I'm the most important Finger, really special. Numero Uno. I do more than the rest of you. I'm the smartest. I'm the pointer. I'm simply better than you. I'm the First Finger; that's obvious."

So the other fingers thought about what Indy said and didn't like the sound of it. They started looking at each other and making comparisons. They started thinking, "Who is the best?"

So Theo spoke up: "Indy, you are not the best, or the most important. I'm the best, obviously. I am bigger than you; I'm stronger than you. I'm bigger and stronger than any of you. Obviously I am the most important Finger. Who do you think they refer to when they say, 'Give him The Finger?'"

So the fingers thought and fought, thought and fought, thought and fought. Who is better? Who is best? Who is worst? Who is smartest? Who is strongest? Who is most beautiful? Who is MIF (Most Important Finger)?

Then Ringo spoke up: "Indy and Theo, you are both wrong. I'm the only Finger wearing a solid gold belt. They save the solid gold belt for the best Finger, obviously. You are deluded. Someone better knock you off your high hand. Do you wear a solid gold belt? No you don't. You don't have any belt at all."

Pinky considered all this and felt depressed. He didn't know what to say. The other Fingers seemed superior to him in every way. He was the smallest, the weakest, the least and the last. Even his name, Pink, was a lame embarrassment. Then he found a verse in THE BOOK! It is WRITTEN: "The last shall be first and the first shall be last." Eureka! He is the most important Finger because he is the last. And the last shall be first. THE BOOK said so!

So Pinky told the others and laughed: "I am the most important. You are all mistaken. Haven't you read THE BOOK? THE BOOK says that I'm the first because I'm the last and the last shall be first. It is so WRITTEN. You all are quite stupid."

And so, lo and behold, CONFLICT came and continued. The Fingers continued to compare and compete with each other. They argued and acted angrily. They began to fight with each other more and more. Violence increased as they started to hurt each other. Fingers even wanted to kill other Fingers by amputation!

And so it went. They stopped cooperating. They stopped creating music and poetry. They no longer joined and worked together. They exchanged constructive play for destructive work, trying to prove who is most powerful. They attacked each other. They hated each other. They feared each other. They became depressed and depressing, anxious, arthritic, suspicious and vicious. They suffered. Kill or be killed seemed true.

If one did not kill the other then the next best thing was to control the other. The Fingers each said to the others: "I'm the boss of you."

This went on for a long, long time.

The situation became worse and worse.

Then Hand woke and spoke: "You Fingers stop it! Are you insane? You seem to think you are separate, individual Fingers, and in certain ways you are because it seems you are not the same. But you forgot that you are all connected to me and how we enjoyed making music and poetry. Each of you is important and necessary. I need you all equally. We enjoyed life when we were joining in to play the guitar and type up love poems. Wasn't that a lot more fun?"

"Hmm," the Fingers thought, "that really was more fun."

The fingers realized Hand was wise. And so they made peace. It was a simple and sane choice. They were free to agree.

So, lo and behold, Fingers and Hand are ONE.

> **One brother is all brothers. Every mind contains all minds, for every mind is one. Such is the truth.** [61]

Chapter Seven

WHEN EGOS COLLIDE: RELATIONSHIPS

*J*f I am confused about my identity, how am I in relationship with others? Who loves whom? Who hates whom? ACIM describes two kinds of relationships, special relationships and holy relationship. Holy relationship is based on the Holy Spirit's right-minded thought system of oneness. Special relationships are based on the ego's wrong-minded thought system of separation and neediness. Specialness requires separation. No separation means no specialness.

> **You are not special.**[1]

Even though I'm not special, I believe I am special, until I don't. I'm conditioned from infancy to believe I'm special, different, and separate. In truth, though, no one is special because no one is separate. I have the power of choice; I can choose ego or God, specialness or holiness, but not both, as they are mutually exclusive. Nor can I compromise, keeping what I like of each. My choice is guided by what I believe, especially the belief about my identity.

> **Every decision you make stems from what you think you are...**[2]

The most dangerous beliefs are unconscious. I see my conscious belief in specialness, perhaps denied a little by pseudo-humility. Yet unconscious specialness is more dangerous because it is hidden, unrecognized, and does its damage in secret.

> **...an unrecognized belief is a decision to war in secret...**
> **And many senseless outcomes have been reached,**
> **and meaningless decisions have been made and kept**

143

> hidden, to become beliefs now given power to direct all
> subsequent decisions...All that is ever cherished as a
> hidden belief, to be defended though unrecognized, is
> faith in specialness.[3]

Hidden beliefs direct decisions and I defend hidden beliefs even though I am unconscious of them. The conscious and unconscious beliefs in specialness are the beliefs in separation, and the resulting dualities of differences. Without separation, specialness is impossible. Specialness and separation are the basis of special relationships.

The hidden belief in specialness drives the decisions of the world and the results of this are not so hidden: endless conflict and war, and endless in its various forms: between two individuals, between two families, between two cities, between two nations, between two races, between two religions, between two sexes. As a separate being, specialness defines me as different, superior, or inferior. From difference arises judgment. From judgment arises condemnation. From condemnation arises attack. From attack arises suffering. The human herd stampedes down the stairway of suffering.

> But what is different calls for judgment, and this must
> come from someone "better," someone incapable of being
> like what he condemns, "above" it, sinless by comparison
> with it...For specialness not only sets apart, but serves as
> grounds from which attack on those who seem "beneath"
> the special one is "natural" and "just."[4]

Spiritual specialness says I'm more holy than you. Or perhaps I'm "humble" enough to pretend you are more holy than I. Ironically, I take pride in my humility. The hierarchy of holiness requires that you and I be separate, different. What about someone like Hitler? Is Adolph holy too? If I hate Hitler I have confused God's creation and ego. No ego is holy. No ego is unholy either because no ego is at all.

The effect of identifying as special is special relationships of both friends and enemies. ACIM stresses the importance of our relationships; in relationship I experience Heaven or hell. We are healed, together, or we hide in hell, together. There is no individual salvation in ACIM. It is all for One and One for all.

> **No one is crucified alone, and yet no one can enter Heaven by himself.**[5]

How I feel is determined by how I am in relationship. Depression is related to relationship.

> **Whenever you deny a blessing to a brother, you will feel deprived.**[6]

If I deny a blessing to a brother I deprive myself because I deny my Self. Feeling deprived develops into feeling depressed.

In relationship I either agree with the ego's delusional thought system that we are separate beings or I agree with the Holy Spirit's true thought system that we are perfectly integrated into the one Son of God. This is a true co-dependency in that we are dependent on each other for the complete wholeness of our true Self, also called the Sonship, or the Christ. Even if I'm not depressed, I share in the collective, unconscious, separation trauma drama. I am not healed until everyone is healed. Is a depressed person more sensitive to, or aware of, the collective suffering?

A consequence of the separation is that my mind is split, and then split again and yet again until there are billions of brains believing each is special, separate and autonomous. The consequence of this splitting is the world I project and the kind of conflicted relationships I keep, the ultimate cognitive dissonance. The course's teaching is radically inclusive and unconditional. Every seemingly separated person is re-joined in the grand re-union, not in the future, but beyond time in the eternal now.

Everyone is included. *Everyone.* This is a core teaching of ACIM and a difficult one to accept because I have my favorite, special, evil, enemies that I don't like. Inclusiveness is so important the course states that how quickly or slowly I progress is contingent on including everyone, because no one is special.

> The progress of the teacher of God may be slow or rapid, depending on whether he recognizes the Atonement's inclusiveness, or for a time excludes some problem areas from it.[7]

It seems like certain problem people are especially separate from me and I refuse being one with them, and resist including them in Heaven. This stems from confusing ego and mind, or identity confusion. To the extent I exclude anyone, I exclude myself, because we already share the same Spirit, not according to perception, but according to the truth that the Holy Spirit is already present within each mind, uniting us.

> You cannot enter into real relationships with any of God's Sons unless you love them all and equally. Love is not special. If you single out part of the Sonship for your love, you are imposing guilt on all your relationships and making them unreal. You can love only as God loves. Seek not to love unlike Him, for there is no love apart from His. Until you recognize that this is true, you will have no idea what love is like.[8]

Inclusiveness does not mean I include the ego because the ego is an illusion and not real. To say we are one is to say that we are joined because we share the same Holy Spirit.

> When you unite with me [Jesus] you are uniting without the ego, because I have renounced the ego in myself and therefore cannot unite with yours. Our union is therefore the way to renounce the ego in you. The truth in both of us is beyond the ego.[9]

Unitive wholeness includes every mind, but excludes ego, bodies and any other temporary symbols of separation because they are not real. What is not real is not included even if I wanted to include it. Ego and body are excluded not because they are evil, but because they are not real; they are projections. They are temporary symbols of specialness and separation in the dream domain of duality. No more real than the remembered figures from a nightmare dream of twenty years ago. Illusions are not included.

Whether in holy relationship or special relationship, it is in our joining in agreement that "consensus" reality exists as a shared belief. The world is projected by the collective unconscious. If I want to see what shape the collective unconscious is in, I look at the world it is projecting. Relationships can go either way, but only one of two ways and not both, regardless of how much I might will for a compromise. There is no guilt or fear in Heaven. If I want in, the guilty stain of separation is washed until I am cleaner than the purest air. The camel is completely unloaded, and on its knees, to squeeze through the narrow needle gate. I can't drag guilt into the Kingdom. Unconscious guilt is revealed when I realize I'm projecting this guilt onto my brother. Projection reveals what is within, hidden, forbidden, unconscious. So I am released from it as I release my brother from the projection of judgment. I cannot do this by myself, on my own. I need my brother and my own release is tied to his release. My brother is the mirror of myself. Without that mirror I cannot see, nor know, myself. Without my brother to help, my situation is helpless, and hopeless. We are saved together. Egos are not saved. There is no salvation in separation.

As an individual, my creative power is extremely limited. But joined together, our creative power is unlimited. It is like how one's bargaining power goes in the workplace. The union is more powerful than the individual. "Where two or three are gathered in my name" is another way of saying it.

Special relationships are the relationships between egos. These relationships are designed to get something I perceive as lacking. They are based on getting to compensate for deprivation. They are based on needy differences. Holy relationship is based on holiness; it gives and shares abundance, because nothing is lacking. The more I share, the more I receive, in the economy of Heaven. Holy relationship sees through the illusion of separation and recognizes union and radical equality in one Will.

In the United States there is the great idea that "All men are created equal." This is a true idea, but in practice it is hypocrisy: all men are created equal *except* for women, Indians, Blacks, poor people, homeless people, the mentally ill, the developmentally disabled, the sick, gays, Germans, Russians, Chinese, Jews, Muslims, atheists, the unpatriotic, immigrants, illegal aliens, criminals, and any one else who dares to "tread on me." Who is left as equal? Wealthy White Male Anglo Saxon Protestants? This is specialness and separation in action in the slaughterhouse world. Hundreds of millions of humans were slaughtered by other humans. And the killing continues. Body/egos torture and kill each other over ideas of specialness, ideas about identity, race, religion, and nationality. Opposition and conflict, drama and trauma, proves that all men are not equal, not in this world. On earth, equality is exclusive. True equality is inclusive. What happened to Thy Kingdom come on earth as it is in Heaven?

Special Love Relationships

There are two kinds of special relationships: special love relationships and special hate relationships. They are two sides of the same coin.

> The special love relationship is the ego's chief weapon for keeping you from Heaven. The special love relationship is the ego's most boasted gift, and one which has the most appeal to those unwilling to relinquish guilt.[10]

That quote is a warning. Special love relationships are with anyone I think I love and/or like: family, lovers, friends, etc. Special love relationships are the *ego's chief weapon* and *the ego's most boasted gift* because they are so important and so difficult to see as they are. Special love relationships are the ego's best bet because these "love" relationships are the last thing I suspect of blocking love. I think it is love, even though it is secretly anti-love. Special love guards the jail of separation. These special "love" relationships perpetuate hell. They keep my mind in pain. They keep me special. My kids are special because they are *mine*. Luke's Gospel:

> **Now great multitudes accompanied him; and he turned and said to them, "If any one comes to me and does not hate his own father and mother and wife and children and brothers and sisters, yes, and even his own life, he cannot be my disciple."[11]**

In the verse above, Jesus identifies the major special love relationships: father, mother, spouse, children, brothers, sisters. *Even his own life*, is my own specialness on which my special relationships are built.

As an example of a special love relationship, two people meet and "fall in love." They get married, have a home, have kids, care for cars, etc. But sooner or later the honeymoon ends. This is the theme of countless books and movies: *When Egos Collide*. Dream drama.

> **Where both partners see this special self in each other, the ego sees a "union made in Heaven." For neither one will recognize that he has asked for hell.[12]**

Special love relationships can change on a dime into special hate relationships. Flip that dime and sometimes it comes up hate, sometimes "love." The coupled, who were once "in love," now are enemies seeking separation, and pay lawyers to attack each other. The hatred escalates to violence and murder. As for the kids, they are sacrificed on the ego's altar and learn the hard way the ways of the world. When the kids grow up, they get to follow in their parent's footsteps. Considering the number of divorces, that's a lot of moola for cops, lawyers, custody investigators, psychologists, judges, etc. This is the lucrative business of the separated preparing separation packages. Although I can change partners, divorce rates are higher for second marriages than first ones. Divorce rates for third marriages are higher than for second marriages.

The intoxicating and addicting bliss of the beginnings of most romantic relationships is due to its similarity to true spiritual joining. At this stage sweetie is seen as just what I need. Because Adam separated into Adam and Eve, I long for reunion of wholeness. The split of one Being into female and male is a metaphor for one Mind split into many minds. The honeymoon does not last long, does it? I get a short respite from the war of the egos. I get high on this love-drug and feel great. The ego is down but not out. The guilt and fear collision is just around the corner.

> ...everyone who believes that the ego is salvation seems
> to be intensely engaged in the search for love. Yet the
> ego, though encouraging the search for love very actively,
> makes one proviso; do not find it.[13]

Is it not depressing to be deprived of love? This wicked game is the ego's trick. The plain fact is that ego does not, will not, and cannot, love. Ego only pretends to love. It gives to get. The ego's care is calculated in its own best interest. In specialness, love is ever unrequited, despite pretenses.

> The ego's search for love guides you to a journey which
> must end in perceived self-defeat, for the ego cannot
> love.[14]

Joel S. Goldsmith wrote about our relationships:

> Do not be concerned about your relationships with
> people. Consciously maintain your relationship with God,
> and this will take care of everything else...When thought
> dwells on person, place, or thing, you are functioning in
> the dream.[15]

Special love relationships don't work. Egos remain infinitely alone and unreachable. There is a saying: for every beautiful woman there is a man tired of sleeping with her. True love does not tire or fade away. If it fades, there is the proof it is phony.

In the Gospel of Matthew, Jesus is told that his mother and brothers are asking for him. His response makes more sense if I understand the course teaching on special relationships:

> While he was still speaking to the people, behold, his mother and his brethren stood outside, asking to speak to him. But he replied to the man that told him, "Who is my mother, and who are my brethren?" And stretching out his hand towards his disciples, he said, "Here are my mother and my brethren! For whoever does the will of my Father in Heaven is my brother, and sister, and mother."[16]

Who is Jesus in holy relationship with? Whoever does the Will of his Father. When my will is joined with God's, we cannot collide. In this world there is a heavy emphasis on the special love relationship called "family." Millions of children starve and suffer and I'm not too bothered about it. But if my own child is suffering or dying, it is a super big deal. Certain people are "special" to me, more or less. Birth kids and enter fear. Special love means special fear. My children can be hurt, and will be. My children will die sooner or later. Suck it up; welcome to the world. The special relationships in organized crime, referred to as "family," operate on the thinking that my family is primary and your family is disposable. If I really want to hurt someone, I hurt his kids. My identity is tied up in my special relationships.

Special Hate Relationships

Special hate relationships are the flip side of special love relationships, often with the same person. Krishnamurti describes our special relationships as "mutual usage." Lawyers call it "quid pro quo." This for that, tit for tat. Polite politicians know it well: "I'll scratch your back if you scratch mine." The ego gives to get. Special love is conditional love. There is always an "if." It is basically the world of manipulative, separate, calculating, greedy, self-centric, egotistic selfishness, disguised as relationship. I, me, mine.

As many learn the hard way, the special relationship called marriage rarely ends as happy ever after. Let's say about half of the marriages end in divorce. Of the other half, how many are happy? How many resigned themselves to mutual usage? How many lie to each other and cheat on each other? How many secrets separate husband and wife? Divorce happens not only between married partners. It happens between friends, between siblings, between parent and child; it happens within just about any relationship. Some say, well… relationships are supposed to be work. It's hard to be in a long-term relationship. You bet. It is hard because a relationship between two egos cannot work, except as calculated, mutual, manipulative usage. Even if the getting desire is not conscious, it is nonetheless unconscious, though usually it is both.

The fact is, people I am in relationship with are a type of mirror. I project what I do not want to see about myself on to others. Others project onto me as well. There is strong resistance to seeing this. What if the disturbing characteristic of someone who seriously bothers me is actually in me? How could I re-cognize that characteristic in the other unless I knew it already? And this is why I change partners. But I'm only substituting one mirror for another.

> **Your brother is the mirror in which you see the image of yourself as long as perception lasts.**[17]

As long as perception lasts, means as long as time lasts, or as long as I continue dreaming. In the mirror, I do not see myself, I see an image of self. In the process of projection, my unconscious guilt is the filter through which I see my brother and so I believe my brother is guilty.

> **Projection always sees your wishes in others.**[18]

Since the eye cannot see itself, as the knife cannot cut itself, I see my self-image in the mirror of projection, or not. What I project is what I don't want to see about myself. What I project is not a pretty picture.

> You think that you hold against your brother what he has done to you. But what you really blame him for is what you did to him.[19]

The pain in my mind, caused by guilt, is too excruciating to experience directly, and is thus concealed in the unconscious part of my mind and then projected "outside" myself so that I perceive guilt as in someone else, not in me. Ego says the sin I hate is in my brother, not me. If my brother is guilty, he is deserving of attack. This attack is actually self-attack.

> Only the self-accused condemn. As you prepare to make a choice that will result in different outcomes, there is first one thing that must be overlearned. It must become a habit of response so typical of everything you do that it becomes your first response to all temptation, and to every situation that occurs. Learn this, and learn it well, for it is here delay of happiness is shortened by a span of time you cannot realize. You never hate your brother for his sins, but only for your own. Whatever form his sins appear to take, it but obscures the fact that you believe them to be yours, and therefore meriting a "just" attack.[20]

Do I want to shorten the delay of happiness by a span of time I cannot realize? This is accomplished by learning that judgment of my brother is a projection of my own guilt. Does the following quote have anything to do with blessed unions gone awry?

> Suffering and sacrifice are the gifts with which the ego would "bless" all unions. The fury of those joined at the ego's altar far exceeds your awareness of it.[21]

Is that a nod to: "Hell hath no fury like a woman scorned?"

Special hate relationships are affairs with people I don't like, don't love. People who are my enemy. People whom I judge as bad or evil. People I believe hurt me. People I think attacked me or someone I "love." People I used to love. Grievances, grudges, etc. Religious, racial, political, professional, personal, it does not matter. Like the philosopher Sartre said, *hell is other people.* Separation is necessary in order for there to be "other people."

> The special relationship includes a great amount of pain. Anxiety, despair, guilt and attack all enter into it, broken by periods in which they seem to be gone.[22]

How much of my pain revolves around relationships? How many dramas are about special relationships? It appears that for the thousands of years of human history what happens here is one war after another, and multiple wars going on at the same time. One damn thing after another. Many of these wars, maybe most, were, and still are, based on religious beliefs, or the other ways in which we identify as different, special, and separate subsets of humanity, including gender, tribe, race and nationality.

> Only the special could have enemies, for they are different and not the same.[23]

What gives anybody the justified desire to attack other people, enslave them, kill them, and steal the spoils? The way of violence continues as humans "evolve" except that methods of just killing improved efficiency from sticks and stones to nuclear, chemical, and biological mass and mutually assured destruction. Now governments use economic hit men as well as drones. We traded the rack for the water board. We watch in horror as religious terrorists burn people alive. How is this different from the "good guys" dropping napalm bombs that burn men, women and children alive? The Jewish people are special because they are God's exclusive, chosen people. In the

Old Testament, God commands the Jews to attack and wipe out other groups of people, killing everyone, including women and children, and all the animals as well. Such is the fruit of specialness and how we treat each other. According to the Old Testament, God commands genocide. Slaves, obey.

The basis for special relationships is the special self: the me, the constructed idol of self-concept, as discussed in the last chapter on identity. How can this false self be in a true relationship? ACIM describes one side of this self-concept in relationship:

> [Self-concept] presents the face of innocence, the aspect acted on. It is this face that smiles and charms and even seems to love. It searches for companions and it looks, at times with pity, on the suffering, and sometimes offers solace. It believes it is good within an evil world. This aspect can grow angry, for the world is wicked and unable to provide the love and shelter innocence deserves. And so this face is often wet with tears at the injustices the world accords to those who would be generous and good. This aspect never makes the first attack. But every day a hundred little things make small assaults upon its innocence, provoking it to irritation, and at last to open insult and abuse. The face of innocence the concept of the self so proudly wears can tolerate attack in self-defense, for is it not a well known fact the world deals harshly with defenseless innocence?[24]

Jesus did not defend himself and the world dealt him a harsh execution. He knows well what he is talking about. The passage above describes one side of the self-concept I imagine about who I am: the *face of innocence,* and how this face interacts with the world and others, loved or hated. This is the conscious false self (though I believe it is real and who I am). This innocent self needs defense because others attack it.

Then there is the unconscious shadowy self I prefer to forget and deny. This part of self-concept is concealed and the "conscious" face of innocence refuses to see it.

> **Beneath the face of innocence there is a lesson that the concept of the self was made to teach. It is a lesson in a terrible displacement, and a fear so devastating that the face that smiles above it must forever look away, lest it perceive the treachery it hides. The lesson is this: "I am the thing you made of me, and as you look upon me, you stand condemned because of what I am." On this conception of the self the world smiles with approval, for it guarantees the pathways of the world are safely kept, and those who walk on them will not escape.**[25]

The previous two quotes provide a whole psychology of identity and relationship, compressed into two paragraphs. This is the divided self, split between unconscious and conscious. I blame my mind in pain on others, projecting my shame, guilt, and division on to them. This world is built and maintained on the b-lame game. The world is a blame projection.

> **...every pain you suffer do you see as proof that he [my brother] is guilty of attack...Whenever you consent to suffer pain, to be deprived, unfairly treated or in need of anything, you but accuse your brother of attack on God's Son. You hold a picture of your crucifixion before his eyes..."**[26]

When I buy into the blame game, I keep the split-mind in pain, because I remain unconscious of the true cause of pain.

It is in my relationships that I either continue the crucifixion, or receive Resurrection, by accepting the Atonement. In accepting the Atonement guilt is released and I no longer need to project what is not there. The ending of hell is the ending of blame and shame.

> Attack in any form has placed your foot upon the twisted stairway that leads from Heaven.[27]

Blaming is attack. It is self-attack and keeps my mind in pain. It is not the stairway to Heaven; it is the highway to hell.

> A sick and suffering you but represents your brother's guilt; the witness you send lest he forget the injuries he gave, from which you swear he never will escape...the sick are merciless to everyone, and in contagion do they seek to kill... "Behold me, brother, at your hand I die." For sickness is the witness to his guilt, and death would prove his errors must be sins.[28]

Special relationships are based on past grievances, grudges I hold against others, whom I judge as judging me.

> It is impossible to let the past go without relinquishing the special relationship. For the special relationship is an attempt to reenact the past and change it. Imagined slights, remembered pain, past disappointments, perceived injustices and deprivations all enter into the special relationship.[29]

Being in a relationship with someone implies a past, a history. And possibly a continuance into the future. Special relationships need the past, a history. The past is gone but I hang on to it through special relationships. They are "proof" the past is alive and well. "I remember what you did to me."

> The ego cannot tolerate release from the past, and although the past is over, the ego tries to preserve its image by responding as if it were present. It dictates your reactions to those you meet in the present from a past reference point, obscuring their present reality. In

> effect, if you follow the ego's dictates you will react to your
> brother as though he were someone else, and this will
> surely prevent you from recognizing him as he is.[30]

In special relationships I do not see my brother as he is *now*. I see him
as an image I imagined, based on the past. This is not a real relationship. The image of my brother I make is not my brother, no more than
the image of myself I see in a mirror is me. The past is not present
now, but I drag it in, blocking the view of my brother as he is now.

> ...you perceive a brother only as you see him *now*. His past
> has no reality in the present, so you cannot see it. Your
> past reactions to him are also not there, and if it is to them
> that you react, you see but an image of him that you made
> and cherish instead of him...If you remember the past as
> you look upon your brother, you will be unable to perceive
> the reality that is now.[31]

The image of my brother I make and believe, based on the past, is
simply the accumulation of memories and not who he is now. I seek
the continuity of this past image into the future. I literally drag the
past into the future for a sense of stability and continuity. I am hardly
aware of the present, using the now to feel guilt over the past and feel
fear about the future. Grudges, grievances, judgments, attacks, and
conflicts all require a past history held against my brother. The future
is for punishment.

> You consider it "natural" to use your past experience as
> the reference point from which to judge the present. Yet
> this is unnatural because it is delusional. When you have
> learned to look on everyone with no reference at all to the
> past, either his or yours as you perceived it, you will be
> able to learn from what you see now.[32]

If I see my brother through the filter of the past, my view is distorted,
even delusional. I see an image I imagined, not my brother as he is

now. This cognitive construction is a concept of my brother, not my brother.

Because I also see myself through the filter of the past, I cannot know myself as I am. ACIM differentiates between self-concept and Self. One is real; one is not. One God created; one I imagined. The holy instant releases conceptual images of self and other based on the past. One of the reasons why people love babies so much is there is no history, yet. Same with a new romance. But the accumulation of memories starts constructing the image of *other* quickly. This is what it means when I say I "know" someone. In fact, I don't know him. I know an image I imagined based on belief, maintained by memory. The special relationship is between two self-images, two self-concepts. I expect the future to confirm my memory.

Holy Relationship

The solution to special relationships, love or hate, is transforming them into holy relationship. A holy relationship is real and it is not based on images constructed over time. The holy relationship is based on now, the holy instant. It is based on who I am, and who the beloved is, as God created us.

> The miracle enables you to see your brother without his past, and so perceive him as born again. His errors are all past, and by perceiving him without them you are releasing him. And since his past is yours, you share in this release.[33]

The holy relationship is directly tied to my true identity. True identity is *shared*.

> You cannot understand yourself alone. This is because you have no meaning apart from your rightful place in the Sonship, and the rightful place of the Sonship is God. This is your life, your eternity, and your self.[34]

ACIM describes my true identity as the *Sonship*. This is the joining of all minds and wills into union as the one Son of God, the fel-
lowship of Christ. Hence the primary importance of allowing the
transformation of my relationships in order to end hell. In the *Gospel
of Thomas* Jesus says:

> If two make peace with each other in a single house, they
> will say to the mountain, "Move over there!" and it will
> move.[35]

In a single house is code for non-duality. Peace of holy relationship
replaces conflict of special relationship. In the Gospel of John, Jesus
prays for our unity:

> I do not pray for these only, but also for those who believe
> in me through their word, that they may all be one; even
> as thou, Father, art in me, and I in thee, that they may
> also be in us, so that the world may believe that thou has
> sent me. The glory which thou has given me I have given
> to them, that they may be one even as we are one, I in
> them and thou in me, that they may become perfectly one,
> so that the world may know that thou has sent me, even as
> thou has loved me.[36]

Compare the above Last Supper prayer of Jesus to this Jesus prayer
from the last section of the last chapter of the *Text*:

> I thank you Father, for these holy ones who are my
> brothers as they are Your Sons. My faith in them is Yours.
> I am sure that they will come to me as You are sure of
> what they are, and will forever be. They will accept the
> gift I offer them, because You gave it to me on their
> behalf. And as I would but do Your holy Will, so will they
> choose. And I give thanks for them. Salvation's song will

echo through the world with every choice they make. For we are one in purpose, and the end of hell is near.[37]

Sound like the same Jesus?

Special relationships are transformed into holy relationship by the Holy Spirit. How does this change from special to holy happen?

> Because of guilt, all special relationships have elements of fear in them. This is why they shift and change so frequently. They are not based on changeless love alone... The Holy Spirit knows that no one is special. Yet He also perceives that you have made special relationships, which he would purify and not let you destroy. However unholy the reason you made them may be, He can translate them into holiness by removing as much fear as you will let Him.[38]

The Holy Spirit is the author of the holy relationship. I cannot do it, but I cooperate, by inviting Him to remove the cause of fear. A central key to the Atonement and the holy relationship is the holy instant, the freedom from past and future, the freedom from fear, which allows perfect communication. The holy instant is the Holy Spirit's most helpful tool in protecting me from guilt. Guilt is what makes the special relationship attractive.[39] The past is the ego's chief learning device, maintaining memory of guilt.[40]

How the holy relationship works is presented more thoroughly in Part III, where application of these ideas is the focus.

Sidetrack: 1977-1987

I experienced severe depression, know family members with severe depression, and worked as a therapist with many clients with severe depression. The face of depression is quite familiar to me. That's why

I wrote this book. Depression is common and widespread. It is such a great suffering that many depressed kill themselves; many attempt to kill themselves; many consider killing themselves; many wish they were dead. Depressed people understand this. If you are not depressed, you probably know someone who suffers so. You probably know someone who completed suicide, or attempted suicide. How many of us die by slow suicide?

I can be depressed and not realize it. I might think I'm not depressed, or at least not *really* depressed. I might be depressed for a long time and become acclimated to it like the mountain climber becomes used to lack of oxygen. Depression becomes my "normal" state and I manage some form of function, perhaps self-medicating with alcohol or drugs or another avoidance strategy. ACIM describes ways in which I deny depression.

> **Yet some try to put by their suffering in games they play to occupy their time, and keep their sadness from them. Others will deny that they are sad, and do not recognize their tears at all. Still others will maintain that what we speak of is illusion, not to be considered more than but a dream...**
>
> **We speak today for everyone who walks this world, for he is not at home.**[41]

This applies to everyone. Everyone who is not in Heaven suffers because he is not home. Our illness is collective, though many deny it and some claim happiness. I can be deeply unhappy yet deny my unhappiness and seek various distractions and substitutes for happiness. Why is everyone doomed to suffering? Because this world is not our home. Awareness of truth is blocked until it isn't.

> The children of God are entitled to the perfect comfort
> that comes from perfect trust. Until they achieve this,
> they waste themselves and their true creative powers on
> useless attempts to make themselves more comfortable by
> inappropriate means.[42]

My attempts at happiness are *useless,* and I waste myself and my creative power in such attempts. *Inappropriate means* are *anything* I substitute for salvation. Each of us picks his poison. Apparently, the world's ways of wasting continue until perfect trust is realized.

Depression might not be realized until the depression lifts and the definite difference is noticed in hind sight. My experience confirmed this, even before my first major depressive episode at age twenty-seven. As a child my parents considered me to be "moody." I experienced intense feelings affecting me more deeply than most. This is why I preferred art as a means of expression. Words do not serve well in describing intense emotions. To name a feeling is to intellectualize it. The word sad is not the feeling sad. I often considered myself sad, but not all the time. I had good days and bad days. My swings were not serious enough to be considered Bipolar. I did not experience mania. I functioned fine enough most of the time, keeping my problems to myself. I could not consider suicide, a definite mortal sin with no chance to confess. I did well in school academically, but my interpersonal life sucked. I formed few friendships and believed everyone hated me. In elementary school, a sense of rejection saddened me so much that I cried myself to sleep frequently. So the blues became my normal, but not constant, state, and varied in intensity. I might DSM-IV diagnose myself with: "Dysthymic Disorder, Early Onset, With Atypical Features: long-standing pattern of interpersonal rejection sensitivity (not limited to episodes of mood disturbance) that results in significant social or occupational impairment."

I won't forget the first time I took LSD. I was nineteen and it seemed as if happiness found me for the first time in my life. I found everything hysterical and could not stop laughing. What a relief this was! Sadness disappeared. In my case, I did not realize how depressed I was until I felt what feeling *really* happy was like. LSD trips can go in the opposite direction; I was lucky the first time. At the time of this first psychedelic experience I asked my trip buddies, "Can we get more of this stuff?" Over 35 years I took LSD hundreds of times.

So what happened after I left the Abbey in New Mexico at age 21? Still undecided about vocation, I saw that my spiritual seeking was self-centered. New Camoldoli in Big Sur seemed like the best option, but I did not know for sure. My hesitation concerned the Catholic Church, not monastic life. In many ways, the church reminded me of the Jewish religion at the time of Jesus. Jesus is not described as friendly and obedient to the religious leaders. He reserved his harshest criticisms for them – brood of vipers, hypocrites. I wondered if Christianity strayed from the Master's teaching. I did not trust ecclesiastical authority, though I did trust a few holy persons who stayed loyal to the church and accepted its authority. The novice master, Fr. Adam, the Prior, Fr. Bruno, and the recluse, Fr. Joseph, all much wiser than me, encouraged more education before joining the Hermitage, if I did join. So I went back to school for two more years of college.

The first year I went to Foothill College in Los Altos Hills, and majored in music. I enjoyed school for the first time in a long time. I had a lot of energy and took a heavy load of music classes and worked part time as a dishwasher in Palo Alto. I commuted by bike and bus.

In 1977, the novice master at Big Sur invited me to an extended summer retreat of a couple months with a few other young men considering a vocation at the Hermitage. I went to Big Sur for the retreat but a schedule conflict shortened my stay. I struggled with dysfunctional family relationships all my life. My relationship with my father deteriorated and did not recover. I also felt regret about poor relationships with my four brothers. Although I gave up hope of healing the relationship with my father, I wanted to do better with my brothers. I devised a plan to invite them on a backpacking trip, hiking the John Muir trail, from Yosemite to Mt. Whitney, the highest mountain in the continental USA. Eventually three of them made the trip, or parts of it, and I left the retreat half way through to go backpacking with my brothers.

Next I moved to Arcata, California, and started my third year of college at Humboldt State University. I changed my major from music to religious studies. That seemed to make more sense if I decided to join the hermitage. While in school that year, I lived at the Newman Center, a Catholic university organization present at many colleges. I rented a room and I attended daily Mass right across the hall from my room. I played guitar at the Sunday Masses for the Newman community. About this time I met a woman, Dee, two years younger than me at the Newman Center. She wanted to become a Catholic. I became interested in her and encouraged her to be baptized in the church, which she did.

I liked my classes in religious studies and studied good books, like *The Idea of the Holy*, by Rudolf Otto. I started a job as a cab driver and joined a country and western band as the lead guitarist. During this time my right arm swelled up. It turned out that a blood clot, thrombosis, blocked the main vein in my right shoulder. Doctors hospitalized me for two weeks while they tried to dissolve the clot with blood thinners, with no luck. Then they planned to build a bypass of the clot with a piece of vein taken from one of my legs, a vascular plumbing job. A second opinion by a Newman community doctor changed the plan. He advised me to cancel surgery and see if collateral veins developed to relieve the bloody gridlock, and that's what happened.

I dropped out of school at the start of my second year at Humboldt State to take over ownership and operation of Arcata Taxi. The previous owner made an offer and I didn't refuse.

I returned to the Bay Area in 1979. I started working with my brother Robert installing hot tub systems. I learned how to do electrical and plumbing work, installing gas and electric lines to hot tubs. I found a grower of psychedelic mushrooms in nearby Palo Alto and started consuming them frequently. A regular routine established itself. About once a week, usually on Friday evenings, a seminary friend and I met at my house in Los Altos. My room, where several marijuana plants were growing, we affectionately named "the drug den." Friday nights were the weekly holy communion, consuming "flesh of the gods." We weighed out our dosage, usually 2-3 grams, and mixed the dried mushrooms with orange juice in a blender. It is easier to get down that way because the magic mushrooms taste not so magical, and being dried, are hard to chew and pieces get stuck between teeth, prolonging the taste. Immediately after drinking down the fungi juice we psychonauts, soon to be higher than astronauts, would drive to Stanford University. A quick five-mile drive up Foothill Expressway delivered us to the launch pad, so we had time to get there and park the car before the lift-off in consciousness, usually after about thirty minutes. Behind the university there is a large, hilly, greenbelt area with paved trails for miles. At night rarely anyone was there and beautiful views of the Bay Area lights abounded. I often wondered when an atomic bomb would incinerate the nearby military base, Moffett Field. After four or five hours, the mushrooms wore off and the two of us night-crawlers crawled back. We called ourselves the night-crawlers because of our weekly, nocturnal, psychedelic crawls where we tried to "find out" what was going on. We were like worms trying to understand the universe. We were trying find out. Find out what was not clear. While I lived in the seminary, one priest, Fr. Saussotte, seemed different than the rest. He seemed more a mystic. He taught math, a subject I liked and did well in. We shared a love of fishing and he nicknamed me "worms." So being a night-crawler, a worm and no man, suited me fine. I especially loved the difficult to describe change in consciousness I experienced with the mushrooms. It was the closest thing I had to a real spiritual experience. Another mystical experience eluded me and I wondered what, if anything, was wrong.

I remember one mushroom experience that seemed especially good. It happened during the day and in the same open space behind Stanford University. Several of us were having fun with the fungi. Sitting stoned on a stone with eyes closed and the sun shining pleasantly, I experienced a deep peace. No desires disturbed me. Deprived of nothing, I felt completely contented. It lasted only a few minutes, but I experienced it: true peace, and I saw how it related to not wanting anything. It is the opposite of craving. Sometimes a psychedelic experience is spiritual, or perhaps opens the door to the spiritual.

I was gearing up to grow my own mushrooms when I decided to take a break, after a few intense psychedelic experiences. I went for a solo backpacking trip in the usual place, Desolation Wilderness. I brought plenty of mushrooms and marijuana. While alone in the wilderness, I observed the change of consciousness in both directions, going up and going down. I wanted to stay in higher consciousness, but I could not do that by continuing to eat mushrooms. The drug consciousness change is temporary. I always came down. With mushrooms, higher consciousness is not a result of my effort; all I have to do is eat them. Nothing to brag about. Maybe I risked my sanity, yet the sober option seemed more insane. I did not yet realize how the dynamic of unconscious guilt prevented me from staying in Heaven.

During one solo backpacking trip in Desolation Wilderness I saw UFOs in the night sky – not close up – but I became curious about UFOs for the rest of my life. Then I made the stupid decision to spend the next night on top of Pyramid Peak for a better view of the UFOs. The temperature was cool but comfortable at my 8,000-foot base camp, but 2,000 feet higher Pyramid Peak was a different story. I did not consider the temperature difference and had not prepared with proper clothing or sleeping bag. Snow remained on top, with no wood for a fire. I knew it was too dangerous to try a slippery climb down in the dark, especially in my altered state. I basically froze all night waiting for the sun to rise. I imagined a newspaper article about a drugged solo backpacker who died of hypothermia atop Pyramid Peak in Desolation Wilderness. Is there a metaphor here? After backpacking I returned to the Hermitage to talk to the monks about my experiences.

I formed a plan to visit the place of my birth on my twenty-sixth birthday. I drove to and from King City the same day. My birth certificate listed the address of the hospital where I was born. After I arrived in King City I found the hospital. Empty and dilapidated with windows broken or boarded up, the abandoned hospital looked ready for demolition. I found a way into the building and walked around. Next I went to the Catholic Church where I was baptized, named after St. John the Baptist, one of my favorite (wilderness) saints. I went to the baptismal font and renewed my baptism, renouncing Satan and all his works. I went to the parish office and received a copy of my baptismal certificate. This place is close to the Hermitage in Big Sur, directly west over the coastal range, yet there is no road. I imagined that if I joined the Hermitage, I might walk from the place of my birth over the mountains to New Camaldoli.

Meanwhile, back on earth, I struggled in the relationship with my girlfriend, Dee, who didn't like drugs but occasionally partook and turned paranoid. I hesitated making a marriage commitment because such a choice eliminated the monastic option, though becoming a monk seemed less and less likely. I did not want to give up music, marijuana, and mushrooms. My spiritual life disappointed me. I was divided between vocations, not 100 percent sure about being a monk or married. I thought the solution might be to try to love one person, as an extension of the divine love I experienced five years earlier. Dee and I were engaged and then after much struggle I broke off the engagement, feeling terrible about the whole thing. I didn't want to hurt her or anyone, but I did not know what to do. I consulted with a priest about all this who knew us both from the beginning. He was the chaplain of the Newman Center at Humboldt State. It is well known that depression disables decision making.

I underwent my first period of severe depression at age twenty-seven. At the time I considered a variety of things to be at fault, or cause, of the depression. The psychonaut trips blasting into high orbit on LSD and mushrooms, and the re-entry, over and over, wore me down. I used marijuana daily. I attended the psychedelic celebrations civilians called Grateful Dead concerts whenever I could. Since the Bay Area homed the Dead, opportunities to help them make the music came several times a year. In 1980 the Dead took up residence at the Warfield Theater on Market Street in San Francisco for fifteen shows in three weeks. I attended fourteen of those shows as a full time job, driving up to the city five days per week, happy to be participating in the live albums the Dead were recording at these shows.

Getting a taste of Heaven and then slammed back into the sea of sorrow depressed me because I missed what I lost on re-entry. The sense of failure in my relationship with Dee and with a monastic vocation pressed down on me. The overall sense of spiritual failure depressed me and I'm sure psychedelics substituted for the real thing and served as an escape from the pain I felt, if I was lucky. I still believe, however, that the psychedelic experience helps deconstruct conditioning more efficiently than anything else, except direct mystical experience. God was absent, or playing hide and seek, as usual. Depression sufficed to cripple and paralyze me. I became completely dysfunctional, thinking constantly of death. Psychedelics are related to death-obsession as well, because I experienced a type of consciousness death/change whenever I visited that realm. I could not actually choose suicide, but I prayed that God would let me die as soon as possible. My death wish was sincere. Typical of depression, I no longer enjoyed anything. I wanted out. Nothing ever satisfied my longing for the love I experienced at age twenty-one.

This first bout of severe depression was mercifully short. I don't remember how long it lasted, no more than a few months. A cleansing fast and a trip to the Hermitage for a week-long retreat seemed to bring me out of it. I became interested in alternative health, primarily through the writings of Paul Bragg like *The Miracle of Fasting*, and *The Shocking Truth About Water*. Over the years I tried many types of fasting cleanses, and drank only distilled water.

When Dee and I broke up, she moved away. After a few months I went to see her and we were re-engaged. We went on a Catholic "Engaged Encounter," a retreat for couples planning to marry. It felt like jumping off a cliff. I wasn't sure it was the right thing to do but it seemed like the best option. I did it on faith, flying blind. I realized there were no guarantees and trusting God meant risking a mistake. I had tried to play it safe by avoiding such a major risk. Monks take temporary vows, for three years, before final vows – a lifetime commitment. No such option with marriage. We married in 1982, drove to Lake Tahoe for our honeymoon, and hiked in the High Sierras. Things were OK for a while. I felt grateful for life and wanted to procreate children, or at least one child, to share life. I did not learn for ten years that Dee considered our marriage a mistake from the first year. During the first five years of our marriage we lived in Los Altos at the same house where I grew up. The drug den became the lion's den of marriage. I worked various odd jobs, mostly gardening and outdoor carpentry work like building fences and decks.

In 1986 I took a job as a messenger, driving all over the Bay Area delivering packages. I crashed and totaled our Toyota cargo van. I didn't see the car coming and it sounded like the car that broadsided and knocked over the van actually entered into my vehicle.

Eventually the car accident led to a great job with the same company. I delivered airline tickets and traveler's checks all over Stanford University by bicycle. I loved bicycling and enjoyed riding all over campus because my route was mostly off streets and away from cars. I spent spare time at the Stanford library viewing photography books. Dee worked for British Petroleum (BP) in San Francisco and since they were closing their office there, they offered her a transfer to Alaska. I was all for the move. As great as the Bay Area is, it is also crowded and expensive. I don't like traffic. I started making photographs after taking my first class in photography at Foothill College. Developing my first roll of Tri-X film and printing my first contact sheet excited me. I could do this! Alaska: wilderness land, low population, and likely a great place to pursue landscape photography.

In 1987 we moved to Alaska and settled in Anchorage. Dee was pregnant when we moved and in November 1987 our first child was born, a girl, named Alicen. This was a happy time. I wanted a girl. I had four brothers and no sisters. Only my brother Mickey married besides me and they produced two boys. About time for a girl in our family! The next bout of serious depression was about four years away. To be continued.

Chapter Eight

AS THE WORLD TURNS IT BURNS, YOU LEARN

*a*CIM teaches a clear view of the world, a view congruent with the view of Jesus in these quotes from John's Gospel and ACIM. John:

> In the world you have tribulation; but be of good cheer, I have overcome the world.[1]

ACIM:

> *In this world you need not have tribulation because I have overcome the world. That is why you should be of good cheer.[2]*

The difference between these two quotes is that one says we will have tribulation in the world and one says that we do not need to have tribulation in the world. Both are true because we have tribulation before we don't. Both quotes agree that Jesus overcame the world, and because of this, we have hope. John:

> If the world hates you, know that it hated me before it hated you. If you were of the world, the world would love its own; but because you are not of the world, but I chose you out of the world, therefore the world hates you.[3]

John:

> He who loves his life loses it, and he who hates his life in this world will keep it for eternal life.[4]

Jesus here is not advocating hating life. The significant qualifier is *in this world*. In this world, if I want liberation, I take the painful path to hating my life. I might get depressed. Getting to the point of hating one's life in this world is a good description of depression. Getting to this place, what ACIM calls the "lowest point," is necessary for everyone. Until I surrender to this emptying I still hope for some solution in the world. It is a trick designed to continue hell and myself.

> **There is a tendency to think the world can offer consolation and escape from problems that its purpose is to keep.**[5]

Naturally, I look for solutions to my problems in the world. Yet the world is designed so that I keep my problems and thus the world frustrates hope of escape to the point of despair. A depressed person might try many kinds of treatment: psychotherapy, medications, diet and exercise, meditation, mindfulness, hypnosis, electroshock, self-medication, you name it. The guy who developed the quick and easy lobotomy received the Nobel Prize for this therapy! Most of the time these methods attempt to treat brain symptoms, not cause. For some people these methods may help relieve symptoms of depression and that is good enough for a lot of us. I just want the pain to go away. Yet temporary symptom relief is like a prisoner who moves to a different, maybe nicer, cell. He may have a better view through the bars but he is still a prisoner. How many treatments did you try to free yourself from depression? Is the outcome the same?

> **Perhaps you fancy to attain some peace and satisfaction in the world as you perceive it. Yet it must be evident the outcome does not change. Despite your hopes and fancies, always does despair result.**[6]

Always does despair result? That's rough. A hint about the world, however, is given: *as you perceive it.* Or, even if not depressed, I still might search for fulfillment in the world seeking whatever or whomever I think makes me happy.

> **Is it not strange that you should cherish still some hope
> of satisfaction from the world you see? In no respect, at
> any time or place, has anything but fear and guilt been
> your reward. How long is needed for you to realize the
> chance of change in this respect is hardly worth delaying
> change that might result in a better outcome? For one
> thing is sure; the way you see, and long have seen, gives no
> support to base your future hopes, and no suggestion of
> success at all. To place your hopes where no hope lies must
> make you hopeless. Yet is this hopelessness your choice.[7]**

How long do I want to play in the world and keep trying for happiness the world promises, but never delivers? The happy payoff is in the future, yet I never get there. I keep trying different "roads" the world offers, but in so doing I am distracted and delay the solution that actually works. As I continue in the ways of the world, disappointment accumulates into hopelessness. I choose this despair? That's what the course teaches. It is not that I consciously choose despair. But when I choose to pursue the world, I am choosing for despair because there is no hope in the world.

In this world, trials and tribulations prevail over peace and joy because the world cannot satisfy me.

> **When you let your mind be drawn to bodily concerns,
> to things you buy, to eminence as valued by the world,
> you ask for sorrow, not for happiness…There are no
> satisfactions in the world.[8]**

I suffer *bodily concerns* because I identify with a body. If I want what the world offers, I am seeking sorrow. It is not easy to learn *there are no satisfactions in the world*. How do I learn that? Mostly by trial and error. The world is a teasing temptress promising pleasure – just not yet. Frustrations accumulate until, perhaps in old age, it finally dawns on me that there might be a better way. Or else I despair to death and lose this round. Eventually, and inevitably, I will not break down in despair; I will break *through* despair. How long this takes is up to me. Perhaps one's life is hunky dory. The world is being nice to me. My *dreams* are coming true. Success at last! Beware, the Apostle John warns us in his First Letter:

> **Do not love the world or the things in the world. If any one loves the world, love for the Father is not in him. For all that is in the world, the lust of the flesh and the lust of the eyes and the pride of life, is not of the Father but is of the world. And the world passes away, and the lust of it; but he who does the will of God abides forever.**[9]

All the pleasure and "happiness" the world teases is temporary. Who does not die and lives forever? The one who does the Will of God. This is the one who realizes his will is God's Will. One Will is not the wish of the world, where billions of wills conflict.

> **It is hard indeed to wander off, alone and miserable, down a road that leads to nothing and that has no purpose.**[10]

Alone and miserable, going down a road to nowhere, with no purpose, is a pretty good description of depression. Since the world is an illusion, all the choices it offers are illusions as well. It is easy to get tricked into the magic matrix maze for a long, long time, repeating an endless loop, a vicious and useless circle.

ACIM uses the metaphor *idol* to describe an illusionary desire that keeps me searching for a solution in the world, *outside* of myself.

> **Seek not outside yourself. For it will fail, and you will weep each time an idol falls...for all your pain comes simply from a futile search for what you want, insisting where it must be found. Do you prefer to be right or happy?**[11]

When I insist on what I want and where it is, I'm operating out of my separate will, the worldly-mindedness of ego. When I insist I'm right, I opt for misery. This won't work because what ends hell is ending separation. The world is the magic kingdom of separation where the separated celebrate suffering. There is no solution outside of me because there is nothing outside of me. My senses *(lust of the eyes)* say there is something outside of me but perception is part of the idol illusion. It's a trick fooling fools. Would I rather be right, and depressed, or be gratefully happy to be wrong? Open mind is a state of "I don't know." Insistence is idiotic idolatry and absurd if I know I don't know.

> **It is vain to worship idols in the hope of peace. God dwells within, and your completion lies in Him. No idol takes His place. Look not to idols. Do not seek outside yourself.**[12]

When I feel lack of any kind, where do I look for relief? It is usually "outside" myself, in the world, isn't it? Idols take a variety of forms. One form is an illusion about my identity and the identity of others. Other idols include bodies, things, places, situations, possessions, rights. All these forms are substitutes for what truly brings peace. How often do I wish, "If only I had that job," "If only I married her," "If only I owned that house, that car," "If only I lived in that place." If only, if only, if only. If only this world wasn't so cruel.

> **An idol is an image of your brother that you would value more than what he is. Idols are made that he may be replaced, no matter what their form…be it a body or a thing, a place, a situation or a circumstance, an object owned or wanted, or a right demanded or achieved, it is the same…let not their form deceive you. Idols are but substitutes for your reality.**[13]

I substitute things of the world for what is missing: awareness of love, peace, and union. Missing my heavenly home, I get tricked to try endless idols, illusions, substitutes for the truth. I know something is an idol by its appearing outside myself. Whatever I see outside of myself is a projection and not real, and thus can never satisfy. If you meet the Buddha on a road...

> No one who comes here but must still have hope, some lingering illusion, or some dream that there is something outside of himself that will bring happiness and peace to him...The lingering illusion...will impel him to seek out a thousand idols, and to seek beyond them for a thousand more. And each will fail him...[14]

Apparently, I am here because I want the world, the place of separation, where I get to be special me. In the final desert temptation, the devil offers Jesus all the kingdoms of the world and their glory if he worships "me." But his kingdom is not of this world and his response to the devil is "Begone Satan." If the Christ tells Satan to be gone, then Satan is gone. Even so, I can still claim that Satan is not gone.

The wish for separation led to a dream that the separation is real. Idols are lures designed to maintain faith in the dream. The fake worm looks like a real worm to the hungry fish. The happy meal is just around the corner, but watch out for the barbed hook.

> All idols of this world were made to keep the truth within from being known to you, and to maintain allegiance to the dream that you must find what is outside yourself to be complete and happy.[15]

The way of the world, and the way of the ego, is to want more. Everything I want is "outside" of me. Wanting more means I'm deprived and needy. Idols promise more.

> Each worshiper of idols harbors hope his special deities will give him more than other men possess. It must be more. It does not really matter more of what; more beauty,

> more intelligence, more wealth, or even more affliction
> and more pain. But more of something is an idol for.
> And when one fails, another takes its place, with hope of
> finding more of something else...An idol is a means for
> getting more. And it is this that is against God's Will.[16]

If I bite the bait, I get burned. To desire more, or to own more, is to believe in the separation and deprivation. Do I want more depression? Do I want to be more depressed than others? Do I want to win the competition crowning me the king of pain? Do I win some kind of spiritual trophy for suffering more than you? To achieve *more than other men* is the American *dream* of getting ahead, is it not? Who do I get ahead of? Don't worry about the homeless hungry, my wealth will trickle down to them eventually, just not in this lifetime. If my true identity is as the *one* Son of God, the Christ, then how can one person have more, or need more, than another, except in the delusion of separation and specialness?

To seek for more is against God's Will because God already gave all to all. God is all in all. This is the thought reversal the course teaches. Eventually I learn that having is being. I already have everything just by nature of my being. Wanting idols denies the truth that God gives all to all. All the meaningless junk I seem to want, that appears to be outside of me, in the world, is illusion. I want more of illusions that cannot satisfy me and ignore the abundance of being God gives now.

> You do not really want the world you see, for it has
> disappointed you since time began.[17]

Is this what hell is? The craving for more, more, more? More frustration, disappointment, despair, and depression? Real peace does not want anything.

ACIM describes two different worlds. One is the real world. The other is the illusionary, projected world of separation I believe is real.

> Sit quietly and look upon the world you see, and tell
> yourself: "The real world is not like this. It has no
> buildings and there are no streets where people walk alone
> and separate. There are no stores where people buy an
> endless list of things they do not need."[18]

Living in the material world. It lets me down because it's not my
home. Come Christmas, kids compete for material things. How long
is it before they tire of their toys?

> The homes you built have never sheltered you. The roads
> you made have led you nowhere, and no city that you built
> has withstood the crumbling assault of time.[19]

All things must pass. Everything in this world, including the universe
itself, is temporary and passes away. This is a simple, scientific fact,
no matter how much I might ignore it. All form is fiction.

> What *seems* eternal will all have an end. The stars will
> disappear, and night and day will be no more. All things
> that come and go, the tides, the seasons and the lives of
> men; all things that change with time and bloom and fade
> will not return.[20]

Think of all the people, places, and empires already absent. What
is the few years of a human life in this world compared to fourteen
billion years of the space-time continuum?

> The world you see is merciless indeed, unstable, cruel,
> unconcerned with you, quick to avenge and pitiless with
> hate. It gives but to rescind, and takes away all things that
> you have cherished for a while. No lasting love is found,
> for none is here. This is the world of time, where all
> things end.[21]

The world of time is the world of impermanence, where all things end.

ACIM teaches that God did not create this world, a common Gnostic teaching. Many believe God did, in fact, create the world, and not only create it, but saw it as good. Is the world I see good? Is the world God created and saw as good the same world He regretted making and so destroyed with the flood? Is this the God who makes a mistake? The world, and everything in it, is temporary. If God made this world, then He made a place for billions of beings to suffer and die.

> **You who feel threatened by this changing world, its twists of fortune and its bitter jests, its brief relationships and all the "gifts" it merely lends to take away again; attend this lesson well. The world provides no safety. It is rooted in attack, and all its "gifts" of seeming safety are illusory deceptions.** [22]

The world and its idols are deceptions. Is God a deceiver? God did not create the world, but He did create us, His Son. ACIM teaches, again and again, that I am as God created me. God's love is so strong, it does not change, except perhaps to increase, if the maximum increases. It simply continues to extend, endlessly, timelessly. The course addresses the Biblical claim, "For God so loved the world":

> **The world you see cannot be the world God loves, and yet His Word assures us that He loves the World.** [23]

Three back-to-back lessons in the *Workbook For Students* state:

> **The world I see holds nothing I want.** [24]

> **Beyond this world there is a world I want.** [25]

> **It is impossible to see two worlds.** [26]

It is impossible to see two worlds is a declaration of non-duality. It is impossible to see two worlds because there are not two worlds. One is not real, an illusion. Apparently there is another world (the real world) beyond this world, yet I can't have both. Wanting this world, or aspects of it, blocks my awareness of the real world of knowledge, peace, love, and joy.

In this world war of duality, there appears conflict between illusion and truth, between wrong-mindedness and right-mindedness, between the ego's thought system and the thought system of the Holy Spirit, between self-image and Self, between special relationship and holy relationship. God did create the perfect utopia of Heaven. In my wish for independence I seemed to exit paradise, to find out what happens when I try to make my own world, be my own boss. What actually happens is I fall into a deep sleep and lose awareness of Heaven. I become unconscious, like the prize fighter, knocked out by a sucker self punch. Dazed, and dreaming nightmares, amnesia took over. Knocked down, I dived into a coma of confusion for the canvas count.

> **The Son of God believes that he is lost in guilt, alone in a dark world where pain is pressing everywhere upon him from without.**[27]

Notice that being alone, or separate, is a belief, as is the world I perceive as a dark place full of pain where the lonely are lost in guilt. The world is only a cruel claim with no ontological basis.

As far as this world eventually evolving into some kind of utopia, there are surface improvements over the centuries, certainly, but is the dark side simply more insidious by being more subtle? Slavery ended, for the most part, right? Well, is it not more accurate to say we substituted for slavery a minimum wage slavery and a world of disparity where one percent of the population owns 99 percent of the wealth. A few bank billions while billions starve. Psychiatry exchanged canvas straight jackets for chemical ones. Tribes traded local killings for global wars of nations; "shock and awe" of mass destruction replaced sticks and stones. The efficiency of harm and attack continues to evolve. Millions of young girls suffer genital mutilation today. In some places, women have come a long way. One hundred years ago women were not allowed to vote in the United States. Is someone forcing scientists to build biological, chemical, and nuclear weapons? Who is forcing God's kids to keep killing after thousands of years of "Thou shall not kill?" And why would an all-powerful, all-loving, and all knowing God create this slaughterhouse world of pain? Boredom? Entertainment? Too much leisure in Heaven? Some people are atheist because they cannot believe that the Highest Wisdom and Most Holy Love created this brutal battlefield of a world. Am I depressed yet? The world is depressing. I did not say it; ACIM says it.

> There is nothing so frustrating to a learner as a curriculum he cannot learn. His sense of adequacy suffers, and he must become depressed. Being faced with an impossible learning situation is the most depressing thing in the world. In fact it is ultimately why the world itself is depressing.[28]

It is frustrating and depressing because it won't work. Idols trick and tempt me, over and over again, to dream the impossible dream.

Disappointments accumulate into depression, despair, and death. Eventually I learn to give up the world, or keep on suffering. Renouncing the world is sacrificing nothing but illusions and despair. There is a better way.

> An ancient hate is passing from the world. Give up the world! You never wanted it. What happiness have you sought here that did not bring you pain? What moment of content has not been bought at fearful price in coins of suffering? Your experiences here were not free from bitter cost and joyless consequence.[29]

Because of the separation, I lost the awareness of love's presence. So I seek for love in substitutes that cannot satisfy. Not finding it I use pain killers that work on symptoms and not cause. As tolerance increases, numbing power decreases. I seek different and stronger poisons, potions that deceptively advertise relief, yet perpetuate pain.

> **Do you realize that the ego must set you on a journey which cannot but lead to a sense of futility and depression?**[30]

Looking for love and not finding it is the soap opera drama of this world turning and burning into self-defeat, futility, and depression. I pay a heavy price in heavy chains for choosing to believe the ego and wanting what it whispers.

> **There is no gain in the world for of itself it profits nothing. Not only is there no profit but the cost to you is enormous.**[31]

The cost is shame of sin, guilt, fear, suffering, and depressing despair unto death. How happy.

> **You have paid dearly for your illusions, and nothing you have paid for brought you peace.**[32]

If I look for hope in the world, I find despair, because illusions can't bring peace. Hope in the world is hopeless.

> **You looked upon the unreal and found despair. The unreal world is a thing of despair.**[33]

The way out of worldly despair is God's plan for Atonement. Relief is nowhere in the world. I resist giving up the world because I believe renouncing it is a sacrifice. In truth, when I renounce the world, I sacrifice suffering.

> The world you see holds nothing that you need to offer
> you; nothing that you can use in any way, nor anything
> at all that serves to give you joy. Believe this thought,
> and you are saved from years of misery, from countless
> disappointments, and from hopes that turn to bitter ashes
> of despair.[34]

Jesus promises that realizing the futility of the world saves me from years of misery, disappointments, and bitter despair, because I won't want the world, nor its worrying ways. I will no longer expect any relief from the world. Or not. I'm free to continue looking for relief in the world, but ACIM is trying to save me time and save me pain. If I believe the world offers something I want, then I believe in lack because I am deprived. Wanting anything means I'm lacking. Even wanting God implies God is gone. Is Christ needy?

> Let nothing that relates to body thoughts delay your
> progress to salvation, nor permit temptation to believe the
> world holds anything you want to hold you back. Nothing
> is here to cherish. Nothing here is worth one instant of
> delay and pain; one moment of uncertainty and doubt.[35]

What does the mind want for the body other than what is in the world? The body *is* of the world but I am not. The choice to delay or quicken release is mine to make.

Few of us simply see the truth and accept it. Most of us learn the hard way, seeking substitutes and lured by shiny things with hidden hooks. Tranquilized by trivialities or comfortably numb is the best I can do. The temporary fix wears off and I want more, and so it goes, around and around; needy me never stops wanting.

> Thus you think, within the narrow band from birth to
> death, a little time is given for you to use for you alone;
> a time when everyone conflicts with you, but you can

choose which road will lead you out of conflict, and away
from difficulties that concern you not. Yet they are your
concern.[36]

I am free to try whatever tasty tricks the world offers to avoid what I
cannot avoid. All the world's temptations are deceptions, idols outside
of me that prolong pain. I think I can choose a path out of pain but it
does not matter which hell highway I choose; they all are dead ends.

> **Real choice is no illusion. But the world has none to offer.
> All its roads lead to disappointment, nothingness, and
> death…Seek not escape from problems here…**[37]

There is no real choice among all the world's shiny streets. All of the
world's titanic trains derail into destruction regardless of who I think
I am – a rock star, a Bowery drunk, or paralyzed by depression.

> **All of them will lead to death. On some you travel gaily
> for a while, before the bleakness enters. And on some the
> thorns are felt at once.**[38]

It is not a matter of if; it is a matter of when. It is not a matter of finding the right road; there is no right road in the world.

Suicide

I might be tempted to choose suicide upon realizing that all the
world's dark alleys lead to the same meaningless end.

> **Perhaps you would prefer to try them all, before you really
> learn they are but one. The roads this world can offer seem
> to be quite large in number, but the time must come when
> everyone begins to see how alike they are to one another.
> Men have died on seeing this, because they saw no way
> except the pathways offered by the world. And learning
> they led nowhere, lost their hope.**[39]

This is the *lowest point*. This is the point of disillusionment, existential despair, and suicide. Nothing works. The world, my world, crashes completely; I'm a loser. This applies to everyone. Everyone eventually learns that this world does not work. Even though reaching the lowest point can lead to despair, it is also an opportunity.

> **...and yet this was the time they could have learned their greatest lesson. All must reach this point, and go beyond it.**[40]

The word "crisis" contains two meanings in the Chinese pictograph: danger and opportunity. So, excruciating as it is to arrive at this critical low point, it is *the* opportunity to learn my greatest lesson.

> **Learn now, without despair, there is no hope of answer in the world.**[41]

We all reach this place that is the prison exit. If I still hope for peace in this world, then the lowest point is yet to come.

Given all this bad news about the world, is it any wonder I tire of living in it? Depression is so painful that many depressed people kill themselves. It seems like the only solution, a mercy killing, but it's actually a mistake of madness. If I kill myself, I kill the body, and the body is not the problem. Suicide makes things worse because I add more guilt to the guilt already blocking my re-awakening. In suicide the ego wins that particular round, even though the good end is inevitable. Suicide is a drama of delay, which is what the ego wants. It's continuity is contingent on me coming back in serial dreams. Killing myself is agreeing with the ego that I suffer, and I die, because I'm identified with the body, a special, separate, suffering, and hopeless, case. Liberation from separation happens while I appear to be in the separation. If I kill myself, I lose this opportunity to use my life for liberation and must return to try again because I'm not yet ready for Heaven.

> The death penalty is the ego's ultimate goal. You judge
> yourself unworthy and condemn yourself to death.
> Wanting to kill you as the final expression of its feeling
> for you, it lets you live but to await death. It will torment
> you while you live.[42]

If I kill myself, I'm agreeing with the ego's thought system. I am duped. I cannot kill my *Self*, but I can murder the body's so-called life. Thus I must return to finish the purification of guilt. The ego recruits minds for its battlefield world like the government recruits teenagers and high school dropouts to join the army, be all you can be, visit exotic lands, meet beautiful and interesting people, and kill them. Life is not fair and it sucks to be me, so, goodbye cruel world.

> By confusing yourself with the ego, you believe that you
> want death. And from what you want God does not save
> you.[43]

The ego's plan for its own continuity is this: keep flunking, don't graduate. Rinse and repeat. Helter Skelter. Stay in identity-confusion.

There are many stories of people who attempted suicide, but lived. When they report a near-death experience, they often describe an immediate and severe regret about attempting suicide. On the other side they realize that suicide is a big mistake. Guilt and regret increase for such a serious "sin."

> You must learn the cost of sleeping, and refuse
> to pay it. Only then will you decide to awaken.[44]

The cost of sleeping is suffering and the solution is to wake up from restless sleep and end dreaming. Was there ever an end to suffering in this world? Was there a pause in suffering when Buddha, the Awakened One, and Jesus, the Christ, walked the earth? Suicide only seems like a solution to suffering. I cannot kill myself any more than the crucifixion killed Christ.

> **When you are tempted to yield to the desire for death, remember that I [Jesus] did not die.**[45]

Jesus says "when" I am tempted to suicide, not "if." The Resurrection proves Jesus did not die. They could not kill him. He is not a body. He overcame the world's belief in death.

> **As long as you believe the Son of God is guilty you will walk along this carpet [time], believing that it leads to death. And the journey will seem long and cruel and senseless, for so it is.**[46]

Guilt keeps me out of Heaven, or rather, my belief in guilt. Suicide is killing a body and leads to more belief in guilt. I feel guilty for being a failure, guilty for self-murder, and guilty for the pain my suicide causes others. Suicide is the logical end of identity-confusion disorder. I can kill the body but I cannot kill the Self. If I identify as a body, and most of us do, then I can kill myself, because I can kill the body. I will lose everything in this world, including the body, yet I cannot lose being.

> **You have handled this wish to kill yourself by not knowing who you are, and identifying with someone else.**[47]

To make matters worse, killing myself won't end my pain. If I'm guilty of self-murder, then I deserve eternal punishment in hell.

> **Out of the ego's unwillingness for you to find peace even in death, it offers immortality in hell. The belief in hell is inescapable to those who identify with the ego.**[48]

Is there a difference between murder and self-murder? Suicide is not a solution; there is no death.

> **Death is an attempt to resolve conflict by not deciding at all. It will not work.**[49]

The retreat to death is not the end of conflict.[50]

The world is not left by death but by truth…[51]

Swear not to die, you holy Son of God! You make a bargain that you cannot keep. The Son of Life cannot be killed. He is immortal as his Father. What he is cannot be changed.[52]

I might not believe in guilt and punishment in hell after death and so reason that if the body is an illusion and no one can die, then why not terminate the body and get off this crazy pain train? The reason why not is that the body is used by the Holy Spirit for liberation if I let Him.

The body is the means by which God's Son returns to sanity. Though it was made to fence him into hell without escape, yet has the goal of Heaven been exchanged for the pursuit of hell. The Son of God extends his hand to reach his brother, and to help him walk along the road with him. Now is the body holy. Now it serves to heal the mind that it was made to kill.[53]

Do I want to kill the means which returns me to sanity? The ego's use of the body is for pleasure and pain, death and hell. The Holy Spirit has a different use for the body: communication with my brothers.

The Holy Spirit sees the body only as a means of communication, and because communicating is sharing it becomes communion.[54]

I let the ego use the body to attack and condemn or I let the Holy Spirit use the body to communicate truth.

> Remember that the Holy Spirit interprets the body only
> as a means of communication. Being the Communication
> Link between God and His separated Sons, the Holy
> Spirit interprets everything you have made in the light of
> what He is. The ego separates through the body. The Holy
> Spirit reaches through it to others. You do not perceive
> your brothers as the Holy Spirit does, because you do
> not regard bodies solely as a means of joining minds and
> uniting them with yours and mine. This interpretation of
> the body will change your mind entirely about its value.
> Of itself it has none.[55]

The Holy Spirit and I need the body temporarily. I am liberated with
my brother. As I liberate my brother, so I liberate myself. The body is
the means the Holy Spirit uses for communication between brothers.

> Why is the illusion of many necessary? Only because
> reality is not understandable to the deluded. Only very
> few can hear God's Voice at all, and even they cannot
> communicate His messages directly through the Spirit
> which gave them. They [brothers] need a medium through
> which communication becomes possible to those who do
> not realize that they are spirit. A body they can see. A
> voice they understand and listen to, without the fear that
> truth would encounter in them. Do not forget that truth
> can come only where it is welcomed without fear. So do
> God's teachers need a body, for their unity could not be
> recognized directly.[56]

Thus, if I commit suicide, I lose the means of communication with my
brother that the Holy Spirit uses to teach truth. Yet I do not destroy
my potential to communicate. Being born again gives this potential
means again in another body capable of communication with other
parts of my Self who think they are bodies.

> You can wait, delay, paralyze yourself, or reduce your
> creativity almost to nothing. But you cannot abolish it.
> You can destroy your medium of communication, but not
> your potential. You did not create yourself.[57]

I don't know about you, but I hope not to be born again in another body. Suicide might guarantee my return. That possibility alone is enough to convince me to forget about suicide.

No one ever kills himself. Suicide is a dream event that delays waking up. Getting to the lowest point, where I realize there is no hope in this world, leads to suicidal despair, or not. Maybe I get to this point many times before I learn there is another way, an alternative to despair. The solution is not found outside of myself or anywhere in this world. So give it up. Sooner rather than later if pain wearies you.

> Why would you seek to try another road, another person,
> or another place...seek not another signpost in the world
> that seems to point to still another road. No longer look
> for hope where there is none. Make fast your learning
> now, and understand you but waste time unless you go
> beyond what you have learned to what is yet to learn.[58]

It is not enough just to realize there is no hope in the world. If I do not go beyond that, without despairing, I waste time, rinsing and repeating. There is a big difference between "no hope" and "no hope in the world."

> From this lowest point will learning lead to heights of
> happiness...[59]

The *lowest point* is where and when I either commit suicide or turn around. It is the point where I realize that every peace the world promises fails. Duality does not work.

> The learning that the world can offer but one choice,
> no matter what its form may be, is the beginning of
> acceptance that there is a real alternative instead.[60]

What is the one choice offered by the world in a plethora of painful poses? It is the same depressing destination of all the bad byways of the world: despair unto death. So I begin to return to Heaven, the real alternative, after I reach the *lowest point* and realize there is no solution in the world. Not sex, not drugs, not fame, not beauty, not wealth, not pleasure, not prestige, not legacy. Nothing. These are all wrong ways of the world, substitutes for Heaven, idols, designed to lure me into postponing the ending of hell.

What the world offers is puny compared to God's generous grace of the Maximum. Only the Maximum satisfies because God designed me for the Maximum.

> Everything in this world is little because it is a world made
> out of littleness, in the strange belief that littleness can
> content you. When you strive for anything in this world
> in the belief that it will bring you peace, you are belittling
> yourself and blinding yourself to glory…Choose littleness
> and you will not have peace…It is essential that you
> accept the fact, and accept it gladly, that there is no form
> of littleness that can ever content you. You are free to try
> as many as you wish, but all you will be doing is to delay
> your homecoming.[61]

The idea that I can find peace in the world is a strange belief. Peace is an inner state and has nothing to do with the world. World peace is an oxymoron.

ACIM teaches that not only will the world let me down, but that *there is no world*. This is the *central thought* the course tries to teach.

> There is no world! This is the central thought the course
> attempts to teach. Not everyone is ready to accept it, and
> each must go as far as he can let himself be led along
> the road to truth. He will return and go still farther, or
> perhaps step back a while and then return again. But
> healing is the gift of those who are prepared to learn there
> is no world, and can accept the lesson now.[62]

This is a radical teaching, no doubt, and *not everyone is ready to accept it.* In the same passage the course goes on to teach that some discover this truth, that there is no world, on point of death; some find it in experience that is not of this world; and some find it in ACIM. Is the world a virtual reality? Is it a dream? A mental matrix? What happens to the dream world and dream figures when I wake up? Where do they go? Do they seem real when I'm dreaming? Is the world only an image in my mind? The world will disappear like a dream when I awaken.

The roads of the world lead to despair because they lead to a false identity, an identity substitution that cannot work. Illusion leads to illusion, and confusion.

> All roads that lead away from what you are will lead you to
> confusion and despair.[63]

In duality, all attempts to reconcile the two opposite sides fail because there are not two sides, only one Self. The other is an illusion and an illusion cannot be reconciled with what is true, anymore than darkness is reconciled with light. Until I accept that this compromise is not possible I look for solutions in the world and none of them work. Trying to make duality work is futile, and depressing.

> Until you have accepted this, you will attempt an endless
> list of goals you cannot reach; a senseless series of
> expenditures of time and effort, hopefulness and doubt,
> each one as futile as the one before, and failing as the next
> one surely will.[64]

The teaching of ACIM about the world is clear and repeated. Like the ego, the world is not evil; it is an illusion, a projection, not real, a dream world only. Many other teachings encourage embracing the world, changing the world, loving the world, seeing the world as good and so forth. Not ACIM. The problem is not in the world but in my perception of the world. The transformation is in my mind, not in the world. Sometimes, when studying what the course teaches about the ego, special relationships, the world, and the resulting suffering, it seems as if the course is specifically for depressed persons, or anyone who suffers, or anyone weary with the ways of the world. It seems to understand my discontent, desperation, and despair. Maybe it also understands the way out.

> You see in death escape from what you made. But this
> you do not see; that you made death, and it is but illusion
> of an end. Death cannot be escape, because it is not life
> in which the problem lies. Life has no opposite, for it is
> God. Life and death seem to be opposites because you
> have decided death ends life. Forgive the world, and you
> will understand that everything that God created cannot
> have an end, and nothing He did not create is real. In this
> one sentence is our course explained. In this one sentence
> is our practicing given its one direction. And in this one
> sentence is the Holy Spirit's whole curriculum specified
> exactly as it is.[65]

ACIM is not the only teaching declaring the world a dream. Row, row, rowing my boat, gently down the stream, merrily I learn that life in this world is but a dream. The idea that the world is an illusion is common in eastern philosophies and theologies, but this idea is not considered Christian. Yet, even in Christianity wisdom teachers wonder. Fr. Thomas Keating:

> Are we simply God's thoughts, and is this whole evolving
> universe from the Big Bang on in fact an illusion?...Could
> it be that what we are experiencing is just an illusion or
> the most elaborate dream ever?[66]

In this same passage, Keating goes on to quote the famous passage
from Shakespeare's *As You Like It*:

> All the world's a stage,
> And all the men and women merely players.[67]

The notion that there is no external world might be depressing if
the story ended there. In the transition to Heaven I make the perceptual shift to the real world. The real world is still part of perception
and temporary. But the nightmare has changed to a happy dream as
I prepare to let all dreaming go. What has changed is my perception.
Now I see the world through the forgiving eyes of Christ instead of
the ego's eyes.

> God's teachers can have no regret on giving up the
> pleasures of the world. Is it a sacrifice to give up pain?
> Does an adult resent the giving up of children's toys?
> Does one whose vision has already glimpsed the face of
> Christ look back with longing on a slaughter house?[68]

The Free Fine Feast

Imagine you are an ordinary person, working and scraping by,
living paycheck to paycheck. You are on a tight budget and are careful with spending. You don't like your job but you can't afford to quit.
You watch football and drink beer on weekends. Or maybe you smoke
pot and go to rock and roll shows.

Then one day, low and behold, you win the lottery. Suddenly you are a millionaire. Things are looking up. The world is being generous to you.

Another prize included with your lottery win is a free dinner at the most expensive restaurant in the world, world-famous for its delicious food and fine wines. Well, this ought to be a treat. Few but the radically rich dine and wine at this establishment. Brokers, bankers, and billionaires are the exclusive club patronizing this place. You would not try it yourself, but a complementary dinner? Why not enjoy a new experience? You make your reservation.

When you arrive at the restaurant, it is unbelievably fancy. You are seated at their best table with the best view. You have your own personal waiter. There are no prices on the menu. If you need to ask, you can't afford it. This place is for those who don't care what it costs and write it off on their taxes as a business expense anyway.

You order and you are brought old wine and warm, buttered bread. Both are incredible, the best you ever tasted. This place is living up to the hype. This is quite pleasurable. You are enjoying this free fine feast.

You look out the window and see a person there looking in at you and your table. Just a passerby, but he stays there and keeps watching you. Annoying. Then another person comes and stares, and another. You look closer and realize they are poor people. They look like homeless street people. Apparently there are thousands of them in this greatest city in the New World, Modern Yorkshire. The group of gawkers grows as does your grumbling about it. How are you supposed to enjoy this priceless meal with all these hungry homeless humans looking at you?

More and more people come to see what is going on. Soon there is a large crowd. A massive mob is assembling, as far as you can see. Now the wine does not taste so good. Now the food is not so great. Now you are not enjoying yourself so much. In fact, now you start to feel bad. This was supposed to be fun and free. Now you realize more is not much of anything. How can you enjoy more while most suffer less? Well, aren't you supposed to get ahead? Ahead of who? Ahead of them. To drive a better car. To own a bigger house. To get a bigger bank account. This is living the American dream. Capitalism is generous to the rare few. You've made it into the one percent. Congratulations. Enjoy the pleasures you deserve. Those homeless people are not your concern.

You go to your new, luxurious mansion feeling bad. You ate too much and you drank too much and all those homeless people staring at you ruined a fine meal. You go to bed and toss and turn but don't fall asleep. Something is bothering you. You won all this money. You quit your lame job. You have everything you want. But you are not happy. No-thing substitutes for God or Heaven. In fact, you feel pretty miserable. Disparity demonstrates division: separation. What about all those people barely surviving? How can you enjoy your wealth while others suffer? You can't. Why not? Because they are you.

In the Kingdom of Heaven there is no disparity between rich and poor. There is an ever increasing abundance for all. The more that is given, the more that is received. Joy is in sharing, not in having more than another. ACIM describes the true feast:

> The door is open, that all those may come who would
> no longer starve, and would enjoy the feast of plenty set
> before them there. And they will meet with your invited
> Guests the miracle has asked to come to you.

> This is a feast unlike indeed to those the dreaming of the
> world has shown. For here, the more that anyone receives,
> the more is left for all the rest to share. The Guests have
> brought unlimited supply with Them. And no one is
> deprived or can deprive. Here is a feast the Father lays
> before His Son, and shares it equally with him.[69]

Chapter Nine

TIME IS TEMPORARY

*T*he holy instant is now. The holy instant is the closest I come to the timeless eternal while I dream I live in this temporal world.

> The Holy Spirit's perception of time is the exact opposite of the ego's…The Holy Spirit interprets time's purpose as rendering the need for time unnecessary. He regards the function of time as temporary, serving only His teaching function, which is temporary by definition. His emphasis is therefore on the only aspect of time that can extend to the infinite, for now is the closest approximation of eternity that this world offers.[1]

ACIM presents two views of time, one of the ego and one of the Holy Spirit. I am either stuck in the time loop, repeating a futile routine, or, I can use time to end time.

> Time can release as well as imprison, depending on whose interpretation of it you use. Past, present, and future are not continuous, unless you force continuity on them.[2]

The Holy Spirit's use of time is to hasten the ending of time. There is no continuity of past, present, and future except the illusion of continuity forced by the ego's wrong-mindedness. The past is gone and the future is not yet, not ever. Only belief in past and future allow the illusion of continuity of time. My choice is to believe either the ego or the Holy Spirit.

> The purpose of time is to enable you to learn how to use time constructively. It is thus a teaching device and a means to an end. Time will cease when it is no longer useful in facilitating learning.[3]

Right use of time is the means of ending time, just as right use of concepts ends concepts. Time is useful to learn the truth about time, and this seems to take time. What's so terrible about time? It's not terrible but unreal, like the ego. The ego wants more time; the Holy Spirit uses time to transcend time. The Holy Spirit uses time to correct mistaken choices and undo all unconscious guilt. Then the need for time is over. When it is time for me to die, do I want more time? More time to suffer?

The story of "me" requires a past. Special love or hate relationships require a past. Judgment requires a past. Grievance requires a past. Guilt requires a past. Every problem I imagine requires a past. Why do I hold on to the past? For the continuity of "me." How do I hold onto the past? Memory, and the special people proving the past true.

Try this thought experiment: compare a memory of a past event and a memory of a dream. Notice anything? They have a peculiar similarity. They are both memories. One I consider a "real" memory and the other one I consider "not real." How "real" is any memory? Is the memory of eating ice cream as real as eating ice cream? Is the memory of a migraine as real as having a migraine? Remember one of the best experiences of your life. Is the memory of that experience as real as the experience itself? What about memory of pain? The memory of pain is mellow compared to actual pain. A memory is like a photograph. Is a photograph of me who I am? No, it is an image. My memory of anything is a memory of a memory of a memory of a memory all the way back to the event, person, or place remembered. As time fades away, memories pile up.

Fear feeds on the future and the fear-filled future feeds on guilty memories from the past. Time's fear feeding frenzy ends with the release of guilt. The present moment, the holy instant, is the escape hatch, the portal, into eternity. Here and now I am released from the balancing act of karma. On the tightrope of time I balance past and future because I fear falling off the time line.

> Guilt feelings are the preservers of time. They induce fears
> of retaliation or abandonment, and thus ensure that the
> future will be like the past. This is the ego's continuity.[4]

Guilt over the past sin furthers fear of future penalty. Because of my
guilt I fear retaliation. Or if not that, abandonment. This is what I
anxiously anticipate. Fear of the future is the fear of the just retaliatory
God, or the God who abandons me in permanent hell. Love-blocking
fear is how the ego keeps the karmic time loop repeating and keeps
me out of timeless Heaven, or eternal life.

> The ego invests heavily in the past, and in the end believes
> that the past is the only aspect of time that is meaningful.
> Remember that its emphasis on guilt enables it to insure
> its continuity by making the future like the past, and
> thus avoiding the present. By the notion of paying for the
> past in the future, the past becomes the determiner of the
> future, making them continuous without an intervening
> present.[5]

The eastern idea of karma, the fundamental law of cause and effect,
is the *notion of paying for the past in the future*. Karma balances the
opposites in duality. Karma is tied to time but I do not need to be.

> "Now" has no meaning to the ego.[6]

Eckhart Tolle couldn't say it better.

> The shadowy figures from the past are precisely what you
> must escape. They are not real, and have no hold over you
> unless you bring them with you. They carry the spots of
> pain in your mind, directing you to attack in the present
> in retaliation for a past that is no more. And this decision
> is one of future pain. Unless you learn that past pain is an
> illusion, you are choosing a future of illusions and losing
> the many opportunities you could find for release in the

present. The ego would preserve your nightmares, and
prevent you from awakening and understanding that they
are past.[7]

Liberation happens now, not in the future. Could I be depressed if I
had no past? If I am interested in liberation and the ending of all suffering, it might help if I know where to look. If I look for liberation in
the past or future, I will not find it because it is not there. Hence the
importance of the holy instant.

Let us forget the purpose of the world the past has given
it. For otherwise the future will be like the past, and
but a series of depressing dreams, in which all idols fail
you, one by one, and you see death and disappointment
everywhere...an endless circle of despair...[8]

Who believes that keeping the past causes a future of serial depressing dreams, death and disappointment: an endless circle of despair,
the circle of time?

The ego teaches that hell is in the future. Hell is its goal.[9]

Sin and guilt of the past cause fear of future hell. For the severely
depressed, hell seems quite real now and for the foreseeable future.
That's why many choose suicide. Annihilation is preferred over hell.

Some people say they do not believe in hell. Good for them because
in truth hell is only a belief. What they likely don't know, however,
is that the fear of just punishment in hell is unconscious as well as
conscious. Therefore there is a discrepancy between the conscious
belief in no hell and the unconscious belief in hell. Hell no, or hell
yes, which is it?

Save time, my brother; learn what time is for. And speed
the end of idols in a world made sad and sick by seeing
idols there.[10]

Do I want to save time? ACIM happened to shorten my time in hell.

How long it takes to awaken from the dream of separation is up to me, except for the mysterious final step taken by God. I have the freedom to delay or advance awakening. Do I want more time? I got it. Do I want to return and live more lives, a series of depressing dreams? I got it. I live as many as I want. If I'm "enjoying" life, I probably want more. True joy, however, is a function of being, not life in this world, or anything external. As long as my idiot self imagines idle idols of future satisfaction, I suffer. Eventually, I will want off the not-so-merry-go-round. If I'm having a tough life, perhaps I chose that life to accelerate awakening. If I'm serious about liberation, I will visit the lowest point. Until that happy day, the karmic clock keeps on ticking and tocking. If things are going great, beware. The danger of another depressing dream is just around the corner.

Although I procrastinate and postpone my awakening and liberation, the silencing of hell's bells is inevitable.

> The word "inevitable" is fearful to the ego but joyous to
> the spirit. God is inevitable, and you cannot avoid Him
> any more than He can avoid you.[11]

When I wait to wake up, however, I also delay the ultimate reunion of everyone, the complete restoration of the Sonship. Waiting to wake up delays the fullness of joy. Waiting and delay imply time. What makes me wait? Fear.

> You can delay the completion of the Kingdom, but you
> cannot introduce the concept of fear into it.[12]

The completion of Heaven requires you and me. You wait on me and I wait on you. I can wait but I cannot bring fear into the Kingdom. Thus the way to minimize delay is to eliminate fear by surrendering the *cause* of fear to God and welcome His plan for Atonement.

In all its forms, from slight worry to full blown panic attack, fear features a future where sad things happen. In this temporal world, the future *is* unstable. The ego's continuity requires fear. Fear delays the completion of the Kingdom because fear blocks the awareness of Love. There is no fear in the Love Kingdom and I cannot bring fear into it. Fear and love cannot co-exist any more than sunlight and darkness. Thus the need for purification. Remember, the cause of fear is guilt and the cause of guilt is the separation. The answer to the separation is the Atonement and the Atonement declares that the separation never happened. A wish for separation led to the dream of separation. The ego wants to delay the Atonement because the completion of the Atonement is the end of time, space, and ego.

Delay is of the ego. Because time is its concept.[13]

Delay is just that, delay. The inevitable good ending of hell is sure. It is just a matter of how long do I want to suffer? Without suffering, I probably would not be interested in changing anything. But even if I'm not consciously suffering personally, can I ignore the suffering of billions? Can I ignore the suffering of even one other person? Those suffering are part of the Sonship, part of my Self.

It is in your power, in time, to delay the perfect union of the Father and the Son.[14]

I procrastinate for a long, long time, or not; the trip through time traps me, or not. ACIM teaches how to minimize delay.

You can temporize and you are capable of enormous procrastination...[15]

My procrastination is keeping me in time and out of eternal, timeless Heaven. Instead of using now, I wait until tomorrow, or the next day, or next year, or next life. The signs outside Heaven say, "No loitering." The fearful loiter.

Love does not require a past or future. Being does not require a past or future. Awareness does not require a past or future. They do require the present, the now, the holy instant. And actually, even that they do not require because the present is already now here. I think I require "something," yet what is "required" is not required because it is already given, freely, unconditionally. In fact the two, the present and awareness, are one, not separate. They are integrally part of each other. The only time I am aware is now.

Time and Miracles

There is an important relationship between time and miracles. Miracles are the method of shortening time.

> **Just as the separation occurred over millions of years, the Last Judgment will extend over a similarly long period, and perhaps an even longer one. Its length can, however, be greatly shortened by miracles, the device for shortening but not abolishing time. If a sufficient number become truly miracle-minded, this shortening process can be virtually immeasurable.[16]**

ACIM came for this. To recruit miracle-minded miracle workers and shorten time. If enough of us become miracle-minded we shorten the time of suffering by such a great amount it is virtually *immeasurable*. That's a big if, right?

How long I suffer is how long I want to pursue the specialness of me. The first words of the course teach that the time I take to awaken is up to me.

> **This is a course in miracles. It is a required course. Only the time you take it is voluntary. Free will does not mean that you can establish the curriculum. It means only that you can elect what you want to take at a given time.[17]**

A miracle of forgiveness undoes guilt over past sin and this undoes the ego's forced continuity of past projected into future.

Miracles are both beginnings and endings, and so they alter the temporal order. They are affirmations of rebirth, which seem to go back but really go forward. They undo the past in the present, and thus release the future.[18]

Miracles break the karmic cycle of past guilt causing fear of future punishment. Miracles hasten the realization that I am sinless, innocent, as God created me. I realize this as I release my brother from karmic-causing guilt. Thus miracles remove guilt and fear of future punishment. Remove the cause and the effect disappears.

Miracles therefore reflect the laws of eternity, not of time.[19]

Miracles reflect the truth that there is no time, no past of sin, no future of fear. The *laws of eternity* transcend the laws of time, and the laws of karma.

Miracles are part of an interlocking chain of forgiveness which, when completed, is the Atonement. Atonement works all the time and in all dimensions of time.[20]

Miracles, forgiveness, the Atonement, and time are all related. The quote also implies different dimensions of time.

Jesus often proclaimed the forgiveness of sins before performing a miracle. True healing is not a physical cure. True healing is the release from guilt: my sins are forgiven. The miracle cancels cause. If the cause of suffering is released, then what happens to suffering? The miracle shortens the amount of time it takes me to realize the timelessness of forgiveness. How long does it take for God to be Himself and extend Love unconditionally? It takes no time at all. It already is. When Moses asked God Who He is, God's answer is *I am that I am.* Not, "I was," nor, "I will be." Likewise Jesus said of himself, *Before Abraham was, I am.* He didn't say "Before Abraham was, I was." Was

Jesus referring to his body, his flesh? *I am* is a statement of timeless now. What seems to take time is my acceptance of the truth.

> **The miracle is a learning device that lessens the need for time. It establishes an out-of-pattern time interval not under the usual laws of time. In this sense it is timeless.**[21]

Miracles achieve the opposite of the ego's plan to procrastinate and continue the time of dreaming. The ego wants to continue in time. Time and the world are the ego's kingdom. True continuity is everlasting, eternal, and not of time which is temporary, the opposite of eternal. The seeming continuity of past into future is temporary because it ends with the ending of time.

> **The miracle is the only device at your immediate disposal for controlling time.**[22]

How miracles collapse time:

> **The miracle minimizes the need for time. In the longitudinal or horizontal plane the recognition of the equality of the members of the Sonship appears to involve almost endless time. However, the miracle entails a sudden shift from horizontal to vertical perception. This introduces an interval from which the giver and receiver [of the miracle] both emerge farther along in time than they would otherwise have been. The miracle thus has the unique property of abolishing time to the extent that it renders the interval of time it spans unnecessary. There is no relationship between the time a miracle takes and the time it covers. The miracle substitutes for learning that might have taken thousands of years. It does so by the underlying recognition of perfect equality of giver and receiver on which the miracle rests. The miracle shortens time by collapsing it, thus eliminating certain intervals**

within it. It does this, however, within the larger temporal sequence.[23]

Inclusive recognition of everyone's equality seems to be taking *endless time.* Miracles shorten time because they substitute *for learning that might have taken thousands of years.* This miracle lesson is radical, inclusive, equality: *recognition of perfect equality of giver and receiver.* Without miracles, learning this takes much longer. Through the miracle of the Atonement, imagined guilt over imagined sins from the memory of past is removed, now, not only my sins but the imagined sins of my brother as well. This saves time. Otherwise I'm caught in a seemingly endless loop of karma, cause and effect, sin and punishment, past and future.

ACIM is not a selfish spirituality, concerned with individual and personal salvation. It is not about me getting to Heaven. It is about the completion of God's creation. God's Kingdom waits for completion and the fullness of joy as long as I wait to accept the truth about the separation and Atonement.

> God in His knowledge is not waiting, but His Kingdom is bereft while you wait. All the Sons of God are waiting for your return, just as you are waiting for theirs. Delay does not matter in eternity, but it is tragic in time. You have elected to be in time rather than eternity, and therefore believe you are in time. Yet your election is both free and alterable. You do not belong in time. Your place is only in eternity, where God Himself placed you forever.[24]

Eternity and time are two different dimensions and only one of them is real; the other is temporary. From the view of eternity, the ego's delay does not matter. But from the view of time, delay means the continuation of suffering. I elected to be in the dimension of time, from which I project/perceive space and its three dimensions.

If miracles are so powerful in shortening the delay of liberation, why don't I see them more often? Did not Jesus promise that we would do the same works as he, and even greater works? Part of the problem is that I do not understand what a miracle is and how it works. Hence *A Course In Miracles* is given to teach what a miracle is, what it does, and how to perform them, in order to save time and stop delaying Heaven. This is a relatively recent teaching. It is public now for forty years, not four thousand.

> **Miracles are everyone's right, but purification is necessary first.** [25]

Purification is necessary because fear blocks love and miracles are expressions of love. People tend to think of a miracle as a type of magic, that changes something or someone, such as a miraculous healing, commanding a storm to stop, or chopping down a mountain with the edge of my hand. This is a misunderstanding of how miracles work. The miracle does not substitute one illusion for another. It does not add a new illusion. It does not improve the dream. A miracle lifts the veil hiding the Truth. A miracle helps everyone return to Heaven sooner.

> **The basic decision of the miracle-minded is not to wait on time any longer than is necessary. Time can waste as well as be wasted. The miracle worker, therefore, accepts the time-control factor gladly. He recognizes that every collapse of time brings everyone closer to the ultimate release from time, in which the Son and the Father are one.** [26]

Why procrastinate? Wasting time wastes me.

Time, along with space, are necessities for the separation. Thus time is part of the dream, and not real. For God a thousand years is like one day and one day is like a thousand years, according to the Bible. The Holy Spirit teaches how to use time in His way, to choose again, to perform miracles, to allow the healing of my unconscious mind, to practice true forgiveness and remove the fear-causing guilt blocking my awareness of the Truth. Guilt requires time, the past, and fear requires the karmic consequence, future punishment, including hell. Dreams of sin, maintained by memory, are released in the Atonement by the miracle of forgiveness. Time is replaced by the holy instant. Physical perception is replaced by spiritual vision. Consciousness is replaced by Awareness.

Time and Evolution

Notice that the creation stories and John's Gospel start with the three words, *In the beginning.* The term "beginning" implies time and the limitations of time. Whatever begins in time also ends, including the entire universe. What was before the beginning? Nothing. Before and after are terms of time. God and His Kingdom are not before or after time but beyond time, a different dimension. Everything between the beginning and the end is in time, temporary, and only an ego dream. God is not limited. Time is limited. Time began. Time ends. Time is temporary, by definition. The time/space continuum began at the separation. Birth, aging, and death all happen in time. Life everlasting, or eternal life, cannot happen in time. Eternity does not begin or end. Eternity is not endless time, extending for billions and billions of years; eternity transcends time altogether. All of time exists as a little loop within the infinite field of eternal timelessness. God, the Kingdom of God, the Son of God, all exist in an eternal, non-temporal Heaven, outside of time, beyond time. This is eternal life, everlasting life, the endless abundance of Heaven.

Evolution is a time-based idea and proceeds "over time." Thus evolution is a temporary process with a beginning and ending. As usual, ACIM presents a much different view of evolution than those theories of the world.

> Evolution is a process in which you seem to proceed
> from one degree to the next. You correct previous
> missteps by stepping forward. This process is actually
> incomprehensible in temporal terms, because you return
> as you go forward. The Atonement is the device by which
> you can free yourself from the past as you go ahead. It
> undoes your past errors, thus making it unnecessary for
> you to keep retracing your steps without advancing your
> return. In this sense the Atonement saves time, but like
> the miracle it serves, does not abolish it. As long as there
> is need for Atonement there is need for time. But the
> Atonement as a completed plan has a unique relationship
> to time. Until the Atonement is complete, its various
> phases will proceed in time, but the whole Atonement
> stands at time's end. At that point the bridge of return has
> been built.[27]

The sentence from the above quote about the Atonement, *It undoes your past errors, thus making it unnecessary for you to keep retracing your steps without advancing your return*, refers to the ending of karma. Without the Atonement's action of undoing my belief in past errors, I'm doomed to keep retracing my steps. In karmic time, the past determines the future. If I do not use time to advance my return, I waste time, procrastinating. What seems like reincarnation from this side is actually serial dreams, or a series of dramas, stuck in a repeating time-loop.

> The acceptance of the Atonement by everyone is only a
> matter of time.[28]

Even though it is only a matter of time, how much time depends on my willingness to cooperate. If I apply the course teachings, I shorten suffering for everyone. I tend to think of time as moving forward, from past, through the present, and into the future. Time is actually moving backwards. If I am standing still, and time moves past me from the future, then time is moving from future to past. Today is yesterday tomorrow.

> Time really, then, goes backward to an instant so ancient that it is beyond all memory, and past even the possibility of remembering. Yet because it is an instant that is relived again and again and still again, it seems to be now.[29]

Apparently, I cannot remember the beginning of time that is so ancient and *past even the possibility of remembering*. Perhaps, at the ancient beginning of time, memory had not yet evolved and thus there is no way to remember it. Somehow, I relive the instant of separation, over and over, as time seems to continue.

> Your creation by God is the only foundation that cannot be shaken, because the light is in it. Your starting point is truth, and you must return to your Beginning. Much has been seen since then, but nothing has really happened. Your Self is still in peace, even though your mind is in conflict. You have not yet gone back far enough, and that is why you become so fearful. As you approach the Beginning, you feel the fear of the destruction of your thought system on you as if it were the fear of death. There is no death, but there is a belief in death.[30]

Notice a core course differentiation: there is no death, only a belief in death. This is the truth demonstrated by the crucifixion of Jesus and Resurrection of Jesus Christ. Death, where is your sting? Belief in death leads to fear. I fear the Beginning because it is the end of me as I know myself. Annihilation of specialness. Gospel of Thomas:

> Have you discovered the beginning, then, so that you are seeking the end? For where the beginning is, the end will be. Fortunate is the one who stands at the beginning: That one will know the end and will not taste death.[31]

Jesus says that he is the alpha and the omega, the beginning and the end.

> **And now we say "Amen." For Christ has come to dwell in the abode You set for Him before time was, in calm eternity. The journey closes, ending at the place where it began.** [32]

Is the end of time a frightening concept or can I say "Amen?"

Consider time as a circle. A circle does not have a beginning or an end, except by arbitrarily assigning one. But whatever point I select as the beginning of the circle is also its end. A circle is a curving line that ends where it starts. Science is all about measuring things. A mysterious thing about a circle is it can't be measured, only estimated. Mathematicians came up with pi to measure the circumference of a circle. And since pi is an infinitely repeating number, I get closer and closer to a measurement without ever getting there. Strange, is it not? Infinity is in an instant.

The first thing made as a result of the mad wish for separation was consciousness. Thus, consciousness is the beginning we "evolve" back to. Consciousness is all the rage now and the new age movement is all about consciousness. Consciousness is a sort of substitution for, and imitation of, Awareness, and although sharing similarities, it is not the same as Awareness. Consciousness is conscious of form. Consciousness requires the other to be conscious of. Consciousness is the duality of the perceived and the perceiver. Separation means perception of people and objects outside of myself, something not me, the other I am separated from. Consciousness is necessary for perception, the dream domain. Awareness does not perceive form, duality, illusion. Awareness is aware of Knowledge, Truth, Love, and Union that demonstrate no form, and are not objects. Awareness is not individual and separate. With consciousness, however, I have mine and you have yours. I could be conscious and you could be unconscious. Even while sleeping, I perceive people and places, yet my dreams are different from your dreams. In deep dreamless sleep I am conscious of nothing. Hard to remember nothing with no image, no form, no sound. It is intentionally elusive.

> **Consciousness, the level of perception, was the first split into the mind after the separation, making the mind a perceiver rather than a creator. Consciousness is correctly identified as the domain of the ego.**[33]

Consciousness was a necessary prerequisite for the dream of separation to begin. So consciousness was at the beginning, the first stage of the separation. As such, it is also the last stage as I "evolve" back to the Kingdom I never left, except in a nightmare. In the circle of time, the beginning and the end are the same.

One of the hermit-monks I knew from Big Sur, Fr. Bruno, died less than a month ago after 56 years in the Hermitage. He understood consciousness as the domain of a false identity:

> **We are strange creatures: strangers to the ground, not knowing where we stand. Literally, we don't know the first thing, don't know ourselves, who we are. Human consciousness, as we know it, may systematically exclude being truly conscious.**[34]

In course terms the sentence above is rendered, "Human consciousness, as we perceive it, may systematically block *Awareness*." In the return, I go back to the beginning: consciousness, where the *detour into fear* began. From there, original consciousness, God takes the final step, restoring Awareness. Some spiritual teachings confuse this arrival at the beginning, consciousness, with the final step, partly because it is as far as *I* can go in my return. When I return to pure consciousness, it is the closest I come to Awareness, the original and eternal state, that God re-establishes in the "final step."

People tend to polarize into "evolutionist" and "creationist." One is considered scientific and one is considered religious. ACIM is aligned with neither. The course teaches a different view of both creation and evolution. Both the creationist and evolutionist views require a blind faith in something problematic. Somehow, from nothing, magically comes something. How could this happen? Well, creationists say God magically and mysteriously makes the material world out of nothing. How? Don't ask. Can God do anything including make a world so painful that He can't stand it? The evolutionists, on the other hand, say that before the big bang beginning, the entire universe was compressed into a piece of matter the size of a dime, literally. The big bang exploded the dime-sized piece of whatever, expanding it into this universe that is still expanding fourteen billion years later. Now that is a truly BIG bang. No word yet on where the dime-sized whatever came from. Both versions are theoretical beliefs, and require blind faith in how nothing became something. To seek the source of the illusion in the illusion results in more illusion. When a blind man leads a blind man across the street, they both get big-banged by a bus.

A third view tries to integrate both creation and evolution: intelligent design. God is creating the universe *through* evolution. Creation continues. This still does not provide an answer as to how something evolved from nothing. Some scientists say, "Something we don't understand is doing we don't know what." That is the open-mindedness of not knowing.

This universe is a mental projection, a virtual reality; matter is mind stuff manifested as image in the matrix like a hologram. Or, if you prefer, physicality is part of the dream/illusion. It is as real and "solid" as a dream. Well that solves the problem of how something is made from nothing, does it not? There is only Spirit. The rest, all form, all material, is imagined, illusionary, projected, and perceived, by mind and in mind. There is no world; there is no time; there is no outside of myself, nor inside myself. The simplest way to put it using words is *God Is, I Am*. In one poetic word: *Ising*. Or I-sing. Metaphorically speaking, of course.

Beyond consciousness, after the final step, is Awareness. All form is gone. All perception is gone. This might seem frightening. One of the reasons the return to Heaven is taking so long, in time, is that I fear this loss of perception. Annihilation of perception is frightening. Who wants to be Helen Keller? So I awaken gradually, moving mercifully from the nightmare of ego's wrong-mindedness to the happy dream (real world) of the Holy Spirit's right-mindedness, before returning to the one-mindedness of Awareness, without any consciousness, or projection, or perception, of duality, differences, form, or separation. The happy dream is still a dream, still temporary, and still involves perception. It is a merciful transition.

The Holy Instant

I wrote about the holy instant earlier, in its role in giving and receiving perfect communication, with no private thoughts I withhold. The holy instant is the present moment free of past and future. The holy instant is closely related to the holy relationship. They work hand in hand.

> The holy relationship is the expression of the holy instant
> in living in this world. Like everything about salvation,
> the holy instant is a practical device, witnessed to by its
> results. The holy instant never fails. The experience of it is
> always felt. Yet without expression it is not remembered.
> The holy relationship is a constant reminder of the
> experience in which the relationship became what it is.[35]

Apparently, even though I experience the holy instant always, I do not remember it unless it expresses itself in the holy relationship. In this world, the holy relationship is the expression of the holy instant. This is a relationship without past or future. The holy instant is the secret to transcending time, and transcending special relationships that require past and future.

Begin to practice the Holy Spirit's use of time as a
teaching aid to happiness and peace. Take this very
instant, now, and think of it as all there is of time.
Nothing can reach you here out of the past, and it is here
that you are completely absolved, completely free and
wholly without condemnation. From this holy instant
wherein holiness was born again you will go forth in time
without fear, and with no sense of change with time.[36]

Will I do this? Will I think of this instant as all there is of time? Try
it. Where is past or future when I stop thinking about them?

You look upon each holy instant as a different point in
time. It never changes. All that it ever held or will ever
hold is here right now. The past takes nothing from it, and
the future will add no more.[37]

It is a mistake to think of the holy instant as one of a series of
instants, like seconds ticking by on a clock. This is to be tricked back
into time. There is one holy instant, not many. The holy instant cancels
special relationships because special relationships, love or hate, rely
on judgments, that rely on memories, that rely on a past. My history
is hocked by the holy instant.

The holy instant is the Holy Spirit's most useful learning
device for teaching you love's meaning. For its purpose
is to suspend judgment entirely. Judgment always rests
on the past, for past experience is the basis on which you
judge. Judgment becomes impossible without the past, for
without it you do not understand anything.[38]

The significance of the holy instant is stressed. It is the Holy Spirit's
most useful learning device. It releases judgment because judgment
requires the past. Freedom from judgment is the advanced shift from
duality to non-duality. It frees me from special relationships because

specialness requires a past. I cannot learn the meaning of love in the duality of judgment. Love has no opposite. Love is non-dual; love is what God is and what I am. Therefore I am non-dual as is God. God and I are not two.

> In the holy instant no one is special, for your personal needs intrude on no one to make your brothers seem different. Without the values from the past, you would see them all the same and like yourself. Nor would you see any separation between yourself and them. In the holy instant, you see in each relationship what it will be when you perceive only the present.[39]

Through memory I keep the past alive – I remember what you did – this is my blame frame of reference for judging you. Accumulation of memory is the – "me" – the story of me. As Byron Katie asks, who am I without my story? That is, without my history?

> The holy instant reflects His knowing by bringing all perception out of the past, thus removing the frame of reference you have built by which to judge your brothers.[40]

The holy instant is inclusive because exclusiveness requires the past.

> There is no exclusion in the holy instant because the past is gone, and with it goes the whole basis for exclusion.[41]

The holy instant removes the basis for grudges, grievances, and revengeance for memories of what I think happened in the past. The reason for attack, and for defense, is gone.

> In the holy instant it is understood that the past is gone, and with its passing the drive for vengeance has been uprooted and has disappeared. The stillness and the peace of now enfold you in perfect gentleness. Everything is gone except the truth.[42]

The holy instant is now and only now is experience possible, including memory of sin, and including fear of future pain.

Who can feel desolation except now?[43]

I feel depression now. All past depression is a memory and the memory of pain is, thankfully, not pain. Does anyone care about a toothache from ten years ago? Why hold on to past depression? It is not real now. It does not matter how long I felt depressed. Only this instant matters. Both feeling depression and release from depression happen now.

For a miracle is now.[44]

It is easy to fall into the error of hoping for future release. Release is not in time. God is not in time. Heaven is not in time.

God knows you *now*. He remembers nothing, having always known you exactly as He knows you now.[45]

Deeper Down the Time Rabbit Hole

Perhaps the strangest idea ACIM teaches about time is that time is already over. What I seem to experience "in time" is a review of what already happened. The movie metaphor might help here. When I go see a movie it takes place over a certain amount of time, say two hours. Even so, the movie is already made and the ending is finished, even if I'm in the first five minutes of the film. It's over, but I haven't seen the ending yet. Sometimes, I watch a movie I watched before because I forgot how it ended. The course teaches that the script is already written. It is like being a passenger on a train and believing I control the train, make it stop and go, and turn where I want it to go. But the train follows the tracks already laid.

The course also speaks of different dimensions of time. I likely won't be aware of it, but I can switch dimensions of time. This is like a train switching to a different track while I sleep. When I awake

I'm still on the train following a track already laid, but it is a different track. If I learn certain lessons so they do not need repeating, I graduate from further lessons and "change tracks." Thus the course teaches how miracles shorten time, collapsing it. I switch dimensions of time, shortening the time of suffering.

> In order to understand the teaching-learning plan of salvation, it is necessary to grasp the concept of time that the course sets forth. Atonement corrects illusions, not truth. Therefore, it corrects what never was. Further, the plan for this correction was established and completed simultaneously, for the Will of God is entirely apart from time. So is all reality, being of Him. The instant the idea of separation entered the mind of God's Son, in that same instant was God's Answer given. In time this happened very long ago. In reality it never happened at all.

> The world of time is the world of illusion. What happened long ago seems to be happening now. Choices made long since appear to be open; yet to be made.[46]

The Atonement happened at the instant of the separation because God wills it so, beyond all time. In a certain sense, time is a repeating loop. The course teaches that the separation ended in an instant. It also teaches that it happened over millions of years. Be careful of level confusion here. The one instant of separation gets repeated for a long, long time.

> Time lasted but an instant in your mind, with no effect upon eternity. And so is all time past, and everything exactly as it was before the way to nothingness was made. The tiny tick of time in which the first mistake was made, and all of them within that one mistake, held also the Correction for that one, and all of them that came within

the first. And in that tiny instant time was gone, for that was all it ever was. What God gave answer to is answered and is gone.[47]

God's answer and solution to the separation, the Atonement, happened immediately at the instant of separation and took no time. If healing of depression requires time, healing is based on an illusion of future release.

> Salvation is immediate.[48]

God's world is timeless and eternal. Ego's world is temporal and temporary.

> The working out of all correction takes no time at all.
> Yet the acceptance of the working out can seem to take forever.[49]

It can seem confusing and this confusion the course calls "level confusion." The Atonement happened instantly. God does not need or use time. God transcends time. Yet my acceptance of the Atonement seems to take time, in the temporal dream. I'm the one delaying liberation because I resist what already is.

> We have repeated several times before that you but make a journey that is done.[50]

There is no time in Heaven, and no time at all. Yet on my level, in the dream, I believe in time and so it seems real. The holy instant is no past and no future. From this side, it appears to take time to transcend time.

> Nothing is ever lost but time, which in the end is meaningless. For it is but a little hindrance to eternity, quite meaningless to the real Teacher of the world. Yet

> since you do believe in it, why should you waste it going
> nowhere, when it can be used to reach a goal as high as
> learning can achieve?[51]

While I'm dreaming in the time dream, I use time to transcend time
or I waste time going nowhere. I have already wasted a lot of time
going nowhere. From the view of eternity, it does not matter. But from
the perspective of time, wasting time is tragic, continuing suffering.

Time exists as a belief based on memory. I keep the ancient instant
of separation repeating through belief in judgment, attack, sin, guilt,
and fear, because these illusions are based on the past and separateness. When I judge I choose for separation and therefore the instant
of separation continues, or repeats.

> Yet in each unforgiving act or thought, in every judgment
> and in all belief in sin, is that one instant still called back,
> as if it could be made again in time. You keep an ancient
> memory before your eyes. And he who lives in memories
> alone is unaware of where he is.[52]

Memory blocks awareness of the holy instant. Memory presents what
is past. Memory is what continues the instant of separation. This
might make more sense for a guitar player. Electric guitar players often
use a sound effect called a delay. It is an electronic device that uses
memory. There are also tape delays. With a delay a guitarist can play
one note and keep that single note repeating indefinitely. Likewise, I
can delay deliverance by repeating a sad song indefinitely. Imagine a
perfect echo chamber where a loud, frightening bang keeps repeating.

People tend to hope for liberation in the future. This is a trick, an
illusion designed to keep me in the time loop. I was raised on a religion that proposed a future Heaven, maybe, after a future purgatory,
after the suffering behind this "veil of tears." The kids in the back seat
won't stop asking, "Are we there yet?"

> The plans you make for safety all are laid within the
> future, where you cannot plan.[53]

Belief in future liberation is selling out the holy instant, and a futile
attempt to subject God to time.

> Why in the future? And you seek to be content with
> sighing, and with "reasoning" you do not understand it
> now, but will some day. And then its meaning will be
> clear. This is not reason, for it is unjust, and clearly hints
> at punishment until the time of liberation is at hand...
> This is a sacrifice of *now*...[54]

Enlightenment is not time based. It is not in time. It is not part of
the ego's world. It is not in the dream. It is in the awakening from
the dream. To place enlightenment in the future, as something that
will happen, is to sacrifice the now, where enlightenment already is.

> Be not content with future happiness. It has no meaning,
> and is not your just reward. For you have cause for
> freedom now.[55]

The illusion of time and separation exists in my mind. The solution
also exists within. There is nothing without.

> Everything God wills is not only possible, but has already
> happened. And that is why the past has gone. It never
> happened in reality. Only in your mind, which thought it
> did, is its undoing needful.[56]

The whole mess is a meta-mental problem. Although the ending of
time is predetermined, it also exists as an unfolding potential, with
many, perhaps even infinite, possible variations because there are
different dimensions of time. There are many potential "endings."

The revelation that the Father and the Son are one will come in time to every mind. Yet is that time determined by the mind itself, not taught.

The time is set already. It appears to be quite arbitrary. Yet there is no step along the road that anyone takes but by chance. It has already been taken by him, although he has not yet embarked on it. For time but seems to go in one direction. We but undertake a journey that is over. Yet it seems to have a future still unknown to us.

Time is a trick, a sleight of hand, a vast illusion in which figures come and go as if by magic. Yet there is a plan behind appearances that does not change. The script is written. When experience will come to end your doubting has been set. For we but see the journey from the point at which it ended, looking back on it, imagining we make it once again; reviewing mentally what has gone by.[57]

Ask all things of His Teacher [the Holy Spirit], and all things are given you. Not in the future but immediately; now. God does not wait, for waiting implies time and He is timeless.[58]

The emphasis of this course always remains the same; – it is at this moment that complete salvation is offered you, and it is at this moment that you can accept it. This is still your one responsibility. Atonement might be equated with total escape from the past and total lack of interest in the future. Heaven is here. There is nowhere else. Heaven is now. There is no other time.[59]

Sidetrack: 1987-1992

Shortly after moving to Alaska my daughter, Alicen, was born. My wife and I decided to reverse roles and I agreed to be a stay-at-home dad. Dee's income was enough for us to get by on, and by the time we deducted childcare costs from whatever minimum wage I made, it didn't make sense to hand over our baby daughter to strangers paid a minimum wage, in order to slightly increase our bottom line. The shepherd cares more about the sheep than the hired hand. Society says the man should work; his agency and identity is provider. He catches the fish, and the wife cleans the fish, cooks the fish, and cleans the dishes after. There is usually a social stigma for not conforming to the status quo. I was a hard-core non-conformist. Ambition for money did not enslave me. Like a live lobster in a pot of warm water, I did not realize the challenge of parenting until the cook turned up the heat.

Dee and I led separate lives. We spent little time together. When she was at work I watched the kids. When she was home she watched the kids and I worked on remodeling the house or photography. Usually it was late when I finally finished washing the film or prints and she was long asleep. I remember only one night out together without the kids the whole first five years in Alaska.

Before we married, Dee insisted I stop smoking marijuana and I did so for about five years. She permitted alcohol and I became a daily drinker, though it did not seem to be causing any serious problems, yet. Soon after arriving in Alaska I started jamming with musicians, and someone always had weed. Playing music and smoking marijuana seemed to go together. This is true, in general, for generations of blues, jazz, and rock musicians. When I was playing in my first working band, in Arcata, CA back in 1978, I learned that alcohol cured stage fright. There was a fine line though between being loosened up and sloppy. Alcohol was a social lubricant for a person as shy and introverted as me. Drinking was hereditary as well. On my Irish side, my mother's side, everyone drank and smoked. On my father's French-Canadian side, not so much. But if French-Canadian writer Jack Kerouac is any clue, French-Canadians are drinkers too. Catholics also drink, including the priests. Most Catholic social gatherings I went to supplied alcohol. I'm not making excuses for my increasing dependence on alcohol, but I seemed set up for it like a bowling pin. Drinking helped manage the stress and fears of life while all the while abuse crept into dependence. There came a point where I needed to drink as part of the recovery from yesterday's drinking. I learned right away that to do my best in photography I needed to be sober. Same with writing. There is a cliché that writers are drinkers but in my case I can't write, or even read, for long if I'm drinking, and certainly not when hungover. Strangely, sickness blocks inspiration and disables ego at the same time. Have you ever been horribly seasick? There is no energy to argue about anything.

Ambitions about money or career did not afflict me, but the artist in me loved photography and playing music and I did both in my free time. I spent eighteen months doing a major remodeling job in our house, building a darkroom and studio. Now I had a fine darkroom, but throughout construction I had the nagging notion that I labored in vain. I would lose the fruit of my labor if we moved, or by destruction from earthquake or fire. As it turned out, I had use of my dream darkroom for less than three years. I advanced quickly in photography and started to win awards. I finally found a visual art medium perfect for me.

In 1990 my son, Francis, was born. I felt blessed to be a father to one girl and one boy and I loved them dearly. I hoped to extend the same unconditional love I experienced to them. I tried my best to be a good father but I knew that the deterioration of their parent's marriage distressed them. Dee and I didn't fight and so our kids didn't see that kind of thing. I hoped to hide my inner unhappiness from them and protect them from pain, but kids pick up on much more than parents suspect.

Two and a half months after Francis was born, I experienced the strongest grief of my life. Our dog, Otto, died. Grief never hit me so hard. It may sound strange, but many people find that relationships with the most unconditional love are with animal friends, not human ones. Dogs don't judge. Otto was a magnificent dog, my favorite of many canine companions over the years. I even named one of my early bands after him: *Friends of Otto.* I had a framed picture of him on my Twin Reverb amp during gigs.

In 1991 a Russian photography organization invited me to participate in a photographic exchange with photographers from Magadan, Russia. Magadan was a hub supply city for the Siberian Gulag, not far from Alaska. It's so close, in fact, that after a few pitchers of palin alein you can see it from AK! First, four photographers from Alaska traveled to Magadan for three weeks and then we hosted four photographers, and a translator, from Magadan in Anchorage. The experience was powerful. I was raised in the prime of the cold war and communist Russians were the enemy. They were *atheists!* The Russian's friendliness and generosity flabbergasted me. The fear of Russians was conditioned from childhood. Experience proved conditioning wrong.

The airport for Magadan seemed more like a military base. When we landed all I saw were military planes. The customs agents, dressed like soldiers, never smiled. A team of about a dozen photographers and friends met us at the airport with a private bus to transport us to Magadan, about an hour's drive. We were on the bus for about five minutes, taking turns talking through a translator, when the bus pulled over and everybody started getting off the bus. What was this? We appeared to be in a wilderness area with no reason to stop. Then our new Russian friends popped open the champagne bottles to toast our arrival. Then the vodka. The Russians I met liked to drink, and smoke, and it's no wonder. People living in arctic regions drink more than average. Maybe its the long, hard, cold winters? Maybe drinking was a way of escaping the fruits of the now collapsing communist system. We saw grocery stores with nothing in them but a few loaves of bread and a few cans of food. Sometimes drinking does support bonding, because the interpersonal walls of sobriety come tumbling down. Decades of anti-Russian conditioning collapsed in two weeks. Our connection was sudden and strong, despite different languages. I learned not to believe government propaganda about national "enemies." These Russian people were amazing. They all knew more English than we knew Russian. They learned English from listening to western music, such as banned Beatles' records. Strangely, the landscape appeared as run-down as the buildings. I mostly photographed the people and made portraits of a former Gulag prisoner and his family. I won't forget Sergei and Elena. I wonder if in these poignant experiences there is not a past-life connection?

This experience of the warm Russian connections emphasized the coldness of my marriage. I saw my parish priest for spiritual direction and attended a retreat at the local Jesuit retreat house. I sank into my second period of deep depression. My mother visited us and one time she said she thought my wife Dee was abusing the children. She claimed that my daughter Alicen screamed in the bath tub because Dee placed her into water too cold or too hot. Dee denied it and demanded that my mother leave. I felt I should put my kids and marriage first and my mother left. Most mornings Dee rose early to get ready for work and often Alicen was up with her. I often worked late in the darkroom, not starting developing film and printing until after Dee returned home from work. I wearied of hearing Dee screaming at Alicen most mornings. I tried to escape the whole situation by drinking. I isolated myself and stopped caring about photography or just about anything else other than my children. I knew the family situation hurt Alicen and Francis, and seeing no solution, I became deeply depressed. I tried going to daily mass again, but nothing worked. At one Sunday Mass, a man approached my wife and I and asked us how long we were married. Nine years. Then he invited us to help other couples through a program called Marriage Encounter, related to the Engaged Encounter retreat my wife and I attended before our wedding. I replied that we were not a good example. Dee didn't disagree. It seemed a ridiculous pretense to "help" people with their marriage when mine was a wreck.

I stopped going to the obligatory Sunday Mass. I wondered why I felt worse after attending Mass. One time, after Holy Communion, I watched the rest of the congregation taking Communion and walking back to their seats. The down-turned and eye-avoiding faces looked serious and depressed. Perhaps I projected my own depression on them. Never-the-less, I ceased being a practicing Catholic. The undeniable sexism in the church justified my exit. As previously noted, my relationship with the church was precarious for many years. Now I had no use for it except the contemplative dimension. In the future, whenever I visited a Catholic church, like when Thomas Keating came to Anchorage, there was a strange sensation of visiting my past.

Meanwhile, deterioration of my marriage continued. I worried about my kids and felt hopeless for a solution. Parenting is a difficult job, maybe the most difficult job. It's much harder in a bad marriage. The sense of responsibility is huge. Nothing was worse than when one of my kids was hurt or sick. My children's suffering hurt me more than my own suffering. I hoped, in vain, that I could spare my children suffering. Otherwise, why bring them into this world? So they can suffer? As a stay at home father, I found taking care of two kids, one an infant, more difficult than taking care of one child. It seemed like my attention was divided between the two, whereas before Francis was born I was focused on one child.

Once I was downstairs with my wife and son and we heard Alicen crying in pain. I ran upstairs and found her chin split open and bleeding. Standing on a chair at the dining table, she fell off it and slammed her chin into the table. We took her to the ER and I held her head still as the doctor injected the wound with a needle and stitched up the cut. I sure wanted a stiff drink after that. Similar injuries happened with my son. One time he was running in circles in the kitchen, became dizzy, and fell, hitting and splitting his head on an outside wall corner.

Another trip to the ER. One time I was out photographing at one of my favorite spots, Hatcher Pass, with both my kids. As I stood under the dark cloth, composing on the ground glass, Francis approached in tears. I looked down and his thumb was bleeding profusely. That same day I had given him a little pocket knife and he proceeded to cut himself. Injury or illness might happen any time. It is something a parent lives with. My parents had their share of it with five boys. When I was young I fell against a hot stove. I don't remember it, but I still have the burn scars on my fingers. Once, my Mom picked me up from kindergarten. After I boarded the car, the door slammed onto Mickey's hand, leaving a finger hanging by the skin. Somehow my Mother manged to drive the car to a hospital. I had not experienced the death or serious illness of a child, yet, but the fearful possibility of such events waited patiently. I became more vulnerable with kids. The carefree life of being single with little responsibility was gone.

After two children, and my depression, I told Dee I didn't want more kids. Catholics usually grow large families; artificial birth control is forbidden. Being good Catholics, we did not use birth control other than a type of "rhythm method" where the woman monitors her fertility cycle and sexual intercourse is abstained from during fertile days of her cycle. If it is done right it works pretty well and it worked for us. No unplanned pregnancies happened, that I knew about. Then one day Dee said she needed to go to the hospital because she was having a miscarriage. Miscarriage? I didn't know she was pregnant. She wanted more kids and became pregnant. She didn't ask me about it. She deceived me about her fertility in order to become pregnant. She used me as a sperm donor, if indeed I was the father.

I read an announcement in a parish bulletin that a man, Kess, offered a class over several weeks featuring Father Thomas Keating, Trappist Abbott, on *Centering Prayer*. Centering Prayer emerged in 1975, but this was the first I heard of it. Contemplative Outreach is the organization that teaches Centering Prayer, a contemplative Christian meditation, to the laity. The popularity of Transcendental

Meditation, and the fact that many Catholics left the church to find spiritual needs better served by eastern religions and philosophies, led to making available a type of prayer normally reserved for cloistered monks and nuns. I knew immediately I wanted to participate in Kess' class and did so. It turned out that Fr. Thomas was retired and living at St. Benedict's Monastery in Snowmass Colorado, since 1981. I could not escape to the monastery but perhaps the monk could come rescue me. I embraced Centering Prayer wholeheartedly and saw it as a way to get my spiritual life back on track instead of on the back burner. Contemplative Outreach offered ten-day retreats of intensive Centering Prayer at St. Benedict's Monastery in Snowmass and I signed up for one scheduled for May 1992. My idea of a great escape/vacation: ten days at a Trappist Monastery! The person I most wanted to meet: Thomas Keating.

Through Thomas Keating I learned of another contemplative author, Bernadette Roberts. I marveled at her first book, *The Experience of No Self*. She describes wild spiritual experiences unlike any I heard of. She was connected also with two of the monasteries I knew, the Hermitage in Big Sur, and St Benedict's in Snowmass, Colorado. One of the things she said struck me. She said she failed at everything in her life. I wondered if failure was my fate as well. When I started showing photographs in juried exhibitions I noticed how other photographers wanted to talk to me and seemed to respect me without knowing anything about me other than I made nice photographs and won awards. I saw immediately how my ego liked this attention, and how it was dangerous. "Best in Show" means I am surely special. For some, the spiritual journey may be a path of failure. Perhaps I unconsciously sabotaged my success in anything because of the danger that success might derail spiritual growth. The ever-present danger is that I can be as proud of failure as of success. The ego is fond of success, so that I might not consider a better way. Failure also works for the ego, if it leads to despair. Is spiritual pride the worst illusion? Is spiritual "success" the greatest danger? Humility is the honesty that knows I'm not humble.

Two other things happened around the same time. I'm not sure of the dates. From my journal during the Centering Prayer retreat I see that I recently started the *Workbook* lessons in ACIM, so I purchased the book shortly before, probably March, 1992. Also around this time, I received a letter from my brother Gerry revealing that he suffered severe depression for many years. I didn't suspect it. Because of my own battles with depression, I intuited what he endured. His struggle seemed worse than my own. I encouraged him to try Centering Prayer and attend an intensive retreat if possible. I saw his and my own depression as a type of "dark night" of the spiritual journey. Sometimes it is and sometimes it isn't. There can be a type of depression associated with the "dryness" of the spiritual journey or the "absence" of God. There is also a neurotic and self-centered depression that has nothing to do with the spiritual journey.

Gerry did embrace Centering Prayer, attended an intensive retreat before I did, and received direct attention from Fr. Keating, but his depression persisted. For myself, my depression lifted and the retreat was a wonderful experience, as expected. Fr. Thomas Keating was amazing. I didn't get to see him much because of his poor health. I met privately with him once. I visited with him on another occasion when he came to Anchorage. Fr. Thomas exudes an energy of holiness. I think the presence of Christ is palatable in him. In 2015, he is still going, ninety-two years old, a monk for seventy-one years. I also met with the saint, Fr. Theophane. When I embraced him at the "kiss of peace" during the monastery Mass, he said, "Welcome back." I didn't remember seeing him during my previous two visits. Before I left our meeting I tried to give him pictures of my kids, but he did not want the pictures. I said, "So you remember to pray for them," and he accepted the pictures, saying, "I'll tell people they're mine." His great sense of humor made me laugh.

In a intensive retreat like this, one becomes more spiritually sensitive and open. Love is felt on different levels; love for God, love for other people; love for nature and natural beauty. I thirsted for love like the person dying of thirst in the desert. My awareness of God's love remained blocked since 1976. On the human level, I felt not only did my wife not love me, she actually despised me. I did experience a deep love with my children, especially when they were very young, before the seemingly unavoidable walls develop. The special love relationship with Dee shifted to the special hate relationship, just as the course describes. I did not know her abrasive anger was a symptom of her own depression. Someone else told me she was depressed before I suspected it. We knew we needed to make changes, but I more or less resigned myself to an unhappy marriage. As a Catholic, I could not end my marriage, and when I married I determined not to follow in my father's footsteps. He married five times. In fact, fear of divorce, or failure of the marriage, was one of the reasons it took me five years and two engagements to finally make the commitment. In my deterioration – my undoing – my relationships with both wife and the Catholic Church crashed.

A big issue between Dee and myself was money, as it is for many couples. The love of, and desire for, money, is one of the greatest dividers. What do we keep more separate than our bank accounts? Dee resented that I did not make money. The only financial advantage of my photography "business expenses" was as a tax write-off. The cost of doing photography bothered her despite the cost being covered mostly by tax savings. She did not understand, nor support, my passion for creative work and I began to feel guilty about it. Dee's despising of me furthered my sense of failure. I did not provide money as social norms say I should.

The company my wife worked for, British Petroleum, offered employees options for a voluntary severance package. Dee said she had not made a decision, but the deadline came while I was on the retreat in Snowmass. I called home during the retreat and she confirmed my feelings about our marriage. I asked her what she decided about her job and she refused to answer. She also said she hired painters to paint the outside trim on our house. I found it strange she did that without consulting me. I did most of the work on the house myself, including painting and remodeling. Her coldness and secretiveness about a major decision (her job) affecting the whole family convinced me that the divide between us was great and growing.

During the retreat I became attracted to a female participant, a psychotherapist a few years older than I. I felt an intoxicating combination of exhilaration and fear in this "romance." I did not know what to do with it. I had no intention of divorcing my wife, despite our bad marriage, and I could not even imagine leaving my kids. She hadn't married and lived in a different state on the other side of the country. But I longed for love and here was love, apparently. If one is dying of thirst in the desert, it does not matter who brings water. We held hands and I was dizzy. We didn't make love; I was never unfaithful to my wife. Sex had tempted me three times in that year but my conscience did not permit it. Two of the women I met through the Centering Prayer classes taught by Kess, and the other I met in Russia.

After the retreat I flew to Dayton, Ohio to attend the annual Taize conference. Taize is a town in France where a new contemporary contemplative Christian community formed. The Taize community, clearly Christian, monastic and non-denominational, used amazingly inspiring chants in their liturgies. The presence of the Holy Spirit was palpable. In many ways I felt that the Taize movement and Centering Prayer demonstrated a renewal of the authentic Christianity I was looking for – a true, contemporary reformation. I did not travel much out of Alaska and synchronously, the Centering Prayer retreat ended on the same day the Taize conference started.

It turned out that the woman I was falling in love with lived in Ohio. Not Dayton, but she could drive there and I invited her to attend the Taize retreat. She attended and we grew closer. I felt more confused, falling more in love with her, and not having any idea what to do about it. We both fell hard and I felt a lightness, as if I was ten years younger. I could not control this force. Yet here was an unsolvable dilemma: love was sinful, and so was resistance to love. The situation tortured me because on one hand I hoped for something sweet, some solution to my sad situation, and on the other hand I saw no way to realize that hope. No solution. Our shared practice of Centering Prayer supported our bonding in a common spiritual ground. The contrast between this new love and my marriage was stark, as it usually is in these situations. No accumulation of past distorted yet, no history harmed us. It seemed like we didn't have a future either. I flew back to Alaska hoping that somehow we would work things out. We would not, however, ever see each other again. To be continued.

PART III

ENDING HELL

When you want only love, you will see
nothing else.[1]

~A Course In Miracles

Chapter Ten

TRUE FORGIVENESS AND THE END OF GUILT

*T*his chapter begins the final part of this book: applying the ideas presented earlier. Practicing the teaching ends hell. Forgiveness, *as the course teaches it*, is a primary practice in ending hell, and ending depression. Forgiveness erases the claim of guilt that causes suffering. Ending guilt ends depression.

> **The guiltless mind cannot suffer.**[1]

The practice of the idea, not the idea itself, is what proves the idea true. Belief in the idea is not necessary, but practice is.

> **This is not a course in the play of ideas, but in their practical application.**[2]

The course promises that the practice of true forgiveness ends depression because forgiveness ends the cause of depression. Forgiveness recognizes the Atonement. Guilt is gone.

> **Forgiveness is the key to happiness.**[3]

If I could exchange depression for happiness, would I do it? If I could exchange guilt for peace would I do it? This chapter describes the practical application of true forgiveness. The meaning of forgiveness, as the course teaches it, is not the traditional understanding of the word. Before getting to that, what is forgiveness for? It is for healing guilt over the separation that is the source of suffering.

Releasing Guilt

Forgiveness is the remedy for sin, guilt, judgment, condemnation, anger, and attack because guilt and true forgiveness cannot coexist. The original sin of separation led to a sense of guilt enormous and unbearable. The defense mechanisms I use for protection from guilt do not heal it; they hide it. Out of sight, out of mind. It's like having a toilet that flushes directly into a secret basement inside my own house. Although the temporary solution provides relief, the real solution becomes more difficult, because the real problem is hidden in a secret and dark place, a place I don't even know about. I do not know the unconscious, by definition. I do not want to know it because it is a dark and scary place sometimes symbolized in dreams as filled with venomous snakes and spiders barely visible in the dimness. They feed at night, in the cover of darkness.

> The acceptance of guilt into the mind of God's Son was the beginning of the separation, as the acceptance of the Atonement is its end. The world you see is the delusional system of those made mad by guilt.[4]

Guilt makes me insane. The world I see is delusional because it is a projection of collective, unconscious guilt. And so it is a mad, mad world I perceive. It is delusional; it is not real. Guilt is for sin I believe happened, but didn't. The price for believing in guilt is massive madness: awareness of love is lost. I believe God evicted me from the Kingdom of Heaven. If God did this, then I deserved it; I must be guilty.

> For it is guilt that has obscured the Father to you, and it is guilt that has driven you insane.[5]

Unconscious Guilt For Attacking God

Guilt drives me into depression, denying the joy of Heaven. Separation, guilt, and attack on God are all related. The unconscious belief that I attacked God, by separating from Him, and dividing His Son, is the primary source of all unconscious guilt.

> If the ego is the symbol of the separation, it is also the symbol of guilt. Guilt is more than merely not of God. It is a symbol of attack on God...This is the belief from which all guilt stems.[6]

My guilty secrets are revealed for releasing. If I remain unconscious, I remain in darkness, and guilt continues its secret condemnation that keeps me in fear. Darkness (unconsciousness) hides in the absence of light.

> The darkest and deepest cornerstone in the ego's foundation: a secret it guards with its life – its existence depends on it. We must look upon it: you believe that you have crucified God's Son. You have not admitted to this "terrible" secret.[7]

At first glance it might not seem true that I believe I crucified God's son, or attacked God at all. But this guilt is a guarded secret, locked deep in the unconscious vault. It is the deepest foundation of the false self. As a Catholic, I related to the idea of guilt over crucifying God's Son. Catholic churches feature, front and center, a realistic, life-sized sculpture of Jesus nailed and bleeding on the cross, crown of thorns pressed into his head. What is the reason for the torture and killing of the most holy and innocent Son of God, who is also God Himself, the Second Person of the Holy Trinity? The reason for this horror is my sins. I caused this killing to happen. My sins required him to be tortured and sacrificed. The loving Father demanded the blood of His Son to pay for my sins. The Jews created guilt and the Catholics perfected it, goes an old joke that is ironic because it has some truth to it.

Imagine you are a parent with two children. One is the perfect child, respectful, loving, a delight to be around. The other child is the opposite. He is disrespectful, mean and frequently in fights and trouble with the law. What should the parent do? The parent could demand that the good child be slowly tortured to death. In this way the sins of the bad child are washed away by the blood of the good child. Although such logic represents an early stage of human development, many still think this way today. Abraham intended to kill his miraculous son in order to obey God. Humans accepted and practiced human sacrifice for religious reasons then. Since Cain killed Abel, how many murders happened? How many suicides? In the twentieth century alone, humans sacrificed over 100 million people to the twin gods of power and money, also known as the military-industrial complex. Add to those numbers torture, rape, assault, lies, and theft. It is also possible that I committed murder, rape, and torture in one of my serial dream lives and I still hold guilt over these past events. Karma continues consequences of past choices, good or evil, into the future, whether I remember what happened or not. As the karmic cycle balances behavior, I'm a murderer in one life and murdered in another. There is a lot of guilt accumulated in the collective unconscious. We have tried to kill God's son billions of times, and billions of bodies have suffered and died.

The unconscious guilt over my mistakes denies joy. I do not believe I deserve joy because of my unspeakable sin. I believe I deserve punishment and pain. Since I rejected God, God rejects me. I project my rejection of God onto God, making God the One Who rejects me.

> The "attack on God" made his son think he was Fatherless, and out of his depression he made the god of depression. This was his alternative to joy...[8]

Depression is deserved; it is just punishment from a just God. That's what the ego wants me to believe. In fact, sadness is self-punishment, in the hope of mitigating the wrath of God; or, my sorry state is used to blame my brother, so as to avoid my own responsibility.

The Atonement says sin did not happen, but my sight shows sinners sinning, and if I believe sin did happen, then for all practical purposes, it did happen, and I suffer a real sense of guilt, and fear punishment, both consciously and unconsciously.

Do you really believe that you can kill the Son of God?[9]

Because the worst guilt is unconscious, I project it onto others, who are now deserving of my attack. The Jews became the scapegoat for my guilt. They killed the Son of God.

The first attack is mental: judgment. Physical attack begins with a mental attack based on judgment, that is my thoughts about what I think happened, in the past. When I attack anyone, I add to my guilt. I'm guilty of attacking my innocent brother. I do not realize that what I accuse him of is actually within me. I project unconscious guilt unconsciously. It is a vicious and blind circle. Guilt and fear keep me out of the Kingdom of Heaven because God's Kingdom is a Kingdom of Perfect Love, and fear blocks the awareness of love. I cannot choose both love and fear. Weapons are not needed nor permitted on the peace train.

> Peace and guilt are antithetical, and the Father can be remembered only in peace. Love and guilt cannot coexist, and to accept one is to deny the other. Guilt hides Christ from your sight, for it is the denial of the blamelessness of God's Son.[10]

Guilt, Identity-Confusion, and Depression

The ego's continuity depends on my continuing belief in sin and guilt. If I feel guilty, this tells how I identify myself.

> If you identify with the ego, you must perceive yourself as guilty. Whenever you respond to your ego you will experience guilt, and you will fear punishment.[11]

Depression, again, is an identity-confusion disorder, caused by guilt, that then causes fear. This is a simple identity test. If I see myself as guilty, I identify with ego. My true identity is the blameless Son of God who cannot be guilty.

> **The disheartened are useless to themselves and to me [Jesus], but only the ego can be disheartened.**[12]

My mind identifies with either ego or spirit. Only separate self is depressed. Only ego judges. Only ego attacks. Only ego pretends there are many to judge and attack each other.

Spirit, my true nature, is as God created it, and God did not create His Son to be depressed, or suffer in any way. Guilt keeps me from knowing my true identity, and because this guilt is unconscious, I don't know what keeps me from knowing. I believe what I see, the effects. I'm blocked without knowing it.

> **What is there God created to be sick?**[13]

Is there any sense to the idea that God created us to suffer? Is God a sadist, worse than an average human?

> **Your will is lost to you in this strange bartering, in which guilt is traded back and forth, and grievances increase with each exchange. Can such a world have been created by the Will the Son of God shares with his Father? Did God create disaster for His Son? Creation is the Will of Both together. Would God create a world that kills Himself?**[14]

Does God enjoy my suffering as entertainment like humans enjoy violent movies and the virtual violence of video games?

How do I feel when I have a grievance? How do I feel when I hold a grudge? What causes me to keep grudges and grievances? The ego is maintained by grievances and tries to suck me into believing past harm happened, and that the attacker and the attacked are separated and different. This attack deserves my anger and righteous revenge, if I am the victim of attack, or, deserving of shame and punishment if I'm the attacker.

> Idle wishes and grievances are partners or co-makers in picturing the world you see. The wishes of the ego gave rise to it, and the ego's need for grievances, which are necessary to maintain it, peoples it with figures that seem to attack you and call for "righteous" judgment. These figures become the middlemen the ego employs to traffic in grievances.[15]

Belief in grievances births judgment and attack, that are of the ego. The split between "self and other" is part of the ego's thought system of separation, or duality. There are not "others" because we are one. My grievance towards my brother is a projection of my grievance towards myself.

Whatever I do to anyone is done to the Sonship, the Christ, and therefore to myself. All attack is destructive to myself. Depression is mental self-judgment, condemnation, and attack. I am unconsciously angry towards myself for my shameful sin and should suffer for it. So I project my own guilt onto my brother. This is literally an attack on myself.

> All attack is self attack.[16]

I am fooled into believing my dream of separation is real if I attack "others," or am attacked. I do not see that attacking another is attacking myself because the dynamic of projection is unconscious. I feel it, however, as depression and anger.

> The ego teaches you to attack yourself because you are guilty, and this must increase the guilt, for guilt is the result of attack. In the ego's teaching, then, there is no escape from guilt.[17]

This is the vicious circle the ego does not want me to escape from. Guilt results in attack, producing more guilt, producing more attack, etc. For the ego, there is no exit in this recycling and accumulation of grievance, guilt and attack. This game of guilt forms fear.

What if judging self or other contributes to depression? If all attack is self-attack, then I hurt myself when I attack another. If I judge my brother it means I do not understand the relationship between judging and depression. I literally make myself more depressed when I accuse and attack my brother, but I am unconscious of this cause and effect process. So I treat symptoms instead of cause. An unspoken judgmental thought is enough to depress me because the attack thought accuses me. If I realize that judgment causes depression, why would I continue judging? If I persist, it means I want to be depressed. Judgment is a choice for depression.

Guilt and Special Relationships

When guilt is projected it is unconscious attack on my brother and this is separation. You are guilty and I'm not, or at least, you are more guilty. We are definitely different. Special relationships are maintained by belief in past guilt and grievances. If we are one Son of God, who could condemn or be condemned? Duality breeds judgment. Non-duality is freedom from judgment.

> If you did not feel guilty you could not attack, for condemnation is the root of attack. It is the judgment of one mind by another as unworthy of love and deserving of punishment. But herein lies the split. For the mind that judges perceives itself as separate from the mind being judged, believing that by punishing another, it will escape punishment.[18]

Guilt, judgment, and attack are based on belief in separation. The truth is that I am not separate and so I hurt myself if I attack anyone. If I accuse someone of sin I'm choosing for the ego, not for God.

If you attack error in another, you will hurt yourself.[19]

When I mentally attack my brother by projecting my guilt on to him, I actually attack myself because the source of the guilt is within, not without, and my brother is me, not other than me. This whole process happens unconsciously, until it becomes conscious, which then reveals the absurdity of making myself depressed. It is as insane as hitting myself in the head with a hammer. Or cutting off my own ear.

Guilt and Time

Guilt is related to the continuity of past into future. Guilt, over past sin, deserves punishment, in the future. Do the crime and serve the time. Belief in guilt is belief in time. The karmic cycle of guilt and fear is ended by the holy instant, where there is no past or future, only now, as it is in Heaven. If the past is gone, the basis for guilt is gone. If the guilt is gone, the basis for fear of future punishment is gone. If fear of future punishment is gone, fear of a punishing God is gone. The whole thing collapses like dominos falling into each other. Tip the first one and the rest follow easily.

> **You can hold on to the past only through guilt. For guilt establishes that you will be punished for what you have done...**[20]

Ceasing Judgment Means Ceasing Suffering

I cherish judgment because it is a deeply ingrained habit that seems to help me feel I am special, better than my brother, whom I judge as more guilty, or as a worse schmuck than I am. The cost of judgment is the exhausting pain of depression.

> **The strain of constant judgment is virtually intolerable. It is curious that an ability so debilitating would be so deeply cherished.**[21]

The choice to judge is a denial of the truth. I cannot know the truth of myself or my brother if I judge him, or judge myself, which is the same thing. I can reverse wrong-minded thinking into a denial of the denial of the truth. I deny the ego's false accusation, or suffer the consequences.

> **The choice to judge rather than to know is the cause of the loss of peace.** [22]

Judgment is based on ignorance, the opposite of knowing. The course promises peace if I release all judgment.

> **You have no idea of the tremendous release and deep peace that comes from meeting yourself and your brothers totally without judgment.** [23]

Guilty or Not Guilty?

As the course repeats, I choose between two thought systems about what is true or not. The ego tries to complicate it, confuse me, and delay my liberation, by myriads of forms of its thought system. The choice, regardless of the form of the lesson, is simple and clear: God's Son is either innocent or guilty. Whichever view (map) I choose leads to a completely different world.

> **The certain outcome of the lesson that God's Son is guilty is the world you see. It is a world of terror and despair. Nor is there hope of happiness in it. There is no plan for safety you can make that will ever succeed. There is no joy that you can seek for here and hope to find.** [24]

Despite deception and accepting the temptation to believe that I am guilty, I learn, sooner or later, the eternal truth that I am innocent and holy. So is everyone.

> And you will learn God's Son is innocent, and see
> another world. The outcome of the lesson that God's
> Son is guiltless is a world in which there is no fear,
> and everything is lit with hope and sparkles in gentle
> friendliness.[25]

God's Son is innocent because this is how God created him; this is God's Will. Some say sin is real since I use free will to choose sin. It is more accurate to say that I fall down while learning to ride a bike. I do make wrong choices in the dream, and these mistakes are easily corrected simply by choosing again, what I truly want, which is the same as what God wants. Sin, and a separate will that chooses against God, seem to happen in the dream but actually do not happen at all. The holy instant demonstrates that there is no past. The Atonement declares that the separation didn't happen and the Atonement is realized through true forgiveness.

Self-Condemnation As Failure

Even though all judgment is self-judgment, while I am in the dream of separation I see a difference between conscious judgment of myself and my brother. There is a self-accusing judgment related to depression. If I judge myself as guilty, is depression self-punishment to mitigate God's just wrath?

> The ego believes that by punishing itself it will mitigate
> the punishment of God.[26]

It is easy for a depressed person to judge himself a "failure." I know I did. The sense of failure comes in different forms: failure of relationships, failure of career, failure at school, failure at sports, failure to thrive, etc. Probably the most painful sense of failure is that of spiritual failure. Now I failed big-time. Now I have failed God. Judging myself increases guilt, fear, and depression. I drop the accusation of failure towards myself by realizing that I do not know, and so, I cannot judge. What if failure is supposed to happen? Could failure facilitate growth? What if I grow faster through failure than through success? Is it true that the more pleasure, power, and success I experience in this world, the less likely I am to renounce the world and accept liberation? This is the purpose of suffering: showing that separation cannot work. The recognition that my state of mind is unpleasant and unwanted is the evidence that convinces me to use my power of choice to choose again, and choose not to suffer. That recognition is painful in itself, but without it why would I choose differently? Suffering may motivate me to find a better way. At the same time, if I view the renunciation of the world as a sacrifice, I introduce fear and defeat the relief of renouncing the world.

The ego wants any and all success, including spiritual success, and takes the credit for what I judge as "successful." The ego does this to keep the game going, keep me in illusion. Joel S. Goldsmith:

> Students are often concerned that their own happiness, peace, and harmony are not complete, that they can bring greater good to others than to themselves. This often brings doubts and fears to the student: doubt that God is still with him; fear that a sense of separation from God may permanently hold him. These things come only that the student never shall be tempted to glorify himself, or take pride in his own understandings.[27]

Self-glorification, success, and pride are ego's intentions. Vanity is verified. Therefore, failure is grace.

At certain stages of the spiritual path there is an emphasis on a strict moral law and I might think that my behavior demonstrates the success or failure of my will power, and thus my devotion. Ramana Maharshi:

> Your idea of willpower is success insured. Willpower should be understood to be strength of mind which makes

it capable of meeting success or failure with equanimity. It is not synonymous with certain success. Why should one's attempts always be attended by success? Success breeds arrogance and man's spiritual progress is thus arrested. Failure, on the other hand, is beneficial, in as much as it opens his eyes to his limitations and prepares him to surrender himself. Self-surrender is synonymous with eternal happiness…success and failure are the results of parabdha [past actions, currently bearing fruit] and not of will power.[28]

My day to day experience of success or failure is a result of karmic action, not my will power. Self-surrender is the surrender of the separate self sense, the me, the ego. Spiritual "success," or worldly success, continues the ego because it breeds arrogance and thus thwarts the surrender of self. I can, as noted before, be as proud of failure as success. Each is a judgment. What I judge as failure may be success. And what I judge as success may be failure.

Put yourself not in charge of this [salvation], for you cannot distinguish between advance and retreat. Some of your greatest advances you have judged as failures, and some of your deepest retreats you have evaluated as success.[29]

Judgment and Perception

One reason I judge is because I believe my perception is true. Can a blind person jury a visual art show? When I believe my senses, I forget that I dream and make the dream appear real. Senses do perceive duality, differences, self and other, success and failure, attack and anger, sin and guilt. Perception provides the basis for judgment. As I am able, I withdraw belief in senses that demonstrate the dream domain.

> You do not seem to doubt the world you see. You do not
> really question what is shown you through the body's
> eyes. Nor do you ask why you believe it, even though you
> learned a long while since your senses do deceive.[30]

I perceive what appears to be consequences of the will to separate: sin, guilt, fear and suffering. I perceive duality, differences, oppositions, good and evil, beautiful and ugly, true and false, all judgments. It is easier to drop judgment if I realize that I do not understand my perception and cannot trust it. What I perceive is a projection. Guilt in, guilt out. Love in, love out.

Magicians are also called illusionists. They create an illusion where I think I see something that did not happen. Slight of hand, slight of eye, slight of mind. Stop allowing perceptual trickery.

> How can you judge? Your judgment rests upon the
> witness that your senses offer you. Yet witness never falser
> was than this. But how else do you judge the world you
> see? You place pathetic faith in what your eyes and ears
> report. You think your fingers touch reality, and close
> upon the truth.[31]

In truth, I am not able to judge, even if I want to. I am advised not simply to drop judgment; I am told that it is impossible to judge in the first place. Judgment is an illusion based on illusions. I cannot judge because I do not know the meaning of what my senses present. If I judge anyone, I am in ego mode, living the dream.

> Can this be judgment? You have often been urged to
> refrain from judging, not because it is a right to be
> withheld from you. You cannot judge. You merely can
> believe the ego's judgments, all of which are false.[32]

The ego is constantly judging, accusing, condemning, defending, attacking. If I catch myself judging, it is a sure and simple sign that I agreed with the ego. The ego proves its position with perception. Literally, eye witnesses declare the verdict: guilty and deserving of death.

I will not use the body's eyes today.[33]

This means I won't believe what my eyes see and thus I lose the basis for judgment.

> **Let not your eyes behold a dream; your ears bear witness to illusion. They [my senses] were made to look upon a world that is not there; to hear the voices that can make no sound.**[34]

Is it not my senses that say something is wrong, that I am sad, that someone is sick? My senses testify that separation is sure, that I am different. ACIM teaches me not to trust my senses because they are false witnesses, perceiving an exterior world not there. My senses witness against the truth that I am still as God created me, and that God created one Son, and created Him perfectly. Early on the course asks me to question the reality and meaning of my perception. The first lesson in the *Workbook* states:

> **Nothing I see in this room [on this street, from this window, in this place] means anything.**[35]

Ending Judgment

If I drop judgment I stop hurting myself. Ending judgment stops the accumulation of more guilt. Jesus in Matthew's Gospel:

> **Judge not, that you be not judged. For with the judgment you pronounce you will be judged, and the measure you give will be the measure you get. Why do you see the speck that is in your brother's eye, but do not notice the log that is in your own eye?**[36]

When I judge anyone I judge myself. I *do not notice* my hidden, forbidden, unconscious guilt, *the log that is in your own eye*, and I project it onto my brother as a judgment. Would I judge a brother if I realized that the fault I see in my brother is not in him, but me?

I also judge according to how I am conditioned, my frame of reference, from the past. I judge according to not knowing, ignorance, blindness. Jesus in Matthew's Gospel:

> **You have heard that it was said to the men of old, "You shall not kill; and whoever kills shall be liable to judgment." But I say to you that everyone who is angry with his brother shall be liable to judgment; whoever insults his brother shall be liable to the council, and whoever says, "You fool!" shall be liable to the hell of fire.** [37]

...it was said to the men of old, refers to past conditioning. Jesus is revising what I have heard, or my conditioning. Anger relies on judgment; *You fool* is actually self-judgment, and I end up in the hell-fire of depression. I am fooled and foolish when I judge my brother a fool.

Many religions present God as a just judge. Justice is served! Yet Jesus says this about His Father:

> **The Father judges no one, but has given all judgment to the son, that all may honor the son, even as they honor the Father.** [38]

God's justice is this: mercy. Just as the Father does not judge, Jesus does not judge because He does only what the Father is doing. Their Will is one. Since the Father judges no one, then Jesus judges no one. If I recognize how the ego's world of pain relies on judgment, would I continue judging? Does not me vs. you and us vs. them require judgment? Does not killing and war, even in self-defense, require judgment? I'm right and you're wrong is the duality of judgment. Why continue judging if I realize that judgment relies on grievance over what I think happened, but didn't? Judgment precedes despair. I consider suicide after judging myself or my life-situation. Would I continue judgment if I recognized that my judgments are projections? Anyone who calls another a narcissist is demonstrating his own narcissism because he could not know what narcissism is if it was not in him. If I identify as being one of the "good guys," then I have embraced judgment and duality.

I practice a serious, long-term, habit of judging. Here is the great addiction; I am dependent on judging. It is hard to drop judgment because it is going to cost all my previous conditioning. Does not my whole identity, relationships, and world depend on judgment, based on memory and learning of the past? How could I live without judgment? Judgment is obligatory in duality and impossible in non-duality.

I stop the increasing of guilt by dropping judgment. So try to give up all judgment for a while. See what happens. The truth is, when I judge/attack another, I remain unconscious of my projected guilt. I feel bad because I attacked someone who truly is still as God created him, perfect and sinless. I make the dream real for myself. This mistake makes me feel depressed; I am attacking myself and opposing God, arguing with God that He did not create everyone perfect. Only in the detour into fear, in the ego's illusionary world of separation, am I not perfect, and different from my brother, guilty as sin.

> **Be innocent of judgment, unaware of any thoughts of evil or of good that ever crossed your mind of anyone.** [39]

When I decide to drop judgment, I stop increasing guilt. The Holy Spirit removes the unconscious guilt I already accumulated through the practice of true forgiveness.

True Forgiveness

How do I drop judgment? Practicing true forgiveness is the antidote for judgment, and the ending of judgment. This is my choice, judge or forgive. Accepting the Atonement for myself is choosing with the Holy Spirit for forgiveness.

> If what you offer is complete forgiveness you must have
> let guilt go, accepting the Atonement for yourself and
> learning you are guiltless.[40]

Accepting the Atonement is accepting God's unconditional Grace of Salvation. It is joining my will with God's Will.

> **The means of the Atonement is forgiveness.**[41]

My part in the Atonement is to practice true forgiveness. True forgiveness allows the Holy Spirit to remove blocks to the awareness of love established by guilt and its consequence: fear.

In the Gospels, Jesus is accused of blasphemy by the Pharisees for pronouncing forgiveness of sins. Only God can forgive and who is Jesus to play God? For Pharisees, then and now, forgiveness is forbidden. Ego fears forgiveness so fiercely that the practice of pardon is illegal and to be punished by torture and death. In Matthew's Gospel Jesus says, however, about God and forgiveness:

> **For if you forgive men their trespasses, your heavenly
> Father also will forgive you; but if you do not forgive men
> their trespasses, neither will your Father forgive your
> trespasses.**[42]

As I give forgiveness, I receive forgiveness. As I give judgment, I receive judgment. ACIM teaches a basic law that giving and receiving are the same. They are the same because we are one. Whatever I give, condemnation or forgiveness, I receive. Whatever I do, I do to myself. Jesus confirms this again when he teaches how to pray in Matthew's Gospel.

> **And forgive us our debts, as we also have forgiven our
> debtors.**[43]

If I do not forgive my brother then I deny forgiveness to myself because my brother is me, one Son of God. I receive forgiveness as I give forgiveness. These ideas are repeated intentionally. Without repetition the ideas do not stick because they are so different from what I learned all my life. I quickly backslide into my old conditioning without a lot of reminders. True forgiveness is radically different from the forgiveness I learned growing up.

Without the acceptance of the Atonement, true forgiveness is almost impossible to practice. True forgiveness, as taught by the course, is difficult to believe and practice without the mind training that replaces wrong-minded thinking with right-minded thinking. True forgiveness is inconceivable to the wrong-minded and is interpreted as a particularly lame form of denial. What is true forgiveness?

> **Let us review the meaning of "forgive," for it is apt to be distorted and to be perceived as something that entails an unfair sacrifice of righteous wrath, a gift unjustified and undeserved, and a complete denial of the truth.**[44]

True forgiveness is the radical recognition that no harm happened in the first place. There is nothing to forgive. From a wrong-minded view, true forgiveness seems to be *complete denial of the truth*. I am denied *righteous wrath*. When I believe my brother hurt me, I want revenge, punishment, prison, or at least an apology and admission of wrong-doing. Sometimes only the death penalty will do. The traditional understanding of forgiveness is that if someone hurt me, I may forgive him or not, but the fact remains, he hurt me. To say otherwise is denial. In the world's wrong-mindedness, true forgiveness is a lame denial of the plain and evident perception (projection) that people hurt each other all the time.

This process of true forgiveness is opposite of the world's version of forgiveness. The world's version of forgiveness says, "Even though you hurt me, I'm going to forgive you." The world's version first makes the offense real, confirming guilt. And even if "pardon" is granted, the ego doesn't forget the offense. Grievance, grudge, and guilt continue my mind in pain. Guilt is not relieved by punishment either. After conviction and serving time, the offender is still guilty of his crime. My pain is proof that you are guilty. You would not need my forgiveness unless you are guilty.

> If you forgive your brother his transgressions, you but add to all the guilt that he has really earned. Forgiveness does not first establish sin and then forgive it. Who can say and mean, "My brother, you have injured me, and yet, because I am the better of the two, I pardon you my hurt." You grant your brother mercy but retain the proof he is not really innocent.[45]

The Atonement proclaims the truth that the separation, and the chain reaction of consequences it seemed to foster, did not, and could not, happen. I am as God created me and God created me as an extension of Himself, impossible to separate from Him. Same goes for you and everyone else, including my so-called enemies. Separation is not, because separation is not God's Will. I can, however, wish to be separated. Just like the 18-year-old who wants to move out of his parents house and get his own place. Just like the prodigal son. But the Will of God is not trumped.

Forgiveness and Projection

Another aspect of true forgiveness is understanding the mechanism of projection. This virtual reality I'm perceiving is being projected in my mind, by the collective unconscious mind, like a dream during sleep.

> Projection makes perception…[46]

I need to understand that not only is the projection not real, but that I share responsibility for making the projection. Projection reveals what is hidden in my unconscious mind. Therefore my brother did not hurt me. The world did not hurt me. Nothing outside of myself hurts me because there is nothing outside of myself, except as an image in a dream, a projection of what is in me. I forgive my own projection, not my brother, whom I mistakenly painted as guilty.

Pilots learn to fly planes on sophisticated flight simulators that make it seem as if they are flying a real plane. If they crash the plane, nothing happens, no plane blows up, no one is hurt. The bullets and bombs in a movie do not hurt the viewer, nor the actors who pretend to die; the silver screen is not damaged. If I watch a movie and see a terrible tragedy, I might feel real emotions even though I know it is make believe. I might find a movie truly funny and laugh my ass off. The actors are pretending; but it seems rather real. One movie production company is called *Dreamworks*. The movie, *Inception*, is all about dreaming, levels of dreaming, and either knowing or not knowing that I'm dreaming. In this world I perceive much more sophisticated "visual effects" than current film technology. Whatever seems to happen in this world, good or bad, is a simulation, and not actually happening and thus not needing forgiveness. If I hurt someone in a dream, do I feel the need to apologize when I wake up?

Because my guilt is unconscious, how do I deal with it? How does healing happen when I don't even know I need it? Once the unconscious part of the mind was theorized, psychologists figured out ways to discover unconscious mind content and thus make it conscious. These methods include hypnosis, interpretation of dreams, and free association. In a way, the client is tricked into revealing what is hidden and the therapist translates the revelation in such a way that the client gains insight into his own unconscious. The divine therapy proposed by ACIM uses projection as the means by which I see what is hidden in my unconscious mind. If I see my brother as guilty of a sin, I projected my own unconscious guilt onto him. Revealed as unreal, guilt is healed. If unconscious guilt is not revealed, it continues its secret work, continuing the guilty mind in pain, continuing its defense by projected attack. Projection provides that revealing, if I'm willing to see it.

True forgiveness, then, is recognizing that:

1. Whatever I thought my enemy or friend did to me did not happen. Or, if I prefer, it only happened in the dreamed drama mind-movie, a simulated, virtual reality, the ego's kingdom of sleepy separation.

2. I help project this mind-movie: I accept responsibility for making this projection, and

3. This projection is grace because it makes conscious the unconscious guilt hiding in my mind that I now let the Holy Spirit heal.

4. I forgive myself this mistake, this mis-perception/projection, and gratefully let it go. The Holy Spirit does the rest, healing the unconscious guilt in my mind, correcting perception and projection. Now I see my brother through the forgiving eyes of Christ. In this way, true forgiveness releases my brother and I together.

Forgiveness is temporary. Forgiveness is for illusions, not for truth. There is no need for forgiveness in Heaven. True forgiveness forgives the *belief* in sin, not actual sin. True forgiveness:

> ...looks on lies, but it is not deceived. It does not heed the self-accusing shrieks of sinners mad with guilt. It looks on them with quiet eyes, and merely says to them, "my brother, what you think is not the truth."[47]

The spiritual teacher Byron Katie teaches the exact same form of forgiveness:

> Forgiveness means discovering that what you thought happened, didn't. Until you can see that there is nothing to forgive, you haven't really forgiven. No one has ever hurt anyone. No one has ever done anything terrible.

There's nothing terrible except your uninvestigated
thoughts about what happened. So when you suffer,
inquire, look at the thoughts you are thinking, and set
yourself free. Be a child. Start from the mind that knows
nothing. Take your ignorance all the way to freedom.[48]

How can she say no one ever hurt anyone? Isn't it obvious that people
hurt each other all the time? What is war? According to perception,
yes. According to God's Will, no. Take your pick. If I start from the
place of *not knowing*, then how do I know you hurt me? I don't know.
Byron Katie's teaching is the same as ACIM. No one hurt anyone
else except in the nightmare dream, therefore no one actually, factu-
ally, hurt anyone else. I certainly can, and do, *think* and *perceive* and
believe that people hurt each other. I *remember* past offenses and yet
the holy instant teaches there is no past except the past I choose to
retain via memory. The ego trained me to force continuity of past into
future. This is the ego's world of time. The past is a ball and chain I
willingly drag around through memory. I remember what you did.
I have a grievance; I hold a grudge. To have and to hold. I *want* to
remember what you did. Your sin proves me better than you. And
in remembering past attacks I defend myself by preparing for future
attacks. Don't fool me twice.

I *perceive* people hurting each other yet the course teaches me
to not believe my perception. Seeming true is not Truth. Ever had a
dream where someone is killed, or some other tragedy happens, a real
nightmare that seems horrible and real while sleeping, dreaming? What
happens upon waking up? What of the terrible event and the char-
actors in the dream, the killed and the killer? Where are they now?
Where did they go? It is no accident that spiritual liberation is called
"awakening," and those liberated called "awakened." Re-awakened
might be more accurate. And with awakening comes grateful relief
that the nightmare was only a dream. Perhaps, the worse the dream
is, the greater the relief is upon awakening.

The course places emphasis on discerning cause and effect. To treat an effect is to neglect the cause and thus the effect returns in similar or different ways. To treat myriad symptoms without curing the one cause is like trying to remove a lawn by mowing it, and watering it. Any treatment that does not heal unconscious guilt is futile. Unconscious guilt keeps me out of Heaven because guilt and love cannot co-exist. Guilt causes me to be depressed now, and to return for more serial nightmares as a separate body/ego, the hero of the dream, until all unconscious guilt is undone. This healing of guilt is the purification, the preparation for re-awakening. Judgment, and its close relatives, condemnation, anger, and attack, are opposed to forgiveness and cannot coexist with forgiveness. If it didn't happen, then what am I mad about?

ACIM teaches that just as the separation took place over *millions of years*, the Atonement takes place over a similar long, or even longer, period of time. Why is it taking so long to wake up from this nightmare? Because the worst guilt is unconscious; I'm not even aware of it. When I judge self or another, I choose for guilt, project guilt, increase guilt, and further delay my exit from the virtual reality, yet I don't know I'm doing this. So it is a hard loop to break out of. Wrong-minded conditioning further reinforces the dream as real. How many people do you know who are fully convinced that what we experience here on earth is a dream? How many people know that there is no world? I am conditioned to believe that 1+1=2. How easy is it for me to drop that belief and instead say 1+1=1? It is not easy to break through conditioning.

I also delay the end of hell because I want to continue exploring the dream world of separation, thinking I might still find salvation somehow, somewhere, someday, in another, better, improved, and evolved future. I want to continue to be me. Will I face the fact? There are aspects of the world I like and prefer to keep, such as perception, pleasure, person, place, or possession. I still want to be "me," and keep what is "mine." I still, literally, want my own separate identity and autonomous will. I continue repeating the tiny instant of separation by continuing to want it. What I want is what I get.

Besides unconscious guilt, conditioning, and a continued desire to be my own boss, another reason why my release seems to be taking so long is that as I approach liberation, the end that is the Beginning, fear of the loss of my entire thought system, including loss of perception, kicks in, delaying my progress. Fear of annihilation. Return to the Beginning means the ego returns to nothing, and if the ego is me, then I am annihilated. The ego uses fear to block the trust in God that is a prerequisite for surrender of "me" because the ego is full of fear. The ego fears its own end. This fear of annihilation is identity-confusion.

So if this world and all the suffering over thousands, perhaps millions, of years, is a dream illusion, what purpose does it serve? What is it for? I needed to learn, the hard way, through the seeming suffering experience of this world of hellish hate, the true effect of separation; how it does not, and cannot work. Perhaps, pre-separation, I did not fully appreciate the Kingdom of Heaven because I did not know anything else, like the older son in the prodigal parable. Perhaps, post-separation, I will appreciate peace, like the younger son in the prodigal parable. Like the Joni Mitchell song, *Big Yellow Taxi*, I don't know what I have until it's gone.

Practicing true forgiveness, and relinquishing judgment, condemnation, and attack, are central to healing depression. It is not enough just to understand it. The Holy Spirit gives me many chances to practice true forgiveness daily. Whenever I feel mad, from a slight irritation to full blown rage, it is another chance to step back and forgive. Making use of those chances is the proper use of time. With the help of the Holy Spirit, I begin to replace the habit of judging with the habit of forgiving. This replaces past guilt and future fear with the perfect present, the holy instant. Try it. That's the way to find out if it works.

> **And that in complete forgiveness, in which you recognize that there is nothing to forgive, you are absolved completely.**[49]

Chapter Eleven

MIND YOUR MIND

*T*hinking is closely related to depression. It is well known that people who are depressed are thinking in negative ways. The quote, *I think, therefore I am,* indicates thinking as proof of existence. Awareness, not thought, demonstrates being. It is a mistake to place thought before being. Being is primary and prior to thought. Yet I identify with the talker in my head, the voice of thought that is "me." I can reverse the equation and put thinking in its proper place.

I am aware, therefore I am. I am, therefore I think.[1]

Thinking is not bad or good. It is a tool, like a knife used by a surgeon to save life, or abused by a depressed person to cut his wrists. Thoughts are either right-minded or wrong-minded depending on whether the thought aligns with the Holy Spirit, or ego. When depressed, do you notice any patterns? Do you engage in ruinous rumination? Fear thoughts, worry thoughts, guilty thoughts, attack thoughts, judgmental thoughts? Thoughts about how unfair things are. Thoughts about what sucks? Critical thoughts? Self-critical thoughts? Self-pity thoughts? Suicidal thoughts?

All wrong-minded thinking is the ego whispering, or yelling, in my split-mind. I learn to accept responsibility for believing my thoughts are true, despite the conditioning that influences how I think. No one chooses for me what I believe is true. I choose to believe the wrong-minded thinking of the ego or the right-minded thinking of the Holy Spirit, but the choice is my own. When I believe that an idea is true, it affects me *as if* the thought is true, regardless of the thought's verity. Like the placebo pill that prevents pain.

> Depression means that you have forsworn God. No one
> can really do this, but that you can think you can and
> believe you have is beyond dispute.[2]

If I believe that I am guilty, I experience the painful nightmare of
depression, even if depression is not possible, because guilt is not true.

> Guilt is a sure sign that your thinking is unnatural.
> Unnatural thinking will always be attended with guilt,
> because it is the belief in sin.[3]

Depression is unreal because all suffering is an illusion based on
another illusion: the belief in sin and guilt, or hell. Yet if I believe
depressing thoughts, I experience depression.

> ...thoughts do have consequences to the thinker...[4]

Right-mindedness *and* wrong-mindedness are powerful, because
mind is powerful. Lies yield power if I believe them.

> It is a mistake to believe that a thought system based on
> lies is weak. Do not depreciate the power of your mind.[5]

The power of mind serves ego or spirit. The false separate self, that
seems to suffer, is made by mind. The ego is also unmade by mind. I
choose to construct or deconstruct ego.

> For it is your mind that believes in it [the ego] and gives
> existence to it. Yet it is also your mind that has the power
> to deny the ego's existence, and you will surely do so when
> you realize exactly what the journey is on which the ego
> sets you.[6]

What jolly journey does the ego set me on? It is a trip through sin,
shame, guilt, fear, anger, judgment, condemnation, sickness, suffering, and death. When I recognize what exactly is going on, I end the
guilt trip that is the ego's journey.

In clinical psychology a method of treatment developed called cognitive-behavioral therapy. This approach places emphasis on thinking and how often thinking misinterprets what happens. Basically, there is what happens and what I think about what happens, or my interpretation of the event or situation. What bothers me is more about my interpretation of the event than the event itself.

Here is a true short story that demonstrates this. One evening I wheeled my machine out of a mall parking lot onto a busy street, making a right turn. I checked oncoming traffic and considered the cars approaching far enough back to safely make the turn. I made the turn and sped up, eyeing the car approaching in my lane through the rear view mirror. The driver flashed his car's lights at me and I flashed into a defensive reaction of road rage. Not severe rage, but I felt the unpleasant adrenaline-anger rush. I did not think I cut him off, but apparently he did. I almost raised my arm out the window to give him the one-fingered salute. Then a car going the opposite direction flashed its lights at me. Suddenly I understood the situation. The drivers who flashed their lights were signaling me to turn my lights on. So these drivers were trying to help. I interpreted it in a different and erroneous way, and I paid the price. What actually happened did not upset me. My interpretation of what happened upset me, which means *I* upset me. I learned by experience a good lesson in cognitive psychology that day.

Often, depressing thoughts are misinterpretations of what happened or is happening. Often, as Byron Katie teaches, these thoughts are not examined, not questioned, not true, and yet capable of making me miserable, just because I believe them. As presented in the previous chapter, these erroneous thoughts are judgments, which are attacks, which lead to increasing guilt and the whole chain-reaction vicious circle. Who controls what I believe? Only I can examine and inquire and see how much I believe the thoughts. Are they even my thoughts? Regardless of their source, the big question is do I believe they are true? Thoughts from the ego are lies. Thoughts from the Holy Spirit are true.

I just heard on the radio that Jimmy Carter, age 90, is diagnosed with brain cancer. His response: "I am looking forward to this new adventure." How many of us think of brain cancer as a "new adventure?" He is a shining example of the truth that it is not what happens that upsets me, but how I interpret it. Lessons 5 and 6 from the *Workbook* state:

> I am never upset for the reason I think.[7]

And,

> I am upset because I see something that is not there.[8]

If I am upset, why am I upset? Not for the reason I think. Perception cannot be trusted; it is dream perception. What I think I see is not there.

ACIM stresses the importance of mind over body. Confusing the two is one example of what the course calls "level confusion." This is also true for confusing the brain with the mind. Thinking precedes behavior and real change is at the level of mind, not behavior. My thinking is my responsibility. Choice is at the level of thought.

> You may believe that you are responsible for what you do, but not for what you think. The truth is that you are responsible for what you think, because it is only at this level you have choice. What you do comes from what you think.[9]

Is this not confirmed by Jesus in the New Testament?

> You have heard that it was said, "You shall not commit adultery." But I say to you that everyone who looks at a woman lustfully has already committed adultery with her in his heart.[10]

The act of adultery starts as a thought/desire, in my mind, in my heart. The cause of behavior is the mind and heart's desire. Thinking and wanting steer the wheel of behavior.

Most of the time, thought precedes behavior. The exception is spontaneous action, that is not planned or thought about in advance, and this is rare. If I hike up a trail and suddenly see and hear a rattlesnake, coiled, rattling, and ready to strike, I immediately stop or step back without any thought about it. The action is spontaneous, requiring no planning or thinking. Quick enough the mind kicks in with a worried, "What should I do?" But before the mind kicks in, there is an immediate, and alert, stoppage of mind, allowing spontaneous action. How much of my behavior is premeditated? Wait, let me think about it.

Behavior modification works with symptoms, not source, through positive and negative reinforcement, punishment and reward.

> **You must change your mind, not your behavior, and this is a matter of willingness.**[11]

One of the first things psychology students learn to do in a lab class is to train rats. It is easy enough to change the behavior of mice and men. Commercials are designed by behaviorists to manipulate buying behavior. The change that heals is in the mind, not behavior. Behavior follows mind and not the other way around. I knew a psychology professor who divided all psychologists into one of two camps: shrinks and rat runners. Scientific behaviorism is the answer to Freudian psychoanalysis and all that mumbo jumbo about the unconscious mind and psychic structure, whatever that is.

I do not realize the creative power of my mind to make a whole world of pain, to project a dream of suffering, because this creative power works in the collective unconscious.

> **Few appreciate the real power of the mind…the mind is very powerful, and never loses its creative force. It never**

sleeps. Every instant it is creating. It is hard to recognize that thought and belief combine into a power surge that can literally move mountains...You prefer to believe that your thoughts cannot exert real influence because you are actually afraid of them...there are no idle thoughts. All thinking produces form at some level.[12]

Literally move mountains? That's what it says. It is the combination of thought and belief that is so powerful. If I do not believe a thought, it loses power. If all thinking produces form, what does that say about form? What is form? Form is a product of thought. Form is imagined. Form is a manifestation of image, no more solid than a thought.

Your Father created you wholly without sin, wholly without pain and wholly without suffering of any kind. If you deny Him you bring sin, pain and suffering into your own mind because of the power he gave it. Your mind is capable of creating worlds.[13]

God does not want, and did not create, robots. God created me with the freedom to love and create. I use freedom in a way that chooses God or guilt, love or fear. Recognizing my responsibility is recognizing the creative power of mind. It does not work to avoid my own responsibility and expect Jesus to magically make everything better.

If I [Jesus] intervened between your thoughts and their results, I would be tampering with a basic law of cause and effect; the most fundamental law there is. I would hardly help you if I depreciated the power of your own thinking. This would be in direct opposition to the purpose of this course. It is much more helpful to remind you that you do not guard your thoughts carefully enough...I cannot let you leave your mind unguarded, or you will not be able to help me. Miracle working entails a full realization of the power of thought in order to avoid miscreation.[14]

It does not help if Jesus heals a symptom without healing the cause. That is why Jesus proclaimed forgiveness before a healing. When the cause is healed, symptoms disappear. When I realize the creative power of my mind, I guard my thoughts. I watch my thoughts with alert vigilance, like the fisherman who carefully watches the water for the first subtle movement of the camouflaged trout. Who is it who watches and guards my thoughts? My identity shifts from being the thinker to being the watcher of thinking. I guard my thoughts because I don't want to miscreate misery with mad-mindedness. Watch your mind.

> **You are much too tolerant of mind wandering, and are passively condoning your mind's miscreations.**[15]

The miracle worker understands the power of the mind to manifest, either by creating or miscreating. A miracle is not a magic trick that denies the fundamental law of cause and effect. Miracles work at the level of cause and not effect. Using miracles to change effects is a misuse of them, or magic. So, to miraculously remove the effect of sickness, without removing the cause, is to do a disservice. It means I do not appreciate the power of mind to cause these effects. It means tampering with the most fundamental law of cause and effect.

The practical application here is watch your mind. Watch your thinking, like a cat, watching the mouse hole, waiting for the mouse. Guard your mind like the Secret Service guards Barack Obama having a beer in a Baghdad bar. Knowing the power of mind, do not give power to egoistic thinking by believing it. This takes vigilance, but how I feel improves if I catch negative thoughts and drop belief in them as soon as possible. Do not believe the lies of the ego. No more catastrophic thinking! Just to become aware of patterns of negative thinking is a big step forward. Most think on cruise control, and so don't watch the thought speedometer.

Whenever being drawn into negative thinking, ask the Holy Spirit to exchange the ego thought for a holy thought. Repeat the good news: *I am not upset for the reason I think,*[16] and *I am as God created me.*[17]

As Byron Katie teaches, inquire about a thought that upsets, "Is it true? Can I know for sure if it is true? How do I feel when I believe the thought?" This is guarding my mind. Cease to believe the ego's lies.

Sidetrack: 1992-2005

I started studying ACIM In mid-1992 and would not understand the teachings about special relationships, projection, and true forgiveness, for more than twenty years. After I returned home from the Taize conference in Ohio, tension increased between Dee and myself. After a few days I went to see Father Don, the parish priest. On the way there Dee asked what I wanted to discuss with him. I told her I was going to talk about a separation. Now, it seems stupid to tell her that but I couldn't lie if I wanted to. From then on, she was feral. I accept full responsibility for the failure of my marriage, but the hostility, violence, lies, and legal moves of the divorce were her doing. It is rather frightening when one is faced with a completely unhinged, unreasonable person, who considers herself above the law. The most discouraging thing was that she did not care how her hostility affected our children. The most heartbreaking thing was damage to our children. Even though I was the primary caretaker, Dee insisted adamantly that she have sole legal and physical custody of our children. Her insanity led to a logical end: violence. Once she surged her car at me in a parking lot, forcing me to jump out of the way. The kids were in her car when this happened. Twice like a coward she kicked me from behind, once when I stood on ice holding two-year-old Francis.

One event sealed the deal. Days after I told her I wanted a separation, she came home with Alicen and said she took our daughter to a doctor for an examination. "Examined for what?" I asked her. Dee told me she had Alicen examined to see if I sexually abused her. No evidence for abuse existed but just that Dee suspected it proved to me that after a fifteen-year relationship, ten married, she did not know me at all. I lost it, and yelled at her that our marriage was truly over, and that she now proved that it was already dead, long dead. I removed my wedding ring and flipped it in the air towards her like a worthless piece of junk. Later, in court, she falsely accused me of abusing Alicen. Fortunately the court saw right through it. False accusations happen often in acrimonious divorce proceedings. Dee went through three or four lawyers in the process.

Apparently I did not know her either because the viciousness and persistence of her anger stunned me severely. Dee said I was not the children's biological father. She planned to prove it with genetic testing, but didn't follow through. She lied so much, I didn't believe it. Isn't it true, though, that fathers don't know? I'm sure it happens all the time. If the mother is with multiple sex partners at the same time, she might not know for certain who the father is. Dee's own mother reproduced eleven children with four or five different men. For some of the children, she did not know who the father was. Dee told the custody investigator that she knew our marriage was a mistake in the first year. Her need for control was absolute. She disappeared with our children for a few days, staying at a friend's house. She refused to let me know where they were and refused me access to our children.

Because I stayed at home as primary caretaker, Alicen and Francis were with me every day. We did not use daycare and the few times we had a babysitter was when my Mother was there. Dee emptied our bank accounts, changed our credit cards to her name only, and changed the locks on the house within a week of my telling her I wanted a separation. She controlled the purse strings because she needed complete control. We shared one vehicle and she changed the ignition on that. I got around on a bike. She even set up the phone to block long-distance calls. She called the woman I fell in love with and told her that I was stunted. I didn't even think about that kind of stuff, like locking me out of the house and lying to police. Dee's out of state brothers made harassing phone calls, calling me a pervert.

Her attempts to control absolutely stunned me. She insisted on choosing my apartment. She met with some of my few friends and tried to turn them against me. I was not prepared for it in any way.

She started selling off stuff. She sold my nice Trek road bike that my brothers had chipped in on to buy as a wedding present. She hired a lawyer and filed for divorce, making her the plaintiff and myself the defendant in our divorce case. I should have seen it coming, but it happened with the suddenness of a car wreck. Given the severity of her attacks, I thought she might be glad to divorce me. My hope and plea to her, in writing several long letters, with the hope of minimizing the damage to our children, fell on deaf ears. Of course such a train-wreck of a marriage does not happen overnight, as it so seemed. Years of ignoring and denying the problems in our marriage resulted in a massive derailment. We didn't fight in our marriage because we seldom communicated. Years of lame communication, frustration, and resentment erupted like the violent volcano dreams our son Francis had.

After many months of police interventions, legal battles, custody investigations, and psychological evaluations, our divorce was finalized in 1993. As far as the trial went, the court awarded what I asked for, joint physical and legal custody of our children and about half of our property. Being the control freak she is, Dee insisted, unreasonably and insanely, on sole custody of Alicen and Francis and 100% of our property. Because her demands were so unreasonable, she ended up firing several lawyers who tried to reason with her about the law.

Dee argued in court that she did everything and I did nothing and thus she deserved 100% of our assets. She refused to take into account that the down payment for our house in Anchorage came from my share of the profit from selling the house in Los Altos. Ownership of our house in Anchorage was in her name only. I didn't care whose name it was in. She also refused to acknowledge the work I did do, beyond taking care of our children. I did several things to help us save money. Instead of paying for garbage service, I hauled our garbage to the dump. Our steep driveway was impossible to drive up after a snowfall. Instead of paying for a plow service, I cleared the driveway with a snow blower after each snowfall. I did the weekly grocery shopping at

Costco. When we had guests over for dinner, I did the cooking. I did extensive remodeling and painting on our house, including adding structural support underneath the house. I enjoyed making things and I built beds in the back yard for growing flowers and vegetables. I built a playhouse for our children. Dee refused to acknowledge any of my work and proved she did not appreciate anything I did. I will not describe the worst of it, that involved our children directly.

Most divorce cases are settled out of court. Ours went to trial because Dee refused to settle. Shortly before the trial, the report of the Guardian ad Litem on custody issues recommended sole custody to me based on her evaluation, observations, and the psychological assessments of us both. Even with this going against her, Dee still refused to negotiate an out of court agreement. After the "Conclusions of Law, and Findings of Fact," I went back to court several times because she refused to comply with the final divorce agreement. In the final agreement, Judge Andrews absolved Dee of paying child support based on the legal logic that she would work half-time while I worked full-time, and assumed that our incomes would then be about equal. Yet the minimum wage I made did not equal her half-time income. She didn't work part-time. She continued to work full time.

We shared custody of the children on a week/on week/off basis and lived near each other. She kept the house and I rented an apartment. Within a year she moved twice, further destabilizing the lives of our children. I wish we had the wisdom to keep the children in one house, the only house they knew, and the house Francis was born in, and then have Dee and I alternate weeks in the house, rather than make the kids move each week. One Sunday I drove to her house to pick up the kids for their week with me and no one answered the door. I never knew what to expect with Dee, but this was strange because there were no tire marks in the snow on the driveway. This meant that no car had driven on it since the last snow, several days prior. Later in the evening I went back and there was still no answer and no answer on the phone. The next day I called her work and the first person I talked to said she no longer worked there. Then someone else came on the phone and made strange excuses and refused to answer my questions. I went back to her house and still there were no tire marks in the driveway. Not knowing what happened, my fears gradually increased. I talked to her neighbors and they said that the previous week a moving van had moved the furniture out of the house.

I went to the police, and they started an investigation. I sent out about a hundred letters to every local moving company and others who might know something, with pictures of the kids and Dee, asking them to respond to the police if they knew anything. The mover who loaded their furniture contacted the police. My divorce lawyer started the legal wheels moving and the court ordered full custody to me and a "Writ of Assistance" for the Alaska State Troopers to find and return my children. Eventually we learned that she stored her furniture and an agency managed her properties. She had her car shipped to Seattle and flew with the kids to Seattle under false names.

The Anchorage Daily News did a couple stories about the situation. The newspaper tried to tie the disappearance of the children and Dee to a previous story they had done a few months before. I often entered juried photographic exhibitions. In a recent exhibit, a dual portrait of Alicen and Francis, two 8X10 color Polaroids in one frame, was accepted into the exhibit and hung in a gallery. Typical of her need to control, Dee objected to the photographs being in the show and demanded removal. She told Francis that it made him look stupid. The newspaper picked it up as a censorship issue. My lawyer saw the article in the paper and offered, pro-bono, to get a court order to return the photographs to the exhibit. Dee didn't show for the hearing. The court ordered the photograph re-hung in the exhibit. So the journalist suggested that Dee had left with the kids because of this; but the truth, later learned, was something else. I agreed to doing interviews with the newspaper in the hope that the publicity might help find my children. To have my personal life made public in the newspaper was humiliating.

At one point, the Alaska State Troopers called me and said they thought they found Dee and our children living with a man in a remote location in Alaska. They asked me to prepare to drive out and pick up my kids. I became excited about this soon-to-end nightmare as I waited for the troopers to call back and tell me where to go. When they called back they apologized and said they did not find Dee or the kids. Apparently Dee had a relationship with this man that ended. He referred to her as "that crazy woman." I didn't learn his identity although apparently his first name is the same as my son's because my kids called him "Big Francis."

My lawyer subpoenaed my ex-wife's bank records and after about five weeks found use of her credit card in Wyoming. I made plans to fly out and search myself. The Anchorage police were not doing much, considering it more a domestic than criminal case, and leads in Alaska had come up empty. I flew to Denver where my brother Gerry joined me and we rented a car and began our own investigation. We drove to Newcastle, Wyoming and talked to a police detective. We learned that she opened a post office box there, nothing else. We staked out a local elementary school when the kids were getting out, but no luck. Apparently she set it up to receive her mail in a different town than where she lived, making it harder to find her and the children. We decided to try the next major town over, Rapid City, South Dakota. On the way there I watched the traffic in the opposite direction for her car. On a Friday afternoon about four PM we arrived in town. We immediately noticed a church steeple and checked to see if it was a Catholic Church. It was. Catholic parishes often include elementary schools and I figured that Dee would enroll Alicen and Francis in a Catholic school. The teachers and principal were in a after-school meeting. I explained the situation to a staff member and the principal came out to talk to us. I showed her the court orders, pictures of the kids, newspaper stories, and she said my kids were enrolled in their school! We found them, and relatively quickly and easily.

The police came and said I could get my kids Monday after appearing before a judge. I called the DA in Anchorage and he talked to the police. My brother and I found a motel to wait out the weekend and gave the number to the police. A few hours later the police called and said I could come get my children. Gerry and I drove to where they were living and I was reunited with my children. Francis was friendly and affectionate, happy to see me, but Alicen scowled with anger. Their apartment was in disarray. After we left, Rapid City police arrested Dee. She was charged with two counts of felony custodial interference.

My brother Gerry was with me when we picked up the kids and afterwards he asked if I noticed Dee was pregnant. I hadn't because I was focused on the kids and barely looked at her. Her explanation for absconding with our children was that she was pregnant and embarrassed about it since she was not married. The Alaska DA tried and convicted her. When I testified at the Grand Jury hearing, a drummer friend I jammed with was excused from the jury. She didn't reveal the identity of the father, but my kids thought he was "big Francis." Later she married a strange Muslim guy named Rich, and they had another kid, Dee's fourth. Their marriage went into one of the worst and prolonged custody battles ever in the state of Alaska. It went on for over five years. I guess what goes around comes around.

After our separation I worked for a while in retail at Eagle Hardware and Garden. I tried to make a living at photography but failed. Commercial photography is one thing; I was doing fine art photography. I made money but not enough. I disliked selling my work. After being awarded full custody of the kids I wanted a better means of making a living. Now that I had full custody, Dee payed $25.00 per month child support, per child. This token amount allowed her to tell the judge she was paying child-support before her trial and sentencing for custodial interference (absconding). Soon after her trial she stopped paying child support altogether. Nothing raised her rage more than having to pay me money. In the court system I experienced sexual discrimination against the male. The judge, Dee's lawyer, the custody investigator, and the Guardian et Litem, were all women. Dee got away with perjury, assault, and rigged child support orders based on false information. I was so sick of the legal system of injustice that I did not continue legal moves to receive child support.

I had three years of college, so I planned to return to college, finish up a bachelor's degree pretty quickly and find a decent job. Because I practiced photography, I enrolled at the University of Alaska Anchorage as an art major. I had taken two photography classes there before completing my own darkroom. Because I changed my major three times in the first three years of college I pretty much started over. Now forty years old, I returned to school full time. Then I figured an art degree might not help much towards a real job, and since I was looking at four years to get a bachelors degree anyway, I changed my major one final time to psychology. Transpersonal psychology interested me. I thought psychology might be better for a job. I read a lot of Ken Wilber, who influenced me significantly. I was a "Wilberian" before I was a "Rogerian." Ironically, the psychology professors didn't mention transpersonal psychology, or Wilber, though I did in my papers and presentations.

I completed the four years in three by going to school full time in the summer as well as the fall and winter semesters and maintained a 4.0 grade point average. I ended up with 193 semester credit hours, not including classes I audited. Thus it took seven academic years (1972-73, 1976-1977, 1977-1978, and 1995-1998) of full time college to graduate with a bachelor's degree in psychology. Because of the variety of classes I took, I truly had a liberal arts education. UAA offered a two-year master's program in clinical psychology and professors encouraged me to apply. I took the Graduate Record Exams and did well, especially in the psychology test, and started the program. I liked the program and most of the psychologists I trained with impressed me.

During graduate school, on Christmas vacation, I broke my back sledding with my kids. We had a plastic sled that fit two people. The conditions were hard ice, and we sledded down a steep hill into a large field. On a run with my son, the sled became airborne and I landed hard on my ass. The impact compression fractured two lumbar vertebrae. Serious pain, physical and mental, followed. When bones break, the core skeletal structure of the body is compromised. Besides the pain, there is a depressing disability. I had no insurance, so I called a community health center that charged on a sliding scale depending on one's income. It was too late to get in that day, so I waited until the next morning to go in. I washed ibuprofen down with whiskey to deaden the pain and toughed it out.

I remember my father being at my trailer then. He had suffered two strokes and verbal communication was limited. I wondered if somehow our poor relationship had something to do with the synchronicity of his visit and breaking my back. The injury depressed me not so much because of the physical pain, but because the damage was permanent. When I broke my wrist in second grade, that healed. This break did not heal back to normal. Vertebrae were crushed and could not grow back. I lost an aspect of my health unrecoverable. I lost about a half-inch in height. Chronic back pain issues continue. I remember looking out the window into the front yard that night and seeing the dark shapes of three large moose lying in the snow. I imagined these strong animals were sending strength.

Despite the injury, I did well in graduate school, maintaining my 4.0 GPA. After two semesters of unpaid internship at a local community mental health center, the agency hired me on as a psychological associate, a bachelor level job. I needed to complete a thesis to finish my masters degree, though all course work, practicum, and internship were finished. One's thesis had almost no practical implications for clinical work. Thesis is important if one is going to work in an academic setting and do research. The team that hired me was the same team I worked for during internship. We served the most severe and chronic mentally ill. These people were often homeless, in and out of Alaska Psychiatric Institution (API), or in and out of jail, and on a pile of medications. I managed two schizophrenic clients who had murdered people but I didn't feel in danger. I built relationships with clients and it was then I started becoming disillusioned with the mental health system. Here also, in 2000, I became a daily cigarette smoker partly because the clients smoked and I started smoking with them.

Next in the saga of special relationships is a big one. A woman I knew, a senior in the psychology undergraduate program, was twenty-six years old, extremely smart, and one of the most beautiful women I ever met, no exaggeration. Clare was married and I didn't consider her anything but a casual acquaintance. After she graduated she planned on getting a PhD in psychology, an option unavailable in Alaska then. She decided to work in the field for a while before starting graduate school and took a job at the same community mental health agency where I worked. Clare worked on the same team as me, with the same job title, so we started to spend a lot of time together. My mates knew I was a fine-art photographer because the university had bought several prints and I exhibited at the university gallery, including a solo show. Clare asked if I could photograph her for a graduate school application. I was delighted to. It turned out she had modeled before.

Soon she revealed that her husband recently moved to Portland, Oregon, and wanted a divorce. I put Clare on a pedestal for her rare combination of beauty, brains, runner's body, kindness, and uncanny social skills, something I lacked. I could not understand why any man in his right mind would want to divorce this woman. It did not make any sense. Well, as they say, one thing led to another. Besides the divorce situation, she started to suffer serious health problems, physical and mental. She lost a lot of weight. I became her transitional lover and support person. She described herself as "your crazy girlfriend," and even spoke of packing it all in and spending the rest of her life in a mental institution. I fell in love head over heals knowing the chance of it lasting was slimmer than Clare's body, though she sent confusing messages, sometimes seeming madly in love with me and at other times distant and cold. Even though I studied psychopathology, I didn't suspect she suffered a serious mental illness until near the end of our relationship. Clare appeared too together, if a bit driven. She knew how to hide her illness, and use it to her benefit. We wrote long emails to each other that could fill a book. I photographed her a lot and dreamed of creating a whole body of work just on Clare. So I juggled all this – graduate school, kids, working full time with schizophrenics, a second career in photography, and the love of my life.

After about a year together, a prestigious graduate school program accepted Clare and she set off to become a forensic psychologist. I helped her move out of state to start the program and her divorce was finalized. I wanted to move with her but logistics prevented it. Shortly after moving, her health took a turn for the worse; she postponed graduate school and moved back. Not long after, she met a man her own age and I saw painfully she preferred him over me, though there was a period of indecision. Now I see that in many ways her new lover was more compatible with her than I was. The writing was on the wall. I knew it was over for us, but I held onto some irrational hope that eventually she might see how much I adored her and come back. That didn't happen and the final couple months were among the most painful of my life. I am embarrassed to say it took many years to recover, if I did ever recover. I did not have another long-term relationship or remarry.

A couple years later, my daughter Alicen, now fifteen, was hospitalized for suicidal behavior. Visiting her at the hospital was tough. She behaved disrespectfully and refused to cooperate with staff. She made light of the whole thing and did strange things, like crawling under a small table. My ex-wife and I met with Alicen's treatment team. I had not seen Dee in a long time and she looked severe, strained, and ill herself. After Dee left the meeting, a clinician asked about Dee, "Does she have a diagnosis?" I replied, "I don't know, but she should." A few years later, Dee was involuntarily hospitalized at Alaska Psychiatric Institute (API) in Anchorage.

By now, I was a functioning alcoholic, though I rejected labels like alcoholic that I believed stigmatized people more than helping them. I had been drinking regularly since my twenties. I drank heavily after my divorce. For about a year after the break up with Clare, I drank heavily again. Then I quit drinking for seven years. I did it on my own; cold turkey replaced wild turkey. It was not hard to quit. I used the Motivational Interviewing counseling method on myself. Because of my clinical work, I was familiar with the residential and out-patient substance dependence treatment programs available locally. I disliked these places intensely and would not voluntarily admit myself to one. I preferred death by drug overdose over entering a "recovery" program.

I gave up on finishing my thesis. I didn't care about much of anything. I continued with my job and the funny thing is, I started to experience problems at work *after* I stopped drinking. While drinking, shaking the boat did not interest me. Sober, I became a problem. I was in my position about three years when I wrote a paper called *On the Treatment of Schizophrenia and Other Psychotic Disorders*, and circulated it around work. Mistake. It was not for school, just something I personally wanted to do. I based it on my experience working there, my education, and my own extracurricular reading and experiences. Our inability, or worse – unwillingness – to help clients, other than to maintain a drugged and unhappy state, frustrated me. If pharmaceutical maintenance kept clients out of the hospital or jail, it is deemed successful and cost-effective. Most clients hated the medications and referred to them as poison. Most clients used tobacco and any other substance they obtained. Medicating the mentally ill is the bread and butter of the agency. Maybe things have improved since I left. The psychiatrist's work was to prescribe medications. That was it. I know because I accompanied clients to their appointments with the psychiatrists frequently. Recovery was out of the question. Therapy meant medication compliance, therapeutic or not. Treatment demanded expensive, life-long medication, providing a steady and lucrative income for psychiatrists and pharmaceutical companies. "Best practices" are advanced because we use Thorazine and Lithium in place of lobotomies.

In the paper I proposed a growth possibility, based on Abraham Maslow's hierarchy of needs. Soon after that, the agency suspended me without pay and tried to fire me, claiming I had violated client confidentiality. I lived paycheck to paycheck and cashed in my vacation pay to make ends meet. I had talked to a client's lawyer because the client asked me to talk to the lawyer; but before I did, I did not check the client's chart to see if there was a written release. The issue involving the lawyer was that the client hated the drugs and wanted to get off them, which the agency did not advocate. I obtained a letter from the client supporting my claim that the client had asked me to talk to the lawyer. I showed up for the meeting with the president of the agency with two lawyers, one my brother Robert, and the other was the Governor appointed Director of the Office of Public Advocacy, a big legal gun, and let them know that if they proceeded to fire me I would sue them.

They backed down and I resumed my old job, but under strict supervision. For unknown reasons, my supervisor and leader of the team had resigned by the time I returned to work. Most of the staff supported me, knowing me to be a client advocate. The team welcomed me back with applause at the team meeting the morning I returned. My coworkers knew that politics pushed the agency's action against me, as usual. Yet after returning to work, the agency made things difficult. If they couldn't fire me, they could drive me to resign, and

I did so as soon as I found another job.

A non-profit agency running a therapeutic community in a women's prison, Hiland Mountain Correctional Facility, hired me as a primary counselor. I liked this job. At times, however, the clinical staff seemed more interested in being guards than counselors. Sometimes the women were treated more like criminals than clients. For a Rogerian, who believed in unconditional positive regard for the client, this authoritarian attitude toward clients seemed counter-productive. There were already plenty of guards there. I spoke up and challenged certain things that struck me as non-therapeutic. Someone presented a quote of "wisdom" chosen each day for the community. I didn't know where the quotes came from, but one I reacted to was, "If you feel an emotion, you have already failed." This quote seemed so ridiculous I spoke up about it. These women already had a hangover from irrational authority and didn't need more of it from the clinical staff.

On the last day of my three month probation period my supervisor followed me into my office with another staff member to witness and told me to resign immediately or be fired. I did not expect this; there was no warning; no suggestion I needed to correct my job performance. When I asked the reason she said I was "saying things," and she had to protect the community. I saw there was no point in even discussing it further and agreed to resign, preferring resignation over termination. Politics as usual, I assumed. With hindsight, I think she feared that some incident might happen leading to a malpractice suit. A therapist is at risk of being accused of illegal behavior such as breach of confidentiality or sexual activity with a client. So here I am in a women's prison; I'm an available male and the only male counselor. I'm 48 years old, single, not even a girlfriend, and in good shape from my daily 20-mile bike rides. The women liked me. I treated them with respect. I think they decided to can me before something could happen. Or perhaps she thought I might rile the women up against the way things were.

I don't know the truth about it. Within thirty minutes I went from starting off a new day at a new job I liked to resigning and leaving the prison for the last time. There was no closure with clients and I don't know what staff told my clients, though they watched as I exited the building, escorted by staff, with a cart holding my personal property. Later, I talked to my supervisor's supervisor and he offered to re-hire me but I declined, figuring I would try something else after two near-firings in six months. After I left, my supervisor left her position, as had happened with my previous job. It turned out that my supervisor, an attractive woman in her thirties, was in a relationship with her previous supervisor in the same agency, he in his fifties. I remember the morning I drove to work, the same day my boss forced my resignation, it snowed so hard that at times I could not see the freeway right in front of me. The blindness of that drive mirrored being blindsided by my boss less than an hour later. The stress of job termination depressed me because I had children to support. A week after I resigned I crashed my car.

As perhaps the reader can tell, the world was beating me up pretty bad. The damage accumulated. Everything failed. I decided to have another go at making a living with photography. Follow your bliss and the money follows, or not. I worked hard at it, spending long days in the darkroom. I won the Juror's Choice Award for Best in Show in the most prestigious juried photography exhibit in the state. The Alaska State Council on the Arts awarded me two grants. A call came for submissions to be considered for reproductions to hang in the rooms of the new Alyeska Prince Resort in Girdwood, Alaska. Four images were selected from submissions of hundreds of photographs by the best photographers in the state. Two of my photographs were selected. I applied for and received an artist residency at Isle Royale National Park in Lake Superior. This was the high-point of my photography career. Three of my photographs from the residency were published later in a book, *The Island Within*, featuring artists from Isle Royale residencies, along with a short essay I wrote. The Alaska State Museum in Juneau presented a solo exhibition from my artist residency at Isle Royale National Park. Three galleries, two in Alaska and one in Portland, Oregon, represented me but sales were few and far between. The three major museums in the State of Alaska purchased prints for their permanent collections, but I was not making a living. Fine art photography equipment and materials are expensive and the old fashioned dark room work is time consuming. At various exhibits of my photographs in galleries and museums over the years, I didn't sell enough prints to cover the cost of exhibits.

So I started auctioning my prints on eBay. I started an international fine art photographer's union called The Contact Printer's Guild, and we took out full page ads in a photography magazine, *Black and White*, that previously published a showcase of my work. I ended up selling and shipping over a thousand prints in two years but I didn't achieve prices permitting a living. I only covered the significant expenses. My biggest satisfaction was the work itself. I knew I did high quality work and other well-known photographers confirmed it. It is simply a hard way to make a living and there are few who do it successfully. How many living fine art photographers do you know? I identified with Vincent Van Gough, who perhaps sold one painting in his life, struggled financially with support from his brother, suffered depression, searched spiritually, and ended up shooting himself, after cutting off one ear. A hard life, but great paintings. I also identified with Edward Weston, one of my favorite photographers, who struggled financially, unable to sell enough prints at $25.00 (that now go for hundreds of thousands of dollars). He was poor, divorced, raised kids, and lived not far from where I now live. One of his favorite places to photograph was Point Lobos, a favorite place for me as well. Financial success and aesthetic success do not necessarily go hand in hand. I also worked part-time teaching photography classes at the university.

My financial struggles continued and I took a job working with a different population, the developmentally disabled. I was familiar with this population. In the seminary, part of our training included service in the community and I volunteered at a local agency serving the developmentally disabled. I gave swimming lessons and helped at dances the clients loved. My own band played for a couple of these dances in the mid-eighties, before I moved to Alaska. It was fun and as far as the clients were concerned, we might as well be the Beatles. They enjoyed dancing to the music as much as deadheads do but without taking acid. Developmentally disabled children were Helen Schucman's favorite population to work with.

In 2004 I received a call from the psychology department at the university asking if I wanted to finish the masters degree...the five year deadline loomed less than a year away. I had already decided not to complete the thesis, but a professor told me there was now a retroactive, non-thesis option. In order to graduate I would take one more class and write a comprehensive paper demonstrating my knowledge of clinical psychology. Doable. I did well in classes and the paper I wrote about the treatment of schizophrenia could serve as the basis for the paper requirement. In 2005, at age fifty, I finally finished my masters degree in clinical psychology. I had nine years of college under my belt and the student loans to prove it. If I made the regular payments, I would not be out of debt until my eighties.

Regarding special relationships, I had relationship problems all my life, as already described. The reader may note that much of my more serious special relationship drama began about the same time I started studying ACIM, or after. It looks like it didn't seem to help much, right? This is true, it didn't help much at the time, but later it explained a great deal. I started the course only weeks before the divorce situation hit the fan. There simply wasn't enough time to even begin to absorb the core course ideas around identity and relationships. I wonder about the timing of this. I can only speculate as to the outcome if I had started studying the course a few years before the divorce.

The divorce experience confirmed the course's teaching about special relationships. I had direct proof of how a special love relationship changes into a special hate relationship. Forgiving my ex-wife is my most difficult forgiveness lesson, and I continue to work on it. Although the course claims to be the most efficient means of liberation, that does not mean it is quick. It is a long process, but still faster than other paths. In practical terms, this might mean one more lifetime instead of fifty. In my case, it might take longer than most because of my extensive religious conditioning. Also in my case, various events distracted me from consistent study. I studied regularly for a while, then something would happen, such as the divorce, to derail my progress. I stayed with the course, but not with a full commitment, having reservations, and not really understanding much of the teaching. As mentioned, to this day I discover a passage in the course that impresses me as personally poignant and wonder why didn't I see it before? Did I just forget it? Maybe my mind was not ready to hear it? Somehow, it didn't stick. Hence the need for study. For example, here is a course quote I recently discovered, not remembering it from the previous twenty-three years of course study:

You forget in order to remember better.[18]

I participated in the spiritual smorgasbord, tasting a little of this and a little of that, without being committed to any one path. Eclectic spirituality. I tried to integrate various teachings and continue to do so in this book. ACIM stands on its own, yet truth is universal and keeps popping up in different forms. I heard a humorous comment by Joel S. Goldsmith in one of his taped talks. He said someone from the tenth century plagiarized his twentieth century book, *The Infinite Way*. Joel laid his body down the year before Helen started scribing ACIM and I wonder if he helped out. He employed the ideas "God is" and "Sonship" before the course did.

My lifelong pattern of poor relationships was self-evident and I accepted being a loner. Maybe solitude called me after all. Even when I wanted a relationship to work, it didn't. As much as I loved my children, I could not prevent their pain, nor my own about them. After the ideas in ACIM about relationships became more clear to me, I recognized that all these problematic relationships, from parents, to brothers, friends, wife, children, lovers, were, all of them, special relationships. They were based on images of self and other as separate, and special. They were built on the accumulation of past encounters forced into continuity by memory. Getting what I think I need motivates special relationships. A relationship between two egos is doomed. I tried, I faked it, but I didn't make it. Unless a relationship is holy, the ego uses it to maintain ego. I, like most of us, learned this through a lifetime of special relationships. The solution is to invite the Holy Spirit to enter the relationship and transform it into a holy relationship, but I did not understand that yet. A hard pain reigned over me. To be continued.

Chapter Twelve

JOINING: THE UNITIVE TEACHING OF NON-DUALITY

*J*magine a celestial choir including everyone singing a harmonious and grateful song. All those "different" voices lend to blend and create one incredible harmony I cannot make alone.

When I am ready to end hell, I choose again, this time for joining instead of separation. Joining is the reversal of the separation. In joining, I am not liberated alone; we are liberated together. In joining, the special relationship becomes the holy relationship. Noah did not bring a single animal into the ark; it was pairs. Jesus sent out his disciples two by two. I could ride around the world on a unicycle but I arrive faster on two wheels, and maybe even faster on a tandem bicycle. I do not enter the Kingdom alone; I enter with my brothers, all of them. This is the unitive way. I cannot enter Heaven if part of myself is missing. The Kingdom of Heaven is the Kingdom of Holiness. It is the Kingdom of Wholeness. Completeness of the Kingdom is Wholeness of the Kingdom. It is Holy because it is Whole.

The injunction "Be of one mind" is the statement for revelation-readiness.[1]

Revelation-readiness means a mind ready to meet its Creator, face to face, metaphorically speaking. This is the perfect communication, Holy Communion, beyond thought and words. This means that guilt and fear, supported by separation, and preventing joining, are gone.

I join my mind with yours to be of one Mind, the Self, with one Will. This joining is a willing agreement with the truth of the Atonement. It is a sharing not only in agreement with the truth; it is a sharing of being. One mind is my true identity. Since the Holy Spirit is already in each mind (that seems to be separated), we are already one. When I will to join, I realize the truth of oneness now, instead of the illusion of separation that was. Union does not happen in the future. It already is so, now. The Holy Spirit reveals what is already so by removing the blocks to my awareness of unity. Those blocks are part of the dream of duality. One Mind is non-dual. One Will is non-dual. Non-dual is Heaven. Joining is the prerequisite for Heaven.

> **To be one is to be of one mind or will. When the Will of the Sonship and the Father are One, their perfect accord is Heaven.[2]**

The ego's autonomy is relinquished, and my will is re-joined to God's Will. My joining with my brothers is preparation for the ultimate reunion: the *Unity of unities*.

> **And now the mind returns to its Creator; the joining of the Father and the Son, the Unity of unities that stands behind all joining but beyond them all.[3]**

The perfect accord of one Will is the end of conflict in all its forms, the perfect peace beyond rational understanding. In Heaven, the re-joined rejoice.

Does it make any sense to oppose God's Will? No, but I still want to be my own boss. It is not easy to give up my own will. Monk's vows include poverty, celibacy, and obedience. Thomas Merton said obedience is the most difficult vow to keep. Surrendering one's will is more difficult than surrendering sex or money. Jesus joined his own will to the Will of the Father, realizing one Will. Luke's Gospel:

> **And then he withdrew from them about a stones throw, and knelt down and prayed, "Father, if thou art willing, remove this cup from me; nevertheless not my will, but thine, be done."[4]**

How difficult is it to surrender one's will? Jesus sweat blood over this. It is not easy, yet I do not do it. I simply desire this joining of wills and offer my willingness for it to be done. God does it when I am willing.

The Holy Trinity is a way of presenting the paradox of non-duality and relationship. Love implies two or more who share love, yet there are not two, only one. It is impossible to provide a satisfying intellectual answer regarding non-duality. The language of duality cannot say it. The Trinity is three in one. 1=3. 3=1. This truth derails rational thinking. This is mysterious until I experience it. Then I don't need a rational explanation.

> **All sense of separation disappears. The Son of God is part of the Holy Trinity, but the Trinity Itself is One. There is no confusion within Its Levels, because They are of one Mind and one Will. This single purpose creates perfect integration and establishes the peace of God.[5]**

The Father, Son, and Holy Spirit are perfectly integrated as One because they share one Mind, one Will, and one purpose. Don't worry about not understanding it. It is beyond dualistic thought. If I think I understand it, I don't. Never-the-less, the idea of non-duality might seem frightening to a mind that does not, and cannot, understand it. Surrender, that seems like the sacrifice of my unique individuality, is based on trusting God and the humility of knowing I don't know.

It is understandable I might fear giving up my will. It seems like I'm giving up personal freedom, like becoming a prisoner who cannot do what he wants. Yet the desire for personal freedom leads to this warring world of conflicting wills. What do I want? If I want to be my own boss I suffer. If I surrender my own will, God liberates me into the bliss of union. Why is the choice between bliss and suffering so difficult? Is there war in Heaven?

When I see that the wish for personal freedom is the wish for separation that causes misery, I change my mind. I choose again, this time with the Holy Spirit, and for joining. In fact, there is only one Will, God's Will, and it is shared by the one Son of God. My own autonomous will is part of the separation dream and not true. The true joining is a union in which I recognize that my brother is me. We are the one Son of God. I am the one Son of God. We are equal and this ontological condition includes everyone. Conflict of me vs. you requires we be different in desire, and divided by separate wills. Heaven is free of conflict and free of fear. Thus is re-joining the way to drop conflict and prepare for the greater joining, the *Unity of unities*, that is God's Will. If we are one, then conflict becomes absurd, meaningless. The drama of conflict starts within, as an idea based on identity confusion. The correction of confusion is the mind-training ACIM advocates. This is a reversal of conditioning. This is the shift from wrong-mindedness to right-mindedness, in preparation for one-mindedness. When I join my brother I renounce the separation and in so doing renounce sickness as an illusion of the separated.

To be aware of this is to heal them because it is the awareness that no one is separate, and so no one is sick.[6]

Separation and sickness require each other. If I'm depressed and you're not, then we are separate and different. Depression is ended as separation is ended. Even though the separation ended the instant it started, the *belief* in separation is canceled by joining.

Joining is not doing something new. We are already joined eternally, beyond time and space. We share a common mind, a common will, a common identity, as Spirit. Re-joining is the "undoing" of blocks to the awareness that we are already one. It is the awareness that no one is separate.

Joining and the Holy Encounter

ACIM offers practical means to practice the teaching. Whether I recognize it or not, each encounter with another person is a holy encounter, an opportunity to remember my Self. Every encounter is another chance at liberation by liberating my brother. The trick is to remember because my habit is not this way.

> **Whenever two Sons of God meet, they are given another chance at salvation. Do not leave anyone without giving salvation to him and receiving it yourself.**[7]

Any time I meet anyone is another chance to remember unity. This includes casual encounters that seem unimportant.

> **Even at the level of the most casual encounter, it is possible for two people to lose sight of separate interests, if only for a moment. That moment will be enough.**[8]

Joining means *to lose sight of separate interests* – one Mind, one Will. In any encounter with any person, I have the option of recognizing it as a holy encounter, where I meet myself and bless myself as I bless my brother. Accepting the Atonement means I am innocent and so is my brother.

How to apply this teaching? In any encounter I remember that my brother shares the same Holy Spirit as I. I might greet him silently in my mind: "You and I are one in Christ. You are holy, innocent, and perfect, just as God created you." Try practicing this and see what happens. When I worked as a therapist I taught clients to practice what I called "the secret blessing." Practicing this meant to say, in one's mind, "God bless you," to each person one met. This automatically softens the encounter and kindles kindness. If I say "God bless you," I feel better. I feel blessed as I bless. "God bless you" means "God bless me" because we are one.

Joining, The Holy Encounter, and the Holy Instant

The different teachings of the course reinforce one another. There is a direct relationship between the holy encounter and the holy instant. The holy encounter happens in the present moment, the holy instant, because I cannot join with my brother, as he is, if I see an image of him I constructed from memories. I do not join with the past. I join with my brother as he is now, free of past and future.

> Would you recognize a holy encounter if you are merely perceiving it as a meeting with your own past? For you would be meeting no one, and the sharing of salvation, which makes the encounter holy, would be excluded from your sight.[9]

If I see my brother through the filter of the past, I cannot join with him because I don't see him as he is. I see an image I constructed. Illusions are not joined. My brother is the same as me, still as God created us. The encounter is holy when I remember that my brother is holy and our salvation is shared. If I see my brother through the filter of his history, then I do not see him as he is now, and joining is blocked.

Joining and the Holy Spirit

We are already one, yet our awareness of unity is blocked in the dream of separation. We are already one because the Holy Spirit is already in everyone's mind and He is not divided.

> The Holy Spirit is in both your minds, and He is One because there is no gap that separates His Oneness from Itself.[10]

What is in my mind: the Voice for God, or the Holy Spirit, is in your mind, and all minds. Although this is the truth, my awareness of it is blocked by my belief in separation. The Holy Spirit already unites us. I don't need to do anything but want it, and accept it. The real preparation is desire, wanting to join. If I truly want it, then accepting it is easy and natural.

Joining, Simplicity, and Non-duality

The world is complex and complicated, as is the collective ego, which made that world. Spirit is simple. Spirit is unitive.

> Complexity is not of God. How could it be, when all He knows is One? He knows of one creation, one reality, one truth and but one Son. Nothing conflicts with oneness. How, then, could there be complexity in Him?[11]

ACIM is not complicated, though it might seem so at first. Duality is complex. The one became two and the two became ten thousand and the ten thousand became ten trillion. One is not complex. One is simple. In math, no matter how many times I multiply one by one I get one. If I try to add to one, I get duality. ACIM uses the word *one* 1,556 times.

> It is God's Will your mind be one with His. It is God's Will that He has but one Son. It is God's Will that His one Son is you.[12]

Non-duality is God's Will, without an opposing will. I may not know it yet, but it is also my own true will. Duality is the illusion of opposing wills, this world of wars and continuous conflict. Resistance requires two wills for one to resist the other. If I resist God's Will, what can I expect? If God's Will is my perfect happiness and I resist It, am I happy?

Joining and Inclusiveness

Earlier I described an important insight at age twenty-one, when I realized my spiritual seeking was selfish. It was all about me getting to Heaven. Various authorities, and my own interpretations, fear-conditioned the belief that some people go to Heaven, and others, even most, go to hell. Few find the narrow gate, and the smooth street selling hell is wide and welcoming. This teaching that excludes many from Heaven, the great divide, is ancient, and many believe it. This idea of eternal damnation fills minds full of fear. ACIM solves the selfish spirituality of personal salvation. We are saved together. Your salvation is my salvation and vice versa. It is all-inclusive and mutually dependent.

> Now are we one in thought, for fear has gone. And here, before the altar to one God, one Father, one Creator and one Thought, we stand together as one Son of God.[13]

Not one mind is excluded because excluding one mind denies the wholeness, the fullness, the completeness, of the Sonship, which is also called the Christ. If Christ is not whole, then the Holy Trinity is not whole. If a single sheep from the flock is missing, joy is not full. Heaven is not happy if part of God's Son is cast out.

> As long as a single "slave" remains to walk the earth, your release is not complete. Complete restoration of the Sonship is the only goal of the miracle-minded.[14]

Excluding anyone denies *complete restoration of the Sonship*, and this means I deny my own liberation. My brother is not separate from me; he is me. If the complete Sonship is not restored, then Heaven is not whole.

> It should especially be noted that God has only one Son. If all His creations are His Sons, every one must be an integral part of the whole Sonship.[15]

Although my true identity is as one Son, in the dream I appear as a separate individual among many; perception presents bodies and brains as if separate, yet perception is illusion.

> In this world, because the mind is split, the Sons of God appear to be separate. Nor do their minds seem to be joined. In this illusory state, the concept of an "individual mind" seems to be meaningful. It is therefore described in the course *as if* it has two parts; spirit and ego.[16]

Note that *as if* is emphasized. The course uses ideas that my split-mind is capable of using for healing. A trick is not true, but it is designed to seem true, like a dream seems true while I'm dreaming. Split-mind projects the schism I perceive.

If a single mind is excluded, then God's Son is not complete. God's complete and perfect Holiness is wholeness and needs every one of us. The Good Shepherd leaves the whole herd to find the one lost sheep. Does it make any sense that God creates a mind, knowing that His creation, created as He wanted it to be, created to be His dwelling place, is to be damned in hell for eternity? Some people view wisdom-logic like a pre-rational child understands a quadratic equation, and say it's not supposed to make sense. However, please consider this: God created us as an extension of Himself. We share His Being, His Spirit, and His Love. Since God is Sapient-Intelligence Itself, we share His Wisdom. I use this intelligence or not. The limits of logic do not mean I ignore God-given Wisdom.

At the beginning stages of writing this book, I almost gave it up because of hostile and angry reactions from people when I shared the ideas verbally. I figured that since my own methods of sharing seemed so inadequate, what is the point of talking or writing about it? So I thought I was off the hook, no need to write this book. Almost immediately after coming to this conclusion I came across this passage from the course that helped me realize that my original intention for this book, to share, is valid and worth doing, regardless of the reactions of others.

> **Many thought I [Jesus] was attacking them, even though it was apparent I was not. An insane learner learns strange lessons. What you must recognize is that when you do not share a thought system, you are weakening it. Those who believe in it therefore perceive this as an attack on them. This is because everyone identifies himself with his thought system, and every thought system centers on what you believe you are.**[17]

If even Jesus experienced resistance, who am I to expect different?

The Master received resistance to the point of crucifixion. I tend to interpret a teaching as personal attack when it does not support my pre-existing thought system. My identity seems attacked and naturally I defend my self-concept, just as I might defend myself from a mugger. Watch out for the mental mugger! Sharing ideas is how we grow. What does it mean to be a "fisher of men?"

> To your tired eyes I bring a vision of a different world,
> so new and clean and fresh you will forget the pain and
> sorrow that you saw before. Yet this is a vision you must
> share with everyone you see, for otherwise you will behold
> it not. To give this gift is how to make it yours.[18]

Sharing is having. If I do not share the vision of love, peace, and joy, with everyone, then I block my own awareness of love, peace, and joy. If I withhold peace from a single mind, then I exclude myself. When I am exclusive, I align with the ego and *delay* the completion of God's Kingdom. In this world there is emphasis on identifying enemies, whom I attack, or from whom I defend. The dualistic separation of friend and foe drives the greed and will to power of the military/industrial complex, investing trillions of dollars to profit from destruction and death. Soldiers are disposable pawns, worth little, and paid little, to kill on command. Jesus in Matthew's Gospel:

> You have heard it was said, "You shall love your neighbor
> and hate your enemy." But I say to you, Love your enemies
> and pray for those who persecute you, so that you may be
> sons of your Father who is in Heaven; for he makes the
> sun rise on the evil and on the good, and sends rain on the
> just and the unjust...You, therefore, must be perfect, as
> your heavenly Father is perfect.[19]

When Jesus says that we must be perfect, does he mean that we are already perfect or that we must become perfect? Does this Father sound exclusive? Clearly, He is inclusive, and His inclusiveness is perfect. When Jesus says, *You have heard it said*, is he referring to religious conditioning? Eye for an eye? Hate your enemy? God does not see the difference between good and evil because this polarity is a false dichotomy; these differences are part of the dream illusion and not true. Some sincere Christians come armed to argue that Jesus supports exclusiveness in the New Testament. Let's look at a few examples.

The Theology of Eternal Hell

There is the dualistic belief in separation of the saved and the damned. God's love is unconditional. God does not love the way humans love. God does not discern between the duality of good and evil any more than does sunlight or rain, according to Jesus. God excludes no one. God's perfection is demonstrated by His non-judgmental acceptance of everyone, the just and the unjust, the good and the evil. Good and evil are my beliefs, not God's.

In telling the story of the last judgment, Jesus teaches that the blessed going to Heaven were not aware of showing any kindness to him. Perhaps they hadn't even heard of Jesus, like a Buddhist who hadn't heard of him: "When did we see you...?"

> And the King will answer them, "Truly, I say to you, as you did it to one of the least of these my brethren, you did it to me."[20]

If the least are included as God's brethren, then why not everyone? The least included the hungry, thirsty, strangers, naked, sick, and those imprisoned. Today, in America, that means convicts and homeless people, right? As I treat anyone, so I treat Christ, and so I treat myself because together we are the one body of Christ, the Sonship. Some may argue that, well, yes, it does say that in the New Testament, but keep reading a little further and you see that the King also says:

> Depart from me your cursed, into the eternal fire prepared for the devil and his angels.[21]

What do I do with that? Remember what was said about interpretation. My interpretation comes from my frame of reference, which comes out of past learning. Who are the cursed, those who are sent to burn in hell, eternally? They are horned animals we call goats, metaphorically speaking. At the beginning of this story, the Son of Man separates the nations from one another like a shepherd separates the sheep and the goats. Sheep on the right and goats on the left. Like the political world. Separated and opposed.

What are the goats guilty of? They did not feed the hungry, nor provide water for the thirsty, nor welcome the stranger, nor clothe the naked, nor visit the sick and imprisoned. These were certainly not socialist goats. Whatever they neglected to do to the least, they neglected to do to Christ. In other words, these goats are selfish and believe in separation because they ignore the suffering of others. The goats are egos, e-goats. They do not accept oneness because oneness ends ego's autonomy and ego fears that ending like I fear heights. When ego is relinquished, the separation is relinquished. The ego is not saved. It is simply not real; it is a self-made concept of self as separate. Many make the mistake of identifying as a separate individual and believe that this individual is either saved or damned. Thank God that the ego departs into an eternal fire. It will not return. Each of us is both goat (ego) and sheep (Spirit).

The subtle serpent tempts us to eat the forbidden fruit of duality (knowledge of good and evil). Adam and Eve were tempted to eat this fruit in order to be like God. This temptation happened after the first separation into male and female had already happened, weakening the Son of God. Wiley serpent tempted me to "usurp" the Authorship of God and re-make myself as separate and autonomous. The devil's dualistic do-over is in opposition to how God created me: as one with Him; as His dwelling place. Literally, God lives in me. Even so, I wanted me to be the boss of me. I wanted to be "like" God, my own boss, rather than one with God. To be "like" God is to be separate from God. This goes back to my sense of identity and confusing the self-concept/ego I made for the Self God creates. *Workbook* lessons 201-220 begin and end with this sentence: *For I am still as God created me.* The self-concept as separate self I imagined is a derivative illusion, a mental image, temporary as time. I am free forever of the ego in the Kingdom of God because there is no time, and no separation, in Heaven.

Beware religious practice that postpones liberation. In another New Testament passage, interpreted as exclusionary, Jesus says:

> Not every one who says to me, "Lord, Lord," shall enter the kingdom of Heaven, but he who does the will of my Father who is in Heaven. On that day many will say to me, "Lord, Lord, did we not prophesy in your name, and cast out demons in your name, and do many mighty works in your name?" And then I will declare to them, "I never knew you; depart from me, you evil doers."[22]

I looked for the Biblical passage that says if you accept Jesus Christ as your personal Lord and Savior, you will be saved, but I did not find it. These *evil doers* claim that they prophesied in Jesus' name, performed exorcisms in Jesus' name, and did many mighty works in Jesus' name. On that day it is *many* who complain about their exclusion. Many means separation of the one into the many. Many is an illusion because there are not many, but one. One who does the Will of the Father is united to the Father. Their wills are joined as one Will. Christ does not "know" the legion of egos because they are not real.

The following passage shows also that evil-doing egos are quite capable of religious activities and even religious leadership. Jesus in Matthew's Gospel:

> For I tell you, unless your righteousness exceeds that of the scribes and Pharisees, you will never enter the kingdom of Heaven.[23]

The scribes and the Pharisees were the religious leaders at the time of Jesus. Jesus said that not only did they fail to enter the Kingdom themselves, they also prevented others from entering. Beware wolves in sheep's clothing. Today, from many religious leaders, we hear calls for judgment, condemnation, and attack, do we not? Seems like Christians want more wars with Muslims and vice versa. Catholics and Protestants at war in Ireland. Hindus and Muslims at war in India. Jews and Muslims at war in the Middle East. These are contemporary conflicts. The crusades continue. Are the current war-mongering religious leaders the scribes and Pharisees of our time? War, and its fruits, are big business with huge profits in power and money.

If God's love is unconditional, how are there conditions that include some and exclude others from the Kingdom of Heaven? It is true that belief in guilt keeps me out of Heaven, yet this human condition is temporary and illusionary, and it is not God who excludes, nor is exclusion God's Will. What is excluded from the Kingdom are illusions of identity, separation, sin, shame, guilt, fear, and suffering. People who insist God's love is limited are insisting on a blind belief based on not-knowing. They have not yet experienced God's love in this human life, or do not remember it if they did experience it. Yet I do forget what is before the separation wish. The only way to know the nature of God's love is to experience it. The experience of God's love blows away systematic theology. It is easy to tell if any preacher knows, by experience, the love of God, by the words that come out of his mouth. Either he knows or does not know, remembers or does not remember.

The religious idea of exclusivity is related to the next six quotes spoken by Jesus in John's Gospel from the Last Supper:

> **I am the true vine, and my Father is the vinedresser.**
> **Every branch of mine that bears no fruit, he takes away,**
> **and every branch that does bear fruit he prunes, that it**
> **may bear more fruit. You are already made clean by the**

> word which I have spoken to you. Abide in me, and I in you. As the branch cannot bear fruit by itself, unless it abides in the vine, neither can you, unless you abide in me. I am the vine and you are the branches. He who abides in me, and I in him, he it is that bears much fruit, for apart from me you can do nothing.[24]

Here Jesus teaches me to abide in Him, the Christ, as a branch is connected to the vine. Where does the vine end and the branch begin? I bear fruit that glorifies the Father if I abide in Christ. God's glory is completed when I bear much fruit, a metaphor for Divine Love. Pruning is the purification that cuts clean. I am already connected to Christ, but the ego is not. Jesus again:

> Greater love has no man than this, that a man lay down his life for his friends.[25]

Jesus is the master example of this kind of love and I learn to love in the same way:

> This is my commandment, that you love one another as I have loved you.[26]

How do I keep this commandment? By laying down my life as a separate individual. If I want and welcome this surrender, I abide in Christ, abide in the Father, abide in divine Love (the non-dual unitive state).

> As the Father has loved me, so have I loved you; abide in my love. If you keep my commandments, you will abide in my love, just as I have kept my Father's commandments and abide in his love.[27]

Keeping the Father's commandments means my will is joined to the Father's Will so that there is one Will. What was the commandment again? To love one another. How to love one another? As He loved us. How did He love us? By laying down his life. Did Jesus commit suicide? To lay down one's life is not to commit suicide. It is not laying down the body. If I lay down my separate ego self, my own will, then I abide in Christ, as Christ, which is abiding in the Sonship, which is abiding in the Holy Trinity, which is sharing one Will with the Father, which is Heaven.

One individual grape does not make much wine. All the grapes are joined together to make the one wine. Am I ready for the crush? This is the transformation of the many into the One. Jesus uses the word "abide" over and over again. He uses it ten times between verses four and ten. This is unitive language. Abiding is the opposite of separation, and the ending of the "fall" from unity. ACIM uses the words abide, abides, abiding, and abideth 117 times. The result of joining is abiding. Abiding is a stable joining that does not fade away. God created me to abide in me. Abiding is mutual. God abides in me and I abide in God.

> **These things I have spoken to you, that my joy may be in you, and that your joy may be full.**[28]

The result of this abiding in each other, in Christ, in the Father, is the wholeness of the completion of the Kingdom of Heaven, which is also the fullness of joy. Joy is not full, whole, or complete, without everyone.

This beautiful unitive teaching of abiding and love has another side, as in the last judgment story, already discussed.

> **If a man does not abide in me, he is cast forth as a branch and withers; and the branches are gathered, thrown into the fire and burned.**[29]

How does the hell-fire and damnation get in there when God's love is supposed to be unconditional? Remember, *interpretation*. What exactly gets tossed into the fire? A branch that does not keep the love commandment to lay down one's life; it does not abide in the vine that is Christ, and thus it is a branch that cannot bear the fruit of love. The ego is the branch that does not want to join. The ego does not want to lay down its separate life. The ego's whole identity is as separate. In other words, the self-concept that is a separated self, the ego, the special self, the private self with an independent will, does not, will not, and cannot abide in Christ. The ego cannot bear grapes that join to make the love-wine, the Good Wine.

So what happens to the non-abiding branch? It is burned in a fire. What happens to wood (form) burned in a fire? Something appearing solid (form) shifts into smoke and disappears. Notice one more important detail. The branch is not thrown directly into the fire. First it withers. Then all the withered branches (egos) are gathered, burned, and disappear. Since the transforming fire is eternal, the separated branch, that is only an illusionary concept, won't return. The purifying fire is in my mind because the ego is a belief in my mind. This is the True Good News about the Good Wine of salvation. The course refers to the above verses from John 15:

> The branch that bears no fruit will be cut off and will wither away. Be glad! The light will shine from the true Foundation of life, and your own thought system will stand corrected. [30]

My own thought system is pruned of wrong-mindedness. Be glad! Why? Because it is Good News. The ego is burnt toast. The ego is dust. Ashes to ashes. Hell is ending as ego ends. I can spend a long time trying to make the ego obey the love commandment, but it will never happen. Thus, if I am confused about my identity I waste time trying to reform an illusion. A reformed ego, a pious ego, is still ego.

This withering of the false self before final consumption in the fire is a necessary and merciful process. What happens if I try to burn a green branch? I get a smoking mess that takes much longer to burn, and may not burn completely. When the the branch is completely dried out, the fire consumes the dead branch quickly. The withering process takes longer than the final fire. The pruning (undoing) is the purification process I undergo in the shift from wrong-mindedness to right-mindedness. The ego's dying of thirst in the desert of this world is bound to be experienced as painful, but a slow burn of green wood is more painful. When the branch is completely withered and dry it does not even feel the fire. It is thoroughly dead. It is fairly common for people on the spiritual path to experience dryness in their walk. The desert is a literal metaphor for dryness. Once my mind is purified, dryness is relieved by the clean, living water coming from within, the spring of eternal life. There is no water in the world. One Baptism is with water; one is with fire; one is with Spirit.

How long it takes to wither the ego is up to me, as studied in the chapter on time. But much better to wither the ego completely first, before the fire. Thus seen, dry suffering is merciful because it is less painful. Imagine a fresh-cut Christmas tree in a living room. The tree is separated from its roots in the earth and is dead or dying. Yet it looks green for a long time and seems alive. In my spiritual life I undergo a cleaning and healing process in which ego is cut off, but it sticks around for while, taking its time to wither. Eventually the process is complete and the separate self sense disappears forever in the eternal fire. In truth, there is no hell, just as there is no ego, except in the temporary dream of separation.

Joining and Forgiveness

I won't want to join with a brother whom I believe hurt me. Grievances and grudges prevent joining. Hence the role of true forgiveness as a prerequisite for joining.

> **Forgiveness takes away what stands between your brother and yourself. It is the wish that you be joined with him, and not apart.** [31]

Without true forgiveness the holy instant of joining is delayed. Inevitably, I will join my brother, but why wait? If I delay joining, I prolong pain. I may "forgive" someone who I believe dissed me, but do I will to be joined with my "attacker?" True forgiveness, realizing there is nothing to forgive, encourages joining. Here is a test to see if I truly forgive. Do I want to join with whom I "forgave?"

> **Today we practice true forgiveness, that the time of joining be no more delayed.**[32]

Enlightenment is mutually dependent. Enlightenment is not for individuals. Enlightenment is the release of my self-concept as individual and separate from my brother. How can illusion become enlightened? Not gonna happen. Darkness does not become light. Darkness disappears in light.

I receive forgiveness by giving forgiveness. A core course teaching is that giving and receiving are the same. Through true forgiveness I welcome joining joyfully because both my brother and I are released together from the hell of guilt, fear, anger, accusation, and attack.

> **This is your brother, crucified by sin, waiting release from pain…Join him in gladness, and remove all trace of guilt from his disturbed and tortured mind.**[33]

Without true forgiveness I share in ego-madness and continue a guilt-disturbed and tortured mind, a mind in pain, that is depression.

> **Brother, you need forgiveness of your brother, for you will share in madness or in Heaven together. And you and he will raise your eyes in faith together, or not at all.**[34]

Without forgiveness, joining and the benefits of joining are delayed. Remember the time factor. The greater joining is inevitable, but I may choose to delay it, or not. The course is given to save time, and end hell, sooner rather than later. Miracles save time and each joining is a miracle.

> **So do the parts of God's Son gradually join in time, and with each joining is the end of time brought nearer. Each miracle of joining is a mighty herald of eternity.**[35]

Joining and Identity

If depression is an identity-confusion disorder, then knowing my true identity ends depression. I discover my true identity through joining because my true identity is *shared*. Even in traditional Christian theology there is one Body of Christ, not many.

> **Remember always that your Identity is shared, and that Its sharing is Its reality.**[36]

Although I share the same being with my brothers and with God, I might prefer to identify as an individual, as special, as different. This wish to be what I am not is a temptation. God's identity is as Sharer, and He created me to share as He does.

> **Being is known by sharing. Because God shared His Being with you, you can know Him.**[37]

When I join my brother, my identity is transformed from a separate self image to the shared one Self, the Son of God, the Christ. I cannot know myself alone because my identity is shared and unitive.

> **The Holy Spirit teaches you that if you look only at yourself you cannot find yourself, because that is not what you are.**[38]

I am not an individual, separate self. I need my brother to learn this. My liberation is yours and your liberation is mine.

Joining and the Holy Relationship

The holy relationship is one of the most practical tools ACIM gives for joint liberation, just as the special love relationship is the ego's most important tool. In the holy relationship, I know my holiness by joining.

> **Do you not want to know your own Identity? Would you not happily exchange your doubts for certainty? Would**

> you not willingly be free of misery, and learn again of joy?
> Your holy relationship offers all this to you…All this is
> given you who would but see our brother sinless.[39]

The holy relationship demonstrates innocence, not specialness. Here is the shift from duality to non-duality, from differences to sameness, from judgment to forgiveness, from guilt to innocence, from the self-made image of separate self to the oneness of Sonship called Christ. In the holy relationship I recognize shared holiness, shared identity, shared mind, and shared will. God is Holy and God shared His Being through creation. Everything God created is holy because everything that God created is an extension of God. Thus, my being is holy just as God's Being is holy. My brother is holy, and so am I. Holiness created nothing but the holy. When I join my brother in holy relationship, I join with my Self. I agree with the Holy Spirit that we are holy and share God's Being.

> A holy relationship is one in which you join
> with what is part of you in truth.[40]

The holy relationship is a mirror of the union of the Father and the Son. This is how I start acclimating to Heaven.

The Holy Instant and the Holy Relationship

The holy instant is the present moment without past and future. The holy instant allows true and transparent communication, mind in mind, with no private thoughts, and no interference from the past, guilt, or fear. This perfect and holy communion is the opposite of separation, where I keep thoughts hidden from my brother.

> So in each holy relationship is the ability to communicate
> instead of separate reborn.[41]

This holy communication is described in the next quote as *For what one thinks, the other will experience with him.* Fear might block this *happy fact*, and I might find it to be a heavy burden to relinquish the privacy of my seemingly separated mind with its private thoughts. In joining, I surrender the privacy of separateness. Is it not true I like my privacy?

> **This is the function of your holy relationship. For what one thinks, the other will experience with him. What can this mean except your mind and your brother's are one? Look not with fear upon this happy fact, and think not that it lays a heavy burden on you. For when you have accepted it with gladness, you will realize that your relationship is a reflection of the union of the Creator and His Son. From loving minds there is no separation.[42]**

The holy relationship reflects the perfect and holy communion of the Father and Son. Does the Father keep private thoughts from the Son, or the Son from the Father?

The holy relationship is the practical means of remembering the holy instant.[43] The holy relationship testifies to the truth of oneness. In the holy relationship I am grateful for my brother, without past or future, without fear. Transparent communication is Holy Communion, or common (shared) union.

The holy instant transforms the special relationship into a holy relationship because past and future of the relationship are relinquished. Grudges, grievances, guilt, and fear are no more. Fears about the future of the relationship are released. Judgment of the other is dropped because the basis for judgment is in the past. The holy relationship is the reminder of, and the expression of, and continuing of, the holy instant, now. The holy instant is present now. Yet if it is not expressed in the holy relationship, I am likely to forget it. I slip back into the ego's world of past and future. The holy instant is present when I attack my brother, but I lose the benefits of it, because attack is based on the past. If I judge or attack I forget the holy instant.

How to Join In Holy Relationship

The transformation of relationship from unholy to holy is a process accomplished by the Holy Spirit with cooperation from us. It begins when we invite Him into our relationship.

> **You undertook, together, to invite the Holy Spirit into your relationship. He could not have entered otherwise.**[44]

In Heaven, there is no need to force anything. God does not force anything. There is only one Will, without opposition. The Holy Spirit enters a relationship by invitation only. Inviting the Holy Spirit into a relationship means we desire the relationship to be holy instead of special. Ideally, but not necessarily, the relationship then changes to serve the goal of holiness.

The Holy Spirit's goal of joining in the holy relationship is holiness. This goal is achieved by mutual healing of mistakes through forgiveness. Joined in the shared goal of holiness, each looks on the other as sinless and as created by God.

> **Yet reason sees a holy relationship as what it is; a common state of mind, where both give errors gladly to correction, that both may happily be healed as one.**[45]

In the holy relationship we give up errors gladly. Judgment, guilt, fear, and attack are all errors we agree to give up together. If we share a common state of mind or will, conflict ends. In the special relationship, conflict arises as I insist on being right.

The holy relationship is difficult at the beginning because the contrast between the goal of the old, unholy relationship, and the goal of the new, holy relationship, is so stark. Since the holy relationship is just beginning, it is not yet stable. It's like learning to ride a bike. Until I learn to balance on two wheels, it's easy to fall.

> In all its aspects, as it begins, develops and becomes
> accomplished, it represents the reversal of the unholy
> relationship. Be comforted in this; the only difficult phase
> is the beginning. For here, the goal of the relationship is
> abruptly shifted to the exact opposite of what it was.[46]

Remember that the goal of the unholy relationship, the special relationship between two special egos, is to get, based on perceived lack and needs. It is based on deprivation. It is mutually manipulative, with each seeking his own benefit, despite pretenses. How often is it said or believed, "I need you," "I'll die without you," or, "I'll kill myself if you leave me." Needy drama is a sure sign of ego. The holy relationship is not based on need or deprivation drama. In it we share abundance of being, needing nothing in return. In it we see no differences; we see a holy equality. The holy relationship welcomes holiness, wholeness, oneness, the natural state of being before the dream of falling into separation. We join so that the fullness of joy is realized, together.

The shift of goals, from getting to giving, happens quickly, as soon as the Holy Spirit is invited into the relationship.

> This invitation is accepted immediately, and the Holy
> Spirit wastes no time in introducing the practical results
> of asking Him to enter. At once His goal replaces yours.
> This is accomplished very rapidly, but it makes the
> relationship seem disturbed, disjunctive and even quite
> distressing...Many relationships have been broken off at
> this point, and the pursuit of the old goal re-established in
> another relationship. For once the unholy relationship has
> accepted the goal of holiness, it can never again be what it
> was.[47]

At the beginning of the holy relationship the old goal still holds attraction, so there is conflict between the old and the new, the special and the holy. There is danger of the relationship being aborted. Because of the change of goals introduced by the Holy Spirit, the ego is frustrated and threatened. Once the Holy Spirit's goal of holiness is established, it does not change. The relationship changes to fit the new goal. If not, the relationship becomes unbearable.

> The temptation of the ego becomes extremely intense with this shift in goals. For the relationship has not as yet been changed sufficiently to make its former goal completely without attraction, and its structure is "threatened" by the recognition of its inappropriateness for meeting its new purpose.[48]

I did not understand this spiritual dynamic when I married. I recognized the problems, poor communication, distance between us, conflicting wills, but I did not know the solution.

The course teaches how to get through the beginning challenges of a holy relationship:

> This is the time for *faith*. You let this goal be set for you. That was an act of faith. Do not abandon faith, now that the rewards of faith are being introduced.[49]

This faith is faith in the Holy Spirit and what He is doing. It is faith that the Holy Spirit knows how to complete what He starts. It is also faith in the beloved.

> Have faith in your brother in what but seems to be a trying time. The goal *is* set.[50]

The ego is not going to like this transformation to a holy relationship and fights against it by rationalizing against the holy relationship with this idea: find someone else.

The substitution of a new relationship to replace the old one is the old ego trick called "falling in love." At the same time I fall in love with a new other, I fall into separation from the old other. Wife becomes ex-wife. Ego succeeds in maintaining the continuity of its dream. Remember what is the ego's primary weapon in its arsenal to maintain itself: the special love relationship. So the course emphasizes: don't listen to the ego and keep faith:

> Have faith in Him [the Holy Spirit] Who answered you. He heard…Now He asks for faith a little longer, even in bewilderment. For this will go, and you will see the justification for your faith emerge, to bring you shining conviction. Abandon Him not now, nor your brother. This relationship has been reborn as holy.[51]

One of the ways I listen to the ego is to find fault with my brother and blame him for challenges. If I comply with the ego's temptation to find fault with the beloved, I forget the holy instant and reestablish the past.

> You will find many opportunities to blame your brother for the "failure" of your relationship, for it will seem at times to have no purpose.[52]

Despite so-called best intentions, most relationships start out as a relationship between two egos. After the honeymoon, honey, comes the ego collision, sooner or later. "Asshole!" Instead of blaming my brother, I am grateful for him. Without my brother I am not liberated. Without my brother there is no holy relationship. Without my brother, I remain stuck in a hellish depression.

> Have you been similarly grateful to your brother? Have you consistently appreciated the good efforts, and overlooked mistakes? Or has your appreciation flickered and grown dim in what seemed to be the light of the mistakes? Perhaps you are now entering upon a campaign to blame him for the discomfort of the situation in which you find yourself. And by this lack of thanks and gratitude you make yourself unable to express the holy instant, and thus lose sight of it.[53]

If I attack my brother, I live in the past and I lose the benefit of the holy instant. The holy instant is expressed in the holy relationship, so that I remember and receive the benefits of the holy instant: sinlessness, guiltlessness, love, peace, joy, and freedom from fear. The condition blocking the benefits of the holy instant is attack on my brother, judging him as guilty. Attack may be as subtle as a passing critical thought, or blatant as calculated and intentional harm. This violent condition is standard in special relationships.

Faith rides me through the rough patch when beginning a holy relationship. Help comes from the Holy Spirit, if I want it and ask Him, and let Him.

> **When you feel the holiness of your relationship is threatened by anything, stop instantly and offer the Holy Spirit your willingness, in spite of fear, to let Him exchange this instant for the holy one that you would rather have. He will never fail in this.**[54]

Notice that ACIM instructs me to seek help from the Holy Spirit *instantly*. If I wait, or procrastinate, I allow the threat to take root and establish itself; I introduce time into the situation, denying the holy instant. ACIM promises that the Holy Spirit helps me if I let Him. Also, my partner helps me because in the holy relationship we are one. So we do not experience fear or forgiveness alone, but together.

> **But forget not that your relationship is one, and so it must be that whatever threatens the peace of one is an equal threat to the other...it is now impossible for you or your brother to experience fear alone, or to attempt to deal with it alone.**[55]

It is useful to know in advance how to join in holy relationship, what challenges to expect, and how to deal with those challenges. That advance knowledge of the territory is what a good map provides.

Joining and Time

ACIM came to save time. That is, to shorten my time in hell. ACIM offers different means, more efficient means, to reach the same spiritual truth that takes longer, using other means. The course's holy methods are practical: Holy Spirit, holy instant, holy encounter, holy relationship, miracles, forgiveness.

> **Your way will be different, not in purpose but in means. A holy relationship is a means of saving time. One instant spent together with your brother restores the universe to both of you.**
>
> **Here is the ultimate release which everyone will one day find in his own way, at his own time. You do not need this time. Time has been saved for you because you and your brother are together. This is the special means this course is using to save you time.**[56]

The emphasis on love by Jesus in the New Testament is the same as the emphasis on joining in holy relationship in ACIM. I lay down my life as a separate individual to join in love.

Joining in One Will and Healing

Joining in the holy relationship is how I heal with my brother. I cannot achieve healing alone. Healing is shared; we join in healing together. Hence the fruit of gratefulness for my brother.

> *When I am healed I am not healed alone. And I would share my healing with the world, that sickness may be banished from the mind of God's one Son, Who is my only Self.*
>
> *When I am healed I am not healed alone. And I would bless my brothers, for I would be healed with them, as they are healed with me.*[57]

In order to heal depression and replace it with joy, I share my healing and bless my brother. I heal as he heals. I realize happiness by surrendering my autonomous will, leaving only God's Will. If I remain devoted to my own will, I won't be happy.

> But it is given you to know that God's function is yours, and happiness cannot be found apart from your joint Will.[58]

Happiness and healing are realized in knowing there is One Will, one function. God's one Will is not for suffering. If there is one Will for Love, how can sin, sickness, and suffering exist? Is pain God's Will? If God is all-powerful, then there is no other power. Therefore, pain is an imaginary and confused claim of separation.

> This holy relationship has the power to heal all pain, regardless of its form. Neither you nor your brother alone can serve at all. Only in your joint will does healing lie. For here your healing is, and here will you accept Atonement. And in your healing is the Sonship healed because your will and your brother's are joined.[59]

Sickness is a symptom of separation. If I end the cause of sickness: separation, through joining, then sickness ends. Joining is the antidote for separation. Joining is exchanging illusions of me for the truth of Sonship. Don't try to heal depression. Allow healing of the cause of depression.

> Uniting with a brother's mind prevents the cause of sickness and perceived effects. Healing is the effect of minds that join, as sickness comes from minds that separate.[60]

Would I rather keep my own independent will and stay depressed or surrender personal will and be healed? Depression *comes from minds that separate.*

Joining in the Wrong-minded Way

Until I stop it, I join in a mistaken way. I can join in agreeing that the dream of separation is real and so experience that dream as consensus reality. This is the view the world shares. The creative power of joining makes worldviews, for better or worse.

> It is the sharing of the evil dreams of hate and malice, bitterness and death, of sin and suffering and pain and loss, that makes them real. Unshared, they are perceived as meaningless.[61]

I support illusions by believing lies are true. I join in specialness or holiness, but I cannot join with both, and I cannot compromise by choosing parts of each. Truth and lies are mutually exclusive. Either I dream or I am awake, not both.

> This course is easy just because it makes no compromise. Yet it seems difficult to those who still believe that compromise is possible.[62]

Compromise makes the course difficult because compromise is impossible. Compromise means I still want my own will. Non-duality is uncompromising. Jesus in Luke's Gospel:

> No servant can serve two masters; for either he will hate the one and love the other, or he will be devoted to the one and despise the other.[63]

The *Gospel of Thomas* agrees:

> A person cannot mount two horses or bend two bows. And a servant cannot serve two masters, or that servant will honor the one and offend the other.[64]

I seek a compromise because I am not yet vigilant *only* for God. I still want something or someone outside of me, in the world.

Sickness requires separation, and separation requires sharing, or joining in agreement, that we are separate, and agreeing some are sick, while others are not. The miracle is a correction in perception so I understand that my brother is not separate and is not sick any more than Christ is sick. Or, I choose to agree with my mistaken perception, and join my brother's belief that he is sick.

> To believe that a Son of God can be sick is to believe that part of God can suffer...Do not side with sickness in the presence of a Son of God even if he believes in it, for your acceptance of God in him acknowledges the Love of God he has forgotten. Your recognition of him as part of God reminds him of the truth about himself, which he is denying.[65]

Miracles correct mis-perception. If my brother believes he is sick, I do not share his belief. Instead, the miraculous view is, "We are part of God and God is not sick."

> No mind is sick until another mind agrees that they are separate. And thus it is their joint decision to be sick.[66]

Joining is a type of agreement, a sharing in a belief. If I agree someone is sick, I agree with the ego instead of the Holy Spirit. I disagree with God and worship the false idol of mistaken identity as separate.

> Sickness is idolatry, because it is the belief that power can be taken from you. Yet this is impossible, because you are part of God, Who is all power.[67]

If I am still as God created me, then why would I agree with the sick self-image made by the ego? Did God create His dwelling place as sick and depressed? What kind of God is that?

If I appear anxious, it is not because God is punishing me. It is because I judge my brother as guilty, and different from me. This judgment is agreeing with the accusing ego's judgment. In finding fault with my brother, I support specialness, not holiness, and I suffer for this mistake.

> Only this is certain in this shifting world that has no meaning in reality: When peace is not with you entirely, and when you suffer pain of any kind, you have beheld some sin within your brother, and have rejoiced at what you found there. Your specialness seemed safe because of it.[68]

How I feel tells me whether I joined in the right way or the wrong way. If I feel a loss of peace, or any kind of pain, it means I joined in agreeing with the ego's lie that separation and sin are real. If I join in the wrong way I give the gift of guilt to my brother and to myself. Specialness is protected by judging my brother. I know I am better than you because of your sin. If I join in the holy way I give the gift of forgiveness to my brother and myself. The end of guilt is the end of hell is the end of my mind in pain. Heaven or hell exist because they are shared. Sharing is joining in belief that something is true. My being is the result of God's sharing.

> Except you share it, nothing can exist. And you exist because God shared His Will with you, that His creation might create.[69]

My creative ability is because of God's sharing and willing that I be creative, as He is. If I share the belief that my brother is sick, then, for all practical purposes, he is sick. I misuse my creative ability to share a projection of separation and sickness.

> Do not allow your brother to be sick, for if he is, have you abandoned him to his own dream by sharing it with him…Thus you are joined in sickness.[70]

Join in love or join in sickness. Join in truth or join in illusions. Join in Atonement or join in separation. I am vigilant about which way I join. Joining in the mistaken way is my habit and easily slips back if I'm not careful. I join, moment by moment, in agreeing the dream is real or agreeing the dream is a dream.

> **Like you, your brother thinks he is a dream. Share not in his illusion of himself, for your Identity depends on his reality. Think, rather, of him as a mind in which illusions still persist, but as a mind which brother is to you.**[71]

My brother might dream he is depressed. If I agree with him, I doom him and myself to a continuation of hell. If I agree with him that he is sick, I join with the ego and believe in separation, and thus I suffer. My Identity depends on my brother's Reality, not his ego.

There is an emotionally powerful story of joining in holy relationship in the book *Grace and Grit* (1991) by Ken Wilber. I encourage anyone interested in holy relationship to read this book. If you are like me you won't be able to put it down. They were enlightened *together*.

In the life of Rumi, the great Sufi mystic, is a wonderful example of joining in holy relationship. Rumi was a respected religious scholar when, at the age of thirty-seven in 1244, he met Shams of Tabriz. Shams was looking for this Friend. According to the stories, a deep, mutual recognition happened and the two disappeared together for months. Rumi translator, Coleman Barks, describes their joining:

> **There are various versions of this encounter, but whatever the facts, Shams and Rumi became inseparable. Their Friendship is one of the mysteries. They spent months together without any human needs, transported into a region of pure conversation.**[72]

The *region of pure conversation* sounds like the perfect communication of the holy instant, with no private thoughts, mind in mind. After Shams disappeared the second time, Rumi in his grief searched for him until he realized:

Why should I seek? I am the same as he. His essence
speaks through me. I have been looking for myself!

The union became complete. There was full fana,
annihilation in the Friend.[73]

Rumi:

Out beyond ideas of wrongdoing and rightdoing,

there is a field. I'll meet you there.

When the soul lies down in that grass,

the world is too full to talk about.

Ideas, language, even the phrase *each other*

doesn't make any sense.[74]

ACIM:

God indeed can be reached directly, for there is no
distance between Him and His Son. His awareness
is in everyone's memory, and His Word is written on
everyone's heart. Yet this awareness and this memory can
arise across the threshold of recognition only where all
barriers to truth have been removed. In how many is this
the case? Here, then, is the role of God's teachers. They,
too, have not attained the necessary understanding as yet,
but they have joined with others. This is what sets them
apart from the world. And it is this that enables others to
leave the world with them. Alone they are nothing. But in
their joining is the power of God.[75]

Chapter Thirteen

RESPONSIBILITY

*G*od did not create me slave or robot. God created me to share His Love and Being, which are the same. The freedom to accept God's grace is mine to give or not. Hence my responsibility. Who is responsible for the world of pain I see? Who is responsible for all the suffering of billions of humans over thousands of years? The answer ACIM gives is challenging:

> This is the only thing that you need do for vision,
> happiness, release from pain and the complete escape
> from sin, all to be given you. Say only this, but mean it
> with no reservations, for here the power of salvation lies:
>
> *I am responsible for what I see.*
> *I choose the feelings I experience, and I decide*
> *upon the goal I would achieve.*
> *And everything that seems to happen to me*
> *I ask for, and receive as I have asked.*[1]

It seems unrealistic to admit responsibility for the insanity I see, the suffering I experience, and every awful thing that seems to happen to me. Isn't it somebody else, or God, or the devil, who does it? All my suffering I asked for? Why would I ask for suffering? Did Job ask for suffering? The resistance to accepting this is enormous. This is a radical teaching. I resist this teaching because it seems counter-intuitive. It does not seem true because the process happens unconsciously.

> **Certainly sickness does not appear to be a decision. Nor would anyone actually believe he wants to be sick.**[2]

322

An open mind, knowing I don't know, facilitates consideration of this idea. Is depression an unconscious decision to be depressed?

Workbook Lesson 196, *It Can Be But Myself I Crucify*, explains the shift from external blame to responsibility. ACIM teaches that the fear of God is the final obstacle to peace. If I suffer now, it must mean God is justly punishing me. Fear of God manifests in the guilt-driven horror over the permanent punishment, of the most painful severity, I have coming. Accepting responsibility for what I experience means I do not worry about God punishing me now or in the future. Recognizing this truth ends the fear of God because I accept responsibility for my suffering. What hurts me are my thoughts, not God, but I won't see the truth of this until the shift into truth is accomplished.

> **Until this shift has been accomplished, you can not perceive that it is but your thoughts that bring you fear, and your deliverance depends on you...**

> **For once you understand it is impossible that you be hurt except by your own thoughts, the fear of God must disappear. You cannot then believe that fear is caused without.**[3]

If I learn that I am responsible for the dream projection, then I am the dreamer, and not the victim of the dreamed world. The world is not beating me up; I unconsciously project this world and then believe it's real. My perception is a projection, yet seeing is believing.

How is it I crucify myself, and why would I cause myself to suffer? The fundamental law of cause and effect is also known as the law of karma. The suffering I experience in this life is a balancing of my forgotten mistakes in this life or a past life. If I am a bully, I learn how it feels by being bullied. If I drink a gallon of gin do I blame God for the hangover? This karmic law is operating in the dream, not Heaven. As long as I am in the dream, I'm subject to the law of karma.

Karma means I reap what I sow. It is not that I consciously asked to be depressed, but I did ask for it through my choices. I fail to understand cause and effect. I fail to understand the power of mind to create or miscreate. I fail to understand how my judgments are me pleading guilty. I am unaware of unconscious guilt that causes fear and suffering. I am likely unaware of past decisions bearing fruit now. Accepting responsibility releases guilt because in realizing that I only hurt myself, I stop believing that I hurt others, outside of myself. I no longer need fear divine retaliation or punishment for what I thought were my attacks on others, in the world, outside of myself.

> **If it can but be you you crucify, you did not hurt the world, and need not fear its vengeance and pursuit. Nor need you hide in terror from the deadly fear of God projection hides behind.**[4]

When I see that the enemy is within, I understand what "split mind" means. Before accepting responsibility, reality is split into objective exterior (others, the world, God) and subjective interior (me). This is duality. I blamed suffering on exterior sources, be it the punishment of God or the attack of my enemies, or perhaps Satan is testing me like he tested Job: "Hide Your Love from him and see how long he lasts." The cause of problems seems outside of me, or not me. The one is split, not ontologically, but in my belief and perception. This split is the false claim of separation into duality.

> **When you realize, once and for all, that it is you you fear, the mind perceives itself as split. And this had been concealed while you believed attack could be directed outward, and returned from outside to within. It seemed to be an enemy outside you had to fear. And thus a god outside yourself became your mortal enemy; the source of fear.**[5]

Eckhart Tolle describes reaching this point right before his transformation. The thought came to him, *I cannot live with myself any longer*,[6] and examining this thought he realized the split. There seemed to be two of himself. The one who can't stand living with the other. Split-self is a false self-image, because split-mind is part of the dream of separation. The split within my mind is projected as the polarized world of opposites I perceive and believe is real. The message of responsibility for erroneous belief and perception is repeated and unambiguous in the course.

> **Deceive yourself no longer that you are helpless in the face of what is done to you…It is impossible the Son of God be merely driven by events outside of him. It is impossible that happenings that come to him were not his choice. His power of decision is the determiner of every situation in which he seems to find himself by chance or accident. No accident nor chance is possible within the universe as God created it, outside of which is nothing.[7]**

My power of decision determines what I experience. Nothing I experience is caused by chance, coincidence, or a simple twist of fate. Every effect has a cause and I think the cause of grief is outside myself, yet it is not there.

When I use my power of decision to give all my own choices, or my will, to the Holy Spirit, I embrace responsibility. My responsibility is the power of decision, my free will to choose. Yet I cannot choose on my own, even if I wanted to. I decide with either the ego or the Holy Spirit. This is my freedom and responsibility. Even my willingness to give all decisions to the Holy Spirit is graced by the Holy Spirit. I willingly give the power of decision to the Holy Spirit to decide for me. This means I agree with the Holy Spirit that I do not know how best to choose and I surrender decision to One Who does know how best to choose.

> And yet, you *cannot* make decisions by yourself. The only
> question really is with what you choose to make them...
> You will not make decisions by yourself whatever you
> decide... For they are made with idols or with God.[8]

Hence the importance of realizing that I don't know. Without realizing that I don't know, surrender of my own choice, or will, is resisted. If I stick to "I know best," then I am not yet ready to surrender my will to God, to step back and let the Holy Spirit lead the way.

> Step back in faith and let truth lead the way. You know
> not where you go. But One Who knows goes with you.
> Let Him lead you with the rest.[9]

If I choose with the ego, I suffer painful consequences. If I choose with the Holy Spirit I experience peaceful consequences. Either way, it is my decision that causes the effects I seem to experience. My decision is my responsibility. The dynamic of decision is in my mind. Yes, my mind is conditioned to the status quo. Yet only I can choose again. If I will not choose again, then I'm a person predetermined to pain. Knowing I don't know facilitates letting go of control and surrendering my will to the One Who does know. If this surrender is forced, it is meaningless. Voluntary surrender is my responsibility. True surrender is wanting to surrender. Surrender sacrifices suffering. Until surrender is unconditional, it is not surrender.

> Never was so much given for so little. In the holy instant
> is this exchange effected and maintained...Yet for this,
> the power of your wanting must first be recognized. You
> must accept its strength, and not its weakness. You must
> perceive that what is strong enough to make a world can
> let it go, and can accept correction if it is willing to see
> that it was wrong.[10]

Remember the holy instant, the present moment with no past or future? The law of karma requires past and future. The holy instant frees me from the past and frees me from fear of future consequences. Otherwise I am stuck on the wheel of karma, the circle of time, sometimes stepping forward and sometimes stepping back, but not liberated from it. The power of my wanting is the heart-power of desire, will. Thought combined with belief moves mountains, literally. I am responsible for this power because I choose to decide with the Holy Spirit or with the ego. What I want determines what I experience. Before I surrender I desire surrender. This wanting is the union of my will with God's Will because this is what God and I want. It is a shared, common, Will.

> **You would do well to look at confusion clearly: you are responsible for what you think because it is only at this level that you can experience choice.**[11]

I am responsible for what I choose to believe. The course is mind-training that replaces wrong-minded thinking with right-minded thinking. How I think guides what I choose.

> **For you do have control over your mind, since the mind is the mechanism of decision.**[12]

Mind directs decision. I believe ego thoughts or I believe holy thoughts. I am conditioned with wrong-mindedness and hence the need for purification. My power of decision is not a choice for specifics. The only valid choice is to surrender all choice to the Holy Spirit so that the Holy Spirit makes all choices. My responsibility is to surrender responsibility to the One who is responsible. This makes perfect sense when I realize Spirit knows best and I don't.

In the dream of separation, my mind is split because I made a special vault in my mind to seal off unbearable guilt. This split is within my own dreaming mind. One part is called conscious and the other is called unconscious. This cognitive cracking is caused by the first fracture that seemed to smash the Sonship into smithereens. Then the heartbreaking pain over this breakup splits mind into unconscious and conscious, as a defensive attempt to forget the fall. Then this dualistic division is projected as if it is outside of me. My mind is split from your mind because I'm not you and you're not me. Healing this mind-split is the goal. The re-joining of the fragmented parts of the one Son of God is the movement from duality to non-duality. It is returning to the non-split, shared Will.

One part of the healing of my mind is through my remaining freedom to choose between the thought system of the ego, or the thought system of the Holy Spirit. This is mind-training, mind-healing, the exchange of wrong-mindedness for right-mindedness. When sane, I choose Love over fear, harmlessness over attack, innocence over guilt, Heaven over hell, Truth over illusion, true forgiveness over grudging grievances. I make all these choices at once with the single choice for the Holy Spirit. I give my power of decision to the Holy Spirit to decide for me, because I do not know how to decide on my own. If my mind is split between what is conscious and unconscious, and the unconscious is hidden from me, then how can I decide? How do I even know my mind is split when one part is not conscious? Realizing I cannot decide, I give the decision to the Holy Spirit to make for me. Before that, I joined in agreement with the ego. Should a blind person decide when to cross the street or trust his best friend Guide God?

Surrender is achieved by desire. I do not decide or choose; I simply want. What do I want? Because part of desire is unconscious, I do not know what I really want. According to the law of attraction, people manifest what they focus on. The reason why it seems not to work is because focus is conflicted between unconscious and conscious desires, and I am unaware of this dynamic. The poor man tries to manifest a Mercedes but unconsciously keeps hidden his inheritance of his dad's belief that the love of money is the root of all evil. So the lord of manifestation does not buy me a Mercedes-Benz.

If I dream I am depressed, it is because I unconsciously wanted this as mitigating self-punishment, or I believe I am depressed because of a source outside myself. Either way, I do not consciously see depression as my desire. The dream of depression is also a way of projecting blame onto my brother: "See what you did to me. I'm sad because of you." Projection of blame is conscious and unconscious. I can choose again, correcting past mistakes, or I delay the ending of hell. Which do I want, Heaven or hell? Since I am not aware of the conflict between unconscious and conscious desire, I surrender decision to the Holy Spirit, who is aware of all levels of desire and knows what is best for everyone. The best decision: yield.

> **What is temptation but a wish to make the wrong decision on what you would learn, and have an outcome that you do not want? It is the recognition that it is a state of mind unwanted that becomes the means whereby the choice is reassessed; another outcome seen to be preferred. You are deceived if you believe you want disaster and disunity and pain.**[13]

I learn I don't want hell by making mistakes and experiencing the effects of those mistakes: pain, suffering, depression. Otherwise, how would I know? Temptation says, "Try this." In my ignorance I try it. Then I know that I do not want it because it produces an unpleasant state of mind. Who learns how to ride a bike without falling down? What happens before the toddler takes his first step? What kind of parent punishes his child for stumbling while learning to walk? Who smacks down his child for mispronouncing a new word? Mistakes are teachers.

When I am depressed, however, it is most difficult to realize I'm responsible for how I feel. I might refuse this idea immediately, and severely. I sure did. It's reasonable to resist responsibility for pain. It seems cruel to tell someone he is causing his own depression. Why would I do it? Why would I choose to suffer so? It seems to make no sense to say I'm doing this to myself. I simply would not do this to myself, would I? It's hard to accept that my suffering is a decision, a choice I make. I am chronically caught in wrong-mindedness, and the ego intends to keep it that way. The decision to be depressed is unconscious. Hence it does not make conscious sense. Yet, if my judgment of my brother makes me depressed then it is my own thinking that makes me depressed. I am responsible.

> **The resistance to recognizing this is enormous, because the existence of the world as you perceive it depends on the body being the decision maker.**[14]

What I resist is the realization that sickness, or depression, is my choice, a function of mind and not the body.

From a body-identification view, I would not choose depression or any pain. The ego consuls thus: I'm the victim of a genetic brain disorder, or some other, external source. Other people, like my parents, brain-damaged me. I'm doing time for their crime. That idea gets me off the hook of responsibility. The cause is not myself; the cause is outside of me. I'm a victim. In truth though, the body is not responsible; it makes no choices; the mind chooses. The brain does not choose. The brain is like a computer. The computer behaves how it is programmed. The programmer is the decider, not the biological calculator. The reason why the resistance to recognizing responsibility is so enormous is because it completely reverses the ego's wrong-mindedness, also known as conditioning.

> **For sickness is an election, a decision.**[15]

Thus, if I mis-identify as a body, I resist recognizing that my mind elected for sickness. This is level confusion. The body is effect, not cause. The mind is cause. If I identify with the body, then I am not responsible for my depression because my body is not responsible for sickness or depression. The issue of identity keeps coming back.

Depression is not a brain/body disorder. It is a mind disorder, a decision, based on an identity-confusion disorder.

> **First, it is obvious that decisions are of the mind, not of the body. If sickness is but a faulty problem-solving approach, it is a decision. And if it is a decision, it is the mind and not the body that makes it.**[16]

What problem is this *faulty problem-solving approach* trying to solve? Guilt, and the fear of punishment. Future punishment might be mitigated if I punish myself, for I am guilty. God, and other people, may have mercy on me because I suffer so much. This is the ego's problem-solving approach.

Sickness is also a way of blaming my brother, whom I see as *outside* me. Responsibility is not blame. Blame is attack. Blame accuses, condemns, and increases guilt. Neither is responsibility self-blame. It is counter-productive to increase my own guilt. Yet in the shift from blaming someone or something outside myself to accepting responsibility, I first shift the blame within.

> *Only you can deprive yourself of anything.* Do not oppose this realization, for it is truly the beginning of the dawn of light. Remember also that the denial of this simple fact takes many forms, and these you must learn to recognize and to oppose steadfastly, without exception. This is a crucial step in the reawakening. The beginning phases of this reversal are often quite painful, for as blame is withdrawn from without, there is a strong tendency to harbor it within. It is difficult at first to realize that this is exactly the same thing, for there is no distinction between within and without.[17]

Recognizing my responsibility is so important the course calls it *the beginning of the dawn of light,* and *a crucial step in the reawakening.* This crucial beginning step is *often quite painful* because instead of blaming my depression on an external situation or person, I blame it on myself. This is the same mistake, believing in blame, but blaming a different brother, me, and believing my brother and I are different. It is still blame, and guilt producing. Now it seems even worse that I cause pain for myself. Now there is no external excuse.

Blaming myself is not the same as accepting responsibility. One produces a painful guilt. The other is a necessary and crucial step in my reawakening. Responsibility is the relinquishment of blame and attack. Responsibility is relinquishing illusions of guilt. Blame makes guilt real. If guilt is not real, why would I blame anyone, including myself? The Atonement knows that the ultimate sin I feel guilty for did not happen. Responsibility realizes that my brother did not do this to me. No one else hurts me like I do. Responsibility accepts that I do this to myself by choices I made, tricked into believing the dream is real. In a certain sense, mistaken choices are necessary to learn the consequences of those choices. Wrong-minded choices are easily corrected by letting the Holy Spirit make the correct choice instead. Thus guilt is decreased, not increased, when I accept responsibility for what I believe. No one else accepts the Atonement for me.

Accepting responsibility is the end of judgment and condemnation; it is the shift from illusion to the truth. It is the way out of hell. This is central to the thought reversal, and shift in perception, the course aims at, and it ain't easy. Now, perhaps, I realize that there is no solution in the world, perceived as outside of myself. There is a cost that I might refuse to pay for this recognition of responsibility:

> What does this recognition "cost"? It costs the whole world you see, for the world will never again appear to rule the mind. For with this recognition is responsibility placed where it belongs; not with the world, but on him who looks on the world and sees it as it is not…Yet to accept this release, the insignificance of the body must be an acceptable idea.[18]

The cost is the whole world I project/perceive, a price I might not be willing to pay. I confuse this cost as sacrifice, but the sacrifice of an illusion is no sacrifice at all. Is the sacrifice of suffering too expensive? Responsibility means I no longer accept the role of victim, nor attack a brother by blaming him.

> **These patients do not realize they have chosen sickness. On the contrary, they believe that sickness has chosen them. Nor are they open-minded on this point...To them the separation is quite real.**[19]

I *do not realize* depression is a choice because the decision is unconscious. Because of my closed mindedness, ignorance, and enormous resistance to accepting responsibility for my suffering, I need help.

> **To them God's teachers come, to present another choice which they have forgotten...Very gently, they call to their brothers to turn away from death: "Behold you Son of God, what Life can offer you. Would you choose sickness in place of this?"**[20]

I am responsible for my mis-perception of sickness and suffering, including depression. It is not done to me. I am not a victim. It is not situational. It is not genetic. It is not random fate. God created me to be creative and yet, in the separated state, I miscreate by projecting a whole world of separation, guilt, and fear, from my mind, and in my mind. There is no outside world; it all takes place in the mind-movie, and this is, naturally, hard to accept. In the darkness of depression the light of truth is blocked. I irresponsibly claim no responsibility. This is the danger of getting stuck in suffering.

> **There is no need to suffer anymore. But there is need that you be healed, because the suffering and sorrow of the world have made it deaf to its salvation and deliverance.**[21]

Suffering leads to breakdown or breakthrough, despair or hope. If suffering leads to despair, the process is not complete. Yet without suffering how would I know I made a mistake somewhere in the first place?

Perhaps I don't understand *how* I create my own suffering. My god-like creativity is producing impressions of suffering. I, and no one else, am responsible for my thinking, my wanting. This is how I make the perception of suffering, with the creative power of mind, desire, and belief. Suffering is a perception, which is a projection, that I make. Pain is in my mind and pain ends in my mind. The message of suffering: separation does not work; separation leads to suffering.

> **Do not deny yourself the joy that was created for you for the misery you have made for yourself.**[22]

Besides *how* I do it, *why* do I do it? Why do I deny myself joy? I deny myself joy because I believe, unconsciously or not, that I do not deserve joy because the separation did happen; I did sin against God, and I'm guilty and fearful of the punishment that I do deserve. God is justly punishing me and my guilt is why the world is so cruel, for is not God just? And if God is not doing it, I choose suffering in the hope of mitigating God's future punishment and perhaps achieve salvation through the sacrifice and suffering of purgatory. I self-flagellate because I believe in sin and punishment. I believe my guilt is real. I believe separate bodies are real. My mind is in so much pain from the guilt over my mistakes that I choose suffering. I believe in sin and guilt. I deserve suffering. I desire suffering. I project the unconscious. I project pain. I perceive pain. This kind of confused thinking means I joined in agreement with the ego's accusing lies. It means I do not yet accept the Atonement. It means that I choose to be in time instead of eternity. Because guilt over separation is unconscious, I don't even know I do all this. That suffering is voluntary is a radical spiritual teaching. I might not be able to understand it right away.

> Watch your mind for temptation of the ego, and do not
> be deceived by it. When you have given up this voluntary
> dispiriting, you will see how your mind can focus and rise
> above fatigue and heal.[23]

My dispiriting is *voluntary*. Don't worry if this idea seems too difficult to accept. Resistance to the idea is normal in this world, where illusions rule. Consider it and try to experience how it works before disagreeing or agreeing.

I am responsible for the whole chain reaction of consequences following from the first mistake. Fear is one of those consequences, caused by my choices, particularly the choice, or wish, to separate from each other and from God. If I choose to judge or attack a brother I will feel fear, and be responsible for causing fear. My feelings show which way I chose.

> When you are fearful, you have chosen wrongly. That is
> why you feel responsible for it.[24]

If I feel fear, it means I made a wrong choice. If I criticize my brother, then I choose, again, with the ego, for separation. It is my responsibility to reverse this and give the choice to the Holy Spirit. This is working with respect for cause and effect and not magic miracles.

> The correction of fear is your responsibility.[25]

How do I correct fear? Fear is a symptom and it does no good to correct symptoms. It is my responsibility to understand the source of fear. This means that if I seek simply to remove fear, I seek release from a symptom, not the cause. The course's core teaching about cause and effect is essential to remember. It does no good to simply remove fear without healing its cause, and understanding this truth is my responsibility. If fear was magically removed without removing the cause, then fear resurfaces, perhaps in a different form. Fear is the alarm clock feeling telling me it's time to wake up and choose again. My erroneous desire to separate is exposed by feeling bad.

> You should ask instead, for help in the conditions that have brought the fear about. These conditions always entail a willingness to separate. At this level you can help it.[26]

I do not fight fear. I ask for help with the conditions that brought fear about. My willingness to separate is the cause of guilt, that is the cause of fear. This chain reaction is unconscious until it isn't.

The Atonement says the sin of separation did not happen. The holy instant declares that there is no past, where sin happened, and no future where the guilty are punished. The holy instant cancels karma. If I believe it did happen, then that belief is my responsibility. This means that my suffering, an effect of my separation belief, is also my responsibility.

> You can but hurt yourself. This has been oft repeated, but it is difficult to grasp as yet. To minds intent on specialness it is impossible.[27]

If I believe in specialness I am still devoted to the ego's wrong-minded system of thought. If I am special, I am separate and the victim of suffering. Others hurt me. I hurt others. God punishes me for my special sins, especially the original sin. Responsibility remains difficult to grasp. I remain unconscious.

> Suffering is an emphasis on all that the world has done to injure you...the dreamer is unconscious of what brought on the attack against himself, he sees himself attacked unjustly and by something not himself. He is the victim of this "something else," a thing outside himself, for which he has no reason to be held responsible...he cannot escape because its source is seen outside himself.[28]

As long as I believe the problem is outside of me, I delay liberation. If the cause of fear is outside of me, I am not responsible for it and I can't do much about it. Believing illusions doesn't lead to salvation. If I correctly identify the source, or cause, a real solution is possible. Otherwise I continue the world of pain, as the ego intends.

When I blame the cause of my suffering on my brother, I blame him out of my ignorance. Blame is joining in agreement with the ego's wrong-mindedness, the way of the world.

> The "reasoning" by which the world is made, on which it rests, by which it is maintained, is simply this: "You are the cause of what I do...and what I suffer from is your attack."...it seems sensible, because it looks as if the world were hurting you.[29]

The way of the world is to blame others for my problems and pain. This blame is a projection, a judgment, a condemnation, and attack; blame is my own free, though often unconscious, choice. If the true cause is unconscious, I can't deal with it because I am not even aware of it. Recognizing the dynamics of projection, I am graced with a glimpse of the unconscious. All blame and attack is self-blame, self-attack, because this blaming is a projection of my own guilt. I attack my own guilt by projecting it onto my brother and attacking him. I do this to myself. The ego's game is to keep the secret from me, keep me unconscious, ignorant, sleeping, forgetting, and not responsible.

> Once you were unaware of what the cause of everything the world appeared to thrust on you, uninvited and unasked, must really be. Of one thing you were sure: of all the many causes you perceived as bringing pain and suffering to you, your guilt was not among them. Nor did you in any way request them for yourself. This is how all illusions come about. The one who makes them does not see himself as making them, and their reality does not

depend on him. Whatever cause they have is something quite apart from him, and what he sees is separate from his mind. He cannot doubt his dream's reality, because he does not see the part he plays in making them and making them seem real.[30]

Responsibility is so challenging because of the unconscious mind factor: *The one who makes them does not see himself as making them, and he does not see the part he plays in making them and making them seem real.*

> *You* are the dreamer of the world of dreams. No other cause it has, nor ever will.[31]

This shift, from being the victim of the nightmare world, to being the dreamer, is huge, and what is meant by accepting responsibility.

> No one asleep and dreaming in the world remembers his attack upon himself.[32]

If I am responsible for making all this up, then I no longer blame my brother for it, nor blame the world, nor blame God, nor blame the devil, nor the ego. Until I accept responsibility, I believe the ego's lies. This is the *secret of salvation.*

> The secret of salvation is but this: That you are doing this to yourself. No matter what the form of the attack, this still is true. Whoever takes the role of enemy and of attacker, still is this the truth. Whatever seems to be the cause of any pain and suffering, this is still true.[33]

It is all my projection. The course hammers this idea and there is nothing vague about it. The secret of salvation is not only that I do this to myself. The secret is also that I keep the secret from myself.

> Salvation is a secret you have kept but from yourself...you chose but not to listen, not to see.[34]

The lesson of responsibility is repeated until I get it.

> This single lesson learned will set you free from suffering, whatever form it takes. The Holy Spirit will repeat this one inclusive lesson of deliverance until it has been learned, regardless of the form of suffering that brings you pain...And you will understand that miracles reflect the simple statement: "I have done this thing, and it is this I would undo."[35]

Responsibility stands on two legs; one is responsibility for the suffering I experience: *I have done this thing*, and the other leg is my responsibility to accept the Atonement and end the suffering I project/perceive: *and it is this I would undo*. The lesson comes through pain, in many different forms. Depression is one of those forms. I am responsible for choosing depression and I am responsible for choosing again for joy instead.

If the truth is that I cause suffering to myself, and I deny this truth, what solution is there? Accepting responsibility is not easy, but continuing in depression is worse.

> The miracle does not awaken you, but merely shows you who the dreamer is...Yet if you are the dreamer, you perceive this much at least: That you have caused the dream, and can accept another dream as well. But for this change in content of the dream, it must be realized that it is you who dreamed the dreaming you do not like.[36]

If I want to change the dream of depression I first realize that I dreamed it; I projected it; I believed it. If I dreamed it, I can dream a different dream. This is the movement from unconscious to conscious. Unconscious content that becomes conscious is no longer unconscious and thus no longer projected. What is chained in the dark vault of unconsciousness attempts escape via projection. When unconscious content is released, it no longer needs to escape. When I no longer believe that the sin of separation is real I am free from guilt. When I am free from guilt, I no longer believe in, and fear, punishment. When punishment becomes absurd I no longer punish myself or my brother with sickness. Blame no longer makes any sense. Freedom is another word for nothing left to hide in the dark dungeon. The prisoner is released. The shift from the nightmare to the happy dream is not the end goal. It is a transition before re-awakening from all dreaming.

Do I believe I cause my depression? Probably not. If I suffer depression, it is a sign I do not yet take responsibility for it, because uncovering the true cause, myself as the dreamer, myself as the projector, is the revealing allowing healing; then the dream can change because I direct the dream, happy or not.

> Those who are sick do not love themselves. If they knew
> the truth about themselves, they could not be sick.[37]

If I do not love myself, who is responsible for this lack of love? If I know the truth about myself, about what I am, about my Identity, then I will not be depressed. If I know and love myself I cannot be sick.

> To identify with the ego is to attack yourself and make
> yourself poor. That is why everyone who identifies with
> the ego feels deprived. What he experiences then is
> depression or anger because what he did was to exchange
> Self-love for self-hate, making him afraid of himself.
> He does not realize this. Even if he is fully aware of
> anxiety he does not perceive its source as his own ego
> identification, and he always tried to handle it by making
> some sort of insane "arrangement" with the world. He
> always perceives this world as outside himself, for this
> is crucial to his adjustment. He does not realize that he
> makes this world, for there is no world outside him.[38]

Ego-identification (or identity-confusion disorder) leads to either depression or anger. Depression and anger are basically the same attack in different directions. Attack directed towards others is expressed as anger. Attack of anger towards myself is felt as depression. Depressed persons often appear angry or irritable. If I am depressed I identified with the ego, and not as God created me. I attack myself with anger. I blame self or other but I do not accept responsibility. But, *He does not realize this.*

> All attack is self attack. It cannot be anything else.
> Arising from your own decision not to be what you are,
> it is an attack on your identification. Attack is thus a way
> in which your identification is lost, because when you
> attack, you must have forgotten what you are. And if your
> reality is God's, when you attack you are not remembering
> Him. This is not because He is gone, but because you are
> actively choosing not to remember Him.[39]

I accept responsibility, or, I argue with God and insist God is wrong. If I insist on being right, making God wrong, then heroin might be the best bet. Escape the pain. Forget about the cause of pain, and better luck next time around. Should I oppose God's Will with my confusion and ignorance? I literally cannot oppose God's Will because my will is already one with God's Will. I imagine, however, that I do control a will that opposes God's Will. I pay a heavy price in pain for believing that nightmare. I choose to stop believing illusions whenever I want to. It does not take time to achieve this; it takes willingness. In this world, it seems to take time to come to that place of willingness to surrender my personal will to God and re-join God's Will.

> There is no peace except the peace of God, because He has
> one Son who cannot make a world in opposition to God's
> Will and to his own, which is the same as His.[40]

When watching a movie in a theater, how are the images made? They are projected by a projector. It is a perceptual illusion. I see what appears to be movement, a motion picture. Yet it is a series of still pictures, shown at twenty-four pictures per second, which is too fast for the eye to notice. It is literally a visual trick projection/perception. How a movie is perceived is derivative of how the world is perceived: projection. Whether in a movie theater or out in the projected world, all I see are images. What is needed for the projection to take place? Darkness (unconsciousness). In light, the projection cannot be seen. Drive-in movies are projected at night. What is seen in dreams are mental images. When I sleep my eyes are closed. I prefer darkness for sleeping.

I might think that I don't want to project a world full of suffering and conflict. Yet what I project comes from the unconscious mind and does not need to make any conscious sense. What is perceived through projection is based on what is hidden within. Garbage out means garbage in. When the unconscious mind is purified of guilt I won't project guilt. When I no longer desire separation I won't project separation. I no longer believe in separation. I no longer perceive separation.

When you want only love, you will see nothing else.[41]

When I will only for love, then only love is known. This is the purified state. This is God's Will.

Blessed are the pure in heart, for they shall see God.[42]

The word "heart" is associated with desire, what I want, or will for. Heart may also be interpreted as "the unconscious." I employ both conscious and unconscious desires, wishes. When the unconscious heart is purified of illusionary beliefs in separation, guilt, and fear, only love remains. Conflict between unconscious and conscious desire ends. The split between unconscious and conscious ends as the unconscious becomes conscious. Guilt and fear do not exist because love is all there is and love has no opposite. Having a pure heart means a heart that treasures one desire. With one desire, there is no conflict and no opposition. True responsibility ends the projection of responsibility. True responsibility means the end of hell is near.

> **When you are willing to accept sole responsibility for the ego's existence you will have laid aside all anger and all attack, because they come from an attempt to project responsibility for your own errors.**[43]

Accepting responsibility means I understand that all my attacks are attacks on myself. I attack myself for my own unconscious guilt, that I refuse to see, by projecting it onto the mirror of my brother, whom I do see. When I recognize what is happening I drop anger and attack as absurd. Even if God graces me with a glimpse of this dynamic, it is easy to forget in the heat of the moment. Remembering takes practice.

It seems cruelly frustrating that I cause my own depression, yet how long will I continue doing this? If I can cease doing this, why not? How long should I wait before quitting sickness?

> **How long, O Son of God, will you maintain the game of sin? Shall we not put away these sharp-edged children's toys? How soon will you be ready to come home? Perhaps today?**[44]

> **Remember that you are deprived of nothing except by your own decisions, and then decide otherwise.**[45]

ACIM is practical because it teaches how to apply the teachings. It is the application that permits the ending of hell. The course gives specific instructions in how to change my choice.

> **Say this to yourself as sincerely as you can, remembering that the Holy Spirit will respond fully to your slightest invitation:**

I must have decided wrongly, because I am not at peace.

I made the decision myself, but I can also decide otherwise.

I want to decide otherwise, because I want to be at peace.

I do not feel guilty, because the Holy Spirit will undo all the consequences of my wrong decision if I will let Him.

I choose to let Him, by allowing Him to decide for God for me.[46]

Notice, again, that how I feel tells me what's going on. If I am not at peace, that feeling reveals I made a wrong turn; I am lost. I turn around and make the right turn or I waste gas searching in circles, afraid to ask for directions. A good map helps. This is the meaning of repentance, to turn around, to make a different choice. The final section of the final chapter of the *Text*, is titled *Choose Once Again*.

> **Trials are but lessons that you failed to learn presented once again, so where you made a faulty choice before you now can make a better one, and thus escape all pain that what you chose before has brought to you. In every difficulty, all distress, and each perplexity Christ calls to you and gently says, "My brother, choose again."**[47]

The result of accepting responsibility for mistaken choices is relief. Now there is a way out. Now I can make a better choice. I repent by choosing again, this time with the Holy Spirit, by surrendering my choice to the Holy Spirit and letting Him choose according to God's Will.

ACIM takes an even stronger stand than just I am doing this to myself. If I insist on being guilty, depressed, or any other form of illusion, it is blasphemous. It does not work to argue with God.

> **If God knows His children as wholly sinless, it is blasphemous to perceive them as guilty. If God knows**

His children as wholly without pain, it is blasphemous to
perceive suffering anywhere. If God knows His children
to be wholly joyous, it is blasphemous to feel depressed.
All of these illusions, and the many other forms that
blasphemy may take, are refusals to accept creation as it
is. If God created His Son perfect, that is how you must
learn to see him to learn of his reality. And as part of the
Sonship, that is how you must see yourself to learn of
yours.[48]

My thinking, my decisions, my choices, my judgments, my attacks and
condemnation, my wish to be separate in body, mind, and will, the
world I project, and thus my wish to suffer, are all my responsibility.
To choose again, this time the right way, is also my responsibility. I
am not a programmed robot with no choice of my own. I am programmed by conditioning yet I can choose again. But I do need help
and the Holy Spirit is here and now ready and willing to help. My
responsibility is a little willingness to invite His help on the way. Byron
Katie about my responsibility for suffering:

I sometimes say that you move totally away from reality
when you believe there is a legitimate reason to suffer.
When you believe that any suffering is legitimate, you
become the champion of suffering, the perpetuator of it in
yourself. It is insane to believe that suffering is caused by
anything outside the mind. A clear mind doesn't suffer.
That's not possible.[49]

The proof is in the practice. The ideas alone are not enough. If I
want to end hell, and relieve my mind in pain, I apply these ideas. Try
it. If the course is true, and I am responsible for my own suffering,
and I cannot accept this as true, then what happens? I cannot know
if the course is true without trying it. What have I to lose? Maybe I
have depression to lose.

Who would profit more from prayers alone? Who needs but a smile, being as yet unready for more? No one should attempt to answer these questions alone. Surely no teacher of God has come this far without realizing that. The curriculum is highly individualized, and all aspects are under the Holy Spirit's particular care and guidance. Ask and He will answer. The responsibility is His, and He alone is fit to assume it. To do so is His function. To refer the questions to Him is yours. Would you want to be responsible for decisions about which you understand so little? Be glad you have a Teacher Who cannot make a mistake. His answers are always right. Would you say that of yours?

There is another advantage, – and a very important one, – in referring decisions to the Holy Spirit with increasing frequency. Perhaps you have not thought of this aspect, but its centrality is obvious. To follow the Holy Spirit's guidance is to let yourself be absolved of guilt. It is the essence of the Atonement. It is the core of the curriculum.[50]

Sidetrack: 2005-2010

We left the story of my spiritual journey in 2005 when I graduated from UAA. Shortly after graduating, I took a clinical position in Kotzebue, Alaska as an itinerant therapist. My supervisor assigned me to serve the village of Selawik, Mavsigvik – a remote wilderness family recovery camp, and Kotzebue. In the mental health field there is a lot of employee turnover. In bush Alaska the turnover rate is even higher. When I arrived in Kotzebue the counseling services center had a supervisor and four itinerant therapists. Soon, two more therapists were hired. Then, within three months, many of the clinical staff left. One therapist was fired and two resigned. The supervisor resigned.

The director of the behavioral health department resigned. A fourth therapist moved up to the directors position. After three months, by default, I became the senior therapist. Soon enough I became the counseling services supervisor.

I didn't like being a supervisor and I didn't like the inter-office politics. The agency, Maniilaq Association, received a SAMHSA Garret Lee Smith Grant for youth suicide prevention. I applied for the job of managing this new grant and after jumping through some hoops, was hired. In less than two years I had three jobs at Maniilaq. This job lasted till June, 2010, when I left Maniilaq. The program was named "Project Life," to place emphasis on life, not suicide. This job suited me well. I helped people use creative mediums of photography, music, video, and writing, as a means of discovering and expressing their values. The Center for Digital Storytelling trained me in Berkeley, and the Marin Headlands, California, in 2007. The man who started digital storytelling, Joe Lambert, impressed me. Here was a guy making a difference. On that training trip I attended an evening with Byron Katie and her husband, Steven Mitchell. Another synchronicity. They appeared at a church in Berkeley a block away from the motel where I was staying. I did not know about it ahead of time. She signed a book I bought for my daughter and Steven signed a book I bought for my brother Gerry.

Also during that trip, my brother Gerry and his wife Donna took me to a Ratdog concert at the Fillmore in San Francisco on Saint Valentines Day. I had a blast and gratefully realized that Grateful Dead music was still rocking. Although a big fan of the Dead, I pretty much stopped going to shows when I moved to Alaska in 1987. I hoped to take my kids to a Grateful Dead concert sometime. When Jerry Garcia died in 1995, I figured it was over. The Ratdog show demonstrated that this psychedelic jam band music keeps on keeping on. Eventually My daughter joined me for several Furthur concerts in San Francisco and Los Angeles. After fifty years of touring, the remaining members make sure the music never stops.

Over three years, the Project Life team presented thirty-nine digital storytelling workshops in eleven villages of the Northwest Arctic Borough and Point Hope which produced 566 digital stories by 432 persons, mostly youth. Each year the workshops increased in popularity as we returned to the villages. For the most part, I managed to run the program and fly under the company political radar. But traveling to the villages meant living out of a suitcase for a week at a time. Most villages did not enjoy motels or restaurants. Staff usually slept at the village clinic, with access to a kitchen, or at the school in sleeping bags. We worked mostly in the village schools.

I traveled outside of Alaska as well for annual suicide prevention conferences in Bethesda, Maryland, Portland, Oregon, and Albuquerque, New Mexico. I presented at the 2007 Canadian Association for Suicide Prevention (CASP) in Yellowknife, Northwest Territories. I presented at the Hope and Resilience in Suicide Prevention Seminar, Nuuk, Greenland in 2009. To and from Greenland, I enjoyed a few days in Copenhagen, Denmark, the most bicycle-friendly city I have seen. Besides these out of state and out of country conferences, there were many within the state and I traveled to Juneau, Kodiak Island, Anchorage, and Glen Allen.

During this time I discovered two new authors I liked. One is Keith Varnum. One of his books, *Inner Coach Outer Power* describes many incredible experiences and a fascinating spiritual journey. I wanted to meet him, and since he offered workshops I signed up for one at his home in Phoenix, Arizona. I used vacation time to attend the workshop and visit friends and relatives within driving distance of Phoenix. Although I enjoyed the workshop and especially liked meeting Keith, my spiritual questions remained unanswered. I also visited Sedona and the Grand Canyon. The other author is Thom Hartmann, another writer with an amazing spiritual journey. I especially enjoyed his auto-biographical book, *The Prophet's Way*.

Meanwhile, back in Anchorage, my daughter Alicen, now eighteen, finished her training as a massage therapist at a vocational school in

Anchorage. Shortly after graduation she had her second involuntary hospitalization. This time it was for a Bipolar manic episode that became psychotic. I knew my daughter was moody but I did not suspect Bipolar Disorder. I had seen her withdrawn and abrasive and I chalked it up to normal teenage angst and rebellion. I hadn't seen her manic. I wasn't sure what to make of her first hospitalization at fifteen. Adolescent growing pains?

Now it seemed more serious. I was heartbroken by my daughters illness. Over the next ten years she was hospitalized many times and tried many kinds of therapies, none of which helped for long, if at all. Her suffering was my suffering. A situation in the mental health system, a focus on pharmaceuticals, which I knew well, became personal with my daughter. Although I had done plenty of self-medication, I never used psychiatric medications. Alicen tried many different psychiatric drugs without relief. She also suffered severe side effects from the meds. I know from clinical experience there are times when medications are the professional option in a crisis situation. This is different from permanent drugging. After seven years of sobriety, I said the hell with it and started drinking again.

In 2008 my son, Francis, moved to Kotzebue to live with me. My ex-wife's second husband, Rich, physically abused Francis, and Dee tried to cover it up. He stopped living with his mother and dropped out of High School. He stayed with my brother Robert for a while. Francis started getting into trouble and without my knowing it started smoking and selling marijuana. He pretended that he was not interested in pot at all and I naively believed him. Francis is intelligent and entrepreneurial. He snowboarded, skateboarded, and started a skateboard business. He enjoyed computers and trained himself to build web sites. My brother Robert discovered Francis' marijuana stash and we figured living in the bush with me was the best bet for Francis. The day he was to fly to Kotzebue, he tried to steal a computer in Anchorage. Fortunately for Francis, he was under eighteen, and my brother Robert, a defense attorney, worked with youth offenders.

My brother managed a release from the youth detention facility and Francis flew to Kotzebue. More grief over my kids' problems pressed down on me.

My trips to the villages to present digital storytelling workshops had me away from Kotzebue for five days at a time. I left Francis, now seventeen, on his own. One Friday I returned from a village and received a call from airport security in Anchorage. They detained Francis for having a suspicious object in his luggage. They were waiting for a search warrant. With out my knowing it, he had flown to Anchorage to obtain marijuana to sell in Kotzebue, where pot prices were outrageous. Nothing brought me down more than the serious problems my children faced. Now I know that special love relationships are the ego's supreme method for maintaining the dream.

When the grant ended in 2010, I wanted an extended vacation. I decided on a long bicycle tour like I did at age eighteen, and this one also involved biking through Canada. I decided to ride solo from Anchorage to Mexico. In Banff, Canada, I switched to the Great Divide Mountain Bike Route, a mostly off-road ride all the way to Mexico. For the second time I cycled the Icefields Parkway between Jasper and Banff. I thought it would be like backpacking on a bike, which seemed perfect for me. Because of my broken back I could not haul a heavy backpack any distance. I pieced together a full suspension mountain bike and a Bob trailer and prepared for the trip. I left Anchorage in July and finally arrived in Mexico in October. No bad accidents on this cycling tour, though I did fall once and had several encounters with bears, on both the paved and off-road sections. It was quite an adventure, but I will not write more about that trip now.

My son experienced a spiritual conversion and joined a Baptist Church. This was a significant and positive change for Francis. I didn't like his "gun toting" pastor, nor the fundamentalist approach, but this was much better than Francis becoming a career criminal. He was more polite and respectful as well. Before his conversion, he and a friend were drunk and driving at high speed on a rural road.

The car went off the road and down a steep ravine and into trees. Miraculously, they were unhurt and walked away. A year later, Francis showed me where the crash happened. The car was still there in the ravine, wedged between two trees. It was amazing they survived and Francis considered it a sign that God watched over him. Francis was devoted to his new faith and the church community became his family. The church employed him to build their web site, and he practically lived at the church. He wanted to become a pastor. Apparently his time in Kotzebue had a serious effect on him because he dreamed of going back to Kotzebue and starting his own church for teenagers. To be continued.

Chapter Fourteen

HOW TO PERFORM MIRACLES

*J*f you glanced through the *Contents* and jumped to this chapter like a curious monkey, it probably won't make much sense. The background of the previous chapters is needed to get this one. This chapter serves as a review of the ways one applies course teachings. It is the application of ideas that allows healing, not the ideas per se. It is not necessary to believe or agree with the ideas. Try it and see if it works. See if you might miraculously heal depression by releasing guilt through true forgiveness. In ACIM, Jesus is recruiting miracle-minded miracle workers in order to save time and hasten the complete restoration of the Sonship, which is also the ending of hell.

To become a miracle-minded miracle worker, I freely volunteer. It is not forced on me. Everyone is invited, but not everyone accepts the invitation.

> I cannot choose for you, but I can help you make your own right choice. "Many are called but few are chosen" should be, "All are called but few choose to listen."[1]

If I agree, there is a process to go through, a purification. Egos with miraculous powers would be a worse disaster than what already is on earth.

Freedom From Conflict and Fear

Fear blocks love and miracles are expressions of love, so freedom from fear is essential for miracle-mindedness. Guilt over the sin of separation causes conscious and unconscious fear that blocks awareness of love. The course teaches of inner conflict, conscious and unconscious, that cause miracle-blocking fear. Cognitive dissonance is a form of guilt.

> It is essential, however, that you free yourself from fear
> quickly, because you must emerge from the conflict if you
> are to bring peace to other minds[2]

The course teaches about a specific, fear-causing, inner conflict occurring in two ways. The first is doing things that contradict each other. The course calls this conflict the strain of *conflicted behavior*. It is an example of duality. Conflict requires duality. The presence of this conflict is indicated by the presence of fear.

> Fear is always a sign of strain, arising whenever what you
> want conflicts with what you do. This situation arises in
> two ways: First, you can choose to do conflicting things,
> either simultaneously or successively. This produces
> conflicted behavior, which is intolerable to you because
> the part of the mind that wants to do something else is
> outraged.[3]

The second conflict is more subtle. The first kind of conflict shifts to the second sort of conflict by changing behavior. I do what I think I should, but I don't really want to. The problem is not in behavior; it is in the mind.

> Second, you can behave as you think you should,
> but without entirely wanting to do so. This produces
> consistent behavior, but entails great strain. In both cases,
> the mind and the behavior are out of accord, resulting in
> a situation in which you are doing what you do not wholly
> want to do.[4]

The miracle worker needs to be free of this cognitive dissonance because conflict causes guilt, which causes fear, which blocks the expression of love that the miracle is. When I do what I *wholly* want to do, my will is God's Will. This lesson in conflict, guilt, and fear is likely to be overlooked and I need reminding until I get it.

> The Holy Spirit cannot ask more than you are willing
> to do. The strength to do comes from your undivided
> decision. There is no strain in doing God's Will as soon
> as you recognize that it is also your own. The lesson here
> is quite simple, but particularly apt to be overlooked. I
> will therefore repeat it, urging you to listen. Only your
> mind can produce fear. It does so whenever it is conflicted
> in what it wants, producing inevitable strain because
> wanting and doing are discordant. This can be corrected
> only by accepting a unified goal.[5]

My split-mind is conflicted between the personal (egoic) will for separation, and the Voice for God, both within my mind.

The solution to this conflict-driven strain and miracle-blocking
fear is suggested in two phrases in the above quote: *undivided decision* and *unified goal*. These terms refer to the joining of my will with
God's Will so that there is One Will, and thus undivided will: non-
duality. God's Will is the Will to extend Love and create. Creation is
what happens when Love is extended. If I experience fear of any kind
it means I think I opposed God with a choice not in congruence with
God's Will to Love. This conflict is corrected when I catch it, hope-
fully sooner than later.

> The first corrective step in undoing the error is to know
> first that the conflict is an expression of fear. Say to
> yourself that you must somehow have chosen not to
> love, or the fear could not have arisen. Then the whole
> process of correction becomes nothing more than a series
> of pragmatic steps in the larger process of accepting
> the Atonement as the remedy. These steps may be
> summarized in this way:
>
> Know first that this is fear.
>
> Fear arises from lack of love.

The only remedy for lack of love is perfect love.

Perfect love is the Atonement.[6]

Perfect love and fear cannot co-exist. Therefore, miracles and fear cannot co-exist. In defense of my imperfect love, I reason that I am only human, which means I'm imperfect. Perfect love may seem unreachable to me, yet it is God's Love that is perfect. God created me as a perfect channel for His perfect Love. This is God's Will, whether I believe it or not. So, part of becoming a miracle worker is to be purified of the conflict between desire and behavior. This means I first become aware of this conflict/fear.

How to Become Miracle-Minded

To become a miracle worker, I first become miracle-minded. To become miracle-minded I invite the Holy Spirit to make it so. I agree to it and my desire for it is the joining of my will with God's Will. Preparation to become miracle-minded is the process of purification: an exchange of ego's wrong-mindedness for the Holy Spirit's right-mindedness.

Complete restoration of the Sonship is the only goal of the miracle-minded.[7]

This is the ambition worth cultivating: the *complete restoration of the Sonship*. I am miracle-minded when my only goal is this restoration. Here is a summary of the means to become miracle-minded, the prerequisite to becoming a miracle-worker. The order of the ideas is not important. They are co-dependent and mutually supportive. They weave together to create the big picture.

1. Atonement. I invite the Holy Spirit to help me accept the Atonement for myself. The Atonement is God's answer to the separation. Simply put, it says the separation did not happen. God gave the Atonement at the same instant the idea for separation occurred.

God cannot wait because waiting implies time and God is not in time because time is a temporary illusion. Accepting the Atonement for myself means agreeing with the Holy Spirit that the separation did not occur; there is no past; there is no sin; there is no guilt; there is no fear; there is no punishment; there is no suffering; all mistakes made in the dream of separation are easily corrected by choosing once again with the Holy Spirit. This is the transformation from wrong-mindedness to right-mindedness. If I accept the Atonement for myself, the twin towers of dualism collapse.

> **Nothing has ever happened to disturb the peace of God the Father and the Son. This we accept as wholly true today.**[8]

2. Open Mind. Be aware of the challenges to being open-minded. Be willing to question past conditioning. Be willing to say, "I don't know." This is easier said than done. Each of us (including the writer) is conditioned and claims a frame of reference, a world view, that filters and interprets the now that is ever new. Because of conditioning it is almost impossible to keep an open mind. I cannot do it myself so I ask the Holy Spirit, who is already in my mind, to break it open. Expect the ego to resist its own demise. I desire to receive a beginner's mind but the Holy Spirit does it. Then, freedom from the known. To know I don't know is all I need to know.

3. Cause and effect. Understand the fundamental law of true cause and effect, means and ends, source and symptom. Correcting my confusion about cause and effect amounts to a complete reversal of my thought system. Do I really expect a true healing of depression without understanding the cause? I am free to pursue symptom relief any way I want, and as long as I want, but ultimately I might want to get to the bottom of it. Remember, delay maneuvers prolong pain.

4. Separation/dream. Recognize that the wish for separation is the prime cause of this world of pain, the detour into fear, including all consequences of separation: sin, guilt, fear, suffering, time, space, bodies, private minds, autonomous wills, differences, judgments, competition, conflict, anger, attack, inequalities, specialness, deprivation, and disparity. These consequences are claims or beliefs, but not true. The Atonement reveals that the separation did not happen, but until I accept the Atonement for myself, the separation and its effects seem painfully real.

5. Identity. Be willing to allow identity to be shifted from body to Spirit, from ego to Mind, from autonomous will to one Will, from self-image to Self, from separated to joined, from self-made to God-created, from special to holy. In some ways, ACIM seems to be primarily about identity. Depression is an identity-confusion disorder. If I am confused about my identity then I am confused about everything that builds on that identity. Find out what I truly am and I'm done. That's the whole teaching of Ramana Maharshi. ACIM tells what I am but saying it is not enough. Experience, not words, reveals the truth. Language and the conceptual map I use are tools I use like a compass, to point me in a certain direction, and give instruction on how to use the map. I cannot apply the ideas if I do not know what the ideas are in the first place. Applying ideas leads to the experience of what I am and what God is.

6. Holy instant. The holy instant is the Holy Spirit's primary means for learning about love. Abide in the holy instant, the present moment, without past or future. The course teachings about time are radical but make a lot of sense if I study slowly and carefully. Belief in the past causes a lot of grief. Fear of future punishment is no fun. Ever wonder why depression and anxiety are the main courses of the time-based fear feeding frenzy, often served together like bacon and eggs? The holy instant is the portal to eternity. The holy instant allows perfect communication, Holy Communion,

with no private thoughts. Past and future seem to exist only at my ignorant insistence. In the holy instant, the basis for judgment (the past) and the basis for fear (the future), are gone.

7. Holy encounter. Remember the holy encounter whenever meeting anyone. This takes a lot of practice. In order to get as good at the holy encounter as Jimi Hendrix was at playing the guitar, it takes practice. And more practice. And still more. Mainly I practice to *remember.* Remember, there are no differences between my brother and myself. There are no separate interests. The holy encounter is the holy mirror where I meet my holy, whole, Self. In the holy encounter I meet the one holy Son of God, the Sonship, the Christ, the Body of Christ, who is my Self, who is perfect. The Holy Spirit in me recognizes the Holy Spirit in you: *Namaste.* Radical equality means *everyone is included.* The inclusion of everyone is a statement of non-duality. If I exclude any mind, I choose duality and conditional love. Exclusion requires a condition for exclusion based on the past. Inclusion is God's non-dual Will. Don't fight it. And forgive yourself quickly when you forget. Everyone forgets, frequently.

8. Holy Relationship. Invite the Holy Spirit into special relationships so that they are transformed into holy relationship. Joining in the holy relationship is the opposite of separating into personal selves. Joining leads to the ultimate reunion, the *Unity of unities.* This is the relational shift from needy getting justified by deprivation, to needless giving justified by abundance. The holy relationship is the expression of the holy instant, necessary in order to remember and benefit from the holy instant. Relationships are a huge part of the course and directly related to the course's emphasis on identity and forgiveness. I accept that my brother and I are still as God created us: holy, pure, sinless, perfect, one with God and all creation in every way. I join into the Christ. These ideas take a long time to sink in. Be patient and grateful, because eventually, we all realize holiness, even though we are holy already. This is true now, not

in the future. Joining is how the Holy Spirit manifests the holy relationship, through the holy encounter, expressing and remembering the holy instant. Got that? Good. If not see # 1-7 above.

9. True forgiveness. This is the *primary* practice for undoing unconscious guilt. Practice true forgiveness: I realize that what I thought happened to offend me, did not happen; I recognize that I projected what happened from my unconscious mind, revealing what needs healing in my mind. As the forbidden hidden is revealed I release my brother in innocence; I release myself in innocence. Every projection is another chance to reveal what is hidden, to make conscious what is unconscious, another chance to practice true forgiveness. This revealing allows the Holy Spirit's healing of unconscious guilt. If I look at it right, projection makes the unconscious conscious. The Atonement functions through forgiveness. There is no past. No one ever hurt anyone else. Example of a grateful prayer for forgiveness:

> *Holy Spirit, I thought my brother disrespected me. Now I see that I disrespected him and projected my guilt on to him. Now I see that the self-accusing belief in sin is hiding in my mind. Now I see the true cause of guilt, an unconscious belief. Now it is no longer unconscious. Now I release this belief to You and thank You for the Grace of the Atonement, which I accept for myself. As my brother is freed from the guilt I laid on him, so am I. Holy Spirit, I am grateful for your Grace. Amen.*

10. Non-duality. Drop all judgment, condemnation, attack, and anger. To be able to release all judgment is an advanced state. A pure heart is vigilant only for God. Don't worry if it seems to be an unattainable goal. God promises it to us and God keeps His promises. Like the course says in one of its more humorous sentences:

The case may be fool-proof, but it is not God-proof.[9]

Jesus shares a similar idea in the New Testament:

> **Jesus looked at them and said, "With men it is impossible, but not with God; for all things are possible with God."**[10]

11. Responsibility. I am responsible for projecting the bad dream. As I allow the Holy Spirit to heal unconscious guilt, I stop projecting it. I can't project what is not there. I am responsible for my choices. I am responsible for what I experience, including depression. It is a key, primary, and challenging idea. Don't worry if it does not make sense right away. I need not believe the idea. I need not agree with the idea. I consider the idea, and try it, to see if it works. I am responsible to accept the Atonement for myself. I am responsible to surrender responsibility to the only One Who knows how to be responsible.

That, in a nutshell, is how to become a miracle-minded miracle worker.

How to Heal Depression

A miracle worker does not confuse miracles with magic. He understands how miracles work. A miracle worker invites the Holy Spirit to teach him right-mindedness. A miracle worker is prepared to perform miracles by evolving from wrong-mindedness to miracle-mindedness.

> **I have already said that miracles are expressions of miracle-mindedness, and miracle-mindedness means right-mindedness.**[11]

A miracle worker recognizes the oneness of God's Will. What I *really* want is what God wholly wants. This union, or wholeness of Will is reflected by the miracle. God's Will is for joy, not depression. What God wants is in the best interest of everyone, including me and you. God's Will is not contingent on anything. Why oppose my own best interest? In the dream there are many wills in conflict, as well as the inner conflict of my own split-mind.

> The Holy Spirit is the motivation for miracle-mindedness;
> the decision to heal the separation by letting it go…The
> miracle itself is a reflection of this union of Will between
> Father and Son.[12]

The expression of love that is the miracle demonstrates God's Will to
Love, that I joyfully join. The miracle is the healing of the separation
by seeing it as illusion and gratefully letting it go.

A miracle worker ceases identifying with his body and he refuses
to believe what the body's senses tell him. A miracle worker no longer
identifies as a separate mind, the ego. A miracle worker quits believing
in a separate autonomous will. Likewise, a miracle worker does not
share the belief with others that they are separate bodies, minds, and
wills. A miracle worker stops believing that anyone, including himself,
is special, or sick, except as a bogus and blind belief, a false claim.

A miracle is a loving service that takes place in the mind. The body
may follow or not. It is about the mind, not the body.

> Miracles are expressions of love, but they may not always
> have observable effects.[13]

Observable effects has to do with perception, the realm of the senses,
the visible body. What does it mean to stop believing what my senses
say? My eyes and ears may tell me someone is sick, someone is hurt,
someone is suffering. My senses and the ego's illusionary ideas say
that I am a separate body with a separate mind. The course teaches
me to deny sense perceptions, and deny ego's thoughts. My senses are
mis-perceiving. Senses are not sensible. Ego thoughts are trickery and
delusional. The movie is not real. Senses are part of the dream, presenting pseudo-evidence that the dream is innocent like the lawyer
defending a guilty client. God says that His Son is one, perfect and
free, still as He created him. My senses say something sad. Ego says
something smart but stupid. Who is right? Which way do I *want*? If
God is not lying, and surely He is not, then my senses are wrong if

they say God's Son is sick. Miracles correct the perception, or claim, or belief, that God's Son is sick. Miracles heal by correcting perception. Perception is projection, not real. What I perceive is coming from within. A split mind projects the sick mind, a dream of duality. When I accept the Atonement for myself, I agree with the Holy Spirit that I am still as God created me, perfect and one. Split mind is an illusion. I recognize that perception is deception until the split-mind is no longer split. Mr. Goldsmith understood not trusting the senses.

> There is only one way to pray, and that is to ask yourself, "Do I believe my eyes or do I believe the mystics of the world, those people who have had an intuitive contact with God and who have had the revelation that evil does not exist as a reality and that there is no law of sin and disease?"[14]

Do I believe my eyes or the mystics? Do I know better than the holy ones? Do I want to argue with God?

A miracle worker cooperates with Jesus in performing miracles. He works miracles through me.

> When you perform a miracle, I [Jesus] will arrange both time and space to adjust to it.[15]

I do not choose what miracles to perform. Miracles are not personal. Otherwise I might make mistakes is the direction of specialness.

> I [Jesus] am the only one who can perform miracles indiscriminately, because I am the Atonement. You have a role in the Atonement which I will dictate to you. Ask me which miracles you should perform.[16]

I ask which miracles to perform to avoid the mistake of being motivated by selfish, or personal, will.

> The impersonal nature of miracles is because the
> Atonement itself is one, uniting all creations with their
> Creator.[17]

The miracle is impersonal because it does not recognize specialness. Because of special relationships, I compromise miracle-mindedness. When I prefer to heal one person over another (such as a friend or family member), I am tricked back into specialness. I cooperate with Jesus because He is in charge of the whole plan of Atonement and selects when and where a miracle is appropriate.

> ...the action aspect of the miracle should be controlled by
> me [Jesus] because of my complete awareness of the whole
> plan. The impersonal nature of miracle-mindedness
> ensures your grace, but only I am in a position to know
> where they can be bestowed.[18]

If miracle working becomes personal, it is under my conscious control and might be misguided. Don't make it personal, or special.

> Miracles are habits, and should be involuntary. They
> should not be under conscious control. Consciously
> selected miracles can be misguided.[19]

My grace is ensured by keeping it impersonal and involuntary. It is not my personal will that directs miracles, but God's holy, shared, Will.

A miracle worker does not confuse wrong-mindedness with right-mindedness. This is also called *level confusion*. For example, *Workbook* Lesson 284 states: *Pain is impossible.* I might feel frustrated by this claim and feel like throwing the book across the room, out the window, and into the river. Of course pain is possible; I perceived pain many times, even now. This is level confusion. The course does not always say what level it is referring to when it makes a statement. So, to avoid level confusion, understand the statement *Pain is impossible* this way: "In Heaven, pain is impossible." Pre-separation and post-separation, pain is impossible. Remember, the purpose of pain is to prove the body real. If the body is not real then pain is not real. While I believe that the separation is real, then pain is possible, as it is in this world. Pain is impossible but the dream of pain is possible. The miracle worker is careful about this level confusion. The miracle worker realizes that the patient is not sick even though he dreams he is sick. A miracle corrects dreams of pain. Mis-perception changes to proper perception. To be able to say, with conviction, that pain is impossible, represents a mature stage in the spiritual journey. Lesson 284 describes that process:

> **Loss is not loss when properly perceived. Pain is
> impossible. There is no grief with any cause at all. And
> suffering of any kind is nothing but a dream. This is
> the truth, at first to be but said and then repeated many
> times; and next to be accepted as but partly true, with
> many reservations. Then to be considered seriously more
> and more, and finally accepted as the truth. I can elect to
> change all thoughts that hurt.[20]**

The stages or process of accepting truth: (1) first the idea is just words, (2) then the words are repeated many times, (3) then the idea is accepted as partially true, with reservations, (4) then considered seriously more and more, (5) and finally accepted as the truth. I am not expected to get it that pain is impossible the first time I hear it. It appears to take a while in the dream of time and space.

The miracle worker affirms what is already true: the Son of God is always as God created Him. As such, healing is not necessary because my brother is already perfect, as God created him, *now. Instead of healing a sickness, perception of sickness is corrected.* Mr. Goldsmith understood how to perform miracles.

> **That is the way to treat [heal]; that is how to go about the
> world being a blessing and a benediction. You do not treat**

people and you do not try to realize the Christ in them.
You realize the Christ as the only being.[21]

Realizing Christ as the *only* being is another statement of non-duality.
The miracle worker helps the Holy Spirit relinquish unconscious guilt
by performing miracles of true forgiveness. Miracles demonstrate
that the Atonement is true. Why did Jesus often say, "Your sins are
forgiven you," before a healing? Guilt is the cause of fear and fear is
the cause of sickness. Remove guilt via true forgiveness and the cause
of fear and sickness is removed. Without a cause, sickness cannot be.
Jesus had the ability to connect with another person is such a way that
the person realized true forgiveness. This is the miraculous healing:
freedom from guilt.

A miracle worker realizes that he does not change anything. He
simply sees what is already true and does not agree with or share the
perception, or projection, of the illusion of separation and suffering.
Joel S. Goldsmith:

> It is not as if the practitioner [miracle-worker] were really
> trying to heal something when he is asked for help. The
> help that he is expected to give is the realization that such
> conditions do not exist as reality.[22]

Miracle workers express love by performing miracles. The course
teaches that love is received in prayer and shared by performing
miracles. The miracle worker gives as he receives and knows that
both are the same. When one gives love, one receives love. When one
gives peace, one receives peace. When one gives joy, one receives joy.
Thus in the giving and receiving of all good things do they increase
for both the giver and the receiver. This is the abundant economy
of Heaven: ever increasing Love, Joy, and Peace. The giver and the
receiver are not separate or different. Miracles are giving love to Self
and receiving love for Self.

> But your remembering is his [your brother's], **for God
> cannot be remembered alone. This is what you have
> forgotten. To perceive the healing of your brother as the
> healing of yourself is thus the way to remember God.**[23]

When I see the healing of my brother as my own healing, I remember the truth. The miracle worker helps his brother who is temporarily confused and believes wrong-minded ideas that deny the truth.

> **Miracles are merely the translation of denial into truth.
> If to love oneself is to heal oneself, those who are sick do
> not love themselves. Therefore, they are asking for the
> love that would heal them, but which they are denying
> to themselves. If they knew the truth about themselves
> they could not be sick. The task of the miracle worker thus
> becomes *to deny the denial of truth*. The sick must heal
> themselves, for the truth is in them. Yet having obscured
> it, the light in another mind must shine into theirs
> because that light is theirs.**[24]

A miracle worker is the "other" mind shining the love-light of truth into a mind who is denying the truth of the perfection of God's creation, and thus denying love. The same light is in everyone's mind but in some the light is blocked. Thus the miracle worker gives "back" to the receiver of the miracle what is already his.

In Joel S. Goldsmith's book, *The Art of Spiritual Healing*, published in 1959, his approach to miracle working is the same as that taught in ACIM.

> **No treatment [healing] is ever given to anyone or to any
> condition. As you move about this world, inevitably aware
> of it's frustrations and tragedies, you never treat anyone or
> any condition. Never! It is the claim that is presented to**

you that received the treatment, and that claim is always the belief in a selfhood or condition separate and apart from God.[25]

Miracles heal the *claim* of separateness, sin, guilt, fear, and suffering, not illness itself.

When I wake up from the dream is up to me, and miracles save time, or lead to a sooner awakening:

> The basic decision of the miracle-minded is not to wait on time any longer than is necessary.[26]

Joel S. Goldsmith echoes this idea in a specific way:

> If somebody should come into my thought this very minute while I am writing this book, he would receive a treatment immediately. I would not dare to wait even one minute to give the treatment because there is only one time to correct the belief and that is when it comes to me. That is the time for the reinterpretation, or unfoldment. The secret of healing is in reaction – in this immediate reinterpretation.[27]

So much for procrastination. *Immediate* action is *now*. Waiting is for the future. If I wait, I deny the holy instant. Waiting requires the illusion of time.

Miracles are not magic tricks that hide symptoms. Miracles heal at the level of cause, which is the belief in the separation. The miracle worker knows that this belief is an illusion and does not share it. The miracle worker does not substitute one illusion for another. The miracle worker sees the truth that God's creation is already and always perfect, beyond time. The amount of time it normally takes for someone stuck in duality to realize that he is not special, and that he is equal to his brother, and released from all sin, guilt, and fear, is shortened by the miracle.

He [the miracle worker] **recognizes that every collapse of time brings everyone closer to the ultimate release from time, in which the Son and the Father are One.**[28]

The miracle worker knows his brother as God created him, beyond time, and already perfect.

It may seem like there is a lot to do in order to become a miracle-minded miracle worker. It may seem like it might take a long time to get there. But remember, time is an illusion. I use time to be liberated from time. How long it takes is up to me.

> **It is not time we need for this. It is but willingness. For what would seem to need a thousand years can easily be done in just one instant by the grace of God.**[29]

It might seem as if I need to be highly advanced to perform miracles, but this is not so. There are requirements though. If I am fearful, I first allow the undoing of the cause of fear before working a miracle. A state of fear is a state of wrong-mindedness. Because a miracle is a correction, the giver of the miracle needs to be right-minded, even if it is a temporary right-mindedness. The receiver of the miracle does not need to be right-minded. In fact the miracle is performed to restore his right-mindedness.

> However, as a correction, the miracle need not await the right-mindedness of the receiver. In fact, its purpose is to restore him to his right mind. It is essential, however, that the miracle worker be in his right mind, however briefly, or he will be unable to re-establish right-mindedness in someone else.
>
> The healer who relies on his own readiness is endangering his understanding. You are perfectly safe as long as you are completely unconcerned about your readiness,

but maintain a consistent trust in mine [Jesus]. If your miracle working inclinations are not functioning properly, it is always because fear has intruded on your right-mindedness and has turned it upside down.[30]

ACIM teaches me not to rely on my own readiness and instead trust the readiness of Jesus.

I am right-minded when I accept the Atonement for myself. That is the prerequisite for performing miracles with Jesus as the director.

> *The sole responsibility of the miracle worker is to accept the Atonement for himself.*[31]

By accepting the Atonement for myself, I understand that the separation and its consequences (sin, guilt, fear, suffering) did not happen. My depression is not real, except, perhaps, in a depressing dream. Depression is a belief, unconsciously wanted, with perceived (projected) effects of pain. Depression is a false claim. Christ is not depressed, and you and I are Christ. My suffering is temporary and passes, as does everything time and perception present. The awareness of the Atonement is shared with the receiver of the miracle. The giver of the miracle extends the truth of the Atonement to his brother, through true forgiveness, allowing the Holy Spirit to heal his guilt. The giver of the miracle sees his brother as innocent, equal, perfect, and still as God created him. The miracle worker gives his right-mindedness to his brother who is lost, for a moment, in wrong-mindedness. That is performing a miracle, a correction in perception, a correction in belief. *Your faith has healed you.* Healing happens in the mind, not the body.

> **All forms of not-right-mindedness are the result of refusal to accept the Atonement for yourself. If you do accept it, you are in a position to recognize that those who need healing are simply those who have not realized that right-mindedness is healing.**[32]

If my mind is right, I am healed. The only thing wrong is a belief in my mind, a desire in my heart. Understood correctly, a miracle does not "do" anything. The miracle does not change anything. The miracle acknowledges the perfection of God already present, now. It results in a correction of perception, in the mind, now. Perception is corrected by ending projection. Projection is ended by releasing unconscious guilt.

> **Can you to whom God says, "Release My Son!" be tempted not to listen, when you learn that it is you for whom He asks release?[33]**

Chapter Fifteen

I NEED DO NOTHING

*𝒥*f it is true I need do nothing then what is the point of this book? And what is the point of ACIM, or any other spiritual methodology? Are not miracle workers doing something? The teaching that I need do nothing seems counter-intuitive and yet it is one of the most advanced teachings. It takes a while to get this teaching, and until I do, I keep on doing. Doing precedes non-doing. It is similar to Krishnamurti's *choiceless awareness*. Choiceless means I do not make a choice. I do not judge as to good or evil, as it is in the desert of duality. What Krishnamurti learned is that my own effort in spiritual growth is quickly, and unconsciously, taken over by the ego and becomes spiritual ambition, or spiritual materialism, spiritual gaining, seeking spiritual success. Spiritual pride (pious egoism) follows directly on spiritual "success." In 1946 Krishnamurti said,

It is truth that frees, not your effort to be free.[1]

God frees me. My effort for freedom is disguised, or not-so-disguised, ego-effort. Effort implies time and future liberation after my effort. Ego wants the dream to continue.

The alpha spiritual achiever seeks his own spiritual superiority in the competition of separate soul seekers. Separate selves means one is more holy than another. The hierarchy of holiness. The ego presents a persona of piety. The Cistercian monk, Father Thomas Keating, tells the story of an alpha male who joined a monastery and went from drinking his buddies under the table in the world, to fasting them under the table in the monastery. Spiritual competition to achieve the specialness of superiority. To be better than. This is perhaps a stage in the transition to mature spirituality, which is non-doing instead of doing. Experiences interpreted as "spiritual" are easily usurped by

371

the ego and become the evidence of my spiritual specialness. I must be special to God because He gave this experience to me and not you. Monks call it vainglory. The glory of heroic me.

ACIM stresses the danger of my own doing, including "spiritual" doing, as being selfish ego activity.

> The holy instant is the result of your determination to be holy. It is the answer. The desire and the willingness to let it come precede its coming. You prepare your mind for it only to the extent of recognizing that you want it above all else. It is not necessary that you do more; indeed, it is necessary that you realize that you cannot do more. Do not attempt to give the Holy Spirit what He does not ask, or you will add the ego to Him and confuse the two. He asks but little. It is He Who adds the greatness and the might. He joins with you to make the holy instant far greater than you can understand. It is your realization that you need do so little that enables Him to give so much.[2]

My determination is to *let holiness be*, not make it happen. I want it more than anything else to the point of wanting nothing else. Remember the power of my wanting? It is necessary to learn I cannot do more than desire the holy instant, and be willing to receive it. Only desire and willingness is my doing and even that much is a bit of an illusion. The non-dual desire is to desire *only* this, *above all else*. Seeking *first* the Kingdom of God. If I try to do more I *add the ego to Him and confuse the two*. My own effort is ego effort. Grace means gift. All I do is desire and accept the gift. God does it, not me, when I want it more than anything.

> Come to it not in arrogance, assuming that you must achieve the state its coming brings with it. The miracle of the holy instant lies in your willingness to let it be

what it is. And in your willingness for this lies also your acceptance of yourself as you were meant to be. [3]

ACIM calls it arrogance to assume I attain anything. The attainment is of God, not me. My little part is simply the willingness to let it be so.

Even the strength of my *little willingness*, to accept what already is, does not come from me, but from God, because this is God's Will, the way He designed it to be.

> God did not create His dwelling place unworthy of Him. And if you believe He cannot enter where He wills to be, you must be interfering with His Will. You do not need the strength of willingness to come from you, but only from His Will...You have been wrong in thinking that it is needful to prepare yourself for Him. It is impossible to make arrogant preparations for holiness, and not believe that it is up to you to establish the conditions for peace. God has established them. [4]

To do nothing, I don't know helps. What should I do? I don't know what I should do. If I don't know what I should do, perhaps the best action is non-action. I don't even choose because I let the Holy Spirit choose for me. The course teaches me to not confuse God's role and my own. I am arrogant when I interfere with God's Will by preparing myself for Him. I am His dwelling place whom He created as He willed. That is, worthy of Him. Who am I to improve on what God created?

> In preparing for the holy instant, do not attempt to make yourself holy to be ready to receive it. That is but to confuse your role with God's. Atonement cannot come to those who think that they must first atone, but only to those who offer it nothing more than simple willingness to make way for it. Purification is of God alone, and therefore for you. Rather than seek to prepare yourself for Him, try to think thus:

I who am host to God am worthy of Him.

*He Who established His dwelling place in me
created it as He would have it be.*

*It is not needful that I make it ready for Him, but only
that I do not interfere with His plan to restore to me my
own awareness of my readiness, which is eternal.*

I need add nothing to His plan.

*But to receive it, I must be willing not to
substitute my own in place of it.*

And that is all. Add more, and you will merely
take away the little that is asked.[5]

The only thing to do is to *not interfere* with God's plan, which is a non-doing. Interfering, by substituting my own plan, is doing something. If I add more than simple willingness, *I take away the little that is asked.* The first page of the *Text* states that miracles are my right but *purification is necessary first.* The above quote states that purification is done by God. Purification is *for* me, not by me, nor of me. If I try to do it, effort becomes ego activity that produces fear.

And it is only fear that you will add, if you prepare
yourself for love. The preparation for the holy instant
belongs to Him Who gives it. Release yourself to Him
Whose function is release. Do not assume His function
for Him.[6]

Goldsmith:

The light shines. The word reveals that when the
stumbling block is no longer needed, it is removed. *You*
need not move it, change it, or remove it – it is removed
when it is no longer needed.[7]

The stumbling blocks I might try to remove are *needed* until the Holy Spirit removes them. Thinking that I must prepare myself for God is an ego trick that delays liberation by making it a future event *after* purification.

> Never approach the holy instant after you have tried to remove all fear and hatred from your mind. That is its function. Never attempt to overlook your guilt before you ask the Holy Spirit's help. That is *His* function. Your part is only to offer Him a little willingness to let Him remove all fear and hatred, and to be forgiven.[8]

Will I step back and let God do His Will?

Is choosing doing? The only free will I still enjoy, in this world, is the freedom to choose, or my power of decision. This is the power of wanting; I choose what I want. The choice is a simple one between Heaven or hell, though presented in a myriad of forms: Holy Spirit or ego, Self or self-image, love or fear, Atonement or separation, right-mindedness or wrong-mindedness, forgiveness or judgment, holiness or specialness. In more advanced stages comes the realization that even the belief in choice is an illusion because this "choice" is between what is real and what is not real, and what is not real does not exist, so I can't choose it. *Workbook* Lesson 138 explains that, from the level of truth, there cannot be a decision between two ways because there are not two ways, only one way. But on the level of this world, it seems as if I must choose. Beware level confusion.

> In this world Heaven is a choice, because here we believe there are alternatives to choose between...
>
> Creation knows no opposite. But here is opposition part of being "real." It is this strange perception of the truth that makes the choice of Heaven seem to be the same as the relinquishment of hell. It is not really thus.[9]

Creation knows no opposite, is a statement that creation is non-dual. Here, in this world of opposites and duality, I seem to have a choice, but *It is not really thus.*

While I still live in the dream of duality I need the illusion of choice to start moving in the right direction towards the spiritually mature stage that is "choiceless" awareness. Thus I use time and choice to release time and choice. If I do not use these temporary tools, I get stuck in the dream loop maze that seems endless and inescapable.

> Choice is the obvious escape from what appears as
> opposites. Decision lets one of conflicting goals become
> the aim of effort and expenditure of time. Without
> decision, time is but a waste and effort dissipated.
> It is spent for nothing in return, and time goes by
> without results. There is no sense of gain, for nothing is
> accomplished; nothing learned.[10]

Decision lets one of conflicting goals become the aim of effort and expenditure of time, means that I use my power of decision to choose one of two goals to focus on. If I do not make this decision, I founder, waste time, and accomplish nothing, remaining conflicted between two opposing and mutually exclusive goals. The choice is between what *appears* as opposites.

> And even this but seems to be a choice. Do not confuse
> yourself with all the doubts that myriad decisions would
> induce. You make but one. And when that one is made,
> you will perceive it was no choice at all. For truth is true,
> and nothing else is true. There is no opposite to choose
> instead. There is no contradiction to the truth.[11]

After I make the one choice for God I learn there is no other choice to make and thus no choice possible. If there is no other voice than that of the Holy Spirit, then I do not choose. There are not two voices to choose between. There seems to be this choice at the beginning and this is necessary as I make the transition from duality to non-duality. This world is the fruit of the tree of knowledge of good and evil, the world of duality, the world of opposites, and the world of judgment between what is good, or not, what is true, or not, what is beautiful, or not. I start from where I *seem* to be, duality, where a choice between opposites *seems* valid.

It is possible to transcend duality in this world and hear only one voice. This is a most advanced state.

> That is why you must choose to hear one of two voices within you…The Holy Spirit is in you in a very literal sense. His is the Voice that calls you back to where you were before and will be again. It is possible even in this world to hear only that Voice and no other. It takes effort and great willingness to learn. It is the final lesson that I [Jesus] learned, and God's Sons are as equal as learners as they are as Sons.[12]

Jesus says that to get to the point where one hears only the Voice of the Holy Spirit, *and no other*, is the final lesson he learned. I learn the same lesson, for: *God's Sons are as equal as learners as they are as Sons.* Learning the lesson of non-duality takes *effort and great willingness.* It may seem that the ideas *I need do nothing*, and effort and great willingness are contradictory. In fact, they represent different stages of the journey. Before I come to truly know that *I need do nothing*, I add effort to willingness, or try to increase a little willingness into great willingness by my own effort, not realizing it all comes from God.

Another way to look at it is that non-doing, non-interfering, non-judgment – these non-dual ways of being – take effort and great willingness *at first* because they are so different from my usual way, which is to follow my own plan by my own effort. In other words, it takes effort and great willingness to do nothing. It is harder, at first, to do nothing than to do something. Also, I learn that I need do nothing by first trying to do and finding out that my own doing does not, ultimately, work. I learn the way of non-doing through doing. I learn to give up doing by trying to do. Otherwise, how might I know that my doing, my own effort, does not work?

I tend to think and experience that there is a conflict between God's Will and my own will, and this conflict is the struggle and effort of the spiritual life. This illusion of duality seems true at earlier stages but the more advanced state sees that this effort to cooperate with the Will of God, and deny (sacrifice) my own will, is, in truth, an illusion. There is no choice between wills because there is simply One Will that I share with God (non-duality). I only seem to control a will that opposes God's Will in the dream of separation. *Workbook* Lesson 74 emphasizes this teaching as the central idea towards which all the lessons are aimed:

> **God's is the only Will. When you have recognized this,
> you have recognized that your will is His. The belief
> that conflict is possible has gone. Peace has replaced the
> strange idea that you are torn by conflicting goals. As an
> expression of the Will of God, you have no goal but His.**[13]

Conflict of wills is a belief during the dream of separation. If God's Will is the only Will, then conflict is impossible. When the war of wills ends, peace is no longer blocked, and conflict that causes fear ceases. I stop fearing God, and I start trusting God. As an expression of God's Will, I am God's Will. Creation is God willing me into existence. As an extension of God's love, I am Love as God is Love. In what seems to be the duality of two in love, One Love is shared by all in all.

ACIM teaches why I develop from duality to non-duality in stages: the sudden shift from duality to non-duality, from perception to knowledge, from consciousness to Awareness, is too frightening, and fear blocks the awareness of Love.

> **Yet what is true in God's creation cannot enter here until
> it is reflected in some form the world can understand.**

> Truth cannot come where it could only be perceived with fear.[14]

Most people fear losing one of the five senses. So imagine losing all five, plus the mental senses. This happens when God takes the final step and perception is exchanged for Awareness. This is beyond the near-death experience where people report a continuing of a type of perception in a different world, populated by many. What I perceive as an outside world, before or after death, is an illusion I understandably fear to lose. There is no physical world, only a mental world that imagines a physical world. This is a big leap and thus the movement from duality to non-duality, from effort to non-doing, is achieved in stages. If I am atop a tall building and I wish to exit the tower, I could jump quickly to the concrete, or take the stairs. Walking down the stairs is less traumatic, and less fearful, and less damaging, than jumping. The shift happens in stages, step by step. In God's mercy, my transformation happens so gently and gradually that I might not even notice it!

The Development of Trust

In the *Manual For Teachers*, ACIM offers a description of these stages called *The Development Of Trust*. When I truly trust God, I surrender control, will, and self to God. Without trust, this surrender is too difficult. The development of trust is in six stages: undoing, sorting out, relinquishment, settling down, unsettling, and achievement. These stages are not discrete and represent a spectrum. The path through these stages is not linear. I might go back and forth between stages as I develop true trust in God. The descriptions of these stages, their challenges, and what completes them, form a useful map of the spiritual journey. I might be able to identify where I am, and learn what comes next. Beware the ego's attempt to take over. The idea of achieving stages appeals to the ego's sense of specialness. If spirituality becomes competitive, it is a sure sign of ego. Also, it is ego at work if I use stage models to compare myself with others, or judge where someone else is in their journey.

The first stage is called a *period of undoing*, and it might feel painful because of perceived changes and losses. I do not actually lose anything, but I might think I'm losing a lot. I tend to resist my own undoing because my self-concept is threatened. I think that the ego actually is me and fear losing it. Undoing is a type of death, or the beginning of the death of the false self. The only thing I sacrifice is illusion of self. A shift is taking place in what I *value*.

> This [period of undoing] **need not be painful, but it usually is so experienced. It seems as if things are being taken away, and it is rarely understood initially that their lack of value is merely being recognized.**[15]

At this beginning stage, I do not understand what is happening and that's why it is usually experienced as painful. Once I learn that all the changes I experience are helpful, trust is beginning and I move to the second stage.

The second stage, *a period of sorting out*, is *always somewhat difficult*, because now I sort out *all things* in my life, based on how supportive they are of the changes in values I learned in the first stage. Some things, even most things, no longer help on the way.

> **...having learned that the changes in his life are always helpful, he must now decide all things on the basis of whether they increase the helpfulness or hamper it. He will find that many, if not most of the things he valued before will merely hinder his ability to transfer what he has learned to new situations as they arise...It takes great learning to understand that all things, events, encounters and circumstances are helpful.**[16]

The fruit of this learning is the *ability to transfer* what I learn to new situations. This learning has practical applications. So after trusting

that all changes are helpful, I sort out *how* helpful all things are according to how they support practical application of my new values. For
example, let's say I value money. As I grow, I may see that this love of
money may conflict with the love of my brother and my love for God.
This is still an early stage and involves the discernment, or judgment,
as to what is helpful or hindering my changes as I let transformation
happen. A hint about a more mature stage is given: I do not yet understand the non-judgment, or non-duality, that takes *great learning.*
Trusting that *every* thing, event, encounter, and circumstance is
helpful is non-duality.

Then comes the third stage – *a period of relinquishment.* This
follows logically because after I sort out what to keep and what to
throw overboard, I actually toss what is judged as hindering, and this
is usually experienced as *a sacrifice.* The learning goal of this stage
is to see that relinquishing what is not helpful is no loss at all. What
might first be perceived as sacrificing something I want, changes to
relief and receiving grace.

> There is, however, no point in sorting out the valuable
> from the valueless unless the next obvious step is taken.
> Therefore, the period of overlap is apt to be one in which
> the teacher of God feels called upon to sacrifice his own
> best interests on behalf of truth. He has not realized as yet
> how wholly impossible such a demand would be. He can
> learn this only as he actually does give up the valueless.
> Through this, he learns that where he anticipated grief, he
> finds a happy lightheartedness instead; where he thought
> something was asked of him, he finds a gift bestowed on
> him.[17]

In order to learn the lesson of this stage one does it: *He can learn this
only as he actually does give up the valueless.* This third stage is still
preliminary because I have *not realized yet* that sacrifice is impossible.
These first three stages of building trust are accompanied by pain,

difficulty, conflict, distress, and grief. My own "best interests" are the interests of a separate me. It seems a sacrifice to give up my own best interests, my own will, yet sacrifice is impossible because it is an illusion and the whole idea of a separate self with separate interests is an illusion. Knowing this in advance helps on the way.

The fourth stage is called *a period of settling down*. This is a stage of relative peace, quiet, and rest, in which the learning of the first three stages is stabilized and integrated. Here I start to see there is way out of hell. Liberation is an actual possibility and not as unreachable as I thought.

> Now he consolidates his learning. Now he begins to see the transfer value of what he has learned. Its potential is literally staggering, and the teacher of God is now at the point in his progress at which he sees in it his whole way out. "Give up what you do not want, and keep what you do." How simple is the obvious! And how easy to do! The teacher of God needs this period of respite.[18]

Giving up what I don't want and keeping what I do want is easy when what I desire is what God desires, Our One Will. Sounds good, right? It is good but I am not finished. I might be fooled into thinking I achieved the goal. However, I am not yet at non-doing.

> He has not yet come as far as he thinks. Yet when he is ready to go on, he goes with mighty companions beside him. Now he rests a while, and gathers them before going on. He will not go on from here alone.[19]

This fourth stage of settling down is a transitional stage to what's next, not the end of the road. This marks a significant stage of the journey because from here I do not go on alone. I gather *mighty companions* for help on the next, fifth stage. Before this I traveled alone, or separate. Gathering mighty companions is the result of joining in the holy instant: holy relationship. Without these mighty companions, the next stage, a period of disillusionment, called *unsettling*, is too difficult.

In the fifth stage, *a period of unsettling*, I learn that I didn't know what I was doing in the earlier stages.

> **Now must the teacher of God understand that he did not really know what was valuable and what was valueless. All that he really learned so far was that he did not want the valueless, and that he did want the valuable. Yet his own sorting out was meaningless in teaching him the difference. The idea of sacrifice, so central to his own thought system, had made it impossible for him to judge. He thought he learned willingness, but now he sees that he does not know what the willingness is for.**[20]

My *own sorting out was meaningless*. The learning goal at this stage is to let go of all judgment. Judgment is used in earlier stages; I assumed that I could sort out the valuable from the not valuable. When I truly trust God, I no longer need judgment, or my own effort. This is what willingness is for, yielding to God. This state of non-judgment is difficult to attain, even with mighty companions. It is a surrender of self, judgment, and effort.

> **And now he must attain a state that may remain impossible to reach for a long, long time. He must learn to lay all judgment aside, and ask only what he really wants in every circumstance. Were not each step in this direction so heavily reinforced, it would be hard indeed!**[21]

The non-doing of non-judgment is such a challenge it *may remain impossible to reach for a long, long time*.

In the final stage, *a period of achievement*, I live in the surrender of non-doing. My understanding is stable and useful in all circumstances, providing peace. I shift from duality to non-duality and no longer judge. *All* things are working to serve the greater good. Including depression. Including ending depression.

> Now what was seen as merely shadows before become solid gains, to be counted on in all "emergencies" as well as tranquil times. Indeed, the tranquility is their result; the outcome of honest learning, consistency of thought and full transfer. This is the stage of real peace, for here is Heaven's state fully reflected. From here, the way to Heaven is open and easy.[22]

Great learning, willingness, and effort are required along the way to the "achievement" of non-doing. *Real peace* results when the conflict of duality ends.

It might seem as if the earlier stages of undoing, sorting out, and relinquishment were wasted, but these stages are part of the development of trust, necessary but not sufficient. I view the six stages as two major movements. The first movement is the first four stages. A person goes through periods of (1) undoing (value changes and accepting all change as helpful), (2) sorting out (what helps from what hinders), (3) relinquishment (letting go of what hinders), and (4) settling down and resting in a relatively peaceful respite. This respite ends the first movement, that might be thought of as preparation for the second movement. The fourth stage is also a transitional stage between the two movements, and is a time of joining with helpers for the second movement.

Why have I not come as far as I thought? During the first four stages, the work is my own, and in the self-interest of my own spiritual success – my personal salvation. It's still all about me. I learned parts of the truth but still identify as a separate self. Disillusionment with my own selfish efforts is learned in the next stage, the fifth stage of the whole process, but the first stage of the second movement. Now I am in the most difficult stage, but not alone, not according to my own will or effort.

In the second movement, stage five, *unsettling*, corresponds to the first three movements and corrects them by releasing judgment. I used my own judgment to do the sorting out of the first movement. Now, in the fifth stage, I do not judge what is valuable and what is valueless. I surrender all judgment to God. When I truly trust God I know that all things work together for the greatest good. I know that *nothing* separates me from the love of Christ. Now I trust God and surrender all judgment.

> What could you not accept, if you but knew that everything that happens, all events, past, present and to come, are gently planned by One Whose only purpose is your good? Perhaps you have misunderstood His plan, for He would never offer pain to you. But your defenses did not let you see His loving blessing shine in every step you ever took. While you made plans for death, He led you gently to eternal life.[23]

The big difference between the two movements is that in the transitional fourth stage, called settling down, I join with *mighty companions* and no longer go forth as a separate individual.

The final stage of achievement corresponds to the fourth stage of settling down, but its peace is deeper and permanent. Achievement is not based on my effort, nor judgment. Achievement is based on the willingness to surrender my mistaken identity, my judgment, my effort, my own thought system, my will. True trust in God permits willingness to surrender. I am grateful for the peace yielding provides. The achievement is God's.

All these stages eventually lead to a place of non-judgment, which is a non-doing. Judgment is a doing. Laying down all judgment means laying down my own autonomous will, and this is probably the hardest thing to allow because I view it as a sacrifice of freedom and uniqueness. In truth it is not a sacrifice; what I *really* want is what God wants because His Will is in everyone's best interest: the complete restoration of the Sonship, which is liberation. In the final stage of achievement my will is surrendered and united with the Will of God, a shared one Will. The collective Sonship, the Body of Christ, is completed, as I, as separate individual, decrease, like the broken branch that withers in a drought. This is non-duality. Not two wills; one Will. Non-duality is without judgment of good and evil. The fruit of the tree of knowledge of good and evil is forbidden to protect Adam and me from pain and death. Eating of the forbidden fruit of duality leads to death, the opposite of birth. In non-duality there is life eternal, with no opposite, no beginning, and no end. Learning to *lay all judgment aside, and ask only what he really wants in every circumstance*, is the goal of the fifth stage that leads to the achievement of peace, and it may take a *long, long time.*

The truth of non-duality is expressed in other spiritual traditions. In his last book, *Unworldly Wise*, Wei Wu Wei shares the wisdom of non-duality in a conversation between an owl and a rabbit. Here are excerpts; first the owl:

> "A famous Indian sage of our times told everybody that what they dubiously call 'realization' already exists, and that no attempt should be made to attain it – since it is not anything to be acquired."

> "And did they believe him?" asked the rabbit.

> "Apparently not," the owl observed, "I am told that yearly every phenomenal biped who is interested, writes, lectures, or reads about it, 'meditates' and practices goodness only knows what in order to acquire it."

> "Only the bipeds do it," the owl pointed out. "The same Indian sage remarked that 'realization', or 'liberation' as they sometimes call it, is 'ridding yourself of the illusion that you are not free.'"

"And even that did not convince them?' the rabbit inquired.

"To be convinced is not what they want," the owl explained, "for that would deprive them of their precious 'selves.'"

"Another Chinese sage, one of the greatest, stated that 'to awaken suddenly to the fact that your own mind is the Buddha, that there is nothing to be attained, nor a single action to be performed – such is the Supreme Way, such is really to be a Buddha'," the owl added.[24]

Mr. Goldsmith on the freedom from judgment that is non-duality:

In the spiritual life, you place no labels on the world. You do not judge as to good or evil, sick or well, rich or poor. While appearances may show forth harmony or discord, by not judging, you merely know IS, and let that which truly IS define Itself.[25]

A fruit of non-doing, or non-judging, is non-reacting because reaction is based on judgment. Goldsmith:

When living out of the center of being, you are untouched by the thoughts, opinions, laws, and theories of the world. Nothing acts upon you because you do not react to the world of appearances.[26]

The world of appearances is the world of perception, illusionary because it appears to be outside of me when in fact it is a projection within my mind.

If I realize the illusion of my own, self-made, autonomous will, which results in suffering, then giving up my own effort makes merciful sense. I stop trying to earn my way to Heaven, whether by works or by the work of faith. Faith is necessary help on the way but it does not save me. Some sincere, but confused, Christians believe that what I believe saves me. My beliefs might delay or speed salvation but they do not save or condemn. Please consider that God saves all, regardless of what I believe or think. That's His Will, and mine when I wake up. I stop trying to do God's job. I cease crying about what God is doing. Who am I to complain? I cease trying to improve on what God creates. I lay down my own arrogance. Instead of trying to steer the train, I relax and let the train follow the tracks. I realize that when I think I steer the train, well, that's an illusion. I am like a toddler in the back seat of a car with a toy steering wheel, believing that I steer the car. My Father is driving the car. Regarding yielding the illusion of control to the true Author, Mr. Goldsmith in *The Infinite Way* writes:

> **Prayer is the inner vision of harmony. This vision is attained by giving up the desire to change or improve anyone or anything.**[27]

> **Be sure your prayer is not an attempt to influence God.**[28]

> **Be sure that your prayer is not a desire to improve God's universe.**[29]

> **Consciousness lives itself – you do not live it.**[30]

Sometimes people on a spiritual path believe that they must do things to make the world a better place. Like the depressionalized person who tries to improve the prison rather than walking out, I try to improve the dream. It is a mistake, however, to try and improve the dream. Goldsmith:

> **Do not expect the power of God to function in the "dream," but rather to break the dream.**[31]

If God functioned in the dream, it means that God is buying into the illusion. Goldsmith:

> **Do not contact God to adjust, change, or heal the dream. The understanding or awareness of God breaks the dream.**[32]

Many believe that God is going to improve the dream, make things better. This is confusion because God does not improve the dream; God ends the dream. Earlier on the spiritual journey I prayed for material things, temporary things, that are part of the dream and valueless substitutes for what I perceive as lacking. Goldsmith:

> **Even in metaphysics and spiritual practice, the vision has been on more and larger fish in the nets, instead of on leaving your nets and following *me*.**[33]

For example, if I pray for someone not to die, I bought into the illusion that death is real. God is not aware of illusion. I learn not to ask God to act as if illusions are real.

When it comes to performing miracles, and healing, non-doing is still the rule because illness is not healed; illness is illusion. If I think illness is real I interfere with truth and insist that the past, and my perception, are true. The miracle worker does not make this mistake.

> **Step gently aside, and let healing be done for you. Keep but one thought in mind and do not lose sight of it, however tempted you may be to judge any situation, and to determine your response by judging it. Focus your mind only on this:**
>
> *I am not alone, and I would not intrude the past upon my Guest.*
>
> *I have invited Him, and He is here.*
>
> *I need do nothing except not to interfere.*[34]

This is often where there is confusion about what miracles are and what miracles do. It is easy to think of the miracle as simply improving the dream. That's what the ego would do if it performed miracles. This is confusing cause and effect, a primary course idea. Miracle workers do not perform miracles as something they do: *Step gently aside, and let healing be done for you.* And: *I need do nothing except not to interfere.*

The solution for the cause of suffering, or separation, is God's plan, called the Atonement. This is why the miracle worker's first responsibility is to accept the Atonement for himself. Is that doing something? Not really. It is a receiving of God's grace. It is a temporary solution that God gives, but does not force. When I say "no" it is the ego talking, and when I say "yes" it is God's Will, not my own doing. If it's so simple as non-doing, then what takes me so long to wake up? Doing is an entrenched habit. I find non-doing herculean. I constantly interfere and intrude *the past on our Guest.* This interference prevents the benefits of the holy instant. I like doing and I want control. I want to keep being "me." These are temptations to delay and dwell in duality.

Am I ready to let go of the steering wheel? Or do I want control and fear losing control? The relaxing of all control unto God is an advanced state of non-doing. It is true trust in God. Many religious traditions are about a lot of doing. This means that they are focused on the first four stages of the development of trust in God. That's an appropriate focus for many people, especially those still "enjoying" the world. ACIM emphasizes that it is a different way, and it saves time.

> You may be attempting to follow a very long road to the goal you have accepted. It is extremely difficult to reach Atonement by fighting against sin. Enormous effort is expended in the attempt to make holy what is hated and despised. Nor is a lifetime of contemplation and long periods of meditation aimed at detachment from the body necessary. All such attempts will ultimately succeed

because of their purpose. Yet the means are tedious and very time consuming, for all of them look to the future for release from a state of present unworthiness and inadequacy...

You are prepared. Now you need but to remember you need do nothing. It would be far more profitable now merely to concentrate on this than to consider what you should do. When peace comes at last to those who wrestle with temptation and fight against the giving in to sin; when the light comes at last into the mind given to contemplation; or when the goal is finally achieved by anyone, it always comes with just one happy realization; *I need do nothing.*

Here is the ultimate release which everyone will one day find in his own way, at his own time.[35]

The *ultimate* release is the happy realization, *I need do nothing.* The "doing" way of much spiritual practice requires a *lifetime* of *enormous effort*, and may just be building an ego that prides in its spiritual superiority and specialness. How may lifetimes did I suffer doing that? That inefficient method eventually succeeds, but it is terrapin slow and might not lead to liberation after a *lifetime of contemplation*. Liberation is always later. Eventually, even the person of enormous spiritual effort realizes, *I need do nothing.* Silence and stillness are empty paths of non-doing.

Ramana Maharshi responded to a question about doing things, such as self-defense and reacting to atrocities:

Even capable of stopping attacks, he kept still. Why? The occurrences are known to the sages, but pass away without leaving an impression on their minds. Even a deluge will appear a trifle to them; they do not care for anything.[36]

Ramana also made this funny comment about believing I am the doer of deeds:

> **A passenger on a train keeps his load on his head by his own folly.** [37]

In India and other countries, people often carry things on their heads, sometimes huge and heavy piles of things, atop their heads. So imagine boarding a train and keeping a heavy load on top of your head. The train moves my stuff without my effort. There is no longer any need to carry that weight on my head as if I do the moving. Perhaps, at an earlier stage, I seemed to carry the load to the train.

Krishnamurti said that his secret is: *I don't mind what happens.* This is the non-mindedness of non-judgment and non-reaction. It is choiceless. Non-dual. It is accepting what is. This is a radical acceptance. It is not, "Well I'm going to accept this, even though I don't like it." True acceptance is *loving* whatever is. I accept what is because this is God's Will and mine. I love what is because God's Will is abundant blessing to all.

In the Catholic Church there are contemplative orders, who are cloistered, and whose "job" is to pray. The contemplatives are sometimes criticized for not doing something in the world to serve others, like the active orders that might teach or preach, run retreat houses, run a parish, help the poor, work in a hospital, etc. The nuns and monks often answer these criticisms with a quote from scripture, the story of Martha and Mary, that supports the contemplative's "non-doing." Martha represents those in an active ministry, serving others, and Mary represents the contemplative, who is doing nothing.

> **Now as they went on their way, he entered a village; and a woman named Martha received him into her house. And she had a sister called Mary, who sat at the Lord's feet and listened to his teaching. But Martha was distracted with much serving; and she went to him and said, "Lord,**

> do you not care that my sister has left me to serve alone?
> Tell her then to help me." But the Lord answered her,
> "Martha, Martha, you are anxious and troubled about
> many things; one thing is needful. Mary has chosen the
> good portion, which shall not be taken away from her.[38]

Non-duality: *one thing is needful.* Mary's "doing" is sitting and listening. Mary joins with Jesus while Martha is *distracted with much
serving* "alone," or separated.

In my day to day life I might think that doing is necessary and
practical. I must work. And yet the course teaches that, for the most
part, work is done to earn money to support materialism and consumerism…and my neediness is not satisfied. I want more of what I
don't need or even truly want. Even the wealthy feel deprived. There
is apparently so much surplus money that nations spend trillions on
death and destruction. How much of my doing is about making money
and why? Am I responsible for the death and destruction caused by the
military/industrial complex that my taxes support? There is another
kind of work that happens, not for money, but because I want it. This
is a doing of the heart, of passion, that comes without effort. It is like
coasting down a hill on a bike. Gravity does the work while I enjoy
the free ride.

Think of non-doing as not my own doing. Jesus can do nothing
of his own accord. John's Gospel:

> Truly, truly, I say to you, the son can do nothing of his
> own accord, but only what he sees the Father doing; for
> whatever he does, that the son does likewise.[39]

Jesus joined his will with the Father's Will so that there is One Will.
All doing comes from that One Will, in truth. One Will is the end
of conflict.

Christians argue over the means of salvation, faith or works?
Both sides have the Bible verses to back them up. Those who believe
that works do not lead to salvation, have, in fact, made faith the work

one must do in order to be saved. In the New Testament, Jesus says no one comes to him unless the Father draws him. Thus the work of salvation is actually that of the Father, not me:

> No one can come to me unless the Father who sent me draws him; and I will raise him on the last day.[40]

The *last day* infers the end of time. Imagine that.

The teaching that I need do nothing also involves the course's repeated teachings about body-identification and time:

> To do anything involves the body. And if you recognize you need do nothing, you have withdrawn the body's value from your mind. Here is the quick and open door through which you slip past centuries of effort, and escape from time. This is the way in which sin loses all attraction *right now.* For here is time denied, and past and future gone. Who needs do nothing has no need for time. To do nothing is to rest, and make a place within you where the activity of the body ceases to demand attention. Into this place the Holy Spirit comes, and there abides.[41]

Slipping past centuries of effort sounds pretty good to me. I need do nothing because God does everything. The course promises perfect peace, eternal safety, and the ending of all suffering, on what condition? Grace, that is, God's gift.

> What must I do to know all this is mine? I must accept Atonement for myself, and nothing more. God has already done all things that need be done. And I must learn I need do nothing of myself, for I need but accept my Self, my sinlessness, created for me, now already mine, to feel God's Love protecting me from harm, to understand my Father loves His Son; to know I am the Son my Father loves.[42]

My own doing is meaningless because my separate self does not exist except as an illusionary concept. The need to do is another example of an identity-confusion disorder. Depression is done to myself by my own evil-doing. Why not stop doing this to myself by non-doing? Joel S. Goldsmith:

> The responsibility for you is God's responsibility. Let go, relax, be still, and know that I am God.[43]

Meister Eckhart:

> …it is God alone who accomplishes in a man works wrought from within – the prophet Isaiah says, "Lord… all that we have accomplished you have done for us.[44]

Perhaps Taoism is the way most associated with non-doing.

> In the practice of the Tao,
>
> every day something is dropped.
>
> Less and less do you need to force things,
>
> until finally you arrive at non-action.
>
> When nothing is done,
>
> nothing is left undone.
>
> True mastery is gained
>
> by letting things go their own way.
>
> It can't be gained by interfering.[45]

Notice how Lao-tzu hints at stages before realizing non-action: less and less do I force things until *finally* arriving at non-duality. It is easy to be confused about non-doing. Remember, non-doing is an advanced state. In the stages of the development of trust, the first four stages involve doing. Apparently the earlier stages of doing are necessary steps on the spiritual journey. If I get stuck in these preliminary steps, trust in God is delayed.

How long do I want to wait? *Workbook* Lesson 188 teaches that enlightenment already is and does not wait on time.

> Why wait for Heaven? Those who seek the light are merely covering their eyes. The light is in them now. Enlightenment is but a recognition, not a change at all.

> This light can not be lost. Why wait to find it in the future, or believe it has been lost already, or was never there?[46]

> Here again is the paradox often referred to in the course. To say, "Of myself I can do nothing" is to gain all power. And yet it is but a seeming paradox. As God created you, you *have* all power. The image you made of yourself has none.[47]

> What is the peace of God? No more than this; the simple understanding that His Will is wholly without opposite. There is no thought that contradicts His Will, yet can be true. The contrast between His Will and yours but seemed to be reality. In truth there was no conflict, for His Will is yours. Now is the mighty Will of God Himself His gift to you.[48]

Psalm 127:

> If Yahweh does not build the house, in vain the masons toil; if Yahweh does not guard the city, in vain the sentries watch.

> In vain you get up earlier, and put off going to bed, sweating to make a living, since he provides for his beloved as they sleep.[49]

EPILOGUE

Sidetrack: 2010-2015

After the bike trip (2010) I went to visit my daughter where she lived in Los Angeles. I had no plans, but a plan formed to go follow my favorite band, Furthur, on an east coast tour of thirteen shows. I enjoyed touring and I hoped to do it again the next year if my funds held out. Eventually I needed to work. I returned to Anchorage in February 2011, about six months after I left town on my bicycle. I stayed at my brother Robert's house, renting a room from him. Another east coast tour with Furthur followed in March and April, and then back to Alaska. I did one more tour, this time the west coast, in the summer of 2011.

I stopped doing photography since moving to Kotzebue in 2005. After six years with no darkroom I made the difficult decision to sell all my photography gear. I thought re-establishing a darkroom unlikely and practicing photography too expensive to continue if I couldn't make a living at it. I returned to music and spent months recording original songs. I started with a long-term guitar buddy, Jim, whom I started jamming with when I first came to Alaska in 1987. I stopped jamming with Jim in 1992 because of the divorce. Over the years he became more involved with playing and recording and built a nice studio in his Eagle River Home. I spent a week recording with him and he helped improve my songs significantly, acting as producer. New arrangements of three songs excited and encouraged me. We started well but Jim hoped to finish the songs that week. I couldn't do it and I couldn't take up any more of his time, so I continued on my own, learning to use a laptop to record music.

In 2012 my brother Robert and I clashed. One night driving back from a party I exploded in volcanic rage. What Eckhart Tolle calls the "pain-body" erupted and Robert's pain body responded in kind.

I felt it coming for several months, when on a couple occasions, I felt a sudden anger rise up. It happened first in Las Vegas where I went to see Furthur. It shook me by surprise and I wondered what was going on. I was not used to this. Anger accumulated like a leaking faucet fills a bowl, drop by frustrating drop, until it overflows. Denied pain accumulated like pressure in a pressure cooker. My anger reflected anger from the past with my Father, ex-wife, and others. It took a long time to have a handle on it, and now I interpret it differently through ACIM. The special relationship, the ego's last stand, strikes again. When anger arises it seems to be caused by an external trigger, a person who disrespects me, or an unfair situation. I justify my anger. Yet the course teaches that what I seem to see as external cause is actually a projection from within myself. *I am not upset for the reason I think.* If the true source is hidden in the unconscious, then naturally I blame someone, or something else. Perhaps the layers in the unconscious concealing my mind in pain wore away enough to unblock the volcano. The guilt in the unconscious is so unacceptable that it is blocked and locked, like the contents in a pressure cooker. The tighter the locked lid, the more pressure builds. Once it blows, watch out! Neither of us wanted to live with each other anymore. Time to move, but I didn't know where to go, nor what to do.

I don't remember how, but I learned about people buying old school buses and converting them into motor homes. I figured I would build a bus home and have a place to live without worrying about rent or being a burden. I knew Alaska was not a good place to live in an unheated bus, but I could travel to where the weather suited living on the bus. In an intuitive way I was preparing for my collapse. I started looking for a bus to convert and soon found one near Soldatna, Alaska. I bought a 1991 short school bus, twenty-one feet long, with a living area of less than 100 square feet, but I thought it could work. I worked slowly converting the bus, doing nice woodwork, designing, and redesigning my future hermit habitat as I went along. Once I tore out a whole week's worth of work and started over.

I considered, un-enthusiastically, going back to mental health work. I applied for a few positions and interviewed for two before someone from the Aleutian Pribilof Islands Association called about a clinical job. I interviewed and felt good about this position. It seemed my kind of place. St. Paul Island is remote in the Bering Sea. About 400 Aleuts live on the island. It has a harbor where crab and halibut boats come to unload their catch and use the clinic if needed. If you have watched a TV show about the deadliest catch, you may have seen St. Paul Island. I moved there in October, 2012. My position also served a nearby smaller island, St. George Island, with a population of about 100 Aleuts.

One month before moving to St. Paul Island, police forced Alicen into hospitalization again in Los Angeles, California. I visited her in the LA county hospital and it was the proverbial straw that broke the camel's back. I wanted to show her a short video of her Grandmother and her brother Francis that I made recently and the staff refused to allow this. She complained of physical abuse by staff and no one did anything. No one believes a person who is mentally ill. This "hospital" was the stereotypical nightmare of an institution, and my daughter was trapped in the cuckoo's nest. I believed my daughter and got into it with the head nurse. I threatened to talk to a reporter. He threatened to call the police. Even though I was starting a new job in mental health, I was fed up with the system. I hated how the system mistreated my daughter.

In January 2013 my guitar buddy Jim, same age as me, died of a heart attack. I had few friends and this loss hurt. I grieved, but I appreciated talking with him two weeks before his transition. I rapidly approached a spiritual/psychological breakdown. The mental health system frustrated me and I wanted to use a spiritual approach, but that wasn't in the job description. My inability to resolve dilemmas around clinical work added to my frustration. The agency required me to become licensed and I began communicating with the state licensing board about the process. It was complicated because they did not offer guidelines for people working in the bush. They were in the middle of addressing this issue when I contacted them. The license required two years of weekly face to face supervision with a PhD psychologist. Most remote clinics in Alaska did not have a psychologist. The same thing happened in Kotzebue. Someone from the licensing board said to submit an alternative supervision proposal, but without any guidelines. As I struggled with this, I realized that I no longer wanted to work in the mental health field. I probably realized it since my daughter's involuntary hospitalization the month before I started working on St. Paul Island. So what was the point of jumping through the hoops to become licensed when my heart was not in it? I liked St. Paul Island and developed therapeutic relationships with several clients. I did not want to leave and I could not continue either. I struggled with this dilemma for months before making the painful decision to resign, seven months after I started. I felt guilty about abandoning my clients. I not only resigned my job; I resigned a career in the mental health system that I spent nine years in college preparing for. It was a real low point. I did not know what to do; I just knew I would not keep working in the mental health system.

I did not know what was next, but the bus was almost finished. I loaded it with my possessions and drove south, planning on finding a place to park it near Portland, Oregon. My mother, almost eighty years old, lived near there. Her health was good, but I wanted to be nearby. My mother and I liked Eckhart Tolle and before I left St. Paul Island I bought tickets for us to see him for two days in Mill Valley, Marin County, California. I valued seeing him but I found no resolution to my on-going spiritual crisis.

After the Tolle event I drove my mother and myself back to Lake Oswego and for the rest of the summer I drank and smoked marijuana, both the natural plant and the synthetic stuff that I discovered in Alaska where I could buy it in tobacco shops. My favorite band, Furthur, toured the west coast again. I could not afford to do the whole tour but I wanted to see the three shows at the Greek Theater in Berkeley, California, a favorite outdoor venue where I saw many Grateful Dead shows. The last of the three shows happened on my brother Micky's birthday and that show was the last time I went to a concert, September 29, 2013. One time at the Greek, I had backstage passes and my brother Gerry and I were able to meet Jerry Garcia during the set break. After the shows I headed to Nevada to visit my daughter Alicen, who now lived in Reno.

Two days later I woke up in the ER in Reno, involuntarily hospitalized. I remember when my clinical jobs put me in a position where I involuntarily authorized an involuntary hospitalization, most recently on St. Paul Island. Now I experienced the other side of the fence. I knew how to play the game but now I consummated my refusal of the mental health system. They transferred me from the ER to a psychiatric hospital. Although at one of the lowest and most depressed states of my life, I denied suicidal ideation and they released me in a couple days. The forced hospitalization did me no good. My brother Gerry galloped east from Monterey to the rescue.

We rode back to his place and he convinced me to go on an ayahuasca healing retreat in Peru. I had researched ayahuasca since I learned about it ten years before. The descriptions of ayahuasca experiences I read about made my LSD and mushroom experiences seem like Disneyland. There are many places in South America offering various kinds of retreats and healing with shamans and plant teachers. Previously I paid for my daughter to see a shamanic healer in Los Angeles who trained in South America. I researched several places in Peru and found one appealing to me because of its location. Instead of the jungles of Peru, it is located high in the Andes. I preferred the mountain retreat, but could not afford it. Gerry offered to pay for it but I still did not want to go. I was too depressed to take on something that serious. I wanted alcohol, not ayahuasca. I wanted to escape pain, not transcend it. I didn't think it possible to transcend pain. And the cost to my brother bothered me. He eventually convinced me to go ahead with a retreat in November, 2013. Having about a month to kill before flying to South America, I went back to live on my bus in Oregon, with a bitter taste in my mouth from the events of the past couple weeks.

I tried to avoid my pain with drugs and alcohol. Although obvious to me that using did not help, I hit a point where I did not care anymore. It was slow suicide. I wanted to die many times before but now I was reckless about it. One day I rode my bike to get more whiskey and crashed five times in a few miles, straining my back. My vision seemed permanently blurred. My youngest brother Phillip lived in the area and worried about my behavior. He found me passed out on the floor of the bus when stopping by to check on me. He took me for x-rays after the day I crashed my bike five times. One day Phillip came by and found me passed out in my chair on the bus. He couldn't get inside because the door was closed and had to be opened from inside. His teenage son crawled through a window to open the door. They carried me out and unknown hours later I woke up in my brother's house. He said that in two days my brother Robert would drive me and the bus south to Woodland, California, where my brother Mickey lived. Philip could not deal with me anymore. Robert chauffeured me and my bus south. I stayed in Woodland until it was time to leave for Peru.

I was furious with Philip, feeling like he had no right to force me to move. Yet I was too dope and drink disabled to fight him about it. My brother Mickey's son, Billy, found a place to park the bus while I traveled to seek ayahuasca healing. After that I planned to relocate to Monterey County, where my brother Gerry lived, and where I had some history.

In my experience as a clinician I served many clients with substance abuse and dependence problems. Most were "dually-diagnosed" with a substance dependence problem and and another mental disorder. I came across many people in the business who tended to see alcohol as the big problem, especially in the Native Alaskan community. I disagreed with this opinion and it is one of the reasons why the mental health system frustrated me. I see alcohol and drug dependence as another symptom and not the cause of people's problems. Using did not help, certainly, but the drugs pushed by the psychiatrists did not help either. People who stop drinking without dealing with the true cause of their problems develop another addiction or several, be it smart phones, smoking, eating, internet, television, success, sex, work, etc., all substitutes for Heaven. How many people know that Bill W., who started AA, remained a sex addict and used LSD long after he stopped drinking? He asked for shots of whiskey on his death bed.

In the addiction field people often talk about "recovery." Recover what? My sober state from before that proceeded to dependence? That's going backward instead of forward. Pain is what led to substance abuse and dependence. Pain accumulates to the point of despair and suicide. That does not mean the problem drinker should keep drinking. It means that drinking is a symptom and unless one deals with the cause, which is unconscious, treating the symptom is not much use. It may be necessary, however, to stop numbing oneself if one is to get to the source of the pain. In my case, a lifetime of drugs and alcohol certainly didn't help. Addiction is a prison. Withdrawal is hell. One tries to kill one's sorrows but they have a way of rising from the dead. Tolerance to the poison of choice builds, requiring more and more of the substance to drown the pain. Eventually one becomes completely disabled or dead. It is truly a dirty dead end road, with the same end as any other road the world offers, no matter how much smoother and prettier. The addict has surrendered, without finding hope. The non-addicts have not surrendered, nor have they found hope. Jack Kerouac's book, *Big Sur*, has the best descriptions of the drinker's despair I have read.

I heard a spiritual teacher, Adyashanti, I think, say or write that addicts are close to spiritual truth. I agree with him in that an addict may realize there is no hope in the world. If you are ambitious about success in the world, don't drink or do drugs. ACIM talks about the need to experience the *lowest point* before I turn around and start going in the right direction. This is not the same as the "bottom" talked about in AA. Reaching the lowest point has nothing to do with powerlessness over drugs or alcohol. The lowest point is the realization that there is *nothing* in the world that ever brings happiness. It has nothing to do with alcohol or drugs. Alcohol is just one of the millions of things the world offers as a substitution. The problem drinker does not drink to become happy. Alcohol offers a temporary numbing that demands damage as a price in return. A clear and sober look at this pain-filled, insane world might lead someone to attempt escape in a variety of suicidal ways.

The list of creative people, including the rich and famous, who use drugs and alcohol is long. Many die of suicide, overdose or substance related issues. Why is creativity associated with self-destruction? Users are not interested in drugs or alcohol per se. Substances are means to an end. I want to change my consciousness. Sobriety is not all its cracked up to be. Ordinary, sober consciousness is the suffering state of separation, denied or not. I am miserable because I'm not home and all my efforts to find my way back have failed. Only God satisfies, and I appear God-deprived. This is the human condition and each of us uses whatever means he has to get through the night. Certain means of escape are socially approved of, like money, sex, and success. Dope and drink not so much, yet the money spent on alcohol, drugs (legal, illegal, prescribed, or not) is enormous. Even the advertising budgets encouraging "responsible" use are enormous. Welcome to the world of pain. Blaming suffering on drugs and alcohol is an excuse intended to avoid looking at the real problem.

My brother Gerry drove me to LA for the flight to Lima. I endured a grueling twenty-four hour ordeal flying there. The retreat center is in a beautiful setting in the Andes mountains. The owner, who built the place, impressed me. I attended two retreats back to back. The first cleansing retreat included a special diet, liver flush, enemas, Ayurveda evaluation and practice, and other cleansing activities. This preparation/purification readied me for the retreat that followed with five ayahuasca ceremonies. The first cleansing retreat went well and just being off alcohol and drugs made a big difference. I looked forward to the ayahuasca ceremonies. I had wanted to try it for ten years and I did not fear it. It surely could not make things worse, or so I thought. I considered the retreat a last resort. If this did not work, then what would? I didn't think I could get any lower, but I was wrong.

The night of the first ceremony we gathered in the large yurt and took our places on mats in a circle. The shaman from Iquitos chanted icaros in Spanish. Some of the song/prayers included Christian terms in them like Jesus and the Holy Spirit. I learned that the number one healing plant of the shamans is not DMT-containing ayahuasca, or San Pedro, the mescaline cactus, but tobacco. I had smoked cigarettes since 2000 and quit smoking eight months before, while living on St. Paul Island. Tobacco is used frequently in the ceremony, but I felt no desire to smoke. When it came time to take the medicine, we took turns coming up to the shaman to get our dose. I indicated how much medicine I wanted through a translator. I asked for a full cup, and I could tell the translator wasn't too sure about that for a first-timer, who just completed a liver flush. The shaman poured the thick, dark red liquid into a cup, blew tobacco smoke over it and handed it to me. I prayed my intentions for healing over the medicine and drained it. It is supposed to taste bad but I did not find it too bad. I gave the cup back to the shaman and went back to my place in the circle.

Part of the ayahuasca experience is "the purge." Vomiting is common and encouraged. Everyone had a basin to vomit in. The trick is to keep it down long enough for the medicine to get into one's system. I intended to hold it down as long as possible. I started to feel sick, nauseous, but did not vomit. I did not feel high. No hallucinations and not psychedelic. Then I needed to use the bathroom outside the yurt. The purge goes in both directions. I rose and went to the door. I felt wobbly and made it to the door in the darkness. I put on my sneakers and reached for the door knob. My depth perception tricked me and the door knob appeared closer than it actually was. I kept reaching for it, leaning forward, until I lost my balance and fell forward, hitting my left shoulder against the wall. In the commotion a staff member came over to help. Something was seriously wrong with my arm. I could not move it and felt severe pain. I didn't know what was wrong. I thought maybe I dislocated my shoulder because of the pain and immobility of my arm. I did not think that such a minor fall could do much damage.

I hoped to relocate the dislocation and asked a staff member to try that. He declined because he was high from the ayahuasca. I asked him to get the owner, who was not at the ceremony, to see if he could do it. He came and they took me to my room and he spent a long time comparing both arms and shoulders, trying to see what differences he discerned between the injured arm and the healthy arm. Finally he tried manipulating my arm and shoulder and we heard a pop and I said, "Thank God." I thought he fixed the dislocation. But I still could not move my arm, and the pain continued. They asked if I wanted to go back into the ceremony or stay in my room. I saw no point in going back. I felt too much pain.

The next morning I felt no improvement. A large ugly bruise emerged on the inside of my arm from the arm pit almost down to the elbow. I did not know what to do and asked the owner what my options were. He said he knew a "bone setter" in the closest town, about a half hour taxi drive away, and he would see if he could make arrangements for the bone-setter to come to the retreat. Or I could go to the hospital for a traditional treatment that might include surgery after an x-ray showed what damage happened. He advised against the hospital. I agreed to see the bone setter. He could not come to the retreat, so we took a cab into town. I asked the owner if he thought my arm was dislocated or broken. He said dislocated. Some of that day I cried, not so much because of the physical pain, which was bad, but because of emotional pain. Apparently this last ditch effort towards healing was a wash. I went to the bone setter and sat in line on the street. When my turn came, I met this old, small, kind, and gentle man. He put a sling around my arm and shoulder and squeezed from behind while I pulled on the sling with my good arm. The charge for the bone setter was unbelievably small, a couple dollars. Then we went to a place where a woman measured me for a sling, and sewed it together while we waited. Then a cab ride back to the retreat center on a deeply rutted dirt road, in an old beat up Toyota. I felt every bump in my arm. I did not use any painkillers because ayahuasca ceremony protocols forbid recent use of any drugs or alcohol. While we were in town the owner offered to get painkillers but I declined. I wanted to participate in the remaining ceremonies.

I participated in another ceremony and took a much smaller dose, though the full cup from the first ceremony did not effect me strongly, psychedelically speaking. I was in pain the whole time and did not enjoy the ceremony. I endured the same sick feeling but did not vomit. Two more ceremonies with higher doses and pretty much the same thing happened. The taste did get progressively worse. I did not get high and I just felt sick and in pain. After a few hours of nausea I just wanted the ceremony to end. I did not experience the psychedelic bliss I knew with mushrooms or ecstasy. I opted out of the last ceremony. It felt like this ordeal of flying to Peru, and the expense, was a waste. (It wasn't a complete waste. I enjoyed two hikes in the Andes, one with San Pedro.)

Then followed another long flight back to California in several stages. That was the last time I flew on a jet and I hope not to fly again. I disliked being crammed into the flying sardine can. I disliked airport security. More time is spent getting to the airport, standing in line for security, getting to the gate, boarding the plane and waiting for take off, waiting to get off the plane, etc. than the actual flight. I'd rather ride a bike or take a train. My brother Mickey picked me up at the Oakland airport and we drove back to Woodland. The next day I went to a clinic to have my arm checked out. They sent me for an x-ray, and it turned out that my arm was fractured in two places, both at the shoulder. It looked fairly well set and the PA recommended keeping the sling on for a month more and then rehab. I felt like I came back in worse shape than when I left. Because of my arm, I could not drive the bus to Monterey, nor lift things. I learned to do a lot of things with one arm. I stopped wearing the sling near the end of December but my arm was limited in movement and extension. It took more than a year to get back to almost normal and after two years it still is not 100%. This was my third time breaking a bone and it mirrored the blood clot injury in my right shoulder when I was twenty-three. In late December I was well enough to move to Monterey.

It was about five months before I found a place to park the bus. Like a lot of homeless people who lived in their vehicles, parking during the day was not a problem. Parking at night to sleep was. I played a cat and mouse game with the cops. Several times the police came to the bus and ordered me to move. Move where? The police did not have a suggestion.

I drove north about ten miles to a frontage road for Highway One where I remembered seeing a motor home parked. I found a turn-out and parked in the dark. The next day I saw several motor homes parked along the road, not used much, but in view of the highway. I talked to one homeless vet who said he parked there for a couple years. So I parked there for a few months. One day a California Highway Patrol officer came by and gave me three days to move or be towed. The cop told the other motor home residents the same thing. Camping not allowed. I wasn't camping. No camp fire, no tent, no sleeping outside. I was parking. I think the real issue with the homeless is that the homed don't want to see them. People fear the homeless because they think the homeless are going to steal from them, or worse. The homed fear being homeless themselves.

During this time I did basically nothing but read all day, mostly ACIM, but other books as well. I started each day with a *Workbook* lesson, repeating lessons first studied twenty-two years earlier. As I read I started writing down quotes that were poignant to me and many are included in this book. I enjoyed reading many biographies and autobiographies, and I visited the local public library frequently. My brother Gerry lived nearby and was working on his PhD in philosophy. He had a large book collection and I borrowed many from him. I discovered Gary Renard and read each of his three books four times. I found his books helpful. I could relate to him because of similarities we shared. We are about the same age and started studying the Course at about the same time. We both play guitar. Quotes in this book from the *Gospel of Thomas* are from Pursah's (Saint Thomas the Twin) version in Renard's *Your Immortal Reality*.

When living on St. Paul Island I learned of another spiritual teacher named Leonard Jacobson. I visited his web site and he seemed to be in the same school as Eckhart Tolle, even in his vocabulary. He wrote five or six books. One is *Journey into Now*. I learned he gave talks at his house and lived not far away, near Santa Cruz. So my brother Gerry and I went a few times. I read all his books. I liked this teacher but I had a hard time integrating his and the course's teaching about ego. In one book he wrote that Jesus lived many more lifetimes since the resurrection and recently re-awakened.

I decided to attend his annual retreat. It was taking place nearby and they offered a less expensive camping option. I used the last bit of credit on my card to pay for the retreat. The retreat was a bust. I wanted to leave early but stayed since I already paid for it. In my spiritual search I kept checking out new spiritual teachers, hoping to find what I was looking for.

Another teacher I liked is the post-zen Adyashanti. I read and re-read all his books and watched many videos. I felt a lot in common with him. He grew up on the peninsula in the Bay Area, right near where I did, similar age, the bicycle connection, though he raced and I toured. He loved the Sierras as I did. He reported one visionary experience that happened on a hill next to the seminary where I lived for five years. He is based in the Bay Area but comes to Santa Cruz once in a while and once my brother Gerry and I went to one of his satsangs. It was okay, but ultimately disappointing. Nothing happened, not that anything should happen. Sometimes transmission happens, but not for me.

There is another spiritual teacher in Santa Cruz, Mokshananda, of the bald Buddhist/Wilber variety, who also works as a psycho-therapist. Gerry saw him on a regular basis. I saw him once shortly after the hospitalization in Reno. I started attending weekly satsangs in his home, with my brother. I felt a better connection with Mok-shananda, but did not see much point in continuing. All these things cost money and I didn't have any and I was not comfortable with my brother Gerry paying for everything. I was poor for the most part, most of my life. The starving artist cliché. Career ambition eluded me. Most of these spiritual teachers shared a similar social-economic status. They are relatively wealthy. Some charge high prices for their events, even though they don't need the money. Selling water by the river is now lucrative. Another thing about these spiritual teachers is that most of them did not have children. Only Byron Katie had kids. Mokshananda had his first child when I was seeing him. My most serious suffering seemed to revolve around that most difficult special relationship between my children and me. My children's suffering seems to cause more grief than anything else. That was before I under-stood the course teaching about how I am responsible for everything I experience. I do not blame my children or anyone else for my grief. *My* special relationships are my responsibility.

I kept turning back to ACIM and found that it satisfied my spir-itual thirst better than all the teachers I saw in-person. I believe both Eckhart Tolle and Bryon Katie were influenced by ACIM, though they each seemed to focus on one part of the teaching. I studied under many different spiritual teachers, from different traditions, both in person and through studying their writings or sayings. Almost everywhere I seemed to find confirmation of ACIM, as I have tried to show in the non-course quotes throughout this book. I use the metaphor that a teaching is like a map. This book is another map. Many maps might mix me up, or even prolong the return to Heaven. All the maps help with directions, yet some are more accurate and quicker. There can be confusion in exploring many teachers, because their teachings differ. Fr. Bruno Barnhart:

> A thousand quick messiahs bloom like mushrooms, with glossy smiles and toll-free numbers. The hungry shall eat! The blind shall walk, the dumb shall see: Just come and follow me.[1]

Shortly after the Leonard Jacobson retreat is when the CHP forced me to find a new place to park the bus. I tired of hiding from the police. I wanted a place to park and sleep without worry. I talked to a spiritually-minded homeless lady I knew who lived in her motor home for about ten years in the Monterey area and asked for advice. She knew a lady in nearby Carmel Valley who owned a few acres of land and sometimes helped homeless people by letting them park on her land in exchange for work. I contacted her and we came to an agreement. I grow a vegetable garden near the bus. Now I have lived here for seventeen months and enjoy a quiet and solitary place to park my bus and don't worry about cops telling me to move in the middle of the night. I enjoy watching the birds, lizards, deer, rabbits, and bobcats. A few times a bird flew into the bus. My favorite visitors. Except for it being too warm for my Alaskan tastes, and the insects, it is just about ideal for a hermit life of prayer, study and writing.

After seven months parked here, I decided to write a book about a spiritual approach to healing depression based on ACIM and include relevant parts of my spiritual journey. I started hand writing this book on the 100th anniversary of Thomas Merton's birth. Six months later I purchased a used laptop and began typing. The immersive study and reading of the previous two years, including my breakdown over several months, built up inside me as something to be shared. The course emphasized the importance of sharing and this book is my attempt to share.

What all the ups and downs of my life taught me, over sixty-one years, is that ACIM is true. My life is evidence that it is true. As ACIM describes, I engaged in many delay maneuvers. So often I used inappropriate means to escape pain that kept me in hell. Special relationships brought the most pain into my life, and were the hardest to give up, as the course teaches. The ego invests heavily to maintain its continuity and special relationships are the ego's most essential means to maintain itself. The course explained the 1976 mystical experience described in the *Prologue* better than anything else I read. ACIM also resolved the dilemmas I faced as a result of the dichotomy between that experience and my conditioning. I finally hit the "lowest point" by failing at everything, losing everything, and accepting that there is no solution in the world. Close to despair, I did not care anymore and wished for death. The sad irony about suicide is that in attempting to escape one's misery by killing one's self, liberation is delayed.

Thanks to the Holy Spirit, through ACIM, I shifted from wanting to die to wanting to cooperate with the Holy Spirit and to be purified of unconscious guilt and all blocks to the awareness of love. I accept the Atonement for myself. The holy instant liberates me from my depressing past. I place the future in the hands of God, freeing me of any anxiety over the future. I step back and let God direct doing. Believe it or not, I am not depressed.

Oneness is simply the idea God is. And in His Being, He encompasses all things. No mind holds anything but Him. We say "God is," and then we cease to speak, for in that knowledge words are meaningless. There are no lips to speak them, and no part of mind sufficiently distinct to feel that it is now aware of something not itself. It has united with its Source. And like its Source Itself, it merely is.

We cannot speak nor write nor even think of this at all. It comes to every mind when total recognition that its will is God's has been completely given and received completely. It returns the mind into the endless present, where the past and future cannot be conceived. It lies beyond salvation; past all thought of time, forgiveness and the holy face of Christ. The Son of God has merely disappeared into his Father, as his Father has in him. The world has never been at all. Eternity remains a constant state.[2]

brother hermit time-line

1954	Born in Monterey County, California
1955	Moved to South San Francisco, California
1958	Moved to Southern California
1962	Moved to Cupertino, California
1963	Moved to Los Altos, California
1968	Graduated from St Nicholas School in Los Altos, California
1968-1972	Attended St Joseph High School Seminary in Mt. View, CA
1972-1973	Attended St. Patrick's College Seminary in Mt. View, CA
1973	Bicycle tour from Bay Area to Canada and across Canada
1974	Moved from San Jose, California to San Francisco, California
1974-1975	Auxiliary at New Camaldoli Hermitage in Big Sur, California
1975	Retreats at Trappist monasteries in Vina, CA, Christ in the Desert in New Mexico, Snowmass, Colorado, and Pecos, NM
1976	Member of Benedictine Monastery near Pecos, New Mexico
1976	Experience described in Prologue happens
1976-1977	Attended Foothill College in Los Altos Hills, California
1977	Moved from Bay Area to Humboldt County
1977-1978	Attended Humboldt State University in Arcata, CA
1979	Moved from Humboldt County to Bay Area
1982	Marriage to Dee in Los Altos, California
1987	Moved to Anchorage, Alaska and birth of first child, Alicen
1990	Birth of son, Francis
1991	Photography trip to Magadan, Russia
1992	Began studying *A Course In Miracles*
1992	Centering Prayer retreat at St. Benedict's Monastery in Snowmass
1992-1993	Divorce
1994	Dee absconds with children
1995-1998	Attended University of Alaska Anchorage
1998	BA Psychology
1998-2000	Attend University of Alaska Anchorage as graduate student
2005	Received MS in Clinical Psychology
2005-2010	Live and work in Kotzebue, Alaska
2010	Bicycle tour from Anchorage, Alaska to Mexicali, Mexico
2012-2013	Lived and worked on St. Paul Island, Alaska
2013	Moved from Alaska to Oregon, and then California
2013-2016	Living on the bus in Oregon and California, extended retreat, immersive study of ACIM and writing *God Is*

REFERENCES

The quotes from ACIM are indicated by book and page from the second edition combined volume copyrighted in 1992. T is for the *Text*. W is for the *Workbook For Students*, and MFT is for the *Manual For Teachers*. Thus (MFT 64) means page 64 of the *Manual For Teachers*. In quotes from the *Workbook*, I listed both the lesson number followed by the page the lesson starts on: (W Lesson 162, 307). New Testament quotes are from the Revised Standard Version. Old Testament quotes are from *The Jerusalem Bible*.

Preface. 1. *The Essential Rumi*, Coleman Barks (trans.), p. 52.

Prologue. 1. Mojdeh Bayat and Mohammad Ali Jamnia, *Tales from the Land of the Sufis*, p. 130.

Introduction. 1. Henry Thoreau, *Walden And Other Writings*, p. 8.

Part I: Preparation. 1. Thomas Keating, *St. Thérèse of Lisieux*, p. 27.

Chapter One: A Course In Miracles. 1. T 70. **2.** T 1. **3.** T 5. **4.** T 6. **5.** T 7. **6.** T.7. **7.** T 40. **8.** T 41. **9.** T 71. **10.** MFT 64.

Chapter Two: Words about Words. 1. T 37. **2.** MFT 77. **3.** W Lesson 39, 60. **4.** Luke 10:21. **5.** MFT 77. **6.** Krishnamurti, *Reflections on the Self*, Raymond Martin, editor, p. viii. **7.** MFT 77. **8.** MFT 53. **9.** T 662. **10.** W Lesson 12, 20. **11.** W Lesson 129, 235. **12.** Joel Goldsmith, *The Infinite Way*, p. 155.

Chapter Three: Resolving Dilemmas. 1. W Lesson 276, 434. **2.** T 603. **3.** T 640. **4.** T 647. **5.** T. 17. **6.** T 187. **7.** T 103. **8.** MFT 77. **9.** T 14. **10.** T 244. **11.** T 103. **12.** T 71. **13.** T 314. **14.** MFT 3. **15.** MFT 3 **16.** T 389. **17.** MFT 3. **18.** MFT 3. **19.** W 487. **20.** T 73. **21.** T 70. **22.** T 152. **23.** John 14:25-26. **24.** T 74. **25.** T 73. **26.** John 14:16-17. **27.** T 74. **28.** T 469. **29.** Wei Wu Wei, *Why Lazarus Laughed*, p. xiii-xiv. **30.** ACIM, Preface vii. **31.** John 16:12-13. **32.** T 95. **33.** T 36. **34.** MFT 58-59. **35.** MFT 87. **36.** MFT 89.

Chapter Four: Open Mind. 1. W Lesson 133, 247. **2.** T 296. **3.** T 298. **4.** T 499. **5.** T 227. **6.** T 590. **7.** T 54. **8.** T 617. **9.** T 53. **10.** T 211. **11.** MFT 77. **12.** T 211. **13.** T 617. **14.** Ken Wilber, *The Collected Works of Ken Wilber, Volume One, No Boundary*, p. 508. **15.** T 227. **16.** T 18. **17.** Romans 7:15-19. **18.** Meister Eckhart, *Best of Meister Eckhart*, p. 16. **19.** T 299. **20.** J. Krishnamurti, *Reflections on the Self*, Raymond Martin, Ed. p. viii. **21.** W 2. **22.** T 256. **23.** W Lesson 189, 360. **24.** Lipton, *The Biology of Belief*, p. 132-133. **25.** Stan Grof, *The Transpersonal Vision*, p. 14. **26.** Stan Grof, *The Transpersonal Vision*, p. 34. **27.** T 236. **28.** Genesis 3:16. **29.** Henry Thoreau, *Walden And Other Writings*, p. 3.

Part II: Main Ideas. 1. T 668.

Chapter Five: The Nature of Depression: Cause and Effect. 1. T 665. **2.** T 665. **3.** T 424. **4.** T 431. **5.** T 13. **6.** Meister Eckhart, *The Best of Meister Eckhart*, p. 87. **7.** Meister Eckhart, *The Best of Meister Eckhart*, p. 83. **8.** T 553. **9.** T 63. **10.** Tao Te Ching, Mitchell, (tr.), p. 44. **11.** T 256. **12.** Thomas Merton, *Raids on the Unspeakable*, p. 46-47. **13.** T 236. **14.** Jack Kerouac, *Wake Up*, p. 23. **15.** W Lesson 182, 337. **16.** T 52. **17.** T 13. **18.** T 554. **19.** T 25. **20.** T 244. **21.** T 244. **22.** T 244. **23.** T 244. **24.** T 244. **25.** T 586. **26.** T 376. **27.** T 101. **28.** T 18. **29.** T 18. **30.** T 32. **31.** T 136. **32.** Meister Eckhart, *The Best of Meister Eckhart*, p. 132. **33.** T 547. **34.** T 654. **35.** T 505. **36.** Joel Goldsmith, *The Infinite Way*, p. 162. **37.** Joel Goldsmith, *The Infinite Way*, p. 166. **38.** Joel Goldsmith, *The Infinite Way*, p. 166. **39.** Joel Goldsmith, *The Infinite Way*, p. 165. **40.** Joel Goldsmith, *The Infinite Way*, p. 163. **41.** Joel Goldsmith, *The Infinite Way*, p. 163. **42.** Joel Goldsmith, *The Infinite Way*, p. 172.

Chapter Six: Who Am I: Identity. 1. T 660. **2.** T 160. **3.** T 191. **4.** John 12:24. **5.** *Tao de Ching*, Mitchell (tr.), p. 42. **6.** John 10:17. **7.** Meister Eckhart, *Best of Meister Eckhart*, p. 135. **8.** Meister Eckhart, *Best of Meister Eckhart*, p. 139. **9.** Steven Mitchell, (ed.) *The Enlightened Mind*, p. 191. **10.** Thomas Keating, *Reflections on the Unknowable*, p. 50. **11.** Thomas Merton, *The Other Side of the Mountain, The Journals of Thomas Merton*, Volume Seven, 1967-1968. p. 248. **12.** T 328. **13.** T 415. **14.** T 579. **15.** T 415. **16.** Ramana Maharshi, *Talks*, p. 298. **17.** T 151. **18.** Gary Renard, *Your Immortal Reality*, p. 164. **19.** T 587. **20.** T 587. **21.** Luke

12:22, 24. **22.** Matthew 6:20. **23.** W Lesson 72, 124. **24.** John 6:63. **25.** T 203. **26.** T 58. **27.** T 372. **28.** T 54. **29.** T 56. **30.** T 60. **31.** T 69. **32.** MFT 81. **33.** T 42. **34.** T 54. **35.** T 67. **36.** T 68. **37.** T 54. **38.** T 105. **39.** T 155. **40.** T 310. **41.** T 53. **42.** T 17. **43.** T 21. **44.** T 21. **45.** T 22. **46.** Luke 12:2-3. **47.** T 11. **48.** T 11. **49.** T 202. **50.** T 243. **51.** T 243. **52.** T 243. **53.** T 26. **54.** T 245. **55.** T 57. **56.** T 342. **57.** T 502. **58.** T 513. **59.** T 655. **60.** T 505. **61.** W Lesson 161, 304.

Chapter Seven: When Egos Collide: Relationships. 1. T 502. **2.** T 307. **3.** T 500. **4.** T 500. **5.** W Lesson 134, 251. **6.** T 127 **7.** MFT 55. **8.** T 265. **9.** T 147. **10.** T 341. **11.** Luke 14:25-26. **12.** T 342. **13.** T 223. **14.** T 223. **15.** Joel Goldsmith, *The Infinite Way*, p. 175. **16.** Matthew 12:46-50. **17.** T 127. **18.** T 129. **19.** T 369. **20.** T 651. **21.** T 319. **22.** T 341. **23.** T 500. **24.** T 656. **25.** T 656. **26.** T 565. **27.** T 494. **28.** T 566. **29.** T 347. **30.** T 246. **31.** T 250. **32.** T 250. **33.** T 251. **34.** T 79. **35.** Gary Renard, *Your Immortal Reality*, p. 166. **36.** John 17:20-23. **37.** T 668. **38.** T 312. **39.** T 345. **40.** T 312. **41.** W Lesson 182, 339. **42.** T 22.

Chapter Eight: As The World Turns It Burns, You Learn. 1. John 16:33. **2.** T 56. **3.** John 15:18-19. **4.** John 12:25. **5.** T 653. **6.** T 520. **7.** T 521. **8.** W Lesson 133, 245. **9.** 1 John 1:15-17. **10.** T 550. **11.** T 617. **12.** T 618. **13.** T 619. **14.** T 617. **15.** T 618. **16.** T 621. **17.** T 254. **18.** T 254. **19.** T 254. **20.** T 616. **21.** W Lesson 129, 235. **22.** W Lesson 153, 284. **23.** MFT 24. **24.** W Lesson 128, 233. **25.** W Lesson 129, 235. **26.** W Lesson 130, 237. **27.** T 264. **28.** T 152. **29.** T 637. **30.** T 224. **31.** T 227. **32.** T 413. **33.** T 235. **34.** W Lesson 128, 233. **35.** W Lesson 128, 233. **36.** T 653. **37.** T 653. **38.** T 653. **39.** T 653. **40.** T 654. **41.** T 654. **42.** T 232. **43.** T 233. **44.** T 228. **45.** T 233. **46.** T 237. **47.** T 240. **48.** T 301. **49.** T 104. **50.** T 418. **51.** T 51. **52.** T 616. **53.** T 654. **54.** W 425. **55.** T 105. **56.** T 151. **57.** MFT 31. **58.** T 12. **59.** T 654. **60.** T 654. **61.** T 306. **62.** W Lesson 132, 243. **63.** T 655. **64.** W Lesson 96, 169. **65.** MFT 51. **66.** Thomas Keating, *Reflections on the Unknowable*, p. 122. **67.** Thomas Keating, *Reflections on the Unknowable*, p. 122. **68.** MFT 33. **69.** T. 597.

Chapter Nine: Time is Temporary. 1. T 247. **2.** T 251. *3.* T 4. **4.** T 86. **5.** T 246. **6.** T 246. **7.** T 246. **8.** T 618. **9.** T 301. **10.** T 619. **11.** T 55. **12.** T 87. **13.** T 79. **14.** T 324. **15.** T 21. **16.** T 34. **17.** T 1. **18.** T 4. **19.** T4. **20.** T 4. **21.** T 6.

22. T 8. **23**. T 27. **24**. T 86. **25**. T 3. **26**. T 12. **27**. T 20. **28**. T 21. **29**. MFT 6. **30**. T 51. **31**. Gary Renard, *Your Immortal Reality*, p. 164. **32**. T 669. **33**. T 42. **34**. Bruno Barnhart, *Second Simplicity*, p. 37. **35**. T 362. **36**. T 303. **37**. T 435. **38**. T 312. **39**. T 313. **40**. T 313. **41**. T 316. **42**. T 349. **43**. T 559. **44**. T 559. **45**. T 313. **46**. MFT 5. **47**. T 550. **48**. T 559. **49**. T 559. **50**. W Lesson 169, 324. **51**. T 550. **52**. T 550. **53**. T 559. **54**. T 560. **55**. T 560. **56**. T 382. **57**. W Lesson 158, 298. **58**. MFT 71. **59**. MFT 61.

Part III: Application. 1. T 231.

Chapter 10: True Forgiveness and the End of Guilt. 1. T 84. **2.** T 212. **3.** W Lesson 121, 214. **4.** T 236. **5.** T 236. **6.** T 84. **7.** T 240. **8.** T 190. **9.** T 233. **10.** T 237. **11.** T 84. **12.** T 64. **13.** T 601. **14.** W Lesson 73, 127. **15.** W Lesson 73, 127. **16.** T 183. **17.** T 239. **18.** T 236. **19.** T 41. **20.** T 238. **21.** T 47. **22.** T 46. **23.** T 47. **24.** T 646. **25.** T 646. **26.** T 84. **27.** Joel Goldsmith, *The Infinite Way*, p. 161. **28.** Ramana Maharshi, *Talks*, 317-318. **29.** T 383. **30.** W Lesson 151, 278. **31.** W Lesson 151, 278. **32.** W Lesson 151 278. **33.** W Lesson 270, 430. **34.** T 601. **35.** W Lesson 1, 3. **36.** Matthew 7:1-3. **37.** Matthew 5:21-24. **38.** John 5:22-23. **39.** T 648. **40.** T 270. **41.** MFT 77 **42.** Matthew 6:14-15. **43.** Matthew 6:12. **44.** W Lesson 134, 248. **45.** T 569. **46.** T 248. **47.** Lesson 134, 248 **48.** *A Brief Anthology of Byron Katie* p. 60. **49.** T 320.

Chapter Eleven: Mind Your Mind. 1. bh. **2.** T 189. **3.** T 84. **4.** T 222. **5.** T 49. **6.** T 223. **7.** W Lesson 5, 8. **8.** W Lesson 6, 10. **9.** T 29. **10.** Matthew 5:27-28. **11.** T 29. **12.** T 31. **13.** T. 191. **14.** T 31. **15.** T 29. **16.** W Lesson 5, 8. **17.** W Lesson 162, 307. **18.** T 115.

Chapter Twelve: Joining: The Unitive Teaching of Non-Duality. 1. T 28. **2.** T 39. **3.** MFT 84. **4.** Luke 22:41-42. **5.** T 39. **6.** T 184. **7.** T 142. **8.** MFT 7. **9.** T 246. **10.** T 599. **11.** T 546. **12.** W Lesson 99, 177. **13.** W Lesson 187, 354. **14.** T 15. **15.** T 33. **16.** MFT 79. **17.** T 106 **18.** T 668. **19.** Matthew 5:43-45, 48. **20.** Matthew 25:40. **21.** Matthew 25:41. **22.** Matthew 7:21-23. **23.** Matthew 5:20. **24.** John 15:1-5. **25.** John 15:13. **26.** John 15:12. **27.** John 15:9-10. **28.** John 15:11. **29.** John 15:6. **30.** T 51. **31.** T 555. **32.** W Lesson

134, 248. **33.** T 423. **34.** T 422. **35.** T 434. **36.** T 168. **37.** T 137. **38.** T 142. **39.** T 442. **40.** T 455. **41.** T 470. **42.** T 483. **43.** T 362. **44.** T 364. **45.** T 476. **46.** T 362. **47.** T 362. **48.** T 362. **49.** T 363. **50.** T 363. **51.** T 363. **52.** T 363. **53.** T 364. **54.** T 384. **55.** T 384. **56.** T 389. **57.** W Lesson 137, 261. **58.** T 205. **59.** T 481. **60.** T 596. **61.** T 601. **62.** T 495. **63.** Luke 16:13. **64.** Gary Renard, *Your Immortal Reality*, p. 166. **65.** T 185. **66.** T 596. **67.** T 185. **68.** T 508. **69.** T 600. **70.** T 596. **71.** 598. **72.** *The Essential Rumi*, trans. Coleman Barks, p. xii. **73.** *The Essential Rumi*, trans. Coleman Barks, p. xii. **74.** *The Enlightened Heart*, Stephen Mitchell, (ed.), p. 59. **75.** MFT 64.

Chapter Thirteen: Responsibility. **1.** T 448. **2.** MFT 55. **3.** W Lesson 196, 374. **4.** W Lesson 196, 374. **5.** W Lesson 196, 374. **6.** Eckhart Tolle, *The Power or Now*, p. 1. **7.** T 448. **8.** T. 628. **9.** W Lesson 155, 291. **10.** T 448. **11.** T 29. **12.** T 223. **13.** T 647. **14.** MFT 18. **15.** MFT 17. **16.** MFT 17. **17.** T 201. **18.** MFT 18. **19.** MFT 19. **20.** MFT 19. **21.** T 581. **22.** T 192. **23.** T 63. **24.** T 29. **25.** T29. **26.** T 29. **27.** T 508. **28.** T 581. **29.** T 582. **30.** T 583. **31.** T 584. **32.** T 586. **33.** T 587. **34.** T 588. **35.** T 587. **36.** T 593. **37.** T 218. **38.** T 221. **39.** T 183. **40.** W Lesson 200, 384. **41.** T 231. **42.** Matthew 5:8. **43.** T 131. **44.** W 419 **45.**T 63. **46.** T 90. **47.** T 666. **48.** T 192. **49.** Eckhart Tolle and Byron Katie, *Peace in the Present Moment*, p. 22. **50.** MFT 70.

Chapter 14: How To Perform Miracles. **1.** T 43. **2.** T 34. **3.** T 29. **4.** T 29. **5.** T 30. **6.** T 30. **7.** T 15. **8.** W Lesson 234, 409. **9.** T 88. **10.** Mark 10:27. **11.** T 25. **12.** T 75. **13.** T 5. **14.** Joel Goldsmith, *The Art of Spiritual Healing*, p. 95. **15.** T 27. **16.** T 9. **17.** T 10. **18.** T 10. **19.** T 3. **20.** W Lesson 284, 439. **21.** Joel Goldsmith, *The Art of Spiritual Healing*, p. 102. **22.** Joel Goldsmith, *The Art of Spiritual Healing*, p. 98. **23.** T 218. **24.** T 218. **25.** Joel Goldsmith, *The Art of Spiritual Healing*, p. 94. **26.** T 12. **27.** Joel Goldsmith, *The Art of Spiritual Healing*, p. 97. **28.** T 12. **29.** W Lesson 196, 374. **30.** T 25. **31.** T 25. **32.** T 26. **33.** T 666.

Chapter 15: I Need Do Nothing. **1.** Krishnamurti, *Reflections on the Self*, p. v. **2.** T 380. **3.** T 380. **4.** T 181. **5.** T 381. **6.** T 382. **7.** Joel Goldsmith, *The Infinite Way*, p. 168. **8.** T 384. **9.** W Lesson 138, 264. **10.** W Lesson 138, 264. **11.** W Lesson 138, 264. **12.** T 75. **13.** W Lesson 74, 130. **14.** W Lesson

138, 264. **15.** MFT 10. **16.** MFT 10. **17.** MFT 10. **18.** MFT 11. **19.** MFT 11. **20.** MFT 11. **21.** MFT 11. **22.** MFT 11. **23.** W Lesson 135, 252. **24.** Wei Wu Wei, *Unworldly Wise*, p. 60-61. **25.** Joel Goldsmith, *The Infinite Way*, p. 149. **26.** Joel Goldsmith, *The Infinite Way*, p. 149. **27.** Joel Goldsmith, *The Infinite Way*, p. 149. **28.** Joel Goldsmith, *The Infinite Way*, p. 149. **29.** Joel Goldsmith, *The Infinite Way*, p. 149. **30.** Joel Goldsmith, *The Infinite Way*, p. 161. **31.** Joel Goldsmith, *The Infinite Way*, p. 173. **32.** Joel Goldsmith, *The Infinite Way*, p. 173. **33.** Joel Goldsmith, *The Infinite Way*, p. 162. **34.** T 330. **35.** T 389. **36.** Ramana Maharshi, *Talks*, p. 317-318. **37.** Ramana Maharshi, *Talks*, p. 312. **38.** Luke 10:8-42. **39.** John 5:19. **40.** John 6:44. **41.** T 390. **42.** W Lesson 337, 471. **43.** Joel Goldsmith, *The Infinite Way*, p. 145. **44.** Meister Eckhart, *The Best of Meister Eckhart*, p. 136. **45.** *Tao Te Ching*, Steven Mitchell (trans.), p. 48. **46.** W Lesson 188, 357. **47.** MFT 70. **48.** MFT 52. **49.** Psalm 127:1.

Epilogue: Sidetrack: 2005-2015. 1. Bruno Barnhart, *Second Simplicity*, p. 207. **2.** W Lesson 169, 323.

BIBLIOGRAPHY

A Course In Miracles. 2nd Edition. Mill Valley, CA: Foundation For Inner Peace, 1992.

Barks, Coleman. (trans). *The Essential Rumi*. New Jersey: Castle Books, 1997.

Barnhart, Bruno. *Second Simplicity*. New York: Paulist Press, 1999.

Bayat, Mojdeh and Jamnia, Mohammad Ali. A. *Tales from the Land of the Sufis*. Boston: Shambhala, 1994.

Eckhart, Meister. *Best of Meister Eckhart*. Backhouse, H. (ed.). New York: Crossroad, 1996.

Goldsmith, Joel S. *The Art Of Spiritual Healing*. San Francisco: HarperCollins, 1992.

Goldsmith, Joel S. *The Infinite Way*. Los Angeles: Devorss & Company, 1947.

Grof, Stan. *The Transpersonal Vision*. Boulder, CO: Sounds True, 1998.

The Jerusalem Bible. New York: Doubleday & Company, Inc. 1966.

Keating, Thomas. *Reflections On The Unknowable*. New York: Lantern, 2014.

Keating, Thomas. *St. Thérèse of Lisieux, A Transformation in Christ*. New York: Lantern, 2001.

Kerouac, Jack. *Wake Up*. New York: Penguin Books, 2008.

Krishnamurti, Jiddu. *Reflections on the Self*. Martin, R. (ed.). Chicago: Open Court, 1997.

Lipton, Bruce. H. *The Biology Of Belief*. Carlsbad, CA: Hay House, 2005.

Merton, Thomas. *Raids On The Unspeakable*. New York: New Directions, 1964.

Merton, Thomas. *The Other Side of the Mountain, The Journals of Thomas Merton, Volume Seven 1967-1968*, New York: Harper Collins, 1999.

Mitchell, Stephen. (trans.). *Tao Te Ching*. New York: HarperPerennial, 1991.

Mitchell, Stephen. (ed.). *A Brief Anthology Of Byron Katie's Words*. Los Angeles: Byron Katie International, 2003.

Mitchell, Stephen. (ed.). *The Enlightened Heart*. New York: Harper & Row, 1989.

Mitchell, Stephen. (ed.). *The Enlightened Mind*. New York: HarperCollins, 1991.

New Testament. Revised Standard Version. New York: Thomas Nelson & Sons, 1965.

Ramana Maharshi, Sri. *Talks With Sri Ramana Maharshi*. India: Sri Ramanasramam, 2013.

Renard, Gary. *Your Immortal Reality*. Carlsbad CA: Hay House, 2006.

Roberts, Bernadette. *The Experience of No Self*. Boston & London: Shambhala, 1985.

Thoreau, Henry. *Walden And Other Writings*. New York: The Modern Library, 2000.

Tolle, Eckhart. *The Power of Now*. Novato CA: New World Library, 1997.

Tolle, Eckhart & Katie, Byron. *Peace In The Present Moment*. Charlottesville VA: Hampton Roads, 2010.

Wei Wu Wei. *Why Lazarus Laughed*. Boulder CO: Sentient, 2003.

Wei Wu Wei. *Unworldly Wise*. Boulder CO: Sentient, 2004.

Wilber, Ken. *The Collected Works of Ken Wilber*, Volume One. Boston & London: Shambhala, 1999.

The Foundation for Inner Peace

To learn more about *A Course In Miracles*, I encourage you to visit the website of the authorized publisher and copyright holder of the Course, the Foundation for Inner Peace: www.acim.org . While there are many excellent organizations supporting study of *A Course In Miracles*, this is the original one with the greatest variety and depth of Course-related materials, including biographies and photos of the scribes, DVDs, free access to daily Lessons, audio recordings, information about the many languages into which the Course has been translated, and electronic versions of the Course, including mobile device apps.

The Foundation for Inner Peace is a non-profit organization dedicated to uplifting humanity through *A Course In Miracles*. The organization depends on donations and is currently immersed in translating the Course into many languages (26 to date). The Foundation also donates thousands of copies of the Course. If you would like to support more people to benefit from *A Course In Miracles*, donating to the Foundation for Inner Peace or one of the many other fine Course-related organizations would be a worthy endeavor. A portion of the proceeds from this book will be donated to the Foundation for Inner Peace and other organizations proliferating the message of *A Course In Miracles*.

Printed in the USA
CPSIA information can be obtained
at www.ICGtesting.com
LVHW091304151023
761121LV00001BC/56